THE COLORS OF COURAGE

THE COLORS
OF COURAGE

Gettysburg's Forgotten History

Immigrants, Women, and African Americans
in the Civil War's Defining Battle

★ ★ ★

Margaret S. Creighton

BASIC
BOOKS

A Member of the Perseus Books Group
New York

Chapter Six is a somewhat modified version of "Living on the Fault Line: African Americans and the Gettysburg Campaign," in Joan Cashin, ed., *The War Was You and Me: Civilians in the American Civil War* (Princeton: Princeton University Press, 2003). It is reprinted with permission of Princeton University Press.

Published by Basic Books
A Member of the Perseus Books Group

Books published by Basic Books are available at special discounts for bulk purchases in the United States by corporations, institutions, and other organizations. For more information, please contact the Special Markets Department at the Perseus Books Group, 11 Cambridge Center, Cambridge, MA 02142, or call (617) 252-5298 or (800) 255-1514, or e-mail special.markets@perseusbooks.com.

Library of Congress Cataloging-in-Publication Data

Creighton, Margaret S., 1949–
    The colors of courage : Gettysburg's forgotten history : immigrants, women, and African Americans in the civil war's defining battle / Margaret Creighton. — 1st ed.
        p.   cm.
    Includes bibliographical references and index.
    ISBN 0-465-01456-9
    1. Gettysburg, Battle of, Gettysburg, Pa., 1863. 2. Immigrants—Pennsylvania—Gettysburg—History—19th century. 3. Women, White—Pennsylvania—Gettysburg—History—19th century. 4. African Americans—Pennsylvania—Gettysburg—History—19th century. 5. United States—History—Civil War, 1861–1865—Participation, Immigrant. 6. United States—History—Civil War, 1861–1865—Women. 7. United States—History—Civil War, 1861–1865—African Americans. I. Title.

E475.53.C89 2004
973.7'349—dc22
                                                                    2004014003

Text design by Trish Wilkinson
Set in 10.75-point Minion by Perseus Books Group

First Edition
1 2 3 4 5 6 7 8 9 10 / 06 05

CONTENTS

INTRODUCTION

IT IS A STORY TOLD time and again. In the summer of 1863, an army of Confederate soldiers probed its way into enemy country. Veiled by a length of low mountains, it moved into Pennsylvania, and then, at a small town, it turned to face a Union army that had followed it. In a battle that lasted three days, 170,000 men came to blows. They fought on rocky hillsides, charged through wheatfields and orchards, and fought hand to hand. When it was over and the Confederates had beaten a retreat to the South, witnesses to the carnage claimed that it was the bloodiest battle ever fought on the American continent. Some of them argued, even then, that it was the turning point of the American Civil War.[1]

Gettysburg is a tale told in histories and in fiction and film. It is also conveyed, in monuments and museums, at the site itself, to close to two million visitors a year. It is a story so compelling and familiar that for many Americans it has become a defining moment, communicating what courage means, what heroes look like, and how and where war happens.

So well known is this battle's history that it is hard to picture it any other way. But if we shift the focus slightly, and sift the evidence for what also remains of those July days in 1863, different Gettysburgs emerge. Among these is the story told here, in which diverse Americans—people of color, women civilians, and immigrant soldiers—play leading parts, and in which struggles over freedom and contests over respect and recognition provide as much dynamic action as attacks, repulses, and retreats.

These diverse people have been sidelined in conventional battle history—some more than others, certainly—but it is not difficult to place or replace them at the center of Gettysburg's story. German-American soldiers engaged in two critical military actions at Gettysburg, where they hoped to do more than defeat an enemy and stop an invasion. They were deemed "outcasts" in the Army of the Potomac, if not in America as a whole, and they had felt painfully dishonored after a retreat at the Battle of Chancellorsville in May 1863. Now, in Pennsylvania, they hoped to answer those who questioned their courage. Their New England–born corps commander, Major General Oliver Otis Howard, also felt the scorn directed at his men, and it was compounded by his own difficulties. His toughness, too, had come under question, and he struggled against the widespread belief that he was too pious a Christian and too gentle a man to be a successful army commander.[2]

White borough women also actively entered into the Battle of Gettysburg. Many of these women were in the town alone with their children when the battle enveloped them and caught them in military crossfire. During the three days of violence, they faced not only physical ordeals but psychological shock. Many of them rose to the challenge, vigorously opposing Confederate soldiers, using and abandoning domesticity in order to protect their families and their property. Being a woman on a battlefield and being trapped with enemy men in an occupied town was not something any of them had anticipated, and the experience proved a remarkable test of their strength, their political resolve, and their willingness to enter—and influence—the military fray. For immigrant women, it also proved a test of their emotional armor. Pennsylvania Germans came under public attack after the battle for what people said was unpatriotic behavior.

Black women and men were integral to the story of the Confederate invasion. African American residents of south central Pennsylvania faced more than hardship and disruption when Confederates invaded Pennsylvania. Their freedom was in jeopardy. Some of the enemy soldiers who came north in June 1863 hunted down people of color to send south into slavery. Gettysburg's black families—some of whom lived near a place called Cemetery Hill—had labored for generations to build a safe and sustainable world for themselves, and, in the summer of 1863, they saw that world threatened with destruction.

This account not only describes what these different "outsiders" had at stake at Gettysburg and details the part they played in the campaign, but also considers how and why, as Gettysburg became a cherished American narrative, their experiences became peripheral. Acclaim, recognition, and remembrance went to native-born combatants featured in engagements of strategy and maneuver. When writers moved these other people to center stage, as they did on occasion, they tended to use them as foils to their favorite soldier heroes. These are the individuals, we have been told, who hid when the shelling got thick, or who fled at the first sign of violence. Immigrant soldiers were "skedaddlers"; women were "cellar-dwellers"; black civilians were "runaways." And it was not simply historians who marginalized these people. In their effort to seek inclusion in battle memory, these participants sometimes denigrated each other. White, native-born women writing battle accounts, for example, portrayed black civilians, German-American civilians, and German-American soldiers in ways that accentuated their own brave deeds.[3]

The Colors of Courage does not seek to be comprehensive—it focuses largely on Union soldiers and Northern civilians—but, by recasting the battle, it seeks to be freshly inclusive. By bringing diverse individuals forward, and in viewing the Gettysburg campaign through their eyes, it also proposes a new shape to Gettysburg, a reconfiguration of the battle's traditional dimensions and emotional contours.

When we see the battle through the eyes of immigrant soldiers, for example, we come to know the Union army at Gettysburg less as a seamless fighting body engaged with an enemy than as a socially divided set of men beset by internal battles. Thanks in part to the humiliating Union defeat at Chancellorsville, Gettysburg became for many soldiers a test of male fitness and a competition for social acceptance. It was also a contest driven by a belief in right and wrong. Many of the senior German officers fighting at Gettysburg were anti-slavery (as was their Yankee corps commander), and their fight was infused by moral purpose.

When we measure Gettysburg by the yardstick of women's work, the battle's geography shifts distinctly. The circumference of battle expands beyond the familiar Cemetery and Seminary Ridges to include both the borough and civilian farms for miles and miles around. When we take into account women's perspectives, too, the battle's dynamics look different. Women and even girls in the occupied town were fully implicated in the battle's frightful drama, not only as victims of violence but as agents of support and resistance. Seen from the vantage point of civilian women, the battle's chronology also changes. The trauma lengthens from three days' worth of killing to at least three months' worth of recovery and ministration.

Viewed through the lens of African American experience in Pennsylvania, the Battle of Gettysburg expands again. Its boundaries are as wide as the path of its raiding armies, and its time frame reaches back into the past. The battle is both a momentary explosion in 1863 and the climax of decades of threats from below the Mason-Dixon line. It is also less about soldiers fighting soldiers in white man's combat than it is about soldiers preying on civilians, and it has clear and urgent moral proportions. It is a battle all about, utterly about, freedom.

Considering the experiences of these "outsiders," then, requires a reassessment of Gettysburg. It also means reevaluating the preeminent values of the Gettysburg story, not only the principle of freedom, but the telling quality of courage. According to the influential Gettysburg canon (which echoes other war narratives), the kind of courage achievable through the battle's active combat—physical daring—is one of the noblest human attributes. Displays of other kinds of courage are considered less meritorious. Courage that women demonstrated—unarmed, supportive, protective, albeit under fire—is relatively less distinguished. Moral courage, like the principled abolitionism that inspired some soldiers, or that enabled African Americans to persevere in the crisis of the invasion, has also become relatively unimportant.[4]

Adopting the vantage point of these people means challenging the rigid hierarchy of courage. Importantly, though, it does not mean overturning generations of battle history in order to redistribute bravery. Most of the Northern men and women described here did not seek to substitute one narrowly defined battle for another. They wanted to avoid a seesaw of respect, whereby honor credited to one person or group was necessarily withdrawn from another. As proud as they were of their own accomplishments, as eager as some of them were for expanded appreciation, they celebrated with all their hearts the victories of the soldiers on Little Round Top and Cemetery Ridge.

According to some commentators, Gettysburg is the "symbolic center of American history."[5] The perspective of this book thus raises fundamental questions. If Gettysburg *is* a certain set of ideals, with a certain cast of characters, to what degree can it be modified and be recognized as "Gettysburg" at all? The canon—the story of brave soldiers fighting in sequestered space—has enormous tenacity and power, and it speaks to prevailing ideas about the scope of battle and the legacy of war. Can it be challenged? To what extent, too, can slavery be reintroduced into the story of Gettysburg? Many of the men and women described here believed not only in a multidimensional war, but in a war of moral principle. What do their opinions and their convictions mean to us now? How far has Gettysburg's audience come in the last century and a half? How much has it changed?[6]

THE OTHER GETTYSBURG ADDRESS

The narrative offered here differs from most histories of the battle, but the approach it takes is not unprecedented. It is indebted, first of all, to a distinguished historical tribute delivered in the fall of 1863. The speaker who presented this address had been invited to Gettysburg to help dedicate the new Soldier's National Cemetery in November. He was an articulate man, celebrated for the strength of his convictions and for his way with words. And he was not Abraham Lincoln. Forgotten almost as readily as some of the subjects he discussed, the Hon. Edward Everett spoke *before* Lincoln on November 19.

The nearly seventy-year-old Everett, who had served Massachusetts as a congressman, as governor, and then senator, and also been president of Harvard University and secretary of state, had a reputation as one of the best orators in America.[7] The address he gave at Gettysburg was indeed elegant and scripted, and he delivered it, for almost two hours, with premeditated craft. He began by associating the battle with classical battles of Greece. What would have happened, he queried, if the Confederate invasion had succeeded? Would it not recall the invasion of those despots who had sought to "plant the dark banner of . . . slavery on the free soil of Greece?" Everett then brought his oration forward to the beginnings of the American Civil War, and began a long, detailed history of the Gettysburg campaign.[8]

Everett, a long-standing abolitionist, was not shy about engaging in the war's divisive issues, nor was he reluctant to take sides. The success of the Union army at Gettysburg was a sign, he said, that good prevailed. "Victory does not always fall to the lot of those who deserve it," he commented, but in this case, the "triumph" had to be ascribed "to the spirit of exalted patriotism that animated them, and the consciousness that they were fighting in a righteous cause."[9]

In recounting the battle, Everett commended specific people. (In two hours, to be sure, he could cover a lot of ground.) He praised the many valiant soldiers who fought at Gettysburg, including the troops who fought "gallantly" the first day. He spoke of local civilians and what they had endured from the twenty-sixth of June to the following fall—how they had been "shocked with the widespread desolation," how they had spent nights in dreadful anxiety, and how they had dedicated themselves to the care of soldiers. He talked of the sorry aftermath, and he spoke particularly of women—those at home whose labor went beyond "domestic care," and those who worked with the wounded on the fields and in hospitals. Women of the Union, he said, "have entitled themselves to our highest admiration and gratitude." Edward Everett also mentioned free people of color, several times. He acknowledged the black men who served in the United States Army, as well as free African Americans taken into bondage.[10]

President Abraham Lincoln spoke after Everett. He took little time to read from his notes. There were no specifics in his address and there was no town mentioned. He did not refer to the particular battle at hand, nor to that battle's soldiers. He could have been anywhere, following any battle, speaking to any bereaved community. He made elegant references to past deeds and dead men, to Founders' words and Founders' plans. He spoke of principles of equality and of "a new birth of freedom," which many people have taken to be an allusion to the end of slavery. But he made no concrete reference to the war's causes or to the way that the war's purposes had shifted. There was no mention of emancipation, or of a proclamation.[11]

In part because of the beauty of his words, and in part because their spareness left the door open to meaning, Lincoln served generations with his Gettysburg remarks. The fact that he led the Union heroically helped bolster the fame of his address, but it was the words themselves, and what Lincoln left out, that ensured the speech's longevity. For diverse Americans at the time—for border-states Americans, anti-slavery Americans, politically lukewarm Americans—Lincoln's comments carried far. He wanted them to go wide as well. He would be running for reelection within the year, and he could, as one historian has noted, use the Gettysburg podium to help cement his Republican base. He had always been a master at poetic obfuscation—he would not have been such a successful politician if he had not been—and here he could be genuinely and faultlessly politic.[12] And his words would live on—beyond the Civil War, beyond the period of Reconstruction, well into the world of sectional reconciliation. Through the twentieth century, people ascribed multiple meanings to Lincoln's words, and some ultimately used them to honor Confederate and Union veterans and Confederate and Union causes.[13]

While Lincoln's address carried beyond its moment in time, Everett's address did not. The early response to his oration was mixed. Anti-Republican commentators were, not surprisingly, distinctly negative. Everett was cold and long, they said, and, by championing the war's anti-slavery cause, he had helped perpetuate the war and prolonged human suffering. Many Republican editorials were favorable. While some papers thought his oration lacked warmth and that his extended account of the battle was unnecessary, they were generally pleased. Some papers even noticed the way that Everett had acknowledged some of the war's forgotten participants, particularly the country's women.[14] Everett's remarks about women also received positive comment from his co-speaker. Everett had written to Abraham Lincoln after the ceremony, complimenting his speech and asking after the president's sick son. Lincoln returned the message, and remarked that Everett's "tribute to our noble women for their angel-ministering to the suffering soldiers, surpasses, in its way, as do the subjects of it, whatever has gone before."[15]

Edward Everett's oration at Gettysburg, however, became a vanishing act. Ultimately, the statesman seemed too bound to his time and place. Not only was his rhetorical style and long delivery fit for his century, but his subject was topical. And he was partisan. He identified specific heroes. His oration was by no means a diatribe against slavery—it was much more a paean to union—but he mentioned the iniquities of slaveholders and the concerns of "colored people" frequently enough for people to know very well where he stood. So, as the country changed, and slavery and "colored people" became less absorbing concerns to the majority white public, Everett's remarks became known mostly for their windy length. A late-twentieth-century historian would sum up his generation's assessment of the two men and their remarks by commenting that Everett's speech "may no longer be of interest to us on its own merits," but it survives mainly as "the foil to that better thing that followed."[16]

Mr. Lincoln's address was certainly the most beautiful thing delivered that November day, and it justifiably became a sacred text. But Edward Everett cannot be dismissed. By speaking frankly of the war's causes, by honoring the Battle of Gettysburg's multiple heroes, he echoed many of the battle participants themselves—including Union soldiers, women, and African Americans. They might not have personally appreciated Everett, or even recognized their kinship with him, but he pronounced to the public what some of them, too, would later try to articulate.

Many of these battle survivors would ultimately take Everett's words one step further. While he talked about soldiers' "gallant" behavior, they would explain that only some men were so classified. While he talked about how citizens suffered, they would talk about how they took action to mitigate that suffering. While he discussed women's sacrifice and told his audience that women's service was its own reward, they would claim recognition as their reward. While he mentioned black ordeals at the hands of Confederates, they would echo him, but when he spoke of a "helpless colored population," they would speak of their enduring strength.

But just as Everett's oration became a faded occasion, these individuals, too, would disappear from view. And throughout their lifetimes and for generations beyond, their battle for the battle—their efforts to broaden the event's history, and their struggles to complicate popular memory—would be an uphill fight.

THE ADVANCE GUARD

This account takes inspiration from Edward Everett's oration in 1863, but it is also indebted to historians in the late twentieth century who examined the social history of soldiers and who integrated women and the homefront into the story of the Civil War.[17] It also relies on pioneering research into wartime Gettysburg, including very recent work on Pennsylvania Germans, African Americans, women, and civilians in general,[18] as well as on studies of Gettysburg in popular culture and collective memory.[19] Many of these studies acknowledge, implicitly or directly, the ways in which Gettysburg's homefront and battlefield were one and the same.

The narrative here also owes a great deal to scholars who have discussed how battle is deserving of cultural study. Many social historians, for instance, have produced work that goes "beyond the battlefield." Such scholarship is critically important for it increases our understanding of the war's many participants and its complex repercussions. But too often military campaigns remain relegated to military analysts. Battles are also social constructions, of course, and the reasons they are fought, the way they are performed, the people they include, and the way they are talked about reveal a great deal about the broader culture. Above all, then, this work is indebted to those scholars who have encouraged the cultural study of war.[20]

THE SOURCES

Although this book is enriched by historical scholarship, it is grounded in primary evidence, much of it, of course, produced after the battle. It sometimes tells us as much about later circumstances, or about the effects of intervening years, as it does about 1863. Battle survivors had trouble recalling what happened within weeks of the event, not to mention twenty or thirty years later. Witnesses to the Gettysburg campaign are, by the turn of the twentieth century, also witnesses to Reconstruction and reconciliation, and they bring their accumulated perspectives to bear on their memories. Like all witnesses, then, they provide invaluable but not perfect windows into the past.[21]

The story of German-American soldiers and their American commander in the Union army's Eleventh Corps, which opens the book and helps sustain the military action throughout, is based upon army records as well as the diaries and letters and recollections of soldiers themselves. The book's second narrative, which follows the travails of white Gettysburg women, draws on memoirs, diaries, interview transcripts, and correspondence generated by approximately forty local women. These materials provide a good description of how women viewed and experienced the battle, but they are less useful in discussing prewar and postwar experience, and are supplemented by newspaper commentary and military reports. The third story retells the battle through the lens of Gettysburg's black community. This is social history at its most challenging. Much local African American history remains where it originated in the nineteenth century: in tales handed down, or in private collections. And the black community, under siege in 1863, did not have time then, nor the luxury (or interest) afterward, to print accounts of its experiences. This record is thus pieced together from church minutes, pension records, newspaper accounts, military reports, and oral histories, as well as from general accounts of African Americans in Pennsylvania.

As every reader will realize, *The Colors of Courage* speaks of female, immigrant, and black experiences quite generally, although its evidence is particular and limited. Highlighting certain individuals brings personal immediacy to the story but sacrifices broad representation. Focusing on a small group of immigrant soldiers (most of them officers, no less) is to glide over the diverse experiences of German Americans of different rank, from different parts of the United States (and Germany), from different political, economic, and educational backgrounds. Emphasizing five literate, publicly visible women likely means bypassing "ordinary" women—often poor women—who hadn't the skills or time or connections to reminisce in public. And grounding African American experience on church leaders, town "characters," and property owners neglects people who may have been too reticent, too transient, and, again, too poor to register in public. As much as possible, this book tries to mitigate its selectivity by drawing on collective material, but it leaves many social dimensions of the Gettysburg campaign unexplored. Future researchers will no doubt do great justice to other groups of people at Gettysburg, to different sets of immigrants, for example, or to civilian men, to nurses and other volunteers, or to black laborers and black refugees.

THE STRUCTURE

This book dovetails historical narrative with interpretive commentary, and draws on the discrete experiences of fifteen individuals to personalize its story. It also weaves in details of hundreds of other participants. Chronologically, the book is both straightforward, following events before, during, and after the battle, and retrospective, flashing back in time to fill in background. A character list, a brief outline of the Gettysburg campaign, and maps will help orient the reader to events and relevant participants.

The account itself is structured in three parts. Part One includes a brief prologue, which introduces the mid-nineteenth-century town of Gettysburg, Pennsylvania, and then presents, in Chapters 1, 2, and 3, the three major communities that dominate the narrative. It brings each group to the threshold of the summer of 1863. This section thus travels back in time. The first chapter of the book, which focuses on soldiers in the Eleventh Corps, opens in May 1863, and centers on the Battle of Chancellorsville. Here, we learn about the kind of emotions some of these Union soldiers will carry into Pennsylvania, and we become familiar with the book's military perspective. The second chapter begins in June 1863, when women in Gettysburg began to anticipate an invasion. It considers the kinds of expectations that existed for women in wartime. The third chapter introduces the African American community in Gettysburg. Its focus expands to the antebellum period in order to show how the Confederate invasion fits into black history in southern Pennsylvania and to emphasize what black families had at stake in 1863. Part Two (Chapters 4, 5, and 6) centers on the Gettysburg campaign and the battle itself. Part Three (Chapters 7 through 10) discusses the battle's aftermath, the characters' postwar lives, and the way that battle memories were publicly shaped, both locally and nationally.

PRINCIPAL CHARACTERS: SPRING AND SUMMER, 1863

The Soldiers of the Eleventh Corps

Major General Oliver Otis Howard: Thirty-three years old, Otis Howard grew up in Leeds, Maine. A graduate of West Point, he is known for his piety, his abolitionism, and his personal bravery in battle (he lost an arm in 1862). Howard has just been given command of the Eleventh Corps of the Army of the Potomac, with its large cohort of German Americans, and he has high hopes that he and his men can solidify "soldierly" reputations in the spring and summer campaigns.

Major General Carl Schurz: Many men fight in the Army of the Potomac for liberty and union, for personal honor, for money, or out of duty. Carl Schurz has joined the army in large part because he hates slavery. His heartfelt commitment to abolitionism and civil rights was probably shaped in Germany, where he served as a revolutionary "freedom fighter" in 1848. This intense, tireless man came to America as a political exile, and now, thirty-four years old, he labors not only for emancipation but for the acceptance and recognition of German immigrants.

Brigadier General Alexander Schimmelfennig: Like Schurz, Schimmelfennig is a veteran of the German revolutions, and he has been equally impatient to serve the Union cause in his new country. As soon as Abraham Lincoln called for volunteers after the attack on Fort Sumter in 1861, Schimmelfennig began to form a regiment, and he brought distinctive ardor and bravery into battle in 1862. Now this round-eyed, boyish-faced, thirty-eight-year-old general is looking for the same sort of personal success in the months ahead.

Corporal Adam Muenzenberger is a robust-looking thirty-three-year-old who, in 1862, left his home in Greenfield, Wisconsin, to fight for the Union. This shoemaker, a father of four young children, is optimistic about what his regiment of fellow German-American volunteers might achieve. By the spring of 1863, he has suffered some disillusionment, and a personal tragedy, but he is still hopeful that the war will be over soon, that his army will be victorious, and that he will have personally trounced the enemy.

White Women of Gettysburg

Fannie Buehler is a proper Christian woman, committed to "good" causes and to the care of her husband and their six children. Thirty-seven-year-old Fannie, like everyone else in Gettysburg, has been warned about Confederate incursions, and she has convinced her husband, David, a prominent Republican newspaper editor and postmaster, to take flight if the enemy appears. But Fannie also claims to be unconcerned about an invasion. She does not really believe enemy men would have an interest in a small, out-of-the-way town like Gettysburg.

Harriet Bayly: A self-described abolitionist, Bayly is forty-three years old in 1863, and the mother of seven children. Her daughter, Jane Ann, age ten, has recently died. There is plenty that concerns this woman about the prospect of enemy invaders, but nothing compares to her anxiety about her family's farm and the safety of her animals. One animal, a speedy chestnut mare, is, for personal reasons, particularly precious to her and she will do whatever she can to keep this horse out of enemy hands.

Elizabeth Thorn, born in Germany, lives in the gatehouse on Cemetery Hill. Her husband, also a recent immigrant, was caretaker of Gettysburg's new Evergreen Cemetery until he joined the Union army. Now, this determined thirty-year-old woman has to keep up with her husband's grave digging, her own housekeeping, and the care of her elderly parents and her children. To top it off, she is pregnant. She hardly has room in her life to host an army on her hilltop. But she is not going to have much say in the matter.

Sadie Bushman is nine years old. The daughter of a cabinetmaker, the middle child of nine, Sadie lives in the center of Gettysburg. We do not know a lot about Sadie's life before the summer of 1863, but it is likely that she spends her time in chores, schoolwork, churchgoing, and play. It is not at all likely that she does anything connected with army life, except perhaps to help her mother scrape lint or package supplies for soldiers. Sadie Bushman is very young, and it is generally understood that girls of her age will have many more years to mature. Sadie will have three days to grow up, very fast.

Georgia Wade McClellan and her sister Jennie Wade, along with four brothers, grew up next to the Bushmans on the south side of Gettysburg. With a father in the almshouse and little money, the Wades have faced one challenge after another. The girls and their mother work as seamstresses to help support the family, but with the war on and men away, demands and duties have expanded. And now twenty-one-year-old Georgia is pregnant. Her baby is due in the summer, sometime close to the first of July.

Gettysburg's African Americans

Abraham Brian, in his late fifties, owns a farm just south of the borough of Gettysburg, near the north end of Cemetery Ridge. He, his wife Elizabeth, and their children work twelve acres, and Brian has other properties he rents out. His children go to the school nearby, and, unlike their parents, are learning how to read and write. In the late spring of 1863, the family has finished planting their fields with wheat and barley. It is clear that they hope to be around to harvest them.

Mag Palm. The 1860 census taker places Mag Palm and her family in a small wooden house on the northwestern slope of Cemetery Ridge. She rents this house from Abraham Brian. Mag is in her mid-thirties in 1863, a tall, strong woman who works for white families to get by. Her stature and her muscular power appeal not only to employers, but to slave traders. Sometimes, as Mag found out before the war broke out, these are one and the same. By 1863, she has become an extremely wary woman.

Owen Robinson. It is hard to know exactly how old Robinson is in 1863. He was apparently born in Maryland at the end of the eighteenth century. "Daddy" Robinson, as he was known, is a successful confectioner in the borough, and an active member of the AME Zion church. Having been enslaved once, he lives in dread of Confederate invaders, and what they could do to his cherished freedom.

Randolph Johnston has grown to maturity in Gettysburg. Born in 1840, Johnston has been educated in the borough and has intermittently attended the AME Zion church. His family sometimes seems on the edge of acceptance in the black community, thanks to his father's unconventional ways. But in June 1863, Randolph Johnston is nothing if not active and in charge. He has begun drilling men for military work and is ready to offer soldiers to the state of Pennsylvania. Whether Pennsylvania is ready for his help, however, is another matter.

Basil Biggs moved to the Gettysburg area in 1858 in order to give his children a better start in life than he had had. Born in Maryland in 1819, he began working for others at the age of four. He now tenants a farm south of town where he has earned a reputation for helping slavery's fugitives move through on the Underground Railroad. Soon enough it will be Biggs himself who will know what being a fugitive feels like and what it means to be on the run.

It might have been easy to predict that **Lloyd Watts,** who is twenty-eight in 1863, would be a leader of the African American community. He has been committed to "respectability" for a long time, and he has worked hard on everything from his schoolwork to his personal habits, from his romantic life to his spiritual life. He helps support six siblings and a widowed mother with hard labor, and he is committed, heart and soul, to the prospect of emancipation for fellow black Americans.

Catherine Carter and Margaret Nutter. Black history of Civil War Gettysburg is not readily found in archives or libraries. Some of it remains in personal attics or closets or locked in memories of old-time stories. Two women living in Gettysburg in the late twentieth century were not only conductors of that history but personal links to the African American world of the 1800s:

Catherine Carter, who was seventy-seven when she died in 1998, had heard a lot about her great-great-grandmother Mag Palm, especially about how she stood up to her enemies. Carter had her own history with Civil War soldiers, too. In 1938, the last living veterans of the battle came to town for a seventy-fifth reunion and she helped take care of them. A veteran of Jim Crow Pennsylvania, Catherine Carter was also witness to the way that public memory of the battle changed, and did not change, in the twentieth century.

Margaret Nutter, the granddaughter of Lloyd Watts, was Catherine Carter's best friend. The two women had worked together at the veterans' reunion in 1938, and they lived out old age in tandem. Nutter, who died in 2000 at the age of eighty-one, did not spend much time thinking about the battle, or the way that in the Borough of Gettysburg it had visibly revived. It was for her, and many other local people of color, a white man's affair. Nutter's own family history may have made the memory of the battle particularly forgettable. According to the family Bible and family legend, she was descended from a man named Moses Thomas, who was once enslaved by the man who led the Confederate invasion: General Robert E. Lee.

The Louisiana Tigers

Playing a small but significant part in the story to follow are Confederate soldiers in Louisiana regiments. Like soldiers in the Eleventh Corps of the Army of the Potomac, many of the Louisiana men in the Army of Northern Virginia were foreign born. And just as German American soldiers were saddled with stereotypes, these men—many of them Irish—carried burdensome reputations. Louisiana units, often nicknamed "Tigers," were considered some of the wildest, coarsest soldiers in Lee's army. Some Louisiana "Tigers" would occupy the Borough of Gettysburg during the battle, and they would have direct dealings with both resident women and Union soldiers of the Eleventh Corps.

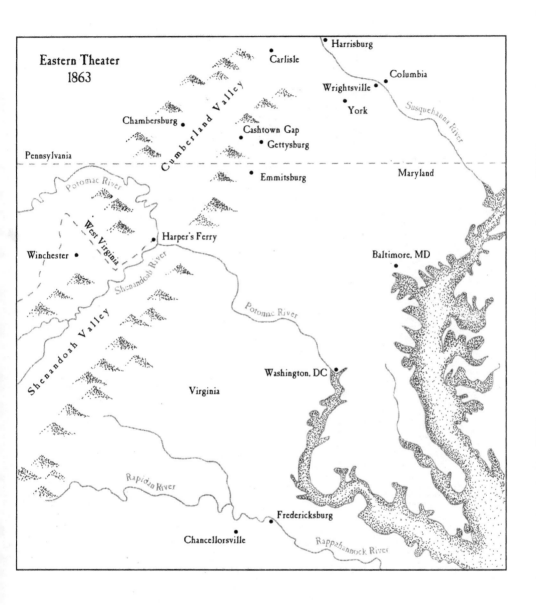

Eastern Theater
1863

Harrisburg
Carlisle
Columbia
Wrightsville
York
Chambersburg
Cumberland Valley
Cashtown Gap
Gettysburg
Pennsylvania
Emmitsburg
Maryland
Susquehanna River
Potomac River
West Virginia
Harper's Ferry
Winchester
Shenandoah River
Baltimore, MD
Shenandoah Valley
Potomac River
Washington, DC
Virginia
Rapidan River
Fredericksburg
Chancellorsville
Rappahannock River

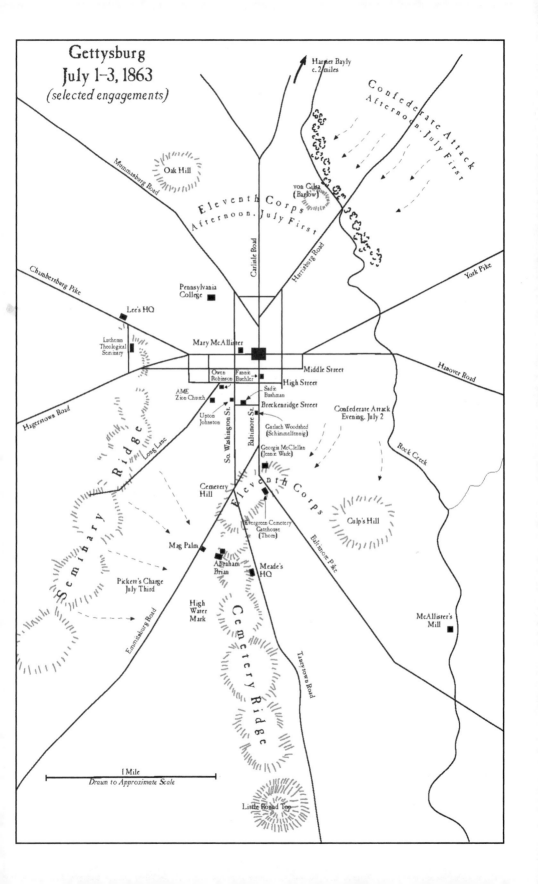

Gettysburg
July 1–3, 1863
(selected engagements)

Harriet Bayly
c. 2 miles

Confederate Attack
Afternoon, July First

Mummasburg Road

Oak Hill

von Gilsa
(Barlow)

Eleven th Corps
Afternoon, July First

Carlisle Road

Harrisburg Road

York Pike

Chambersburg Pike

Lee's HQ

Pennsylvania
College

Lutheran
Theological
Seminary

Mary McAllister

Middle Street

Hanover Road

Owen
Robinson

Fannie
Buehler

High Street

AME
Zion Church

Sadie
Bushman

Breckenridge Street

Upton Johnston

Confederate Attack
Evening, July 2

So. Washington St.

Baltimore St.

Gatlach Woodshed
(Schimmelfennig)

Georgia McClellan
(Jennie Wade)

Rock Creek

Cemetery
Hill

Seminary Ridge

Long Lane

Eleven th Corps

Evergreen Cemetery
Gatehouse
(Thom)

Culp's Hill

Mag Palm

Abraham
Brian

Meade's
HQ

Baltimore Pike

Pickett's Charge
July Third

High
Water
Mark

Cemetery Ridge

McAllister's
Mill

Emmitsburg Road

Hagerstown Road

Taneytown Road

Little Round Top

1 Mile
Drawn to Approximate Scale

THE GETTYSBURG CAMPAIGN, 1863

A Brief Chronology of Military Events

MAY 1–MAY 4: The Battle of Chancellorsville

JUNE 3RD: General Robert E. Lee and his Army of Northern Virginia begin to pull away from the Fredericksburg, Virginia, area as the first step in a bold move to march north and invade Maryland and Pennsylvania.

JUNE 15TH: The first units of Confederate cavalry and infantry cross the Potomac River. The cavalry begins aggressive raiding, including capturing black civilians. The invading force is divided at Chambersburg, Pennsylvania, one set of men heading toward the state capital, Harrisburg, the other east toward the Susquehanna River. Confederate infantry divisions successfully attack the Federal garrison at Winchester, Virginia, in the Shenandoah Valley, and clear the way for the rest of the invading army.

JUNE 26TH: Confederate General Jubal Early's division enters Gettysburg, Pennsylvania, spends the night, then moves east to York. Confederate General Richard Ewell closes in on Harrisburg.

JUNE 28TH: Lee's army, now fully across the Potomac, is ordered to gather east of South Mountain, a northern extension of the Blue Ridge range. Confederate troops engaged in operations at Harrisburg and near York are ordered to return to the Gettysburg area.

JUNE 28TH: The Union Army of the Potomac concentrates near Frederick, Maryland. General George Meade replaces General Joseph Hooker as commander of the army.

JUNE 30TH: The left wing of the Army of the Potomac, under Major General John Reynolds, bivouacs near Emmitsburg, Maryland, just south of the Pennsylvania border. The right wing is twenty-five miles to the east. Union cavalry general John Buford reaches Gettysburg and posts some of his men north and west of town.

JULY 1ST: In the morning, a Confederate division approaches Gettysburg from the west, but its advance is delayed by Buford's cavalry; later, soldiers of the Union army's First Corps arrive on the field and help repulse the Confederates. General Reynolds, commanding the left wing of the Union army, is killed. Both armies gather strength in the afternoon. While Major General Oliver Otis Howard assumes command of the Union troops at Gettysburg, his Eleventh Corps, temporarily under the command of Major General Carl Schurz, joins the fight. Confederates, augmented by infantry divisions arriving from both west and north of Gettysburg, assail the two Union corps and force them to retreat to Cemetery Hill, where General Howard has posted a reserve division. By nightfall, most of the town of Gettysburg is occupied by Confederate troops.

JULY 2ND: The Union army is positioned on Cemetery Ridge, and the Confederates are one mile west on Seminary Ridge. Both armies continue to add to their numbers until the Confederate army has amassed about 75,000 men; the Union army has swelled to about 95,000. From late in the afternoon until early evening, Confederate troops attack Union army positions on Cemetery Ridge and near the Emmitsburg Road. Inventive action by a Union brigade on Little Round Top and the arrival of fresh Union troops help turn back the multipronged assault. Early in the evening, Confederate troops attack the Union right at Culp's Hill, but are repulsed. At the same time, two brigades of Confederate infantry, including Louisianans known as the "Tigers," attack East Cemetery Hill. They briefly capture Eleventh Corps artillery, but are ultimately turned back.

JULY 3RD: A battle over Culp's Hill in the morning results in Union victory. Lee readies his troops on Seminary Ridge for an assault on the Union center. At one o'clock P.M., Confederate batteries open a massive barrage on Cemetery Ridge to weaken the Union position and continue firing for two hours. Union batteries respond, but are ordered to cease firing to save ammunition. The Confederate assault column is ordered forward at around three o'clock, the men advancing toward a copse of trees at the center of the Union line.

Union artillery and infantry fire decimate the attackers, but about a hundred and fifty men are able to push through the Union line on Cemetery Ridge at a place near an angle in a rock wall and the copse of trees known later as the High Water Mark. They are driven back, and less than an hour after it had begun, "Pickett's Charge" is over. Cavalry battles fought east and south of Gettysburg do little to change the day's resounding Union victory.

JULY 4TH: Lee waits for a counterattack, which does not happen, so he begins withdrawing his army from the Gettysburg area. By the 14th, the Confederates are over the Potomac River and back in Virginia. Meade's army follows them south. The Gettysburg campaign, which results in more than 50,000 casualties, is the Army of Northern Virginia's last major offensive of the war.

The Army of the Potomac at Gettysburg contains seven infantry corps, ranging in size from 8,000 to 15,000 men. Each corps is made up of two to three divisions, and most divisions are in turn comprised of two to three brigades. Brigades, for their part, contain four to six regiments. The Army of Northern Virginia is broken down into similar units, but its corps and divisions are larger than those of the Union army.

★ PART ONE ★

THE LAY OF THE LAND;
A SIGN OF THE TIMES

THE LAY OF THE LAND

Some of them were graveled, some were made of dirt, and they came into Gettysburg from just about everywhere. After the war, they would be the subject of serious wonder. People would study them with a bird's eye, looking at the way all ten splayed out from the tight square at the center of town and stretched over ridges and valleys. These were the western roads, observers would say, that the Confederate soldiers marched in on, and these were the northern roads they tramped, too, to fling themselves into the fight. And these were four roads that the Federal army used, double-quicking the last few miles up from Maryland.

Back in the 1850s, before the Civil War, the roads leading in and out of Gettysburg had been less momentous. They were troublesome, certainly, the way they sucked down carriage wheels in a muddy spring, or the way on cold days they glazed over and flipped buggies, or the way they threw up dust in a dry season. Sometimes, too, they had been the conduits of fright—a mad dog, a visitor with cholera, and, worst of all—a slave catcher. But mostly they just brought in the uneventful elements of borough life: a lawyer arguing his case before the county court, a coach with college-bound students, a wagon heavy with the season's harvest.

Gettysburg became an intersection of roads centuries ago, when east–west travelers—Native American originally—walked or rode from the Atlantic Coast through a nearby mountain gap to the Alleghenies and wore a trail through the area. Then in the mid-eighteenth century a man named Gettys took advantage of that dirt byway, bought land, built a tavern and a store, and attracted another dirt road. His son James Gettys laid out the makings of a town in 1786.[1]

3

By the mid-1800s, Gettysburg had grown well beyond its early intersection. It is hard to imagine the place now, when all that remains are black-and-white photographs. But picture how the scene might have appeared to someone standing by the cemetery gatehouse on the hill just south of town in 1863. In early summer, leafed trees veil most of Gettysburg's four hundred houses but can't conceal the spikes of steeples and cupolas. Out beyond the borough, in all directions, lies the rich geometry of farmland: the red dirt of the newly planted earth, the just-cut hayfields, the rolling rectangles of young corn and rye and oats. It is harder to see to the south, to the two boulder-strewn bumps of hills called the Round Tops that anchor the ridge. But to the west the way is clear—past another small ridge, out to a plain, and then beyond to South Mountain, banking around to the north like a slate-colored wall.[2]

Adams County was quilted with farms and orchards, but the Borough of Gettysburg itself was alive with other enterprise. In 1860, the town of nearly 2400 was home to two institutions of advanced learning: The Lutheran Theological Seminary, founded in 1826, and Pennsylvania College, which took in its first students in 1832. The borough was also the county seat, and in 1859 it boasted a big new courthouse. It also had the only banks in the county, more taverns than anywhere around, and its own gasworks, waterworks, and graded sidewalks. It even had that hallmark of modern civilization: railroad service. A visitor from nearby Baltimore was widely quoted in 1846 when he pronounced Gettysburg not only big, but "good looking."[3]

It seems only fitting that in a place with plenty of roads, one of the biggest businesses in Gettysburg became carriage making. In the 1830s, in fact, Adams County was known for producing Conestoga wagons—those canvas-covered "schooners" used to move people and freight across the country. By the time of the Civil War there were at least ten carriage companies in Gettysburg itself, manufacturing everything from cumbersome stagecoaches to jaunty sulkies. Men did the woodworking, painting, and blacksmithing, and women were paid to sew curtains and make lace and braid. Many of the carriage markets were in the South, and when enough vehicles were ready, they were wheeled out of town in a long procession—their new paint and burnished wood covered with white muslin.[4]

In the mid-nineteenth century, white borough residents who were not working in the carriage trade earned a living in other expected ways—as farmers and craftsmen, and as lawyers, doctors, and teachers. Many black men worked without a named skill, and labored for others as a means to credit or pay. White women often listed their occupation as "ladies," and black women frequently worked for these selfsame ladies, as nurses, housemaids, cooks, and washerwomen.[5]

While Gettysburg residents enjoyed the prestige they drew from the seminary, the college, and the carriages, they also were proud of the way they took the mundane aspects of life and made them magnificent. Consider, for example, the way they grew things. Practically everybody in the borough had a garden of some sort, and in the surrounding townships nearly everybody farmed. These farmers did not just produce adequate tubers, suitable crops, and serviceable fruit, however; these men and women saw some remarkable harvests. The local papers trumpeted the outcomes. They described a peach that was eleven inches wide, as well as a nine-pound beet. They reported a head of cabbage nearly four feet in diameter. And they spoke of grains, too: a head of timothy a foot in length; corn stalks over twelve feet tall. Reading the newspapers, one would think that Adams County was the promised land.[6]

It wasn't really perfect, of course. Some people scratched out an existence with dirt that barely covered the diabase, like those who lived on the stony ground along Cemetery Ridge. Others, of course, had no land at all. Gettysburg came close to looking like a pastoral ideal, but it mirrored the rest of America at midcentury in the way that some of its people were independent and well-to-do and others barely got by. The borough's newcomers, many of them immigrants, often took tough jobs and spent time in the poorhouse. Much of Gettysburg's black community, which numbered well over two hundred in the borough and environs, had been laboring for generations with little pay and little promise of improvement.[7]

And even the county's successful farmers had bad years. People grew small and puny vegetables sometimes, and they suffered from blight and drought. Then there was the time, in 1846, when locusts came. Adams County farmers walked out one day in early June to see the ground perforated with holes. The insects had emerged from the ground, sought out trees and bushes and fences, and scraped off their skins and left them lying around like so much scaly litter. Once they had liberated themselves to fly, the pests flew to eat, and they went for everything in sight, including new crops. People in 1846 were grateful that this infestation was not perennial. Locusts, they calculated, came in seventeen-year intervals. They would not have to worry about any invasion in Gettysburg, therefore, until the year 1863.[8]

A SIGN OF THE TIMES

In early January 1863, when people in Gettysburg began to look to the months ahead, they remembered the locusts. It was going to be a bad year, some of them said, for an incursion of bugs. Then, too, Christmas had fallen on Thursday, and this, apparently, was a sign of something to come.[9]

It was wartime now in Gettysburg, and people felt it. Some people felt it with grief. Every week or so, a Gettysburg boy was taken by a bullet or a camp disease and was carried back home in a casket. Others felt it with empathy. Many of the women in town met each other at church or in each others' homes to sew, make preserves, dry fruit, and to pick lint for the soldiers they called "our boys in blue." And a number of Gettysburg residents felt new hope. In January 1863 President Lincoln had formally issued the Emancipation Proclamation, thus helping to turn the war into what black people already believed it was: a fight for freedom. But not everybody in Gettysburg was happy about the prospect of emancipation. The borough, like all of Adams County, was almost evenly divided between people who supported Lincoln and those who questioned his agenda, and social and political opinions grew more bitter and increasingly polarized as the war went on. The Democratic editor in town argued that slavery was a "natural, happy place" for black Americans, and "to bondage they should be returned." He printed stories about what would happen now that the war was revolutionizing society. Negroes, he said, were becoming even more saucy and troublesome. They were "ravishing" white women and girls. They were "swarming" north, depleting town coffers, taking white jobs—they were "locusts."[10]

Occasionally the citizens of Gettysburg felt the Civil War with tangible fear. Living next to the Maryland border, and within marching distance of Washington, they listened and watched for signs that General Lee's army might take the offensive. It had happened in the fall of 1862, when Confederates moved into Maryland. Lee had stopped at Antietam, but later some of his men went farther north, stealing and threatening through the countryside. In January 1863 there was a rumor that enemy horsemen were on their way again. But it was becoming hard to tell which tales were true. Alarms meant sleepless nights, especially when the roads through town jammed with wagons and horses of farmers in flight. The alarms meant anxious days, too, and black women and men kept a lookout down the roads and an ear out for reports of invading Southerners. There was a Home Guard, which was charged with protecting civilians, but everyone knew a sundry lot of local men was no match for regular enemy army.[11]

The apprehension came and it went. Much of the time Gettysburg carried on just as it had before the war. The fall of 1862 saw the usual agricultural fairs, with the standard competitions for the county's livestock and produce. There were awards for the best pen of lambs, the finest loaf of bread, the most delectable pickled cherries. The vegetables and fruit in the county continued to perform to public applause: This time accolades went to a six-foot oatstalk and a thirteen-inch apple. Then, in the spring, Brien's National Circus Show came to town, featuring acts by comic mules, voltigeurs, leapers, and dancers.[12]

During the lulls between alarms, the war seemed a world away. It was not that townsfolk were not concerned with the outcome of battles. Borough residents became apprehensive in April 1863, when the big armies that had eyed each other all winter around Fredericksburg, Virginia, began to stir. Loyal Union families got to worrying again about their boys in the army, and also about the war's trajectory. Things had not been looking good for the Army of the Potomac for some time. The army had not won a decisive battle yet, and nobody knew what another defeat might bring about.

Then in the first week of May, Gettysburg got news that came in mixed messages. The armies had begun campaigning, and there had been a big battle in Virginia, at a place called Chancellorsville. But who had won it? One local paper announced that the Rebels had been taken by surprise, and that the newly polished Union army, under the magnificent General Joseph Hooker, had astounded the Confederates. Finally! But what about this other report, the one that said General Stonewall Jackson had been the shrewd one, and that he had made the surprise attack on the Union flank, and that some cowardly Union soldiers—it was the Eleventh Corps—had run away? What had happened down there?[13]

Chancellorsville, everybody found out soon enough, was a Confederate triumph of remarkable magnitude. But at least—like all of the big battles of this war so far—it was a distant debacle. The Virginia battle brought personal pain to some families in the area, yet its impact was nonetheless muted: It was not felt, seen, or heard. The soldiers who fought down there were mostly strangers in large armies, known through the newspaper's fine print. They did not have much to do with Pennsylvania—their Civil War and Pennsylvania's Civil War were worlds apart. Residents of Gettysburg could sympathize with the men who had dodged or taken bullets, and they could imagine the noise of cannonades and the sounds of shot and shell. They could picture the battle's bloody aftermath. Most of them, though, did not truly know these things. They did not know what gunpowder blasting from thousands of rifles smelled like, or what mortal fear did to one's body and mind, or what it felt like to be at the point of a gun or on the receiving end of a cannon. They did not know what soldiers said when they were cut deeply or torn apart or what they looked like when they died.

They did not know any of these things.

But that was in May.

1

* * *

AN AFTERNOON IN THE BADLANDS

FOR PEOPLE IN PENNSYLVANIA, the Battle of Gettysburg began in July 1863. For many German-American soldiers in the Army of the Potomac, however, Gettysburg began in May. It began in some dense Virginia woods, where they were attacked, suddenly, and where they retreated, precipitously. The retreat fueled nativist suspicion of these men, and they suffered great ridicule. They became the butt of private jokes and the laughingstock of published stories. They were scorned by Union and Confederate soldiers alike. Everyone, it seemed, had a word for them, and it was the word that all soldiers, all men, despised more than any other. It was the word "coward." So when these soldiers moved north into Pennsylvania in late June, they carried with them weighty emotional baggage. They also marched with the determination that they would redeem Chancellorsville, and that they would never, ever hear that six-letter epithet again.

Chancellorsville had actually opened as a promising campaign. General Joseph Hooker, who had taken charge of the Army of the Potomac in January 1863, planned to make a springtime move that would cap his career. With what he believed was the "finest army on the planet," he intended to stage a massive maneuver around Confederate generals Robert E. Lee and Thomas J. "Stonewall" Jackson and take them in the rear as they occupied the heights above Fredericksburg, Virginia.[1]

The planning of Hooker's flank attack had gone smoothly. The early disposition of troops had gone well. By the night of April 30, in fact, everything seemed to be on schedule. Soldiers of the flanking column—three army corps—had marched for four days, crossed two rivers, and were now just where Hooker wanted them: west of a huge brick house that carried the name of a town: Chancellorsville. In tandem with other Union troops in the area—over 130,000 men in all—Hooker would decoy Lee, and then spring upon him.[2]

9

The woods around Chancellorsville on that last night of April rang with the eager noise of men optimistic and ready. At the big house, which became Army headquarters, senior Union officers slapped backs, shook hands, and toasted to their certain success. Generals who were not usually given to hyperbole, like George Gordon Meade, used words like "splendid" to describe the situation. "Hurrah for old Joe," Meade said. "We are on Lee's flank and he does not know it." "Old Joe" Hooker himself issued a general order of congratulations. The maneuvers of the march had given Lee only two options, he said. He "must either ingloriously fly" or he could fight the Union army in a place "where certain destruction awaits him." Hooker described the work of the flanking column as a "succession of splendid achievements," and when his comments traveled the various army camps, and were read into the night air, they were greeted with cheers and shouts and music.[3]

The next day, May first, the weather opened bright. Soldiers, for once not ordered to haul heavy knapsacks and guns, were buoyant. "You have no idea," wrote one man, "how cheerful, how happy, we feel." The rising spirits of that May Day, though, must have lasted only hours—long enough for soldiers to feel unencumbered, to rejoice in dry weather, and to sleep beyond sunrise—but not much longer than that. For by late morning it became evident to everyone that General Robert E. Lee had discovered Hooker's movement. Realizing that what faced him at Fredericksburg was a feint, Lee had attacked the Union front. It wasn't a major assault—the units involved had both recoiled into the brush after the conflict—but it meant the end of the grand plan, and Hooker's troops were now on the defensive. The spring day that had begun so bright had suddenly dulled, and that evening some of Hooker's soldiers slept on their arms, ready for battle, in a mood they had not anticipated.[4]

The place where many of these men were positioned matched that mood; it was the center of a forested Virginia waste called the Wilderness. At one time the area had supported tall trees and been passable, but over the years it had become threatening—seventy square miles of dense, dark, second growth. One Union officer called it "gloomy." Others suggested it was wicked, the way its thorns and brambles grabbed intruders, the way its vines and saplings tripped them, the way its dense thickets and young pines and oaks robbed them of their sight, even in broad day.[5] The Wilderness, where it was hard to get bearings, was a place where someone with daring could plan the unsuspected.

And where someone with daring did. Not far from where Union soldiers slept, Confederate generals Lee and Jackson, sitting together on a log in a clearing, had perfected a plan, a surprise of their own. It would be an attack on the Union right flank. Stonewall Jackson would move in stealth, or as close to stealth as 30,000 men could get. And he would depend on the tangle of the forest for cover.[6]

The next morning, when it was barely light, Jackson put his plan in motion. He admonished his men to silence, and they did their best not to sing, or shout, or cheer. The equipment and weapons the soldiers carried clanked together, and their wagons and caissons creaked and rumbled, but the damp earth muffled much of the noise. Most of the soldiers didn't know where they were going—only that they were fighting thickets to catch Union troops off guard. Even the officers, though, didn't know exactly where in the Wilderness Hooker's soldiers were. But then in the early afternoon, three of them—including Jackson—climbed a small rise and saw what they were looking for. There in a clearing at a crossroads, eating and smoking and with weapons stacked, were enemy men—the Union right flank, all unready. The general said nothing when he saw this, but one of the men with him claimed that his eyes glowed.[7]

THE OUTSIDERS

The men on the flank who were the focus of Stonewall Jackson's rapt attention were the Army of the Potomac's Eleventh Corps. There were close to 13,000 men in that unprepared corps, from all over the northern United States. What gave the unit its character, however, and what people talked about before and especially after May second, were the men of German descent. Over 200,000 German Americans fought in the Civil War for the Union, and 5,000 of them served in the Eleventh. This amounted to less than half of the corps, but to native-born Americans who fumbled with German names and who couldn't understand German language or customs, and who, when the time came, sought scapegoats, the foreignness of these men loomed larger than their numbers.[8]

While many of these soldiers had been born or raised in the United States, others had barely scrubbed their clothes clean of Atlantic salt. They were not the first wave of German immigrants to come to America—tens of thousands had arrived in the middle 1700s, many as indentured servants. What now pushed people from their European homes was, in short, a combination of disasters: agricultural crises, the collapse of rural industries, political conflict. Many Europeans had had their fill of tyrannical nobility and in the late 1840s had organized widespread uprisings against aristocratic states. But revolutionary fighters had been overpowered, and some of the radicals who had led the struggle for a unified, republican Germany faced unhappy choices between prison and exile. Many men chose exile, and these political refugees joined a multitude of others who had the wherewithal to leave home. At the peak of migration in the middle of the century, 100,000 left Germany annually. Many sailed to the United States to shape a free, and solvent, future.[9]

Now, across the ocean, they or their sons were fighting another war, this time to help save a republic instead of establish one. They had myriad reasons for joining the Union army: the bounty money, the regular pay, the fight against slavery, duty to the new country, pride, and honor. Still, they were dogged by accusations that they had been imported and "bought." Confederate officials, especially, accused the United States government of importing "mercenaries" to do the job its citizens would not do. They pictured recruiting agents scouring European cities, looking for poverty-stricken youths, promising civilian jobs, but delivering military service instead. The Lincoln administration certainly opened its arms to immigrants and encouraged recent arrivals to fill states' quotas, and it may have done some dockside recruiting. But the government repeatedly denied that agents routinely preyed on arriving passengers, or that it sent recruiters abroad.[10]

Of the thousands of German Americans who had enlisted in the Union army, and who now, on May second, sat on the wrong side of a Virginia forest, was a certain shoemaker from Wisconsin who had enlisted for three years. Adam Muenzenberger could hardly have remembered his Atlantic crossing—he had only been a baby—and his fatherland, Hesse Darmstadt, was no more than a set of stories handed down. Having grown up in Greenfield, Wisconsin, he was an American. He was proud to enlist in the Union army in the fall of 1862 and eager to fight. At the same time, however, he lived in a Wisconsin community of German-speaking family and friends and fellow Catholics, all of whom held tight to the rituals of the homeland. His regiment, too, the 26th Wisconsin, was filled with first-generation Americans. Adam Muenzenberger was a proud American volunteer, then, but it was as a German American that he coveted honor. It was his German family that he sought to support with his pay, it was his German church that he hoped to fund, and it was when Germans were praised that he warmed with pride.[11]

When he had first joined the army in 1862, Muenzenberger had heard a lot of this praise. His corps commander at the time, Franz Sigel, was German, and he had announced to his soldiers that it "was only through the Germans that anything would be accomplished." Muenzenberger glowed with confidence as he marched through Virginia that fall, looking at insolent civilians and singing along with his regiment, "In the South, in the South, where the German guns explode and the rebels fall." He felt he had plenty of spirited company. "Wherever you meet soldiers, they're German," he wrote home expansively. "And they've all sworn vengeance on the South."[12]

Adam Muenzenberger was as pleased with regimental living as he was with regimental morale. He pronounced his division commander, General Carl

Schurz, "a good man" who cared for the men "like a father." Every two days, the soldier exulted, "we get good wheat bread; the other days we have salt pork and bean soup." Better yet, soldiers of the division enjoyed occasional sausages, and even a spot of brandy for picket duty. Muenzenberger may not have been exaggerating Schurz's attentiveness, for other men also commented that in 1862 the German regiments had less lice, less disease, and got better treatment than other units, and that they took comfort in beer and whiskey.[13]

But then, as quickly as Muenzenberger's enthusiasm for army life blossomed, it withered. In the winter of 1862, military life continued to offer him companionship and still promised him glory, but the 26th Wisconsin had not seen combat. For better or worse, the Eleventh Corps was held in reserve at the Battle of Fredericksburg in the middle of December. The soldiers "do nothing now but picket," Muenzenberger complained, and they survived on hardtack and spoonfuls of coffee. Where were the sausages and the heart-warming brandy now? It had become brutally cold. Disillusioned, the soldier pronounced the war a "big humbug." He also began to be "troubled with lonesomeness." He missed his "true soul," his wife Barbara, and his four young children. He worried about them in the cold Wisconsin winter, when money was "scarce." And at the end of February, his despair deepened when he heard through a hometown friend that his second youngest son, Henry, had died.[14]

When native-born Americans talked about European immigrants in the mid-nineteenth century, they tended to lump them together. They often disparagingly referred to both recent and older German immigrants as "Dutch," an anglicized version of "Deutsch." Other newcomers were simply "German," despite their different religions, their different dialects, or the fact that they hailed from different states. Germany was not even unified as a single country until 1871. Germans were also readily dismissed as abolitionists or as Democrats, when, at least in 1860, they were split politically. A good number of German Americans were indeed anti-Lincoln men who were lukewarm about abolition and who did not like the Republican party's strident temperance platform, its distrust of Catholics, or its equivocation about immigrant and "workingman's" rights. On the other hand, many Germans ultimately supported the Republican Party. They felt so strongly about the wrongs of human bondage or the advantages of free labor and free soil that they overlooked comments from the Republican press about their lager and their schnapps, their "strange" notions of religion, and threw their support to Lincoln. Frederick Douglass was speaking of this set of Germans when he declared in 1859 that "a German has only to be a German to be utterly opposed to slavery. In feeling, as well as in conviction and principle they are antislavery."[15]

German Americans who opposed slavery may not have had much company in the Union army early in the war, but after the Emancipation Proclamation went into effect, in January 1863, more and more native-born soldiers embraced the idea of black freedom.[16] Fewer men were impassioned abolitionists, however, and so those German-American soldiers who brought ardent anti-slavery beliefs to the army stood out. General Carl Schurz stood out. This thirty-four-year-old division commander, who treated soldiers like Adam Muenzenberger with such fatherly care, hated slavery with almost palpable emotion. "This struggle," he commented in a letter, "fills my whole soul. The cause . . . is the cause of my life." It is unclear exactly when Schurz shaped such an abhorrence of slavery, but it is evident that when he arrived in America as a twenty-three-year-old exile in 1852, he was deeply shocked by what he found. As a revolutionary activist in Germany, he had spent his young adulthood fighting for civil rights and social equality. Now, confronted with an appalling system of human oppression, in a republic no less, he almost literally seized the anti-slavery banner.[17]

After honing his arguments by listening to congressional debates, this thin, tall, sharp-faced man began to speak out for the new Republican Party in 1856. Traveling from state to state, he lectured in German about slavery and human rights. Although people sometimes threw stones through the windows of the halls where he spoke, and sounded catcalls to protest his opinions, and even though he was denounced as an "impudent intruder," Schurz was undeterred. To some degree, he reveled in the attention. And he was also not unhappy with the advent of civil war. It meant that the crisis was coming to a head, and that he could participate in the moment when "the old cause of human freedom was to be fought for on the soil of the new world."[18]

Schurz's support for Lincoln and his willingness to promote himself to the president helped earn him a position commanding a division as a brigadier general. While some questioned his "political" appointment and lack of American training, his bravery and leadership at Second Bull Run in the summer of 1862 quieted many doubters. In March 1863, he was promoted to Major General of Volunteers, and given temporary command of the Eleventh Corps.[19]

Carl Schurz had good company in the Eleventh Corps in the fight against slavery. He had enlisted men, like Private Bernhard Domschcke, who served in the 26th Wisconsin, Muenzenberger's regiment. Domschcke, an editor from the Midwest, had co-written a work extolling equal rights for women and men of all backgrounds. Schurz had fellow officers, too, who were committed abolitionists, like Brigadier General Wladimir Krzyzanowski, another veteran of the European revolutions. Krzyzanowski sought to crush the "terrible trade in human flesh." Schurz also had the good company of Friedrich Hecker, who had taken charge of the 82nd Illinois regiment. Hecker, who had been a legendary freedom fighter in Germany, had moved to the American Midwest in the 1850s. When Schurz had visited him in 1854, they had pledged that if ever the anti-slavery cause should need them, they would "meet on the field in a common endeavor." Now they were reunited. Hecker's feelings against slavery infused his regiment. When "The Old Man," as his troops referred to him, read aloud the Emancipation Proclamation at drill on the morning of January 3, 1863, it was greeted, said one soldier, "with great jubilation."[20]

These men may not have had much in common with Adam Muenzenberger when it came to Lincoln or even emancipation. Unlike Muenzenberger, they were also men of education, even of wealth, and most were indifferent to formal religion. But while these European-born soldiers had their differences, they shared a longing for acceptance in America. Carl Schurz, for one, had hoped that finding a home as a foreigner would be relatively easy in the United States. Elsewhere, he had said, "a stranger remains a stranger." He and other immigrants knew, of course, that soldiering was a time-honored way of earning respect and inclusion. Courage under fire was *the* litmus test for American manhood, and a key to true citizenship.[21]

By the early winter of 1863, however, the immigrant men of the Eleventh Corps knew that it might take a long time to prove themselves. The Union army's reverses in the Shenandoah Valley and in eastern Virginia in the spring and summer of 1862 were frequently linked by the press to foreign troops even when those soldiers had fought vigorously. And in the fall, rumors circulated that the Eleventh Corps itself was making a bad show. As one officer put it: "We have been solemnly informed through the Washington papers several times that we have been cut to pieces and driven back to Alexandria." This man took the news with cavalier humor: "In the language of the lamented Webster," he wrote home, "'we ain't dead yet,' having seen nothing calculated to produce death, with the exception of commissary's whiskey."[22]

But this man was not foreign-born. For some men of German descent who yearned to make a brave name for themselves, the stories stung. In early December 1862, Adam Muenzenberger learned that newspapers in his hometown of Milwaukee, both German and English, had reported that his regiment had run away from a battle, abandoning blankets and guns in its flight. Muenzenberger was aghast. His regiment, he protested, had not even seen Southern soldiers except in picket duty, much less engaged them in battle. "Beloved, believe me," he wrote home to Barbara, "we marched back in the same order . . . and with the same packs that we had when we left here. . . . I firmly believe, though, that our regiment would let itself be shot to pieces before it would re-treat. Let me repeat once more, then, that as yet we haven't seen the enemy and that the whole tale is an ugly slander against us." As hurt as he was, Muenzen-berger had lived long enough as an outsider in America not to be surprised. "You know," he wrote to his wife, "we are no Yankees."[23]

To men like Muenzenberger, Yankees were likely Northeastern Protestant Republicans, people who for years had been building antipathy toward the wave of Catholic immigrants—both German and Irish—who had arrived in the United States at midcentury. Yankees included the Protestant elite, which feared "papist" influence, which suspected German "insularity" and social habits, especially drinking, and which distrusted Democratic voters. And they were people of the Protestant working class, black and white, who also disliked Catholics and who competed, or feared that they competed, with upwardly mobile Germans for jobs. "Yankees," as Adam Muenzenberger recognized, were a powerful set of people, and they wielded that power through some of the most influential papers in the country.[24]

Immigrant soldiers sometimes felt Yankee scorn no matter what their reli-gion, or their status. Muenzenberger was a Catholic enlisted soldier, but the bitterness he felt was shared by men of much higher rank. The resignation of German-born general Franz Sigel, who headed the corps from late 1862 until the spring of 1863, was associated with his reputation as a "foreign intruder." Carl Schurz, who took temporary charge of the Eleventh Corps when Sigel re-signed, felt similarly slighted. Schurz expected to be named permanent corps commander, and he let Lincoln know that German-American soldiers antici-pated his appointment. They prefer, he wrote to the president, to "remain in the hands of one of their own. . . . They look at me as their natural head." But other men, most notably Joseph Hooker, resented Schurz's lack of American military training, disliked his abolitionism, and certainly suspected his Ger-manness. Schurz was put back in the command of a division.[25]

THE CHRISTIAN SOLDIER

The man chosen in early April 1863 to command the Eleventh Corps was not someone who knew how a foreigner felt in America. Oliver Otis Howard, a seri-ous, dark-bearded man, had been born in the state of Maine, had attended private Bowdoin College, and was a West Pointer to boot. He had also been successful in rising in rank in the army. But the Yankee Howard did have one thing in common with immigrant soldiers: a driving desire for respect. German-American soldiers, as Adam Muenzenberger discovered, were readily denigrated as cowards, and barely welcome in the army fraternity. Howard also endured criticism of his mas-culinity. He, too, had been questioned about his toughness.[26]

No one had ever seriously questioned General Howard's physical courage. In fact, he literally embodied martial daring. Otis Howard, as he was known to friends and family, had been a brigadier general in the Battle of Seven Pines in Virginia in 1862 when, riding ahead of his troops, he had been shot in his right arm, and had lost it to amputation.[27] It had been a difficult injury for him, and just recently, in March 1863, he had tried to replace the limb with a prosthetic, crafted in Philadelphia. It was an elegant substitute, covered in buckskin to match the color of his pale flesh and tanned soft and smooth. It even sported a hand, elegantly dressed in a kid glove. Howard had taken the arm back with him to the army, and for a brief time he seemed whole again: He used it to carry a lantern and hold a book and brush a hat. He even used his bloodless palm to hold a real knife when he ate. But for all the things it helped him do, in the end it did not work out. It was too short, by an inch or so, and it tired him to wear it. Eventually he stopped strapping it on, and it is unclear whether he ever again, in his entire life, wore it much beyond that month.[28]

From then on, Otis Howard wore an empty, pinned-up sleeve, a sign of personal disappointment certainly, but proof to the world of his battle courage. This did not exempt him from questions about his personal and professional rigor, however. He had heard it said in army circles that he was too young for fast advancement. Being in his early thirties, his youthfulness was undeniable, although he had performed well enough at West Point—graduating fourth in his class—to have taught there before the war broke out. He had also heard, though, that he was considered "too gentle."[29] In a job where one part of the business was the patriotic act of killing, and another part was ordering men into battle, this amounted to calling him an unfit man.

Such comments pained Howard, but they were not new to him. Early on in his training at West Point, in 1851, he had written home that he was "the constant object of slight, neglect and malice." While he may have been targeted for his rural Maine background, or for his relative lack of wealth, or for his willingness to befriend enlisted men, certainly his fondness for Bible classes, as well as his admitted abolitionism, fueled the estrangement. Both piety and abolitionism were considered to be less than stellar attributes by the arbiters of antebellum manhood, and it would have been hard to find more demanding arbiters than the cadets at West Point. What may have made matters worse was that Otis Howard refused to be confrontational with classmates who rebuked him, leading the Commandant of Cadets to urge Howard to "knock some man down." Whether he acted on this advice we do not know, but later on he wrote home that he was on better terms with his fellow cadets, including Robert E. Lee's son, Custis.[30]

When war broke out in 1861, Otis Howard was leaning toward entering a seminary, but he did not hesitate to abandon that plan to become the colonel of a regiment. At the same time, he tried his best to understand the war as a conflict over Christian principles, to be won with God's help by men of faith.[31]

He was well aware that others in the army considered the "Christian soldier" something of a paradox. Boys went to war, many believed, to definitively distinguish themselves from girls and women, and to clear themselves of "womanly" qualities like forbearance and piety. Was there room in the army for a man like Howard? Just the way fellow officers talked about him suggested they had their doubts about his potency. They described him as "slender" and "little" even though he was as tall as the rest of them.[32]

Not every pious general faced Howard's difficulties. Confederate general Stonewall Jackson, who was well known for his intense religiosity, managed to slough off the sort of criticism that stuck to Howard. In part, this had to do with Jackson's personal fierceness—even cruelty—in command, and his almost preternatural military skills. Howard, who had been on the receiving end of Jackson's brilliance in Virginia in 1862, not surprisingly attributed Jackson's success to his Christian faith.[33] And he wondered about the lack of such faith on the part of senior Union officers. Several of them flagrantly broke the commandments—drinking and swearing. Howard knew there were worse sins committed too, as anyone who spent time with General Hooker or General Sickles would testify.[34]

So what was missing in the Union high command, according to Howard, was Jackson's type of piety. Without it, the army lost battles. And what he himself lacked was Jackson's military success. Without it, he was more of a missionary than a convincing member of the fraternity. But there would be future battles, of course, new opportunities to reveal faith and reap victory. What Howard could not know, however, was the irony that lay directly ahead of him in the spring of 1863—the irony of May second. He did not know that the Confederate officer who climbed a knoll in the Virginia wilderness, who saw his unwary men, and who glowed with fierce eagerness, was none other than the Confederate Christian general. He also did not know that the man who helped Stonewall Jackson find a hidden road through the Virginia thickets, along which he would send his attack column, was trained as a chaplain.[35] It would seem, Howard would suggest later, as if God was choosing sides.

Many of the German-American soldiers in the Eleventh Corps met General Howard for the first time in early April. Corporal Adam Muenzenberger explained to his wife that Howard was "from Pennsylvania and can speak German." Carl Schurz got his facts straighter, and was less generous. He saw Howard as a slight, well-mannered young man who did not flaunt his West Point credentials, but who was not "intellectually strong." Schurz claimed that he was not alone in his skepticism. Both officers and enlisted men looked at Howard, he said, "with dubious curiosity; not a cheer could be started when he rode along the front."[36]

It is easy to appreciate the soldiers' diffidence. Howard was hardly likely to understand the immigrant soldiers' estrangement, and he threatened to rob them of their few pleasures. What would happen now to the comfort they took in whiskey, to their expressive need to swear, and to their freedom on Sundays? Was their soldier's life to be centered around sermons and prayer meetings? Was their comfort to be traded for stern encouragement? It appeared to be so. Early on, Howard ordered his men not to do unnecessary work on Sunday, to avoid swearing, and to give up drinking. A number of the men balked. They mocked their new commander, used the Lord's name when they swore, and they teased each other by calling repeatedly for prayers. One soldier summed up the gloom: "Tracts now, instead of sauerkraut!"[37]

It was not that Union soldiers were an ungodly lot of men. The army, in fact, was full of Christian believers. Many soldiers who had been lukewarm about formal religion before the war converted during their service, and men who had been earnest Christians saw their faith intensified. But there was a difference between carrying a Bible and preaching from it, and a difference between being abstemious and exhorting other men to abstain. What Howard wanted from soldiers was often the same things that soldiers' mothers sought: moral rectitude, regular Bible reading, restraint in drinking and speaking. Or, according to some German-American soldiers, it was what Republican social reformers and nativists sought. Many of these soldiers, "free-thinkers" or dedicated Lutherans or Catholics, had spent lifetimes resisting evangelism, and they were not going to stop now.[38]

By the end of April, however, some peace had come to the culturally embattled corps. The spring campaign was about to begin, and Yankees and immigrant soldiers were eager for the same result: success, honor, and an answer to critics. All they needed was one battle, one rout, one charge, or one honorable stand to extinguish the feelings of self-doubt and exclusion. The general who needed a victory to prove that Christian gentlemen could be commanders, and the German Americans who wanted a victory to demonstrate their courage, had common cause.

This optimism ballooned when President Lincoln reviewed the troops of the Army of the Potomac in mid-April. Soldiers in Carl Schurz's division, including Adam Muenzenberger's regiment, claimed they were singled out and praised for looking better drilled and more soldierly than any other unit. The governor of Wisconsin visited German regiments, too. After being serenaded with German songs—*"In Der Heimat ist es Schoen"* and *"Das Treue Deutsche*

Herz"—he had told the men how honored he was. "In my whole life," the governor had said, "I have never before been so proud of my German descent as I am now in the Camp of the Twenty-sixth Regiment." Muenzenberger was thrilled. He was encouraged, too, by General Hooker, who had said that "he thought the war would be over in ninety days!"[39]

Otis Howard felt himself settling in, too, and believed that relations with his foreign-born soldiers were warming. He could not get over the decorations that immigrant men had made for him for the president's review. They had transformed headquarters into a veritable Bavarian village, featuring a main gate draped with evergreen boughs, a landscaped main street, and a moss-decorated tent for Howard himself. The corps commander described his delight to his family in a letter. Sitting at his desk, in front of a small glass of mayflowers he had picked himself, Howard noted how Mrs. Lincoln had personally admired his tent. Furthermore, the president's review had been "perfect." Most important of all, he could report that his corps was "a good one."[40] And he tried to return the favors, too, with attention to the soldiers' comfort. He visited bakeries to check bread, saw that men kept their bedding and supplies clean, and, better than anything, carried more food trains than ever before.[41]

By the end of April even General Carl Schurz had grown expansive. Lincoln's visit had done a lot to soothe his sore ego, and he had made amends with Howard, even becoming "cordial." Then, too, the rain, which had seemed almost constant, let up. So when they were all ordered to march at the end of the month, they moved with enthusiasm. And why not? They were on the offensive against the army of Lee, and there were tens of thousands of them. So even though the soldiers headed off with over seventy pounds on their backs and over their shoulders, their steps seemed light. Schurz claimed that "there was no end to the singing and merry laughter."[42]

Much of the ardor, of course, was abruptly dampened by what General Lee surmised near Chancellorsville on May first. And it was deadened by the way that Lee took the initiative, and then by the fact that the Eleventh Corps—part of Hooker's glorious flanking column—was ordered into a godforsaken place. Some of the soldiers in that place, like Adam Muenzenberger, still hoped for action, but hearing that the Confederate army was massed farther to the east, it did not look likely.

Otis Howard, on the other hand, felt sure there was a big fight looming. And this concerned him. He wasn't worried about how well he would perform—he was well beyond doubting that. What he experienced was a more personal anxiety. He knew that he might be thrown into a bloody battle at just the same time that his wife, Elizabeth, up in Maine, delivered their fourth child. Lizzie, as he called her, had lived mostly alone with the children during the war, and her husband had worried about her: the occasional money problems, the long winters in Maine, the small sicknesses that seemed to take hold of every child and wear her down too. When it came down to it, Otis Howard believed her work was as challenging as his was. "I feel that it is as difficult for you to do your part in this war," he had written, "as it is to do mine." Now he knew that their respective roles in this life, giving birth and making battle, might kill them both, even on the same day. During the evening of May first, he found a minute to pencil home a note to Lizzie. He told her about the long march and the river crossings, and he soberly reflected on the sure fight ahead of him. And he sent her a short prayer: "May God bless & strengthen you. May has come."[43]

ALLES IST VERLOREN

On the morning of May second, Howard settled the Eleventh Corps into a position at the farthest right of the Union line, along a turnpike. The Corps was stretched out for almost a mile and a half—from an old tavern in the east, past a small church in the center, to a farmstead on the far west, and then into deep thickets. Hooker had posted Howard's men out here because, as a corps new to the army, and with a commander new to the corps, the men's fighting caliber was untested, and this position was going to be relatively quiet.[44]

And to many soldiers that morning, it looked quiet. To others, though, including observers in tall trees—many of them German—there were movements they saw that did not make sense. Whatever they were—a flash of steel, a gleam from a gun, a blur of gray or brown—they seemed human and were heading west. The soldiers took their impressions down out of the trees, and sent them from one superior to the next until they found their way to General Hooker. Hooker then sent word to Howard. "Determine your position," the commander said, "in order that you may be prepared for him in whatever direction he advances." Howard replied that he was "taking measures."[45]

The reports did not go away. Soldiers who were farthest in the woods heard sounds where they should not be, and the kind of noises—rumbling noises—that they should not hear. They repeated their concerns to their division commander, General Charles Devens, a Harvard man who had just come to the corps. General Devens, who some said was drinking brandy to soften the pain of a bruised leg, laughed at them and called them skittish. They repeated their worries, too, to their corps commander, and he told them not to be anxious. "For God's sake," they said, when they pleaded to be believed. They were told to be calm.[46]

In the middle of the afternoon, General Howard and his Harvard general and all the others who were telling men not to be frightened by phantoms were vindicated with some good news: General Daniel Sickles had had a good view of the Confederates and they seemed to be retreating. Others confirmed the Confederate retreat, and General Hooker, eager to claim the day as his, ordered Howard to part with one of his reserve brigades in order to help pursue the enemy as it moved away. Howard protested, but complied. He himself would accompany Francis Barlow's brigade to its new position. After four o'clock, then, there was no one in command at corps headquarters.[47]

Through the afternoon, the men of the Eleventh Corps, the right wing of the Union forces, lay in their battle lines. Some of them were positioned behind embankments and rifle pits, some had the woods at their backs, some had the trees to their front, and some were so fully in the Wilderness that it was hard to know forward from rear. Men still heard odd sounds—wheels turning or men shouting or horses rearing—but they had been reassured so often that they must have come to one of two conclusions: that they were badly deluded or—this was the ominous thing—that they were badly used. The men waited. At one point Union skirmishers pushed Confederate pickets back in the woods, and when this happened, a German band in front of Schurz's headquarters seized its instruments and struck up a tune. This was a small taste, it proclaimed with its brass, of the success to come.[48]

And then came the time just after five o'clock.

Finally, soldiers in the corps started to settle down after a nervous day. They built campfires and put kettles on to boil. They listened to bands playing under the shelter of pine trees. Some of them relaxed enough to grouse over a card game, and others lay down for a nap. A few of them gossiped. Many had stacked their muskets along the side of the turnpike, in a line five hundred feet long. Others had unsaddled their horses, and had fed them oats, because the next day they hoped to pursue Lee, and the animals needed strength.[49] At five o'clock the sun was still high in the sky, slanting its white beams through newly leafed trees and picking up smoke in its columns.

It was almost a scene of repose. And what broke it, suddenly, was something entirely benign. Animals burst in unison from the woods at the edge of the clearing—rabbits, deer, and woodland birds.

This, then, signified nothing. One second later, though, and it signified something very, very big. Startling the animals, and sending them through the thick screen of trees and into the clearing were thousands and thousands of enemy soldiers. Like a perverse trick of magic, rabbits became running men.

For some of the Union soldiers on the right flank, the attack was heard, not seen. One man thought it was a thunderstorm, but the sky was blue; another heard the sounds of breaking trees, and realized it was rifles firing in one long roll. Others listened to the horrible yells of the attackers. Having stifled their excitement all day, Confederate troops were liberated to scream as loud as they liked, as they rushed forward to kill.[50]

Howard's men, outnumbered, some of them unarmed, and with rifle shots at their front, at their sides, and even at their backs, decided or felt instinctively that it would be far better to get away than to stand, be killed, or be captured. Leopold von Gilsa's brigade, in General Devens' division, had been hit first, but soon the entire division was in full retreat toward headquarters. Then other men joined Devens' soldiers and they careened together on the narrow road back east to safety, a roiling mass of men and horses and wagons and artillery and cattle. *"Alles ist verloren!"* some of the men shouted. All is lost![51]

When General Howard returned after repositioning his reserve brigade, he tried to rally his troops. The wild firing panicked his horse, however, and it reared, throwing him to the ground. Remounted, with an American flag under his arm stump, he tried to inspirit his men. He and Schurz, all the while being shot at, hurrahed at soldiers to help drive the enemy back. But it was pointless. There was no fight left and there was no help. It was, said Howard, "indescribable panic." Other witnesses concurred. One soldier described the retreat as "headlong." "They had thrown away everything that was loose, guns, knapsacks, caps, and many had no coat and blouse. . . . Nothing could stop them. They were crazed." Another soldier made a more pointed observation. He described the fugitives as crying out "Der wash too many mens for us." A captain in the Third Corps noted that Howard's men, "heads bare and panting for breath . . . pleaded like infants at the mother's breast that we should let them pass to the rear."[52]

One thing that seemed to work against fellow soldiers in flight was to shoot them. According to an artilleryman in the Eleventh Corps, "Gen. Hooker soon ordered the 12th corps to kill every man that run in the 11th. I saw a number of Officers and privates shot." A Twelfth Corps soldier recalled that "we went at it like beavers, first with orders and then with oaths and threats. The fugitives ignored us and kept on, and finally Colonel Cook gave the order to shoot and four or five were shot down. . . . I saw [Colonel Cook] shoot one with a navy revolver at twenty rods; the man fell on his face."[53]

General Oliver Otis Howard did not try to shoot his men—he used exhortation and pleas to try to stop the stampede. It seems he would rather have shot himself. "I felt," he commented later on, "that I wanted to die. It was the only time I ever weakened that way in my life. . . . I sought death everywhere I could." Another soldier who came upon the general "swinging his revolver" and trying to halt his men described Howard in the throes of mortification.

"I'm ruined, I'm ruined," he says he heard Howard say, over and over and over again.[54]

For two hours Howard's corps retreated. The men did not all engage in headlong flight, shot at by Union and Confederate soldiers alike. Some of them "fought desperate" as they withdrew. Eleventh Corps artillery captain Hubert Dilger, who, like so many other officers, had cut his military teeth in Germany, held back a solid line of shooting men with a wild tenacity. His horse was shot from under him, and he commanded on foot. The horses of his caissons were killed, yet he held on, firing and refiring a single gun, slowing the attackers. Dilger's action helped other soldiers from Lieutenant Colonel Adolf Buschbeck's brigade re-form and make a stand. They held back the enemy for what must have seemed an eternity: It was half an hour.[55]

Among the regiments of the Eleventh Corps who did more than run for their lives was one new to battle. The 26th Wisconsin had been attacked by Jackson's men early on. With no trenches to work from, "no cannons or anything else with us," the men were ripped and shattered and riddled, but they stood and responded. "Every round our regiment fired," said Adam Muenzenberger, "mowed down rows of southerners." He rammed "charge after charge into his musket," as his fellow soldiers—men named Manz, Stirn, Burkhard, Weiss, Krueger, Fritz, Luther, Urich, Hermann, and Koch—went down. Realizing that these men were overwhelmed, General Schurz ordered the soldiers to fall back. Nearly every officer of the regiment had a bullet tear through his clothes, and almost half of the men had been hit. But they had been one of the few regiments to withdraw in "good order." And Adam Muenzenberger finally got his moment to fight.[56]

The battle went on beyond nightfall. Stonewall Jackson, the Christian Confederate general and strategist who had set the attack in motion, was mistakenly shot by his own men. But still the contest continued, for two more days, as Union troops bloodied themselves against Lee's army both at Chancellorsville and east at Fredericksburg, to no avail. The Eleventh Corps was ordered to a side line in rifle pits, in a position that exposed the men to enemy fire, but most units were not engaged again. Carl Schurz had hoped for "another opportunity for showing what we could do." And Otis Howard had voted to attack when General Hooker convened his major generals on May fourth to discuss strategy. But Hooker decided to retreat, and the battle was done.[57]

THE DAYS OF INFAMY

On the morning of May sixth, the men of the Eleventh Corps crossed back over the Rappahannock River the way they had come ten days earlier. They had lighter packs now, but no buoyancy, and their high spirits had settled into shock. They made their old camp by nightfall, and some of the men got drunk. Other soldiers began to report home, and to share the brutal images that beat in their heads. One German soldier could not get over the picture of dead men broken like "cut glass," their guts exposed, their limbs gone. He wanted his parents to know that the enemy had attacked "unforseen," and that "we were caught."[58]

It was one hard thing to fight for your life, and another to have to defend yourself again, days later. Howard's soldiers had barely recovered from the battle's brutality when they faced a different threat: the nation's scorn. The cruel news came from everywhere. It arrived from New York, Washington, Philadelphia, Pittsburgh, Chicago, Milwaukee—from cities on the East Coast, from river ports on the Mississippi, and from the farming heartland. Newspapers everywhere proclaimed these immigrants to be the country's cowards. How many ways were there to describe men as frightened animals? Reporters found them all. They told the world the soldiers from Germany had run like a herd of stupid sheep. They said that the soldiers had made a disgraceful stampede. They said these men had been so eager to flee that they hadn't bothered to fire a shot. Yankee newspapers even put Confederate contempt into print. At a prison in Richmond, a Union prisoner had heard his captors say that "had they known that the Eleventh corps was composed of such cowardly poltroons they would have sent a note to Gen. Hooker requesting him to place some troops there that would at least fire one round without running away as these did—they did not want to fight sheep." And it was not simply that these timorous men had exposed their own feeble manhood—they were responsible for the failure of the whole campaign. One New York editor recommended "shooting the entire German brigade."[59]

The recriminations within the country's press became recriminations within the corps itself. Some senior German officers turned on each other, defending their own troops, demanding retractions, threatening court-martial. More often, however, German-born and native-born soldiers exchanged blame and insult. Some native-born officers wondered if they could get away from the immigrants. Boston-educated Brigadier General Francis Barlow, who had been brought over to the corps in April, couldn't bear the thought that the public associated his brigade with the runaway hordes. "Dearest mother & brothers," he wrote home, "You can imagine my indignation & disgust at the miserable behavior of the 11th Corps. It does not appear as plainly as I should desire in the [New York] Tribune letter of May 4th that my Brigade was not with the rest of the Corps." Barlow did not feel it was entirely fair to blame "the Dutch" for the disaster, but he could not "abate [his] contempt" for the German-born men around him. The best Barlow could do in these ignominious times was to imagine the world of refinement that waited for him in New England. "I assure you," he wrote to a friend, "that when I look upon the miserable beasts that I have about me I rejoice to think that there is such a place as Massachusetts."[60]

At the receiving end of such arrogance were men like Alexander Schimmelfennig. This veteran soldier, a short, curly-haired man, given to wearing worn-out uniforms, drew more attention than most immigrant officers for his "Germanness." His name, so definitively, so provocatively German, had once tied the tongue of Abraham Lincoln, and it slipped up other native-born men in the corps, including Howard. Like his fellow revolutionary and exile Carl Schurz, Schimmelfennig believed in the promise of a free and strong American republic. When the country had been threatened in 1861, he moved quickly to defend it. By August 1862, he was leading bayonet charges at Second Bull Run and holding firm against Stonewall Jackson. His resoluteness and valor helped earn him the rank of brigadier general.[61]

The memory of those praiseworthy days must have deepened the wound inflicted by Chancellorsville, and Schimmelfennig took Jackson's attack and the disaster that followed as hard as anyone. He sequestered himself in his tent and, unwilling to talk, told aides he had a headache. His suffering only got worse when he took newspapers in, and he read them one by one, and swore. Schimmelfennig had tried to warn Howard of a flanking attack that afternoon, but headquarters had smiled an "incredulous" smile and told him to "stop reconnoitering." Now it seemed that the contempt that dismissed his concerns that sad afternoon was the same contempt that blamed him. He felt too old for this, and he worried about the "soldierly spirit" of his men. Was it not now broken?[62]

It was Carl Schurz, though, who bore the brunt of the press's assault. As an outspoken abolitionist and political activist, he was a likely target for anti-German and anti-Republican wrath, and he and his men seemed to personify the army's disgrace: It was Schurz's division that had led the flight; it was Schurz's cowards who had thrown down their guns and gone streaming to the rear, demoralizing everyone else.[63]

Carl Schurz was beleaguered, but he was also combative. He protested to Generals Howard and Hooker, and he used his official report to vindicate his actions on May second. He had been worried, he said, that the army's right wing "stood completely in the air," and he had forwarded his concerns to Howard. He had positioned two regiments facing the woods to the west, just in case. Twenty-three percent of his troops—almost 1,000 men—had been killed, wounded, or gone missing. And yet his division, which was not even the first to retreat, was held up to ridicule and was abused by the army "beyond measure."

"We have borne as much as human nature can endure," Schurz wrote in protest to Howard. "I am far from saying that on May 2d everybody did his duty to the best of his power. But one thing I will say, because I know it: these men are not cowards."[64]

Schurz's pain was echoed across America, and German Americans met in cities around the country to issue printed protests. His pain was also felt (which is not to say that it was shared) by General Hooker, who tried to correct some of the press's inaccurate facts, and at least one major paper, The *New York Herald,* retracted. The *New York Times,* no doubt responding to German-American protests in the city, also backpedaled. It reminded its readers that no men had "been truer to the flag" than German soldiers. They had been labeled "mere adventurers enlisting for excitement, or mercenaries fighting for pay . . . [but] these soldiers have served their country . . . with as unselfish an impulse as any Americans." At the same time, the *Times* dared to express the hope that some of these men in the service might lose their Germanness. The military, the paper said, could be "a wonderful school for instilling American ideas, sentiments, sympathies and convictions, and for unlearning a great deal that has been brought over from the old world. . . . The blood that mixes in the battle-field, in one common sacrifice, will be a cement of American nationality."[65] The *Times* could support immigrant soldiers against slander, then, by hoping men lost their immigrant ways.

It would certainly be a long while before soldiers in the Eleventh Corps could imagine anything resembling cultural mixing. General Francis Barlow continued to think of ways to get away from the "Dutch." But his hopes backfired when he became division commander in early June, overseeing the predominantly German brigade that was hit first in the Chancellorsville attack. Now, though, he would be able to break these men in. He would rule his division with "hard knocks & a tight rein" to instill proper discipline. "I expect," he wrote home, "to have to arrest them all the way down until I find some private soldier who will make them do things properly." At the end of June 1863, Barlow had a respite from his dreaded foreign element when the "Dutch Brigade" was detached for other duty. "I suppose I shall have it again in case of a battle," the general complained.[66] He was right.

For their part, German-American soldiers grew even more suspicious of their Yankee officers and commander. Chancellorsville had been an attack on every front, and the damage was deep. What had happened even made painful sense: They had been left out there in the woods alone, to be sacrificed, because they were disposable. "It was all General Howard's fault," wrote a soldier in the 26th Wisconsin. "He is a Yankee, and that is why he wanted to have us slaughtered. . . . He better not come into the thick of battle a second time, then he won't escape." Adam Muenzenberger also found himself discouraged with the high command. The battle had plundered his hope for an easy end to the war and it had punched cruel holes in his community. After marching back twenty-eight miles with his regiment, the sight of his old camp made him sick: "When we . . . pitched our tents we saw only misery. One third of the tents in our camp were empty. And why? Because those who had occupied them were no more. Where are they? Dead! In the hospitals. Captured by the rebels. . . . We have only three hundred men in active service. We crossed the Rappahannock with six hundred."[67]

Muenzenberger blamed the "humbug" generals—particularly Howard—and the "humbug" war, and hoped the "swindle will end pretty soon." "This affair," he wrote, "is nothing more or less than the greatest fraud ever concocted." Muenzenberger felt more and more like a social casualty: a soldier in a ridiculed corps, a poor man overruled by rich officers, an outsider in a hostile America. But he continued to draw comfort from the German friends who wished him well from Wisconsin, and he drew hope from his family.[68]

After Chancellorsville, the Eleventh Corps camped at Brooke's Station, Virginia, as it waited with the rest of Hooker's army to see what Lee would do next. The place seemed desolate. The blight of war had ruined the look of the southern spring, destroying farms, taking down fences, dismembering trees, and the weather—sunny, dry, and increasingly hot—made it worse. The men were ordered to drill, over and over again, and as they marched the dirt became dust, and it deepened and thickened like snow, lying in drifts, and rising into choking clouds. Men waded through it up to their ankles. Sickness circulated through the camps on these rainless days, and up at the corps hospital, some of the wounded men got better, but many did not.[69]

At headquarters, General Howard took as long to recover from Chancellorsville as anyone. Like so many other soldiers, his first reaction to the battle was relief at having survived it. He felt he had never been so exposed to bullets and shells. Then, too, he found out that his wife and baby had lived through the rigors of childbirth at the same time. His jubilation at the well-being of all three of them was such that he suggested to his wife that they name their new son Chancy, after the battle.[70] The name stuck. Whether later he regretted associating his son with one of the worst military moments in his army's history we do not know.

Howard's second impulse had been to give his son a German name, after Frederick Dessaur, a captain on his staff who had been shot while rallying the broken troops. Howard felt bad about the ignominy that rained down upon the German men of the corps after the battle, and he had written to Schurz soon after returning to camp to tell him that he was "deeply pained to find you subjected to such false and malicious attacks." But Howard never came out publicly in defense of his immigrant soldiers, and he never admitted to being at fault himself. Was it that Howard did not honestly believe he had been mistaken that day in the Wilderness? He wrote home to Elizabeth that he "had neglected no precaution." Or was it that he was so sensitive to criticism, so jealous of honor and pride, that he could not admit to being wrong?[71]

Some of the most damaging criticism directed at Howard was delivered by Carl Schurz. And much of it Schurz summed up in a letter he sent to Howard at the end of May. He composed the letter several times, perhaps to get its tone of bitterness, even vengeance, just right. He informed Howard that he needed to tell him "certain things" that he did "not seem to be aware of." They were of a "painful nature." First of all, Schurz had to tell Howard that the men of the corps no longer had confidence in him or in themselves. Were they to enter a battle under him, in fact, "The first thing they will do when placed in a position will be to look behind them, and the accidental discharge of a musket in their rear will produce another panic, another disaster, another disgrace, to yourself, to the troops, to all of us." Even the American troops had lost faith in Howard's command, Schurz asserted, and "whoever may tell you differently, either is deceived or is deceiving you."[72]

The worst was to come. Schurz explained to Howard that the "state of things has led to secret transactions." "The universal desire," he wrote, "is the return of Gen. Sigel to this Corps. He has, of old, the confidence of the men. He was written to by a great many officers and has now expressed his willingness to come back. He is probably at Washington at this moment. I will say to you confidentially that Gen. Hooker was advised of all of this and favors it." Schurz closed his letter by assuring Howard that conveying these truths was "one of the hardest duties I ever performed."[73]

Oliver Otis Howard thought he would never survive this letter. He took everything Schurz said to heart. He believed that "the Germans and the Americans are . . . against me." He believed that Hooker would easily "sacrifice me." And he wondered if he should go home. After all the years of training, all the years of anxious striving and worrying about public regard, it had come to this. "If I could go home where I am loved & be quiet I should like it," he wrote to his wife. He went to Washington and let the army chiefs know that he could be removed: "I said to the President, Sec. of War & to Genl Hooker, if you have anybody else whom you deem better able under the circumstances to command this Corps you must not hesitate on my account to give him the command." Lincoln, though, still had confidence in Howard. "Give him time," the president said, and he kept him in.[74]

Otis Howard also had his own reasons for remaining with the army. Chancellorsville, he believed, had been a judgment from God. It had been a message to the unfaithful officers in the Union army to reconsider a Christian life. Howard begged his brother, a minister in Maine, to use his spiritual energies to help him: "Would that you would plead with our Father to convert the soul of Gen Hooker. It is just what we need. The Rebels are praising God & appealing to Him. We are despising God & trusting in fine looking soldiers."[75]

Howard needed to stay, then, and strengthen officers' Christian spirit. He could also help enlisted men. Men who had faith did not run away, he believed, because they were not afraid to die. That kind of faith had made him a three-limbed man, to be sure, but it had also helped him at Chancellorsville rally his troops under enemy fire. He also had an obligation to all the wives and sisters and mothers who counted on him for his influence. He knew, sometimes all too well, that Christian men and women at home, along with the many commissions and churches and societies they sponsored, did not want to see him leave the army.[76]

Howard had another reason for remaining where he was. Like many of the German officers who now reviled him, he believed he was fighting for something important. Stonewall Jackson may have prayed to the same God, in other words, but not for the same reason. Howard was not a vocal anti-slavery man, but he had been a long-standing one, and he believed in what he would later call practical abolitionism: He wanted to see emancipated people educated, clothed, employed. He also thought that black men should be able to fight in the war even if it might "create hate." And in his words and in his ways in camp he revealed a strong belief in equality before God. He hosted prayer meetings that condemned slavery, and he brought black servants into his prayer meetings as part of the human family to be saved. Howard looked at African Americans with paternalistic concern, but also with generosity and hope.[77]

How much he had seen of racial hatred before he had come down to the South with the army is unclear, but Howard felt it close to home when a young man who worked as one of his servants was offhandedly shot to death by Union soldiers in the winter of 1862. He was also made aware of what slavery did to people. In the summer of 1861 a black woman had made her way through army lines to Howard's headquarters and appeared at his doorstep with an infant and a ten-year-old son. She sought his help. But a "mean ugly woman" claimed the family, and Howard could not get permission to keep her with the army. She said she would "drown herself" before she would go back.[78]

In the end, Howard did not resign because he had work to do so that women and ten-year-old boys did not have to choose between suicide and slavery. There was a "wrong side" to this war that he wanted to oppose. His brother wrote to him from home to remind him of these things and to encourage him not to leave his work unfinished. "A wicked system of oppression & bondage is to be ended," he wrote to the general. "A Nation is to be raised up on fields that have been desolated—to show forth Gods glory—These are great things."[79]

And so Otis Howard stayed on. And proud Carl Schurz stayed on. Like Howard, he would not let his hurt and disappointment steer him from the "splendid goal" and "mighty cause" of emancipation. And men like Adam Muenzenberger, who had far less say in the matter, stayed on too. All of these soldiers would have another chance to work together, to redeem themselves from obloquy, and to help win the war.[80]

2

⋆⋆

THE SEASON OF DISBELIEF

THE GAP IN THE MOUNTAIN

From the Evergreen Cemetery gatehouse where she lived at the edge of Gettysburg, Elizabeth Thorn had a good view of South Mountain, nine miles away to the west. She had a good view, too, of a gap in the ridge, a place where wind and water once eroded the rock, or where, long ago, faults in the earth broke the continuum.[1] This gap appears so inconsequential, and from a distance is such a minor hesitation in the mountain line, that it is hard to imagine that Thorn paid it much attention before the summer of 1863. But by the end of the month of June, Cashtown Gap, as it was called, had become the talk of the town. It had become nothing less than a portal of war, disgorging enemy soldiers by the tens of thousands, and spewing out horses and wagons and caissons—all the moving machinery of battle.[2]

The Southern army that emerged from Cashtown Gap and the Northern army that moved quickly to meet it would converge near Elizabeth Thorn's home. Masses of soldiers would position themselves around her gatehouse, camp in "her" cemetery, and swarm over her backyard. Many of these Union soldiers included men born in Germany, just as she had been. They also included a general, a one-armed soldier, who would ride near her house on the morning of July first. There, up on Cemetery Hill, Oliver Otis Howard would look around at the countryside, even as Thorn certainly did. He would not see it with her eyes, however. He would look at farms and see killing fields. He would appreciate the elevation, but for him it would be high ground, a good place for guns.

Until 1863, Elizabeth Thorn and other white women in Gettysburg had, by all accounts, envisioned a wartime life apart from active battle. They believed, as did most Americans at the time, that men went away soldiering because

33

God and nature had fitted them to fight, protect, and defend, and that women, whom God and nature had fitted to be both pacific and retiring, presided over private domains of nurture and support. Everybody knew the social divisions were not perfect. In this war, in fact, women had moved to the front as nurses, scouts, and spies—even as soldiers in disguise. But everyone also saw that tradition persisted.[3] Most Northern women who served in the Civil War did not travel at all. They supported soldiers from home, by taking on extra jobs, by standing in for their husbands on farms or in businesses, and by raising children alone. They organized local aid societies to send soldiers food, clothing, and medical supplies, and they took part in local ceremonies to honor military troops. From the homefront, they also apprised themselves of political events and military developments in order to be active and involved.[4]

Most women in the North thus labored far from the stage of combat. They could keep their distance, too, because the hallmark of men's wartime work—the actual battle—rarely drew near. While soldiers had brought war to women in the South, and had fought hard in places like Fredericksburg, Virginia, and Vicksburg, Mississippi, and while they had even moved into Maryland, they had left the North largely alone. Confederate cavalrymen had threatened civilians in southern Pennsylvania when they had raided north in 1862, but Northern women, including Gettysburg women, had never been caught in war's worst violence.[5]

And then came that summer, over two years into the conflict. When a battle came to Gettysburg, and women were trapped between armies, they reported shock on all fronts. They saw, some of them all too tragically, that soldiers ran and chased and shot and killed anywhere they felt they could get the job done, inside of town and outside of town and indoors and out. They saw that the arena of battle was broad and complicated, and that they had to be players, too. And so they stepped in. They performed "womanly" duties in the emergency—they cooked, they served, they nursed, and they comforted, but they also deployed domesticity to protest and undermine the enemy. Compelled to enter the physical whirlwind, they reevaluated their alleged weaknesses and the rightful spheres of their work. Courage was required at Gettysburg, they realized, but it was not limited to soldiers.

But in June of 1863, white women and girls in Gettysburg, including the five highlighted here, were still innocent of the trials of battle. In fact, they had been repeatedly told, certainly by parents and by ministers, but most obviously by the press, that war imposed special rules on them, and that battle was out of bounds. This was important assurance, because they had plenty going on as it was without embracing some new, or extraordinary, demands. Georgia McClellan, who lived just north of Cemetery Hill in Gettysburg, was, for instance, heavily pregnant, and yet continued to work for her family and for soldiers' aid. (She had also made no plans to be anywhere but home for her delivery.) Fannie Buehler, a prominent woman who lived in the middle of the borough on Baltimore Street, had a house full of children to cajole and supervise. She had recently taken in two nieces, too, so that they could enjoy a salubrious summer in the countryside. Her opinionated mother was visiting as well. North of town, Harriet Bayly had her hands full as the hardworking wife of a farmer and the mother of seven children. And nine-year-old Sadie Bushman was likely busy in the early summer with household work, school assignments, and Sunday school lessons. None of these women, as the summer progressed, gave much thought to military campaigns. Harriet Bayly thought that battle "may come to everybody else, but not to us." And when Sadie heard the news about approaching armies, it was nothing short of "startling."[6]

Elizabeth Thorn's Cemetery Hill home was a particularly demanding place. The thirty-year-old Thorn, a thin, determined-looking woman with brown hair, watched over three young sons and elderly parents. She had also taken over her husband's job. When Peter Thorn had enlisted in the Union army in 1862, he left behind his work as superintendent of the new town cemetery, and this included grave-digging, managing reinterments, and performing general cemetery upkeep. Now this was Elizabeth's responsibility, and she had to get by with whatever able hands—usually her father's—she could find to assist her. The fact that she was five months pregnant may have slowed her down some, but it did not give her a reason to quit.[7]

Like many women in wartime Gettysburg, Elizabeth Thorn had too little money and too much to do. Compounding the difficulties of her life in the borough may have been her foreignness. She had been born and raised in Germany, just to the east of the Rhine, in Hesse Darmstadt. We do not know how her family, the Mösers, found its way to Pennsylvania in midcentury— whether it was encouragement from a relative, or a friend who wanted familiar company, or whether it was something more in the way of an accidental landing—but by 1854 Gettysburg had become the Möser's adopted home.[8]

Elizabeth Möser Thorn thus had something in common with the soldiers from the Eleventh Corps who would stream past the cemetery and sleep in her backyard on the first of July 1863. In fact, just as men like Adam Muenzenberger and Carl Schurz struggled with an army filled with nativists, she, too, faced community leaders hostile toward immigrants. The fact that early white settlement in Adams County had been dominated by Scots-Irish and German newcomers did little to diminish nativist prejudice in the 1850s. According to Gettysburg *Star and Banner* editor David Buehler (Fannie Buehler's husband), the borough would do well to purge itself of individuals born outside of the United States. Buehler's paper, echoing angry sentiment that was widespread in the country, railed against immigrant indigents who filled local alms-houses, against foreign Catholics with their allegiance to the Pope, and against imported "infidels"—communists, anarchists, atheists. Despite the fact that less than ten percent of Gettysburg's families were actually foreign born, or perhaps because of it, people like Elizabeth and Peter Thorn stood on social probation.[9]

While immigrant men hoped that military enlistment would open the doors to inclusion, German-American women were offered no equally straightfor-ward path to acceptance. American public opinion stressed how important it was for all women to be submissive, undemanding, and domestically efficient, but sometimes suggested that rural German women had a long way to go. Stereotypes of German women often underscored their masculine-ness. They were also seen as crude, stubborn, and stingy. Harriet Beecher Stowe popular-ized some of these images in her fiction before the war. In an essay about hiring a chambermaid, for example, she described a thick-headed, uncultivated "Dutch" girl, who was handicapped by ungainly hands and feet, and who had a habit of staring with her mouth wide open. She carried an air of "stupid won-der." (It is uncertain whether Stowe amended her opinions after her son Fred-erick began serving as a staff officer with the Eleventh Corps in 1863.) Judging from commentary by Union and Confederate soldiers as they entered Pennsyl-vania, opinions such as Stowe's were widely held. They were certainly shared by Gettysburg's *Star and Banner*, which reported before the war that it was be-coming all the rage in Germany for women to wear mustaches.[10]

An immigrant woman who sought a degree of acceptance among the native-born, then, would appear demure, dependent, and self-sacrificing. All this certainly seemed possible for Elizabeth Möser, at least before the war. She married Peter Thorn, also German-born, and together they seem to have skirted social scorn. The couple lived quietly, worked diligently, and raised a family. Evidence suggests that they lived in a conjugal household in a conven-tional marriage and did little to raise public eyebrows. They were Protestants, too, which meant that they might even have shared in, or at least been spared from, the anti-Catholic, anti-immigrant sentiment rising among some of the town's elite. Furthermore, Peter Thorn, in what was certainly a marker of his acceptance in town, was hired as the new cemetery's first caretaker, earning $13 a month. Ever Green Cemetery, as people referred to it at first, was located on "the first hill on the Baltimore turnpike, west side," and it soon became one of the town's most celebrated sites—a commanding resting place for the departed, and a place for Sunday strolls and reveries. The cemetery gatehouse would be home to the whole Thorn family.[11]

The Thorns steered clear of social difficulty in the 1850s, but, like other local immigrants, they continued to suffer warnings. In November 1855, just months after Peter and Elizabeth Thorn had married, the American Party, dedicated to restricting the rights of the foreign-born, staged a political rally in Gettysburg, with some of the most prominent residents of the borough leading a parade. A torch-light parade shortly afterward repeated the demonstration, with women—"American ladies"—waving handkerchiefs and saluting men who carried banners reading "Americans must rule America" and "We want no European paupers or felons."[12]

The Thorns also experienced some ups and downs in managing the cemetery. In 1857, it was alleged that "improper persons" were desecrating the Sabbath and fouling the cemetery by vandalizing gravesites, drinking, and racing through blessed ground in their buggies. The cemetery's board of directors issued public warnings to anybody who might think of creating havoc again, posting signs against misbehavior, including the firing of guns. By 1863, with Peter Thorn in the Union army, cemetery infractions had become Elizabeth Thorn's responsibility. She was probably experienced enough by this time to imagine that cemetery mandates were not perfectly enforceable, but it is likely that she did not picture the sort of man who would make the utmost mockery of its injunctions. General Oliver Otis Howard was a God-fearing man, who honored the Sabbath as earnestly as anyone. But when Howard arrived in Gettysburg in July 1863, and positioned batteries inside the cemetery, he played the part of a battle-hardened corps commander as much as a dedicated Christian.[13]

It was the abrupt arrival of General Howard's soldiers as well as tens of thousands of other armed men that would ultimately put Elizabeth Thorn and her family to the severest test of propriety. German-American women had been put on notice for "unwomanly" appearances and for selfish behavior. Suddenly, however, Thorn would find herself, pregnant, at the very epicenter of battle, where she would be in demand by officers, threatened by gunfire, and surrounded by soldiers on all sides. She and her family would also find themselves homeless, hungry, and destitute. It was going to be very hard for her not to test, and possibly bend, the rules of "American" respectability.

Just down the hill from Elizabeth Thorn, Georgia Wade McClellan anticipated an eventful summer in 1863, but a battle did not have anything to do with it. And she certainly did not contemplate the personal horror to come—no one would have expected that. But this twenty-one-year-old woman probably invested the days of June with more than the average worry. She was, like her neighbor, pregnant, and eight months into the heavy work of bearing her first child. She, too, had a husband fighting for the Union. And she, too, had struggled to get by in Gettysburg. She had spent time at the poorhouse when she was a young child, along with the rest of her family. Her father, a tailor, had had repeated run-ins with the law, usually involving assault charges, and when Georgia was eleven years old, he had been convicted of larceny and sent away to two years of solitary work at the state penitentiary. Shortly after he arrived home from this jail term, his wife had him certified as insane and he was sent off again, this time to the poorhouse, and this time for good.[14]

Georgia Wade, as she had been known when the war began, was a dark-haired girl with a crooked smile. Along with her younger sister Jennie[15] and their mother, she made a living by sewing and mending, and by the time the war began, this work had helped the family move away from want and embarrassment. There was no end in sight to seamstressing, but the family had saved enough to buy a house in the southern part of the borough on Breckenridge Street. And Georgia and Jennie, who were churchgoing girls, began to realize the promise of romantic love. By June 1863 Jennie carried around a letter—somewhere, it is said, in the front of her dress—from an honorable young Gettysburg man named Jack Skelly, and Georgia's sweetheart, a local Pennsylvania College student named John Louis McClellan, had returned from war to marry her in 1862.[16] (By taking on a husband, Georgia Wade may or may not have enhanced her family's respectability. McClellan, according to one historian, had been an "illegitimate" child, and his service late in the war was subject to question. At one point, his sister-in-law reported that he "was tired of playing soldier," and after his second tour of duty, in 1865, he was listed as "absent, in arrest" when his company was mustered out.)[17]

Georgia Wade McClellan's pregnancy, her relative poverty, and her family's difficulties all crowded her days in June of 1863. She never spoke of how she might juggle a battle with her other concerns, but she did not need to. For years, advice givers, including newspaper editors, had spelled out to young women like her what she might anticipate in wartime, and all of it involved staying out of harm's way. Some Democratic editors, unhappy with Lincoln's call to arms, argued that women were not only unsuited for the sphere of war, but opposed to it altogether. Peace was a "loving mother," one editor insisted, and war "an unnatural monster who devours his own children."[18] Republican editors of course disagreed: Female instinct, they argued, was given more to sacrifice than pacifism, and women needed to sustain the Union and encourage enlistment. Shame on the ladies, in fact, who did not take the time to support soldiers at the front. But Republican politicians did agree with their Democratic counterparts that women should perform their wartime work without going anywhere. If they had anything to do with soldiers, it was ideally in a local setting. As soldiers paraded in their hometown, for instance, they could cheer them on, fluttering handkerchiefs from the safety of a porch or a window.[19] Gettysburg women, it seems, concurred with this scheme. When a number of "ladies" presented a flag to the local militia before the war began, they asserted that their sphere "is not amid the rude commerce of camps, and the soul-hardening struggles of political power, but in an humbler path."[20]

Gettysburg women might easily have assented, then, to the idea, promoted in a local paper, that in wartime they should be "A Being to Come Home To." When the "bold warrior" returned, the paper advised, a woman should help him "doff" his helmet, and use womanly hands to pour into his wounds "the healing balm." Local women may have been less eager to listen to incessant instruction, delivered with no sense of apparent irony, that in wartime they must "naturally" bend themselves to greater labor. It was widely supposed that women, with their inherent penchant for domesticity, would enthusiastically take on the extra obligations of soldier's aid work, including producing massive amounts of clothing and bedding, packaged food, and medical supplies. When some Pennsylvania women began to seek recognition or even compensation for what they believed was extraordinary effort, public officials were baffled. Why would a woman be compensated for something that emanated from her heart?[21] Men went off to battle to do unparalleled work, but women who worked at home moved seamlessly from caring for families to caring for soldiers. Or did they?

Georgia McClellan and her sister Jennie Wade certainly needed no lectures on staying home and encouraging soldiers from home base. They supported two brothers who had enlisted in the Union army. And when the 10th New York Cavalry was stationed near Gettysburg in 1861–1862, it appears that the Wade sisters went out of their way to be sociable, engaging hosts. By all accounts, the sisters also did not need lectures on hard work or sacrifice. In fact, judging from the comments of other Gettysburg women before and during the Civil War, neither did anybody else. Even women who had household help claimed to have exhausted themselves. They worked until they were sick or unless they were sick, and through the day and into the night. They were often up beyond midnight sewing and mending; they spent hours darning socks; they mixed, kneaded, and baked bread; they scrubbed and sorted clothes; they planted and pickled, canned, stewed, and boiled; they dusted and they swept. They criticized themselves when they slept in until six in the morning or if they had not worked quickly enough to be done by midnight. And then, in the middle of the day, or at the beginning or end of it, they looked after babies, younger sisters and brothers, not to mention their own mothers, who were themselves sick and tired. On top of this they did work for men who were not even their own men, who were off fighting for the Union.[22]

Gettysburg women like Georgia McClellan needed little instruction in domestic labor and wartime support, but they were offered it anyway. In contrast, they were given virtually no public instruction in performing the ultimate female task: childbearing. Newspapers, so ready with advice for females, rarely touched on this, the most private work that women performed. Nor did newspapers recognize it as any sort of contribution to the Union war effort. Unlike soldier's aid work or other homefront contributions, this labor was entirely invisible, possibly because women would have endured it regardless of war, perhaps because it seemed the most "natural" of all of women's work. But women's childbearing and delivery, which kept the Union future literally alive, actually represented a dangerous struggle, with high casualty rates. It was a rare mother, in fact, who did not lose either her own life in childbirth or any of her children in birth or infancy in the nineteenth century. Indeed, most expectant women approached the moment of delivery fearfully. They cleaned their houses, tidied their cupboards and drawers, and straightened their accounts, not because, as popular sentiment would have it, they were nesting and preparing the nursery, but because they wanted to be able to hand over an organized house if they died. We do not know what Georgia McClellan wrote to her soldier-husband regarding her impending confinement, but it might have sounded like so many other resigned women about to give birth: "It occurs to me that possibly I may not live," or "This life may soon be closed," or "There may be but a step between me and eternity," or "I think that perhaps I may die," or "I have made my will."[23]

Georgia McClellan perhaps drew some comfort from the fact that her mother had given birth successfully seven times, but she also certainly knew that her youngest sister, Martha Margaret, had died as an infant in 1849.[24] There were no guarantees in this business. And so, while her husband engaged in newsworthy battles and faced a noteworthy death, Georgia and other women like her faced quieter, death-defying trials. At least they were supposed to be quieter—childbirth and confinement were traditionally moments of sequestered domesticity. Of all human endeavors, they were the least likely to intersect with the rough and bloody work of armies.

Harriet Bayly could have told Georgia McClellan a few things about childbirth and loss, for in 1863 her grief was raw. She also had lived long enough and seen enough to know that the "rules of war" that kept home and army separated were sometimes broken. She had felt vulnerable and exposed in 1862, for instance, when Confederate troopers had marauded into Pennsylvania. Now, less than a year later, her anxiety intensified. This forty-three-year-old woman, married to a farmer, lived three miles north of the borough, and had borne six sons and one daughter. It was her daughter that she fretted about, and not because she feared what would happen to the girl if soldiers came close—her daughter was dead. What Harriet Bayly worried about was the possibility that enemy soldiers might seize her daughter's pet, a chestnut mare named Nellie.

It had been in March 1862 that Jane Ann Bayly, who was ten years old, had become sick with a severe sore throat. Gettysburg was not known as an unhealthy place. In fact, not many years before, the town had boasted that it was remarkably free from epidemics. Cholera certainly never made a serious claim on Gettysburg. But other diseases, like scarlet and typhoid fever, had insinuated themselves into the borough, and one infectious disease attacked local children especially. It was known as diphtheria.[25]

How did Jane Ann Bayly contract diphtheria? Maybe one of her older brothers brought it home one day, or maybe she had caught it from a classmate. Or maybe it had simply passed to her from the hand of a stranger. The disease, however it found her, may have taken everyone unaware. It might not have looked ominous at first, not even a high fever. But at some point Jane Ann would have become very, very tired, her throat would have become sore, her tonsils would have become swollen, and ultimately she would have struggled for air.[26]

Harriet Bayly never wrote publicly about her daughter's last days, but, thanks to another Gettysburg mother, whose child had earlier died of a throat disease, we might imagine how she felt. This woman had a young son who had been sick, and one night his fever was so high she bathed him in alcohol to cool him down. After she had washed him, she had fallen asleep in the attic room where he lay. When she awoke, at four in the morning, the room was barely light. She looked over at her child's crib. There, she said, was "a white covering thrown over the crib." Her husband then "raised his head and told me that our dear child was now numbered with the dead and that his gentle spirit had passed through the dark valley and shadow without a struggle at 2 oclock it was almost at the same time of night that he was born." She went to look at her son. He appeared cold and shrunken in death and his back was "black and blue." She held him, too, just as she had so many times earlier. She remembered how when she had had him on her lap, alive, she would talk of heaven. She also remembered that he had been a very mischievous boy. She could picture him even now, coming to her with "streaming eyes" after he had been naughty and saying, "Mama I will be a good boy now." "Oh dear," she wrote, we had no idea that he "had so early ripened."[27]

Harriet Bayly carried the same kind of hurt for her daughter into the summer of 1863, and it was made worse by her worries about an invasion. As an abolitionist, she believed in the war's possibilities, and she had, like so many women, doubled her work to support the men in service. With other volunteers, she packaged supplies and food to send to soldiers at the front. Now, however, the war seemed to be closing in on her, and as it did so, she grew increasingly concerned about what enemy men might do to her farm. She knew that Confederate soldiers might want the family's crops, its cows, its sheep— and its horses. "A farmer needs a horse as much as a house," she explained, for it was impossible to harvest grain without one. But one of her horses was no mere draft animal; one of her horses was Nellie. The mother remembered how, a long time back, Jane Ann had seen this mare for the first time: "When she was a tiny bit of a girl, her father came in one morning and said 'Daughter, there's a nice little [filly] at the barn and it is to be yours and you must give it a name.' So she called it 'Nellie,' and it was the nicest little animal we ever had, swift as a bird, gentle as the sound of her own name, and so kind always." The presence of fleet-footed Nellie may have kept grief fresh for Harriet Bayly, but the horse was also a living, breathing link to her lost girl. So of all the things that she did not want to relinquish to an enemy, but of all the things she knew they would want, it was this animal.[28]

Fannie Guyon Buehler, who lived in the center of the Borough of Gettysburg, did not share Harriet Bayly's worries about Confederate raiding. Instead, she fretted about how a visiting enemy might enact pointed punishment. As the news of Confederate activity increased, she sent three of her children to her sister in New Jersey and kept the youngest and the oldest at home. Children, however, seemed the least of her concerns. Thirty-seven-year-old Fannie also planned to evacuate her husband, who was a postmaster and prominent Republican newspaper editor, a likely target for Confederate capture. Then there was her mother, a "red hot Republican," whose thoughts about secession were expressed with "words which were not always wisely chosen." "Had she been a man," Fannie explained, "she would have been among the very first in the attempt to put down the Rebellion." Mrs. Guyon was like a lot of women in Pennsylvania who had become passionately invested in the political fate of the nation, but unlike a lot of those women, she now resided on the borderland. Fannie worried about what might happen when this woman with "intense feelings" met enemies she loathed. Wartime chivalry ideally protected elderly white women from army anger. But why take a chance? Fannie Buehler decided to send her mother away. She obviously believed that a lot was at play in this war—including the fact that old women might take a stand with Confederate soldiers and that soldiers, for their part, might do away with decorum.[29]

Fannie was less bothered by her own predilections. She had for many years positioned herself as the upstanding wife of a town leader and as a churchgoing woman of means and respectability. According to her husband's newspaper, *The Star and Banner,* Fannie shared her husband's opinions about women and their (domestic) responsibilities, as well as his commitment to anti-slavery and temperance. She may also have shared her husband's distaste for German immigrants—the "dregs" of Europe, as his paper put it—and she perhaps served as one of those handkerchief-waving women during nativist torch-light parades. Above all, though, Fannie Buehler was a very careful person. If enemy men were coming, she would see that her children were safe and that the two "targets" in her family were out of town. She did not, it seems, want to experience anything out of the ordinary in these extraordinary times.[30]

Most of Fannie Buehler's children would be spared the Battle of Gettysburg, but two of them were not. As Fannie would discover, it was easier to evacuate family members before armies had materialized than when they surrounded the town, when security was "nowhere to be found." Scores of other children would not be able to leave town in time. As much as Sadie Bushman's parents wanted to send her to safe haven when the shelling began, it did not work, and the nine-year-old girl was trapped.[31]

Sadie entered the summer of 1863 as a schoolgirl, that much we can be quite sure of—but how hard she studied or what she learned, or whether she worked on her penmanship more than on recitation, or on sums more readily than compositions, is anybody's guess. We do know that adults reminded girls like Sadie of the virtues of (some) education, and of course they promoted piety and domesticity. And we know that Sadie was taught something about limits and expectations from her watchful father, and that she probably took instruction on propriety from her mother, from her church, and from her schoolmates.[32] How much anybody taught her about soldiers and what brutal things they could do to each other, however, is another question.

Civil War–era children's books and magazines occasionally talked about war and battle, and, not surprisingly, they put fictional girls and boys in separate spheres. Boys played soldiers, while girls tended to be encouraging handkerchief wavers or helpful nurses. One popular story of the period pictured girls caring for wounded backyard animals, including flies caught in spiderwebs. Children's stories rarely depicted girls encountering enemy soldiers, and almost never equipped them with weapons. Historians suggest that many

Northeastern American children lived up to these models. While some children lived far enough from the front to ignore the fact of the war entirely, others regularly play-acted adult wartime roles. Boys played at killing and dying (some of them, of course, joined the army as drummer boys) and they relished contact with real men in uniform. Girls in Northern communities spent hours winding bandages and scraping lint from cloth for soldiers' dressings or helping stage charity fairs to raise money for the Union army. In Gettysburg itself, girls participated in ritual events honoring soldiers and helped older women organize supplies. Like their mothers, girls sustained the war—war at a distance—with their labor and their sacrifice.[33]

While the nineteenth-century print media rarely pictured girls as soldiers or imagined them wounded on a battlefield, girls were given pointers in the "art" of dying. Detailed published obituaries informed Christian girls like Sadie Bushman how to slip away from life fittingly. Sadie could consider, for instance, the case of a local girl named Louisa Myers. Louisa was "patient and cheerful in her submission to the designs of Providence," and "sought to comfort the sorrowing friends around her." She gave directions for her death, planned the planting of a willow near her gravesite, distributed tokens, and calmly waited for her own passing.[34] When girls died best, then, they obviously died like Louisa, at home, after a slow and diminishing illness. They did not die violently, certainly not at the hands of another human, certainly not in war. Sadie Bushman would have known, well before she was nine years old, that battle was for boys, and that girls, and the women that they would become, had neither the interest in nor the aptitude for such things.

Advice givers presumed that girls like Sadie would remain at home, but they did acknowledge that some females occasionally overstepped boundaries. Should any woman or, God forbid, a girl take it into her head to enter the arena of war, however, she was bound for misfortune. First of all, there was the simple problem of courage: women had none.[35] Second, there was the question of authority and command. Just imagine if a woman were to serve in the army itself as an officer. The idea was laughable, especially since women could not hold their tongues. "A lady officer," explained one writer, "if she wished to give the word 'halt' to her troops, would do it somewhat in this wise: 'You soldiers, all of you, now mind, I order you, as soon as I have finished speaking, to stand still, every one of you, on the spot where you may happen to be; don't you hear me? Halt, I say, all of you!'"[36]

Third, there was the problem of feminine virtue. On this issue editors could point to history, recent and not so recent. In the Mexican War, for instance, a woman had ridden as a captain of lancers, and charged American troops. She had been gallant to be sure; she had also "unsexed herself." Even more recently, in nearby Harrisburg in September 1861, a young girl of "unblemished reputation" slipped into the army unnoticed. She too had "unsexed herself" and was taken home. A girl might aspire to the fighting life, clearly, and she could become a soldier, but she could not at the same time remain a woman. If she managed to successfully hide her "true" sexual identity, who knew what might happen? Why just this past spring it had been reported that a young woman disguised as a man served in the Army of the Potomac even while pregnant, and she delivered a child on picket duty![37]

What happened though, if the war did not stay put? Let's say a girl or woman has done all she could do—said good-bye to a brother, kissed a father for perhaps the last time, and worked, even beyond keeping the farm or family together, to send medical supplies to the front. She has sewed and canned and packaged for sick soldiers everywhere. She is at home and the war is on the battlefield. But then—contrary to all expectations—the battlefield shifts, and it becomes her backyard. What happened when bullets and shells came close?

Events that took place early in the war did not offer much reassurance. In fact, they suggested that the appearance of enemy men might produce nothing short of female frenzy. In April 1861, just after the war had begun, Gettysburg residents learned of the sad consequences of a panic. Borough leaders had just sent the local militia company off to war and had called a public meeting to discuss town safety. Sometime during the meeting, however, two men broke in and announced that Confederates were burning the town of Hanover and moving on to Gettysburg. A horseman confirmed the alarms. Church bells began to toll, residents crowded into the streets, and men ran for a cache of guns. And at least one woman went crazy. A Mrs. Scott, who had a baby in her arms, begged the men not to take the guns—her husband had said not to open the cache. But in their panic, people ignored her, and took the weapons. Mrs. Scott lost her grip. She became, said a later report, "violently insane and started to throw her child in an open well." A man saved the child, but no one could ever save the mother, because she "never regained her right mind."[38]

More optimistic advice for women and girls caught in a battle's crossfire suggested that they might tap into an unfamiliar well of fortitude. If they have imagined that they are inherently fearful and helpless (in part because they have been told this, repeatedly), they might, in certain circumstances, actually summon physical courage. They were not to kill, and they were not to defend themselves with anything akin to a weapon. But they did have the capacity to be brave and protective. "Let real calamity come," wrote one commentator, and see how "her heart strengthens itself—how strong is her purpose. Place her in the heat of battle—give her a child, a bird—anything she loves or pities, to protect—and see her . . . raising her . . . arms as a shield, as her own blood crimsons her upturned forehead, praying for life to protect the helpless."[39]

What, then, were women in Gettysburg to think of themselves? They were supposed to love peace, but to support war. They lacked the physical courage to kill, but they needed the courage to die. They were to seek and expect protection because they were timid and shrinking, but they had to be bold enough to shield others. They were told that they could take comfort in powers that would come naturally to them as girls and women, and that they could take no comfort at all.

If there was confusion about what was expected of women and girls in the extremities of war, and what they were capable of, there was some comfort in thinking that they would not be put to the test. Battles were still mostly fought beyond the bounds of towns and the women who lived in them. The last major battle, as everybody knew, had been in a "wilderness" in Virginia. And while enemy cavalry had recently come marauding, and civilians feared further raids, nobody in the late spring of 1863 imagined vast armies coming close and threatening. So Gettysburg women could continue to believe in their own immunity. They had enough happening as it was, with so many men away. They had, for instance, grave-digging to finish; they had babies to deliver safely; they had farms and families to manage; and some of them were young enough that they had more growing up to do.

AN ENEMY IN THE VALLEY

Gettysburg women could believe in their immunity from battle, but they were not making strategic decisions in this war. Neither, in early June, were many of the leaders of the Union army in the East. It was the Confederate high command who, in early summer, decided to take offensive action. Not long after the battle at Chancellorsville, General Robert E. Lee, still reeling from the death of Stonewall Jackson, but flush and fresh from his victory, proposed to President Jefferson Davis a brazen plan: a massive invasion of the North. It would be a counteroffensive to what was happening in the West, where Union general Ulysses S. Grant was closing in on Vicksburg on the Mississippi River. It might draw the Army of the Potomac away from eastern Virginia, including Washington, where it could be caught off guard. An advance across the Potomac would also threaten key Northern cities, and it could disrupt Northern food supplies and redirect them to the beleaguered people of the South, not to mention to Lee's army itself. It would be as demoralizing to the Northern pub-

lic as the fall of Vicksburg would be to people in the South and it might encourage those tired of the war in the North to try to force an end to it. Such a
move might even gain long-sought-for support from foreign countries, perhaps even nudge Britain into recognizing the Confederacy. General Lee convinced President Davis, and then, after reorganizing his army, the senior
commander acted quickly and with stealth. On Wednesday, June 3, 1863, he
ordered the first of his divisions to move. Ultimately, he would send three
army corps, nearly 80,000 men, along with a supply train that stretched for
sixty miles, up into the Shenandoah Valley.[40]

By most accounts, the soldiers under Lee were a supremely confident army,
fired with success and cocky after winning two major battles in five months,
first at Fredericksburg and then at Chancellorsville. They no longer had the
strategist who had been so vital to their successes, but they imagined a relatively quick end to the war, on their terms, even without Stonewall Jackson.[41]
Some Confederate soldiers pictured intruding into the heart of the North,
even into New York City, where they would plant their cannon on the city's
riverbanks. Others had more modest ambitions. "It is said," one newspaper reported, "that an artificial leg ordered some months ago awaits General Ewell's
arrival in the city of Philadelphia."[42]

The cockiness of the army, however, was not synonymous with its physical
comfort. Many Confederate soldiers marched north carrying little beyond
desperation. Even though they had had a month to rest, and had at least been
supplied with shoes, the rest of their clothes were ripped and torn. The Confederate army was also critically short of horses—there were not enough to
pull wagons or guns, and many of the cavalry traveled on foot. Now, though,
these men entertained some hope. They planned to live off their enemies:
They would eat from their farms, clothe themselves with their shirts and
pants, and commandeer their well-fed animals. They would redirect the hard-
ships of the homefront. They were all too aware that Union soldiers in the
South had not restricted their depredations to the battlefield, that they had increasingly fought in more personal ways—against a farmer's livestock, his
crops, his household possessions. When these Confederate troops marched
away from the South, then, they carried with them the conviction that maybe
it was time their enemies also felt the full impact of war.[43]

3

* * *

DESOLATION'S EDGE

UP IN HARRISBURG IN mid-June, city residents knew the Confederates were coming by the sight and sound of a storm. The clouds billowed from the ground, though, and thunder boomed from a bridge. As far as anyone could see to the south, which was well into the Cumberland Valley, road dust rose into the sky. Closer by, the span over the Susquehanna River rumbled with northbound traffic. Driving the dust and producing the din were refugees from the southern border, moving as fast as they could. They pushed small carts, drove top-heavy wagons, carried calves and sheep, trunks and boxes, bags of flour, and bedding. Adults carried babies who cried to be nursed, and pulled along children who pleaded to be lifted. Behind them, galloping and threatening, rode enemy cavalry. That is why roads pulverized and bridges shook. White people wanted to get out with their possessions before raiders ransacked their farms. Black people wanted to get out before hell swallowed them up.[1]

As the first Confederates to enter Pennsylvania in June 1863, General Albert Jenkins' cavalrymen were on a hard-hitting mission to gather information and round up supplies—to take horses and livestock, to raid houses and barns and fields and orchards. Upon their approach, farmers packed tall covered wagons with food and belongings and headed north, and gathered their horses and cattle and herded them into the shelter of the mountains. Jenkins' cavalrymen were not, however, on a routine scavenging operation. Nor were they simply seeking information about Union troop movements. These troopers were hunting down African Americans. Intent on seizing what they called "contraband," they rode from town to town, chasing and kidnapping black families— some born free and some born enslaved, many of them women and children—in order to send them south.[2]

What black Pennsylvanians anticipated in a Confederate invasion, then, was different from what white civilians anticipated. And what black women

49

feared was very different from what white women feared. White Gettysburg women worried about Confederate incursions but they made no immediate plans to evacuate. A few of them, like Fannie Buehler, even imagined deliberating with Confederate soldiers. African Americans in Pennsylvania did not picture themselves in discussion with the enemy. Nor did they have the time, in June, to speculate on the trials that might lie ahead. They harbored fears that were grounded in generations of peacetime mistreatment and assault, and fears that expanded in the trauma of war.[3] This meant that by the time Confederates moved north, most black families were doing their best to be out of sight. And if they were lucky they were also out of breath, from running north, for freedom.

African American residents of the border country were not necessarily new to the trials of taking flight. Some of them, including black women and men from the Borough of Gettysburg, were familiar with seeking refuge, and for them, the apprehension and peril of 1863 was a tragic chapter in a long story, a terrifying flashpoint on a continuum of danger. What these people of color faced before the Civil War—from the nearby slave system, from their fellow Pennsylvanians—reveals both the momentousness and the predictability of the Gettysburg campaign. On the one hand, they had everything at stake in the invasion of 1863. On the other hand, they had had everything at stake for generations. The history of black Gettysburg in the antebellum years also underscores the will and vitality of the black community. And it underlines the aptness and irony of Gettysburg's popular association—suggested by Abraham Lincoln—with black freedom.

LIFE ON THE FAULT LINE

The Confederate invasion of 1863 represented a horrific new threat to black women and men in southern Pennsylvania. But it repeated a long-standing nightmare. Part of the problem boiled down to the bad luck of geography. Less than ten miles south of Gettysburg, the Mason-Dixon line severed the country east to west. To white people, the survey line that separated Pennsylvania from Maryland was seamless ground, something they passed over without remark and without consequences. To black families, however, the division between the free states and the slave states was nothing less than a chasm. If they were not careful enough, did not look around themselves at all times, did not know their true friends from false ones, they could be taken suddenly, gagged soundless, and dragged into the abyss of slavery. During the 1840s, slaveowners had offered big rewards and big money for both fugitives and free people of likely size and skill. Motivated by high rewards—black artisans could bring up to two thousand dollars, field hands one thousand—white men with sufficient guile and greed went hunting along the borderlands. Then, after 1850, the crisis deepened, because the new Fugitive Slave Law offered federal protection to those seeking escaped property, and the government did little to punish those who took free people and claimed them as runaways.[4]

This operation was the "other" underground railroad, the one nobody talks much about. It also had agents and conductors, and it used houses with sympathizers and depended on forged papers and disguises. And it had plenty of passengers. But there are today no guided tours of secret cupboards or sliding panels in this system; no one points to painted chimneys or colored shutters on these houses. This was the sinister route: the south-bound train.[5]

Margaret Palm knew how this train operated. Three years before the war began, in dead winter in Gettysburg, this young woman—Mag, as she was known—had finished doing laundry work for a white family and it was time to get paid. We do not know what ruse her employer used to keep her waiting, but it was after dark when she finally got her money and started for home. Suddenly, as she crossed an alley, two local men, in connection with her employer, seized her, bound her hands, and tried to wrestle her into a carriage. The carriage even had two horses—all the better to hurry her into slave country. The men, however, had not reckoned on Mag's power. Using the same strength that must have made people want to sell her down south, she struggled and cried out loud. Finally, she counterattacked one of her assailants, and, with the help of a storekeeper who had heard the ruckus, she broke free.[6]

In 1860, Mag Palm lived in Gettysburg, Pennsylvania, with almost 190 other free persons of color, representing eight percent of the borough's population.[7] African Americans living just outside of town added scores to that number, making this community one of the largest and most visible in the area. Its numerical strength, however, belied its vulnerability. Like all black communities in antebellum America, it faced challenges from every direction. It faced the insults of the dominant white press, which drew on "science" and anecdote to pronounce African Americans biologically inferior. It struggled in the white-driven economy, which denied any black man or woman an easy path to independence. It contended with a powerful legal system, which forbade people of color citizenship and gave them only partial justice in court. And for years it coped with the threat of slave traders—men, sometimes men who lived nearby—who would do anything, to anybody, to make money. When Confederate soldiers moved north in June 1863, then, and began abducting people, they brought new capabilities, new motives, and new rapacity, but they also carried out an old practice.

This antebellum railroad, like its equivalent in the Civil War, did not always run smoothly. Traders had had hard luck wresting freedom from Mag Palm. Men who had predatory eyes on a well-known abolitionist named Frederick Douglass as he passed by Gettysburg in 1843 also had hard luck. Douglass traveled by night, stayed indoors by day, and was protected by loyal and faithful friends.[8] But sometimes the reverse underground railroad operated without a hitch. In the summer of 1845, for example, men from the South arrived in Bendersville, about eight miles north of Gettysburg, looking for a woman named Catherine Paine. Paine and her children had been freed two years earlier by a widow who had owned them in Virginia, but when the widow died, a nephew claimed the "property." The men succeeded in locating Paine, and in the middle of a July night five of them drove to the house where the family slept. One of the kidnappers stood sentinel at the front door with a club while the rest of the men used other weapons to gag and bind the mother and children, and force them into a covered wagon. They were below the Mason-Dixon line before the sun was high.[9]

The experiences of Frederick Douglass, Mag Palm, and Catherine Paine point to the tenuousness of black freedom in southern Pennsylvania before the Civil War. Sometimes not even a lifetime of liberty could resist the reaching power of the slave system. People who had once been enslaved were at particular risk for kidnapping, but even those who were born free lived in fear. Nobody knows today how many went missing from the state in the antebellum decades, but one paper reported in 1844 that in a six-month period up to sixty persons had been stolen from the southern part of the state. In Philadelphia alone, sixty black children were seized in a single year.[10]

All African Americans living in the border counties must have wondered how or when or if kidnappers would come. If they read the newspapers, they would know how it happened to others. They would know that hunters came when people were unaware, and unready, and in places they thought were safe. The kidnappers took one person who was sleeping in bed, another who was working in his shop, another who was out chopping wood. They seized one man who was milking a cow, and another who was walking down an empty road—or at least he thought it was empty. Sometimes they approached under false pretenses. Strangers came to one man's door, said their carriage was broken, and said they needed help. They lied. Another stranger extended his hand as a gesture of goodwill. It had a fatal grip. Sometimes they were friends—or they appeared to be friends—and they attacked from behind. And they were never sympathetic. They didn't care if a man or woman had lived in Pennsylvania for decades. Nor did they listen to personal pleas—that a family needed its father; that a woman couldn't bear to see hobbles around her husband's ankles; that a man just wanted to say good-bye to his family, possibly forever.[11] They preyed on adults and they preyed on children. Sometimes slave hunters particularly preyed on children. They were easier to take than adults; some were young enough that they trusted people they did not know, and they had not yet learned to run and hide when a stranger approached them. And they grew and changed. Add a few years of life below the border, and they would not resemble the boy or the girl who had once been free.[12]

Life as an African American in southern Pennsylvania, then, meant being on the alert. But it also meant keeping an eye out for someone else in need— perhaps a person who had been stolen from freedom in the North, like Catherine Paine, or perhaps someone who had emancipated themselves in the South. Indeed, as much as living near the fault line of slavery was frightening, it was also a place of promise, and people on the border did their best to fight the institution whatever way they could. Sometimes, courage rose on impulse. In June 1850, a black man in Gettysburg saw a stagecoach wheeling into town, carrying a white hunter looking for men who had escaped from Maryland. He acted fast. He had no horse of his own, so he took one from a nearby livery stable and rode off to warn the fugitives. With the slave catcher on his heels, he galloped out of town. He won the race, alarmed the fugitives, and returned to town to settle with the owner of the stable.[13]

In Carlisle in 1847, it was not a single man but a crowd of women and men who leaped to the task of rescue. During a hearing to determine whether or not three fugitives—a man, a woman, and a girl—belonged to a man in Maryland, infuriated local women and men gathered in and around the courthouse. When the prisoners emerged, they rushed to rescue them, and in the "melee" that ensued, protesting women were bludgeoned on the heads, and the crowd hurled and received brickbats, paving stones, clubs and canes and "missiles of all kinds." The woman and girl escaped and the man was secured and taken back south.[14] In nearby Lancaster County, the black community was driven by similar anger. In the fall of 1851, a number of residents tried to protect four fugitives from being taken and reenslaved. When the posse came to retrieve the men, the slaveowner was shot and killed.[15]

Slavery's enemies worked spontaneously, as the case required. They also worked secretly and systematically to bring people out of bondage. This operation, the more familiar Underground Railroad, was the liberty train that moved thousands from the South. Pennsylvania was sometimes a dangerous middle passage on the way north, not only because kidnappers patrolled the routes, but because spies and slavery sympathizers kept a keen eye out for refugees. The state also contained numerous Quaker settlements, however, and friendly communities of free and fugitive blacks. Its well-established African Methodist

Episcopal (AME) churches supported the system, too, and traveling preachers carried urgent information about recent escapes and safe routes. Topography, particularly west of Gettysburg, also favored refugees. The South Mountain range could take in slaves in Maryland, shield and harbor them in ravines and woods, and then release them into free farming country in Pennsylvania.[16]

Black Gettysburg residents left only a few signs of their work in the northbound underground, for obvious reasons. We do know that one of the black churches took contributions as early as 1840 for a "slaves reffuge." And the following year the organization acted more formally as the Slave's Refuge Society, publicly flaunting its intentions to the abolitionist press. "We feel it our indispensable duty," the Society had resolved, "to assist such of our brethren as shall come among us for the purpose of liberating themselves, and to raise all the means in our power to effect our object, which is to give liberty to our brethren groaning under the tyrannical yoke of oppression." Many of the men who stood together in this society were free men without property, some of the poorest in the county.[17] It was reported—much less verifiably—that a poor black woman was involved, too. This woman, of "enormous proportions," sometimes wore the sky-blue uniform coat of an officer of the War of 1812. She was active in assisting escaping bondsmen, and protected them and herself with a musket she had bought. She was so notorious that kidnappers sought her out—selling her into slavery would bring money and end a menace, too. Legend had it that she was Mag Palm.[18]

By the time the Civil War began, then, black families in the Pennsylvania border country had been battling the slave system for a long time. They depended in their work on the unequivocal support of black communities, but, just as they would in the Confederate invasion of 1863, they also relied on sympathetic white people. White support in the 1840s and 1850s was often inconsistent and incomplete and, even at its best, it was paternalistic, but when the white and black communities of Adams County worked in concert, they were a powerful force for justice.

In the Gettysburg area, white anti-slavery activity was centered most obviously on the Underground Railroad. Fugitives traveling from Littlestown, south of Gettysburg, for example, learned that they should follow the Baltimore Pike until they came to the crossing of a second stream, then follow it to a grist mill—McAllister's Mill—on the west bank. The white son of the owner recalled delivering rations and clothing to fugitives who hid under the lower floor and in the cog pit of the old mill. After dark, the passengers would then move on, to York or York Springs, to a black settlement called Yellow Hill, or to Quaker homes. Another white boy, living north of Gettysburg, recalled how twice a month or so in the summertime he would hear a tapping on his lower bedroom window, and, without waking anyone else, he would go out into the dark and take families to his barn. His family would feed them and, at dusk the next day, they would start on to the next station, in Carlisle.[19]

The black community in the Gettysburg area could thus count on local white assistance in moving fugitives north. Before the 1850s it also relied on white legislators in the fight against kidnapping. In 1847, the Commonwealth of Pennsylvania not only placed heavy penalties on those who seized free blacks but also forbade enforcement of the fugitive slave law of 1793. Pennsylvania went even further, prohibiting the use of magistrates, justices, jailors, and jails in the recapture and return of runaways. It became, says one historian, "almost impossible for an owner to recover his slave," and a prominent abolitionist newspaper claimed that if any state was a free state, it was Pennsylvania. Then, of course, came 1850, when the federal government issued the newer, harsher fugitive slave law, and not only prohibited interference with slave-hunting, but mandated civilian help. Opposition to the law was intense in Pennsylvania, but many people complied. Others used it as an opportunity to try their hand at kidnapping.[20]

In Gettysburg, white newspaper editors called attention to the plight of refugees and kidnap victims by printing accounts of escapes and near-escapes. They also asked the public to help out. *The Star and Banner* appealed to its readers to assist refugees, even after 1850. Imagine, the paper explained, "a poor, hungry, starving, fugitive slave, wearied and exhausted" who might arrive at the door. He has been reduced to a "panting stag," and he begs for a bit of bread to prevent starvation, or some shelter from "the cold blast or driving elements." "Is there a man among us," the editors pleaded, "with a heart in which lingers a single spark of humanity, that would turn the miserable wretch from his door . . . though a dozen laws, backed by forty marshals, forbade it?"[21]

Many of Gettysburg's white residents, then, cared for the fugitive. But for some people, that is exactly where the concern stopped. Sympathy for the refugee was as much focused on the thrill of the hunt, the chase, and the escape, as it was on the human at the center of the drama. Local reporting of the kidnapping of Catherine Paine, the free woman who was abducted with her children, for instance, suggests a fascination with the wiles of her slave-catchers, the details of their apprehension, and the legal arguments of their trial in 1845. Lost in the shuffle of excitement were the woman and her two children themselves. By the fall of 1846, Catherine Paine remained in Virginia, still unfree, but local editors and their readers no longer seemed to care. It was an abolitionist paper in Philadelphia that noted, in small print, her continued "difficulty."[22]

White attitudes toward the victims of slavery were both contradictory and half-hearted, but some white citizens sought sincerely to help the local free black community. A county anti-slavery society in the 1830s expressed both its unequivocal support of immediate abolition as well as "the destruction of racial prejudice." Then, too, there was Thaddeus Stevens. This intense, dark-browed man, who would become one of the country's most powerful advocates for civil rights and racial equality, moved to Gettysburg in 1816, where, as a lawyer, he defended escapees in court. Known as an elegant speaker, and a witty and wily legal tactician, Stevens was also elected to the state legislature from Gettysburg in 1833. In that capacity, he promoted free public education to black and white children, legal rights for African Americans, and—unsuccessfully—suffrage for black men. He left Gettysburg for Lancaster in 1842, and was ultimately elected to Congress. There he championed racial justice, as consistently and passionately as any American, until his death in 1868.[23]

Most white residents in Gettysburg did not go as far as Stevens in advocating civil rights. In fact, many of them were appalled by abolitionists who, in the 1840s and 1850s, not only countenanced racial equality but supported equal rights for women, German and Irish immigrants, and Native Americans. They were even more distressed by abolitionists who disapproved of the United States Constitution and the Christian Bible because of their equivocation on slavery.[24]

In 1845, people in Adams County, Pennsylvania, got a chance to let a few of these "radicals" know what they thought of their ideas. White abolitionist Abby Kelly, who had criticized the Constitution, came to Adams County, and she had a hard time speaking over the noise of smashing eggs and breaking windows. In Gettysburg, especially, Kelly and her fellow-lecturer got a cold reception. Trying to animate these people in the cause of the slave, they reported, was "like the building of a fire on an iceberg." Where, they wondered, were the usual invitations to board or dine? Why did no one help them secure a meetinghouse or a hall? There was nothing: "Not a single individual took us by the hand, or condescended to bestow the least notice upon us; we truly felt as strangers in a strange land." Their stance on slavery and the Constitution may have played a part in the reception, but the visitors identified another reason for Gettysburg's hostility. "There is a strong prejudice there," they reported, "against women appearing in public, and some who profess to abhor slavery, I suspect abhor woman's speaking as much, or perchance a little more."[25]

There were plenty of white men and women in Gettysburg, then, who may have disliked slavery, but who could not abandon the Christian church as a beacon of enlightenment, even if the Bible was ambiguous on human bondage. There were others, too—including Thaddeus Stevens himself—who would not give up on the Constitution and who sought to work within politics to abolish the slave system. And there were evidently men, and certainly many women, who opposed slavery but who wanted the position and place of women to remain just the way it was.

And there were, finally, many white people who hated slavery and who were happy to help fugitives but who had no intention of sharing their living and working space with the newly emancipated. Their ready answer, it seems, was colonization. Gettysburg's *Star and Banner,* echoing hundreds of newspapers across the country, cheerfully described the scenario: Freed blacks, facing poverty and degradation (and discrimination) in America, were to be sent on ships by the thousands—by the millions if slavery was ended—to the western African colony of Liberia. "The free people of color," the paper reported, "must soon perceive that Liberia presents the only relief from their present disabilities. [It is] the hope for themselves and their children." The paper encouraged contributions to organizations that would facilitate the removal. It also pictured the process of expatriation in glowing terms. In the fall of 1851, it described about fifty ex-slaves along with twelve white overseers rumbling through the center of Washington in two four-horse wagons, on the way to an oceangoing boat. These men and women had been freed "on condition of their emigration to Liberia" and "by their cheerfulness and gayety showed how well they were pleased with their change of circumstances and the prospects which await them." In Gettysburg, this paper echoed the sentiments of the most influential men in town.[26]

Colonization was founded on the belief that black and white Americans would never stand on the same footing, live on the same ground, or share the same successes in the United States. The *Star and Banner* suggested why this was so. It used cartoons and vignettes to portray black men as gullible, clownish, ignorant, and potentially unruly. It presented its readers such frequent accounts of black ineptitude that it offered the "best negro story of the season," and it reported news items describing crowds of free black people in Pennsylvania and elsewhere who displayed "wild excitement" and "wild feeling" or who acted in "tumult and riot."[27]

The editor of the *Star and Banner,* David Buehler, called himself an antislavery man, but he was walking a racial tightrope. On the one hand he sympathized with enslaved African Americans—these people were decent, sensitive humans, deserving of emancipation. On the other hand he and his reporters depicted the free people they would become as thick-skinned comics, with savage underbellies. Buehler did find one way around the paradox of race: He portrayed fugitives as light-skinned, with whom his readership might identify, and potential free blacks as significantly darker and more alien. In July 1855, the paper reported that slave-catchers mistook a sunburned white girl for a fugitive. The fourteen-year-old girl had been driving home a cow from a pasture when she was accosted by two men who forced her into their carriage. The kidnappers dumped her out when they realized their mistake. The paper's message was clear: not only were fugitives people like "us" but "we" could be mistaken for fugitives.[28]

The influential journalists who held a double standard for enslaved and emancipated blacks no doubt established an uncomfortable setting for African Americans in Gettysburg, but they were hardly the most hostile whites around. They acted on behalf of anti-slavery after all; they supported the Republican Party. They would, by 1860, be Lincoln's people. There was another set of whites in town who committed themselves more directly and more energetically to maintaining white supremacy. Much of their spite was unveiled in a Democratic newspaper called *The Compiler*. Its editorial staff was ungenerous to abolitionists and to African Americans before the war, but after 1861 it started to inject its opinions with more venom. Even though it claimed that the war was largely a political, not a social or moral, crisis, it also argued that what had transpired was a race war: nothing less than a contest between blacks and whites for supremacy. Look at what was happening, the paper suggested: Free black men were swarming into the state, robbing decent white men of jobs and, worse, violating the persons of young white girls. Couldn't people see all around them evidence of blacks who were becoming saucy, impudent, and "troublesome"? And then there was Lincoln's travesty, Emancipation, that indelibly linked this war with black power. In March 1863, *The Compiler* printed comments from Union soldiers who were disgusted by the war's "new" aims. "We came out here to restore the Union," said one enlisted man, "not to meddle with the d–d niggers, and I for one . . . if they put the nigger alongside of me to fight, will put a bullet through his black heart."[29]

Opinions like these were hardly confined to Gettysburg, of course. Fears of an African American population surge were widespread in the North before and during the war, and throughout Pennsylvania white people tried to steel themselves against the flood by segregating theaters, schools, churches, coaches, and trains. In 1860, voters proposed legislation that would keep people of color out of the state, and petitions for restricting immigration stood in piles on legislators' desks. Other petitions urged that slavery be reintroduced. Pennsylvania had been the first state to pass a law against slavery, and it was still heralded as the site of relative opportunity and justice for black Americans. But it stood within an inch of looking decidedly Southern.[30]

One day, thanks in part to Abraham Lincoln, Gettysburg would be connected in the public mind with black freedom, and from then on race relations in the borough would receive special scrutiny.[31] Was the link between Gettysburg and black liberty ironic, people would wonder? With regard to the antebellum period, the answer has to be both yes and no. The black community itself was large and strong, and was represented by respected leaders. The seminary and the college attracted powerful intellectuals to the borough, some of whom energetically supported abolitionism, if not black civil rights. The founder of the seminary and the college, Rev. Samuel Simon Schmucker, was himself a committed abolitionist who came to dislike colonization—he could not "swallow the idea that emancipation must go along with expatriation." On the other hand, these institutions continued to draw students from the South, and they were reluctant to antagonize current or prospective clients. Influential white editors were, at best, sympathetic to anti-slavery but unsympathetic to free blacks. At worst, they sought to inflame the public with racial hatred. The black community's strength may have also provoked as much concern as respect among nervous whites. Finally, some residents in Gettysburg had close ties to people in slaveholding states. They had relatives below the Mason-Dixon line, as well as financial connections. Plenty of white Gettysburg merchants, especially in the carriage trade, had markets or suppliers in Maryland and Virginia. These men may have held progressive views on abolition and emancipation, but when they did business with Southerners, money was likely first on their minds.[32]

Gettysburg was a place in the mid-1800s, then, that sent African Americans mixed messages: We appreciate your help, but we encourage you to leave; we support social justice, but within bounds; we stand ready to assist you, to a limited degree. These messages were troubling before the war; in the emergency of 1863, they would become alarming. What the black community wanted then was something more than equivocation or well-meaning pronouncements. It needed assistance in its flight; it needed assurance about jobs; it needed protection. Some white residents would offer this support. Others, though, would regard the threat of Confederate kidnapping just as they had regarded slave-catching in the decades before the war: with distant sympathy, or with amusement. Or they would think of their own predicaments and of the black assistance they depended upon. Or they would simply turn their backs. When waves of Southern soldiers swept up and over the Pennsylvania border, many African Americans would have to turn to those individuals who for generations had been the most consistent and reliable: each other.

THE COMMUNITY

The army of General Robert E. Lee that invaded Pennsylvania at the end of June threatened the persons of African Americans, and the ordeals of black people in Gettysburg can be understood in individual terms—through the story, for instance, of the resilient Mag Palm and the accounts of an entrepreneur named Owen Robinson and a farmer named Abraham Brian. It can be understood, too, in the particular tales of two men who would eventually become Union soldiers—an indefatigable striver named Lloyd Watts, and a fighter named Randolph Johnston.

What people of color stood to lose in the Confederate invasion can also be appreciated by looking at the black community more broadly. Lee's intrusion into the North, and the evacuation that followed, jeopardized economic security and physical and social shelter: It threatened the houses, cabins, and farms that families owned and rented; the jobs that people relied on; the businesses some of them had established; the churches they so tirelessly built. Generations of struggle in Gettysburg, even in the face of suspicion and hostility, had resulted in institutions that people treasured. Of these vital institutions, it was perhaps the AME Zion church, which brought under its roof the majority of the community, that defined as much as anything else the effort and the ambition of black Gettysburg. Today, AME records open a small window onto that church and help humanize the people who, once Confederates invaded, would be regarded mainly as flocks of refugees and mass victims of terror.

To an observer, the incongruities of Mag Palm's life loom large. Mag spent her days bent over the scrubboards and beating the rugs of Gettysburg's well-to-do, but she labored under opinions that said African Americans hadn't the industry to be free. She lived in an African-American community that was as old as the town itself, but she was bombarded with white pleas for people like her to go "back" to Africa. The disjunction between prescription and practice, white opinion and black reality may have lifted in the refuge of her neighborhood, down the dirt lanes and amid the wood houses and log cabins of her friends and relatives. There, dissension and bickering sometimes flared, and Mag had to avoid violence from her husband, even in her own house. But the black neighborhood in Gettysburg's southwest side did its best to shoulder hardship, and to collectively seize life's brief pleasures.

Like most people of color in nineteenth-century America, black residents in the Gettysburg area made a living in 1860 working for others. The women who labored for pay usually did what Mag Palm did: They cleaned houses and washed clothes for white residents. They labored over counters, stood over cookstoves and delivered roasts and pies and puddings and fresh bread. They worked in nurseries, feeding, comforting, and cleaning up after white children. Some of the men made a living by blacksmithing, shoemaking, brickmaking, and preaching. Most men, though, worked as hired hands—day laborers usually—on farms and in the town's hotels. Some of them never stopped working. According to the 1860 census, two of the men hired as laborers were over eighty.[33]

If most African Americans in Gettysburg worked for other people, some of them also worked for themselves. By 1860, some members of the black community had, by dint of hard work, good luck, and savvy, achieved a modicum of independence. Abraham Brian was one of these men. Having lived in the Gettysburg area for at least twenty years, mostly as a day laborer, he was, by the time the war began, a man of land and standing. He still hired himself out to get by, but in 1860 he could look around him at twelve acres of grain and hay fields, at orchards, at a barn and two small houses, and feel the power and pleasure of ownership. Mag Palm and her family were his tenants, renting out a small wooden house at the edge of his property. At home, too, things looked up for Brian. Not long before, he had buried two wives in the space of three years. He had been arrested for fathering a child outside of marriage. Now he and his third wife, Elizabeth, had what seemed to be a long future. Neither one of them could read or write, but they sent their children to school nearby, to get the education that they missed. By the time the Civil War began, then, Abraham Brian had carved out a life that many held as the American dream. There were only a few dark sides to this dream, and one of them was his home's location— and Mag's too—on the western slope of Cemetery Ridge.[34]

Many people of color, like Abraham Brian and Mag Palm, lived in a working world with white citizens. Some of them, like Brian, labored for whites less and less as time went by, while others, like Mag, continued to come and go at the behest of people with lighter skin and more money. All African Americans, though, no matter how many hours of the day they nursed or cooked or labored, or how many nights they slept under a white man's roof, lived in a black world as well. Partly out of their own needs and desires, and partly out of what was handed to them, free people of color sustained a community of their own.[35]

That black community had taken shape generations before the Civil War, but it became especially visible in the mid-1830s, when a separate school for "colored children" opened. The school was staffed sporadically, kept open half the year at most, and lacked sufficient space, desks, slates, and books. But for some, it worked. In 1860, when a census taker came by the borough, all but four black youths under sixteen listed her or his occupation as "student."[36] The community was further strengthened with the founding of distinct black churches. In the 1830s, a visiting African American seminary student named Daniel Payne, disgusted by the pro-slavery pronouncements of the Methodist minister in town, tried to start a separate black church. He also offered a Sunday school class of his own and helped organize societies for the mental and moral improvement of women. When his eyesight gave out, Payne moved away. Many of his plans were unrealized, but he left behind a community increasingly committed to self-protection and pride.[37]

That pride went on display in 1838, when black Gettysburg residents, tired of not being able to sit where they pleased at the white-run Methodist church, and not being able to worship at the altar, moved out. The African Methodist Episcopal congregation they organized—eventually known as AME Zion—would do what other Methodist churches did: offer fellowship, support, and Christian guidance, and encourage values of thrift, self-discipline, and temperance. But it would be black run and operated, and its regulations would be self-imposed.[38]

The AME Zion congregation was powerful and vibrant. It was sometimes beset by dissension and disagreement, but it was also distinguished by solidarity and accord. Its members were profoundly committed to the idea of progress—to the sense that someday, if people worked hard enough, had enough faith and personal strength, things would be better. While the borough's white press disseminated stories and images of black laziness and degradation, AME Zion church members tried to devote themselves to industry and self-discipline. A body of church trustees and class leaders stood sentinel over parishioners, exhorting, approving, and chastising. In the 1840s and 1850s, AME officials set a tough standard of propriety and piety, demanding that members attend church and class with strict regularity, and that they forswear drinking, dancing, gambling, frivolity, and swearing.[39]

Owen Robinson helped lead the black community toward "decorum." Born a slave to a man in Maryland, he couldn't tell people how old he was, but he did know the exact day he became a free man: November 5, 1817. He carried around his manumission papers—he had to in these terrifying days—which told people he was a man of a light complexion, of medium height, who had a scar in his right eyebrow. At the time of the Civil War, Robinson was a confectioner in Gettysburg, selling sweets, savories, and baked goods to the community. In the hot and humid Pennsylvania summers, he also cranked out ice cream. Robinson was not only an enterprising man; he was devoted to self-improvement. A steadfast church member, he made an early stand in the movement toward black "uplift" when, on a winter's night in 1840, he and several others renounced "all spiritus Licuours."[40] It was for Robinson the beginning of a lifelong effort to help himself and fellow African Americans get ahead.

Probably no one worked harder for personal respectability and for collective black dignity in Civil War–era Gettysburg, though, than Lloyd F. A. Watts. Born in 1835 in Maryland, Watts moved to Pennsylvania as a child and worked as a laborer before the war, helping his family—six brothers and sisters and a widowed mother—stay afloat. Lloyd Watts was an ambitious man. In a notebook, he practiced his penmanship, performed mathematical equations, kept track of debts, and composed short paragraphs about how to be a better person. Swearing, he noted, was to be frowned upon. It was "very ungentlemanly" and "cowardly." Every time a man swore, in fact, it revealed his heart to be a "nest of vipers" and "one of them sticks out his head." Novel reading was just as bad. If someone read "high exciting novels on Saturday night till eleven or twelve o'clock," it destroyed the taste for the Bible. He knew; he had tried it "only once" and that was enough. Watts was also a romantic. He wrote ditties about sweet doves and bowers of ladies, and he listed in his journal all the girls "of Col." in the neighborhood. And even though he was dedicated to learning and prayer, he found time for love. In 1861, he married Philena Cameron, the nineteen-year-old daughter of a blacksmith, whose father was prominent in the town's temperance fight and active in the church.[41]

Lloyd Watts navigated the road to respectability so adroitly that he would eventually become a leader, if not the leader of the black community—called on as a church spokesman, a public speaker, and an arbiter. Other men and women did not embrace "rectitude" so easily. They were chastised for infractions ranging from swearing to "withholding money" to adultery. Upton Johnston, a day laborer and a property owner, regularly gave church leaders something to frown upon. He was faithfully involved in the church, but not diligent in attending class. He was seen drinking whiskey. Worst of all, in mid-April 1861, he was found guilty of "immoral conduct." Another church member could not help seeing Johnston, age sixty-one, engaged in "criminal connection" with one Catherine Miles at a third member's house. Worse, a fourteen-year-old girl saw Johnston "at the act" and another, a twelve-year-old, saw him "buttoning up his pants."[42]

Black women were not AME leaders—they did not preach sermons or lead classes—but they were active members of the church. In the decade before the Civil War, women of different ages tested and pushed the limits of authority, wielded the power of complaint, and gave testimony. If in the white world of newsprint they were rarely accorded a single sentence, here they came pulsing to life—feisty, insolent, and daring. Women contested the power of church leaders and the authority of men in general. Sara Jonson said she refused to be led in lessons by one Aaron Constant and "does not consider her self a member of the church." Sarah Thomas also said she refused to be instructed by her leader. She "had no faith in him." Mother Hester Gibson complained of "tolerating improper conduct By Her Leader under her Roof." In contrast to the world beyond, the testimony of black girls and women was in this church heard and respected.[43]

Black women regularly used the authority of the church to discipline and punish each other. Sister Harris charged Sister Thomas with beating her as she returned from church. (Sister Thomas denied having her by the throat.) Sister McGee said that Sister Harriet Peck kept a "disorderly house," and "Sister McClure was at varience with Sisters Williams & Thompson, and refused to break bread with them at Lovefeast." (Later, after some arbitration, they settled and shook hands.) Then in the late fall of 1859, Rebecca Sibbs was accused of grossly immoral conduct, which involved a special trial and witnesses who testified that she called Sally King a "yellow bitch, a bald-face bitch, & a runaway bitch" and that her general conduct was un-Christian and she had "bought & smelt of strong drink." Sibbs was expelled.[44]

Black women relied on the AME Zion church to regulate behavior, and the church did its part in scrutinizing them, and frequently found them wanting. In 1859, church leaders expelled two young women who had, despite repeated warnings from their pastor, visited the circus. A year later, four young women slipped away to the house of John Hopkins, janitor at Pennsylvania College, where he was having "a ball." One Louisa McMullan bet ten dollars she was better than any of the other dancers on the floor. Someone else asked her to go ahead and try it. At McMullan's church trial, she insisted that she was sorry for her conduct and "would not repeat it." The committee of the church generously concluded that McMullan had formerly belonged to a more lenient denomination and must have been confused by the rules of the Gettysburg church. She went unpunished, except for a "severe rebuke from the chairman."[45]

Women thus had a relatively high profile in this AME church. They were rebuked, it seems, more than men, but perhaps this was because they, like white women, were generally more faithful attendees, and thus their falling away was more noticeable. (An account of those who had paid their dues in 1859 lists women to men by well over a two-to-one margin.) Perhaps, too, women had different standards set for them by the all-male leaders. Or possibly these women and girls were vocal and defiant and independent in ways that were widely unacknowledged. For whatever reasons, they struggled against the noiseless or retiring ideal that marked female gentility, and they resisted both male leaders and middle-class mores. They worked, lived, and loved with uncontestable spirit.[46]

There were, however, men and women whose struggles never made it into these prewar records. Why wasn't Mag Palm a vocal or striving member of this AME church? Maybe Mag didn't try. Maybe the church, with all its rules and boundaries and surveillance, put too much of a fence around Mag. She also lived with a man, Alf Palm, who, when he wasn't on the wrong side of the law and in prison, was at home drinking. Mag also bore a child, Josephine, out of wedlock. Perhaps there was more that went on with Mag, too. When the census taker came to her door down by the Emmitsburg Road in 1860, he sized her up as a "mistress-harlot." Was trading sex for money another way Mag survived in a world with limited options and another reason she might have been shunned? Or was this the way a white man registered his disapproval of a black woman who hadn't married her child's father?[47]

The real problem may have been much simpler. Those who had time to study the Bible, to go regularly to church meetings, to meet in associations for social and moral reform were sometimes those who were not at the beck and call of employers and exhausted by daily work. Anna O'Brien worked as a nurse in the household of Robert G. Harper, the editor of the Republican *Sentinel,* and she told church officers that her work kept her from attending classes. Lewis Jones was a laborer, and like many of the black laboring men in Gettysburg he also had no time for religious classes. Mag Palm, even if she had wanted to, may not have had the freedom to join other black women and men in Christian fellowship. She was too busy, too tired, too poor.[48]

Mag's indiscernible presence at church points to some of the fissures—economic, cultural, possibly spiritual—within the African American community in Gettysburg. This is not to say, however, that the church was marked mainly by dissension. If some black residents were missing at church, and if four out of nearly fifty church members in 1860 were complained of, that meant that the overwhelming majority made a commitment to amity, self-discipline, and piety. For all the splits that existed in fact, there was within the community a deep and common sympathy. Years of living on the edge of the Mason-Dixon line, years of personally fighting the slave system, either as a free person subject to seizure like Mag or as a former slave like Owen Robinson, had forged people together. Years of working toward social justice, too, in schools, in church, through family and with sympathetic white neighbors, had led to collective successes and disappointments. Even their disagreements represented dynamic discussions about change that engaged them all.

And now, in the third year of this civil war, the black community in Gettysburg, Pennsylvania, had to ally against more threats and danger. Frightened whites in the state had begun calling for new prohibitions on people of color, demanding a ban on African Americans entering the state and clamoring for free black families to move to some other country, in some other latitude. And they were echoed at the highest political level. Abraham Lincoln, slavery's enemy, continued to endorse voluntary black emigration, and he encouraged members of his cabinet to investigate opportunities for colonies in the Caribbean and Central America. It was not inevitable, nor was it good, he said, that people of African and European descent shared the nation's space.[49]

In the early 1860s, then, all black residents in Gettysburg faced an uncertain future. But that was not the worst of it. When the Army of Northern Virginia moved north into Pennsylvania in the middle of June 1863, they faced peril of another kind. The Confederate army that had bloodied Union men at Fredericksburg and Bull Run—twice—and which had just insulted Union men at Chancellorsville, seemed invincible. What would it mean if the men who sought to save slavery were unstoppable? If they brought with them hatred compounded by Lincoln's Emancipation Proclamation? If they wanted restitution for the "property" that was streaming away from them? What would it mean if they came with guns and horses and like-minded men by the thousands? Would it not seem as if the Mason-Dixon line itself had moved?

When General Lee had brought his army up into Maryland in 1862, it had seized "contrabands." Now, less than a year later, as it swept closer, Lee's army was taking whomever it pleased. What this meant to black families living in southern Pennsylvania was that everything that had been accomplished in months, years, or lifetimes of liberty could disappear in an instant. Everything that had been scraped together, or paid off, or built with blood and sweat and self-sacrifice could vanish. The church, which so many women and men served with such effort and diligence and love, could dissolve. It was hard to know what to do—if and when to go away. If families evacuated, they might lose a log cabin with a dirt floor and a day job with white folk. Or they might lose their businesses and farms. And if they did not evacuate? If they could not or would not get away?[50]

By June, a pall had settled over the community. In the borough itself, Owen Robinson, newly elected steward of the AME Zion church, became visibly anxious. A white boy who knew him, and who liked visiting his restaurant and watching him make ice cream, recalled that ever since the war began, Robinson lived in day-to-day dread of being captured and taken south. Slavery was no imaginary evil to Robinson and his manumission papers gave him little security. When he heard any word of Confederate movement north, he would leave his store, pack his family, and move out. The trick was to know when the threat was real and where he should go.[51]

Randolph Johnston wanted to fight back. This twenty-two-year-old, dark-skinned, dark-eyed man had grown up in Gettysburg and seen his family struggle for respectability. His father was Upton Johnston, one of the black church's toughest cases—recalcitrant with alcohol and notorious with women. Randolph never crossed those kinds of boundaries, but he had not been an easy case for church leaders. He had occasionally violated church discipline—it seems he played cards—and he had been, with a company of others, a "total neglecter" of religious instruction. But the war meant something new for John-ston. Since the first days of the conflict, he had put together a company of sol-diers, had drilled them, had achieved the rank of captain, and had accrued "considerable military notoriety." In the early summer of 1863, Johnston of-fered this "colored company" to Governor Andrews of Massachusetts, who had organized the Fifty-fourth and Fifty-fifth Massachusetts infantry regiments. But Pennsylvania wouldn't let the company go; it would sponsor its own troops of color, eventually. Johnston, however, was ready. With rumors of invaders cir-culating, he offered the services of his soldiers—about sixty men—to the gov-ernor of Pennsylvania. Johnston wanted to stave off Confederates *now*.[52]

According to local legend, Mag Palm remained down in her rented house in mid-June, keeping a lookout to the south and west, and standing ready to warn families of impending danger.[53] She had a good view down the Emmits-burg Road, to be sure, and she had plenty of reasons to be watchful. She had had her brush with slavery before, when the enemies were her fellow Pennsyl-vanians, and she had won the fight. But now her odds were not so good. This would not be a couple of local men she could take on herself. This was an army of soldiers, and it was so big and so powerful it might truly take her away.

☆ PART TWO ☆

4

***

FLYING THICK LIKE BLACKBIRDS

AT JUST AFTER TEN O'CLOCK in the morning of the 20th of June 1863, General Joseph Hooker, commander of the Army of the Potomac, wrote to a man in Frederick, Maryland, asking for help with intelligence. He needed to get scouts to the top of a mountain to look down on the valley to the west. He didn't say how they should make their observations, but he needed to know for sure what was there. And he wanted men who would not be "frightened out of their senses." Hooker knew there might be nothing more than a quiet expanse—vacant fields and a peaceable outcropping of barns. But he was also aware that the sight could be startling, and that the countryside could be swarming with "armed men." He wanted the scouts to hide out in the trees if they could, and watch any soldiers march by, and count them. "Be vigilant and active," he urged. "Use money and it shall be returned to you."[1]

General Hooker and President Lincoln and other members of the Union high command had realized, since the end of May, that the enemy was about to make a move. Some of them wondered if the Confederates might be massing for a brash invasion of the North. More of them, though, speculated about a foray of cavalry into enemy country, or another infantry attack in Virginia. But by the second week of June, there was too much counterevidence to doubt the ominous truth: Confederate infantry were marching into the Shenandoah Valley and heading toward Pennsylvania.[2] Cavalrymen had crossed the Potomac River ahead of the foot soldiers and begun their raiding, including their human hunting, in the middle of June. It took some time, however, for the leaders of the Army of the Potomac to understand where Lee was going, what troops were with him, and what he was after. That is why General Hooker ordered spies onto a mountaintop.

HEAT, DUST, AND LAMENTATION

In early June, before fears about General Lee had been realized, and before the summer's campaign had been scripted, General Oliver Otis Howard and the Union army's Eleventh Corps waited encamped at Brooke's Station, Virginia. They were now a month past the shattering afternoon at Chancellorsville, and some of the men did their best to put it behind them. During the still evenings, when the heat let up and the dust settled down, regimental musicians tuned up their instruments, and soldiers closed their eyes and imagined themselves far away from the army.[3]

At headquarters, however, General Howard was hard-pressed to remove himself from the here and now. He was still troubled by active plans to replace him, still aware that throughout the North immigrant voters were denouncing his leadership, and still feeling wounded by Carl Schurz, whose early friendship now seemed "pretension." Otis Howard could hardly stand to lose any more friends, particularly those with unequivocal loyalty, so it was doubly difficult for him when his horse, Charley, suddenly died, a victim of distemper. "He has been," Howard wrote to his wife on June 6th, "a nice, beautiful, active & faithful friend to me." To top it off, Howard got sick himself. It was dysentery of sorts, and the diarrhea and dehydration were wasting enough that he could not even carry out his duty, and he lay on a cot, under a tent in the shade.[4]

Howard was still recovering when Hooker put the army in motion. The Union commander had received definitive word of Lee's movement behind the Blue Ridge Mountains on the thirteenth of June, and soon afterward ordered four corps to evacuate the camps along the Rappahannock River, and three others to follow. The march north was to be tailored to the Confederates, designed to stay close enough to Lee to thwart him if he launched another attack, or threatened Washington, or penetrated farther north.[5]

Men in the Eleventh Corps successfully ordered their bodies forward, but they had a harder time commanding their spirits. Even though they moved north through a landscape that for once was not picked over, and by farms that seemed intact, and even though they could forage on strawberries and blackberries, the weather was deathly hot—up to a hundred degrees—and rainless. Worst of all was the red dust that rose over them as they marched, like rank fog. Sometimes they covered close to thirty miles a day, their canteens nearly empty. It was hard enough to move their own aching bodies, but, as one soldier explained, "a man in the ranks has to carry his bed & board & his house & drink & his weapons of war." What kept some of them going was a story about four stragglers who had been found in the woods with their throats cut. A number of overheated soldiers, though, couldn't help falling out of line. They grew disoriented, turned bright red, and collapsed in stroke. "O," one soldier lamented, "how hot it was." The mark of success for another man was simple survival. "It is hard work to kill me, for I am tough," he noted in his diary.[6]

Some afternoons, the men heard low thunder off to the north and west, and imagined the relief it would bring, but soon enough realized that the thunder was distant cannonading—the sound of cavalry struggling in the mountain passes. At night, the soldiers traded hot sun for dark melancholy. In the pine forests where they camped, "a deathlike stillness" prevailed, broken only by the sounds of whippoorwills, with their insistent "lamentation."[7]

On the afternoon of June 18th, the thunder proved real. A cold front moved across the mountains, gusted over the corps, flattened the dust, and filled creeks for the first time in a month. Then the fierce sun returned, just in time for the men to pursue a hurried, zigzag march on mountain roads and over makeshift bridges. Late in the night of June 23rd, the corps was ordered toward Harper's Ferry, and the men moved. Then the corps was ordered away from Harper's Ferry, then toward the town once more. No one, it was clear, knew precisely what the enemy was doing behind the mountains.[8]

For his part, Adam Muenzenberger felt like a punished animal. He had been given lighter duties in June, as an orderly, and he appreciated the bountiful countryside with its grainfields and cherry trees, but he and his fellow soldiers were so hot "we scarcely can stand it and yet we have to march with our entire equipment, loaded like a pack mule. You'd think this is a race—and it is, for the southern general, Lee, is marching in the same direction through the Blue Ridge and we have to march rapidly to block his way."[9]

There was probably not much room in Muenzenberger's tired mind for bad news, but that did not stop it from finding him. It must have wended its way from Wisconsin by train, by horse and wagon, in mailbags, then moved to catch him as he marched. It arrived first as a letter that warned that all was not well at home. Ernest, his oldest son, a studious, faithful boy, who prayed loyally for his father, had fallen sick. The soldier grew anxious, and he begged his wife for return mail. "The only consolation I have in this world," he wrote to Barbara, "is to receive a letter from my dear ones at home." Certainly, though, he might have preferred no mail to no consolation. For the mail that found him the next day, June 24th, brought cruel news: Ernest had died.[10]

"Staggered" by the loss of another son, Adam Muenzenberger framed Ernest's death in the way that worked best for him: It demonstrated God's great love. "The Lord tries us in these days of tribulation," he wrote home, and "whom the Lord loveth, he chastiseth." He imagined his wife's ordeal at his children's deathbeds, where it was her "lot all alone to watch the suffering and pain of the children without my being of the least help to you." He assured her that "I will never forget what you have done for our little ones." And he continued to proffer hope. "Be comforted," he wrote. "After the long night the sun must shine again." He repeated it, convinced that it must be true. "Be comforted, dear. After the rain comes the sunshine."[11]

Muenzenberger sought metaphoric sun, but what he and others in the corps got was more real heat. By 5 A.M. the next morning, the 25th, there it was again, "red as opal." But if the hot misery that day was the same as all the other days, at least the progress was different, for by evening most of the men of the Eleventh Corps had crossed over the Potomac River on pontoon bridges. They were out of the Confederate South. And then it really rained.[12]

There was other news, too—finally something for sure. Late at night on the 26th some of the corps pickets, stationed on Turner's Gap on South Mountain, heard the sound of a horse galloping on the dark mountain road. The rider was ordered to halt at fifteen paces. By torchlight he could be seen dressed ominously in gray, but when the pickets ordered him to dismount, he said he was a Union scout, and needed to be taken to corps headquarters immediately. He had to give General Howard a message. The news he delivered meant that all the guesswork, all the stopping and starting, all the backtracking was nearing an end: Lee's army was up in Pennsylvania. Now they had some idea what they were pointing toward, and how far they had to go. Now they knew, too, that Lee was playing his hand in their homeland and that they had to do their damnedest not to play into it.[13]

DREAD ON THE RISE

Fear wore two faces that June in Gettysburg. There was the jaded view of threatening news, which grew out of knowing that rumors of invaders rarely proved true. It had been only a week into the war, after all, that townspeople had been frightened by reports of armed enemies surging up from the South, and in a panic had armed themselves with rakes and hoes to fend them off. The enemy had never appeared. Since then, scares had ebbed with the season, or, to be more precise, with the height of the Potomac. When the river was low and passable, stories would circulate. Sometimes the threats materialized. During the fall of 1862, after the battle of Antietam, Confederate cavalry came marauding as far as Cashtown, eight miles to the west. But the enemy never showed his face in the borough, and eventually the talk of rumors became old talk. The latest alarms to course across the countryside, in the early summer of 1863, even assumed certain predictable rhythms. People came to expect to see the farmers rushing through the borough with wagons piled high with belongings, and ushering their horses away to safety. They grew used to watching storekeepers piling stock, packing sacks and crates. One woman commented coolly that she was simply used to the excitement. Another found the false alarms tedious. "I am getting tired of all this fuss consequent upon border life," she wrote, "the numerous reports do not alarm me. On the contrary I am sometimes quite amused by seeing the extremes to which people will go."[14]

On June 12th, however, after Governor Andrew Curtin issued a proclamation telling Pennsylvanians to prepare for an invasion, even jaded Gettysburg residents took notice. Then on June 15th, it seems, worry intensified. This alarm materialized suddenly, at night. In one house, a mother had fallen asleep when she heard her child cry out. It was a simple enough request: Her daughter wanted a cup of water. But when the woman arose she heard a commotion outside, and looking out a window saw the southern sky illuminated in red. Directly below her, people in the street seemed frightened. "The Rebels are coming and burning as they go," she heard one of them say. Outside Fannie Buehler's house, panic took hold. Enemy soldiers were burning nearby Emmitsburg, and Gettysburg would be next![15]

But later on, the sky shifted from red to black again, and the fire stayed where it was. Everybody found out that it had indeed been Emmitsburg burning, but a local arsonist had torched it, not the enemy. Misapprehended as it was, this conflagration broadcast a visual alarm: This was what an invasion might look like; this was what enemy men might do. And soon enough people learned that over in Chambersburg invaders had actually appeared. Flight through the borough could have told them as much, as black refugees moved hurriedly north. One woman was struck by the sight of people "with bundles as large as old-fashioned feather ticks slung across their backs, almost bearing them to the ground" and by the "consternation . . . as they hurried along; crowding, and running against each other in their confusion; children stumbling, falling, and crying." Another resident described the scene as "sad and pitiful." The children wept, she said, clinging to their mothers' skirts; the "aged" were "frantic with fear." Some of the refugees had the means to ship their belongings by rail; some "drove 'sorry nags,'" and some were too poor to do anything but walk.[16]

For one of these white witnesses, the flight of black families was entertaining. She found it "amusing to behold the conduct of the colored people in town," and offered her readers a sample of some of the anxious voices she heard: "Fo' de Lod's sake, you chillen, cum right long quick! If dem Rebs dun kotch you, dey tear you all up." For another woman the evacuation was bothersome. "Last night," she reported on June 16th, "the darkies made such a racket up and down our house that we could not sleep." And for both of these white observers, the exodus was bewildering. Did the fugitives have real cause for alarm? They believed, said one of the women, that the Rebels had an "especial hatred toward them," and that "if they fell into their hands, annihilation was sure." The other woman was not sure "how much cause they had for their fears." She did admit, though, that *they* believed they were in danger. "It was a terrible reality to them," she said.[17]

White Pennsylvania women pondered black flight with equanimity, but soon enough, they, too, felt dread on the rise. In Gettysburg, people stopped sleeping well, stopped making calls and going to club meetings, and began to quit society as usual. Street life told the change. Residents spent time clustering on borough corners, drawn to the bearers of breaking news. There was plenty of news to hear, too. On June 20th, a Union staff officer appeared and told the townspeople to arm themselves. Newspapers also spoke of a "bloody and desperate foe," hell-bent on "plunder."[18]

Believers began to take action. Beginning on June 21st, parties of borough men took heavy axes and headed toward South Mountain, planning to fell trees across the narrow roads, to block passes and impede soldiers and wagons. They wanted to buy some time. Other men gathered their horses and headed to the hills or toward the Susquehanna River, hoping to hide their draft animals and protect their harvest. The scene through the borough in late June, said one observer, was a "general stampede." Up on the Bayly farm, north of town, the family was in a high state of worry. They had not removed any animals, and they began to fret about "the reckless raiders and their foraging excursions" and to wonder what they should do with their horses, including Nellie. Harriet Bayly encouraged her husband and her thirteen-year-old son to prepare to take the animals and evacuate.[19]

Other families worried about the safety of their men. Fannie Buehler had packed a bag for her husband, a postmaster and "black Republican" editor, because, Fannie said, he was a "marked man." Of decided interest to Confederates were individuals like Buehler who kept the Union buzzing with information and running smoothly—postmasters, telegraph operators, tax collectors. And other white men were not entirely immune from seizure. In 1862, Confederates had expressed little interest in hearing about a man's status as a noncombatant. When they had come up the valley that year, in fact, they had not been at all fussy about the identities of several area men they took hostage and threw into dank Southern prisons.[20]

Some women sent boys and men off with family horses, and others prepared husbands to evacuate. Some households, of course, had no men to consider at all. According to one estimate, over a thousand Adams County men were serving in the army at the time of the invasion, and this meant that many families—like Georgia McClellan's and Elizabeth Thorn's—had no able-bodied men at home. There were certainly men in the area—soldiers who had already served, or who were wounded and convalescing, men who were too old or too young, or who had chosen not to enlist. (Elizabeth Thorn lived with her elderly father and her young sons.) But many women in and around Gettysburg were, by the beginning of July, alone.[21]

Long after the battle, some Gettysburg women would comment on the men who left town in late June. One woman declared that "all the chivalry of the town took its departure," and another claimed that "our homes and hearths were vacated by . . . able bodied fathers, brothers and sons." Outside commentators, too, would weigh in on the fact that many women faced the enemy alone. All of these observers spoke to prevailing ideas about male gallantry—ideas that said that men protected firesides and families. What they did not acknowledge was the fact that most Gettysburg families did not believe that they were stretching chivalric codes. Few of them, if any, anticipated a full-scale battle in their backyards. They worried about raiding parties, certainly, but not about massive engagements. Gettysburg, many residents felt, was of little consequence to army commanders. Infantry might march to a place like Philadelphia or Washington, where the Northern public and the Union president would take notice. Or perhaps troops would march to Harrisburg, the state capital. When one woman in the borough was cautioned about traveling in the area at the end of the month, she responded scornfully. "What," she wondered, "would the rebels ever want to come to Gettysburg for?"[22]

Gettysburg residents, including the men who left town, also had some confidence in emergency protection. Seminary and college students, along with some townsmen, had volunteered to serve as emergency infantry, and on the eighteenth of the month they left for Harrisburg, singing the "Battle Cry of Freedom." There they mustered in with other volunteers as the 26th Pennsylvania Emergency Infantry Regiment. Other men threw themselves into local defense as emergency cavalry. Furthermore, volunteers from Philadelphia, hearing of the distress on the border, rode down to help, too. While some residents of the area saw these volunteers as "raw," or worried that they might be "of little use," others were happy to have them close by. When the emergency regiment arrived in Gettysburg on the 26th of June, the 700 men were fed, sung to, and cheered.[23]

The families who sent men away from the borough at the end of June were not bending wartime proprieties, then. Men left their Gettysburg homes to safeguard family property or to safeguard themselves. They believed a battle unlikely and, in the event of a raid, they knew their wives and children had protection nearby. They also trusted that enemy men, if they appeared, would not harass their women and children—their *white* women and children. But while they were not challenging the laws of chivalry, their departure suggests that they also believed some of those laws to be flawed. Chivalry (and public opinion) emphasized women's frailty. Private opinion may have acknowledged what women could accomplish and endure. One young Gettysburg woman would be taunted by Confederate soldiers about where the men had gone. "Why ain't some of your men here to protect you?" she would be asked by an invading soldier. "They know we can do that ourselves," she replied. Fannie Buehler and her husband had this kind of conviction. She expressed the hope that God would protect her, but she also had faith in herself. When she sent her husband packing, she told him "not for a moment to think of me, as I was not afraid, but would do the best I could." And he, by heading down a borough street "on a dead run," showed that he believed her.[24]

THE VANGUARD

The day that Fannie Buehler expressed her faith in God and herself, and urged her husband to leave town, was the 26th of June, 1863. Late that morning, the 26th Pennsylvania, the emergency Pennsylvania infantry, which was newly armed and barely trained, marched west from Gettysburg. Emergency cavalrymen were in the lead. The men in the regiment did not know where Confederate soldiers were, but they had been ordered to slow the advance of any enemy who moved east through the mountains. Blocking veteran soldiers was a big order for men with little training, and the colonel of the 26th objected to what he imagined would be nothing but sacrifice.[25]

In Gettysburg itself, as people remembered it, the day then seemed to stall. Whether later events put the time into slow motion, or whether people were so nervous the clock seemed to stop, is hard to guess. It was hoofbeats, however, that broke the calm. Emergency cavalrymen, back in town, had hard news: The 26th was running—it had bumped into a force of enemy soldiers, already through the mountains. Worse still, Confederate troops were on their way to Gettysburg. Later, the noise compounded: Wagons thundered back in retreat, and the cavalry, what was left of it, galloped out of town to the east. All that remained now was to wait for the moment that months, even years, of worry had pointed them toward: to see the enemy for real.[26]

That enemy, under the direction of General Lee, had advanced into the heart of Pennsylvania in several columns. The first cavalry and infantry soldiers crossed the Potomac River on June 15th, with cavalry forging ahead up the Cumberland Valley to begin reconnaissance work and aggressive raiding. Two

Confederate infantry divisions headed north toward Harrisburg—Lee had ordered the capital's capture, if feasible. And one division, General Jubal Early's men, moved east, toward York, Pennsylvania, to destroy bridges and railroads and thwart Federal troops should they appear. Gettysburg, thanks to its long-standing position as the meeting place of many roads, was right in Early's way.[27]

At the western end of town, a group of schoolgirls decided to put all the alarms of the day at the back of their minds. Even when their school principal told them to go home that Friday afternoon—insisted that they leave, then and there—they only half listened. They walked to the edge of the town, and waited. Their nonchalance lasted as long as it took them to register the sight of strange-looking horsemen at the rim of Seminary Ridge. The girls ran. An observer noticed how they did not even gather their skirts at steps or mud but flew helter-skelter into the closest hotel.[28]

Fannie Buehler was working on her sewing machine when her eldest daughter rushed in to tell her the Confederates had entered town, but Fannie didn't believe it. Neither did her husband, David, so he went down to the square to see for himself. Confederate foot soldiers were already marching up Chambersburg Street, and a friend shouted out a warning, "David, flee for your life." He picked up a satchel from his wife, who urged him to hurry, and he headed away. Now Fannie would meet the enemy army with a friendly black dog and two children.[29]

North of the borough, Harriet Bayly's son, William, was trying to run away with Nellie the horse. It had been an uneasy morning at the farm. Family and hired hands had hayed fields until it began to rain, around noon. Then thirteen-year-old William, having eaten his noon meal, and feeling little of the general anxiety, found a cool room and fell asleep. He was booted awake, however, with the word that his father wanted him. Nobody needed to convince him that the Confederates were at hand; at the western edge of the farm the emergency troops were running on the ridge. William met his father at the barn and jumped on Nellie. Whipping the mare with his jacket, the boy, with his father and uncle at his side, rode away at breakneck rate. A mud-splashed rider they met told them to get out "pretty quick," as enemy troopers were on their heels. They made it to the refuge of one farmhouse, then rode on to another, and then relaxed and dismounted—just long enough for Confederates to catch up. Nellie and nearly twenty other horses were "rats in a trap." Lucky for them all, then, that they discovered the Confederate pursuers had a weakness—they liked to argue. Some of the Pennsylvania farmers engaged the cavalrymen in a debate about the war, and while the men quarreled, William Bayly and his father crept to the barn, mounted their horses, jumped over a fence, and raced away. This time, they hid well and rode far—nearly thirty miles. When they arrived home two days later, however, Harriet Bayly gave them a mixed welcome. She was pleased to see her family, but not so pleased to see the horses. She was "sorely put out," she said, for there was "no safety" at home. Now they would have to think of a plan to hide Nellie nearby.[30]

While Gettysburg residents held their collective breath that afternoon, and steadied themselves for enemy soldiers, Georgia Wade McClellan began a personal battle. Either the general alarm had hurried her into labor or her baby was simply due to be born. That morning, her body had seized with contractions. Someone had gone into town for a doctor, and he helped Georgia deliver her first child, a son, Louis Kenneth. It was around two-thirty in the afternoon. Georgia's attendants were anxious to help, but more anxious to get away and make sure their own families were safe. Within fifteen minutes of the delivery, the Wade women were by themselves. In another hour, Georgia's mother left as well. "I was locked in the house alone," Georgia said.[31]

Nearby, Elizabeth Thorn contended with six horsemen who came chasing into Evergreen Cemetery, firing revolvers and jumping over fences. She imagined that they would stop at nothing. "I was a piece away from the house when they rode into the Cemetery," she recalled. "I was scared as I was afraid they had fired after my mother." They did not shoot at Thorn's mother, but they did not leave the family alone, either. They demanded food. They also served—though no one knew it at the time—as something of a portent. One of the enemy soldiers, with his mouth full of the Thorn's food, spotted one of their company coming down the pike leading a horse. "Oh, you have another one," he said. "Yes," the soldier replied, "the ____ ____ shot at me, but he did not hit me, and I shot at him and blowed him down like nothing." This, the death of an emergency cavalryman named George Sandoe, was a sad enough affair. A week later, however, it would carry new meaning—one of the first fatalities of thousands.[32]

Confederate cavalry made quick work of Gettysburg, hunting horses, chasing men, plundering barns, and cleaning out stores. They dragged their loot behind their horses, put on several hats at a time, and tied pairs of shoes onto stirrups. Then Confederate infantry marched in. General Early made a formal demand on the town for foodstuffs, clothing, and money, and did not get it. But stores and hotels opened for his men, and they took or traded for what they wanted. They came out with hatfuls of candy, barrels of whiskey, with blankets and shawls and bolts of cloth. Some of this they paid for with Confederate money, some of it they took. They marked the territory, too, by hoisting a Confederate flag in the center of the town diamond, and by serenading residents with enemy music. A regimental band struck up Southern songs—"Hurrah for the Bonnie Blue Flag," "Away Down South in Dixie," and

"The Stars and Bars." But by Saturday morning they were all gone, off to the east.[33]

This first wave of Confederate soldiers left mixed emotions in its wake. Some people felt pity for the soldiers. Fannie Buehler claimed she had never seen "a more unsightly set of men, and as I looked at them in their dirty, torn garments, hatless, shoeless, and foot-sore, I pitied them from the depth of my heart." Another resident was so impressed by the enemy's dirtiness that she said they looked like the street itself; they were so brown and dunlike that she could not see a soldier in front of her tying his shoe, so indistinguishable were man and dust. Women were also overcome by disgust—they were struck by the smell of the soldiers: The humid air magnified the odor of their unwashed flesh, and their rotten and soiled clothes.[34]

The soldiers' sad looks undercut their fearsomeness, as did their eagerness to talk. Were they really thought of as demons? They wanted to know. One soldier asked a woman what she "thought the Rebels were like, whether they had horns." Another man approached a group of women with a sneering look and asked, "Can you tell me what direction those dirty Rebels took? At least that is what you call them." They also spoke to a little boy, in jest. "Bub," they teased him, "would you like to shoot a Rebel?" And they also asked his mother, "Why are you women so afraid of the rebels?" She replied with bravado: "That is news to me. I did not know that they were."[35]

The desire of Confederate soldiers to converse helped to soften their reputation, but it did not dispel women's anxieties. None of these Gettysburg women knew what would happen next. And by reminding residents that they were considered demonic, soldiers raised the possibility that they might be. They also pointed to ways that the Union army violated wartime codes. One soldier commented that they were supposed to treat Pennsylvania women with respect, "not like your men treated our women in Winchester." Another soldier told Elizabeth Thorn that she should not be afraid of them, but that she should also know that war sometimes went beyond boundaries: "They were not going to hurt us," Thorn remembered him saying, "like the yankeys did their ladies."[36]

By pointedly addressing these white women's fears about assault, then, these enemy men may have augmented them. One woman described the invaders as "ugly, rude, hostile soldiers, from whom violence might be expected," and she recalled June 26th, in their company, as "the most uncomfortable night" of her life. Even Fannie Buehler, who chatted civilly with Confederate men, admitted that she, too, was unnerved. When she casually asked one of her "visitors" how long he was planning to stay, he replied, "Why, all summer, of course." This response, said Buehler, "startled me . . . if they were to remain all summer, what should we do?" After putting her children to bed that evening, she flung herself across her bed, bereft.[37]

Rumors, long-standing and recent, probably did not help matters. The Northern public had entertained notions about a rapacious enemy for some time, partly because the abolitionist press had pictured white Southern men as volatile, violent, and lustful. More recent reports about Federal soldiers gave Northern women a reason to fear reprisal, too. Union soldiers had taken an increasingly hard line against civilians in the South, and word was that Confederates had a special interest in avenging Southern women by "insulting" enemy women. All of these stories took a toll on female confidence in Gettysburg. "We girls," wrote one Gettysburg woman, "pictured the most outlandish things which would be done. Children and women went about wringing their hands, alternately bemoaning our impending fate & praying for deliverance." A teenaged girl also wondered what soldiers would do, saying it "was a fearful question to my young mind." Another girl, west of Gettysburg, echoed her. She worried whether Confederate men "would molest the women."[38]

These feelings were heightened when borough women realized that the soldiers who had occupied their town for one night were not simply an independent detachment of troops, but part of a large invading force. Fannie Buehler knew, for instance, what sort of men she had not yet seen, and this worried her. The dreaded Louisiana Tigers, she had heard, had camped on the north edge of town, and, while their fellow soldiers made conversation and foraged for supplies, they had gotten drunk on stolen liquor.[39]

Had Fannie known more than she did—had she been able to see ahead a week, and to picture the men who would actually be crowding her streets, breaking into civilian cellars, and coming contemptuous and insistent to women's doors—she might have abandoned her last shred of bravado. For many of the men who would come chasing into Gettysburg on July first and who would settle down for a stay were Louisiana soldiers.

THE MEN CALLED ANIMALS

Fannie Buehler had obviously framed in her mind an image of Louisiana Tigers, and so, it seems, had many Americans. According to some historians, Louisiana men were the "shock troops" of the Confederacy and represented, by reputation, the antithesis of civility and restraint. Untamed, uncouth, ill-bred, destructive, and disorderly, they were allegedly as wild as a man with a gun could get. In fairness, the Louisiana troops who marched into Pennsylvania in early June carried an association with wildness that many of them had not even been around to create. Early in the war three companies of men had been recruited from the jails and the docks—some would say the dregs—of New Orleans. Many of them were foreign-born. These Louisiana troops were linked with drinking and brawling and unruliness off the battlefield, and with ferocity in combat. At the first Battle of Bull Run—the battle in which one of the units claimed the name "Tigers"—it was said that some of these men abandoned their rifles at a critical moment and fought with knives. Louisiana troops enhanced their reputation for pugnacity when they served under Stonewall Jackson in the legendary Shenandoah Valley campaign. Only a few months later they fought daringly at Second Bull Run in the summer of 1862. They eschewed their knives this time, apparently, and fought with rocks.[40]

In the first week of May 1863, Louisiana troops—now thoroughly reorganized—enhanced their notoriety. While General Jubal Early's Louisiana soldiers clashed with Hooker's Union troops at Fredericksburg, Virginia, other Louisiana men, led by Stonewall Jackson, traversed some wicked undergrowth called the Wilderness, and joined the attack on the Union army's left flank at Chancellorsville.[41]

The Tigers were known not only for their audacity in battle, but for carrying war to civilians. They were accused (probably falsely) of mistreating civilians during the Antietam campaign, and during the winter of 1862–1863, Fredericksburg residents made repeated complaints about Louisiana soldiers stealing and destroying property. Of particular concern were General Early's troops. These men, who were often considered the wildest of the "Tigers," were so unmanageable that Early—not known for an easy temper himself—referred to the men as "a damn pack of thieves." He did appreciate the way they fought, however.[42]

It is doubtful that many of the Louisiana "Tigers" who visited Pennsylvania knew much about the state before they got there, or even that such a place as Gettysburg existed. But even as they marched and fought miles away from that borough, they were associated with some hurt on civilians there. To clear the way for Lee's invasion north, General Richard Ewell had ordered the seizure of the Federal garrison at Winchester, Virginia, in the Shenandoah Valley. Two Louisiana brigades were central to the operation, which included a brash assault on the fortifications around Winchester on June 14th, and, early the next day, an ambush of Federal troops who were trying to evacuate. A number of Gettysburg boys fought for the Federal army at Winchester, and one of them, shot in the arm, died in a field hospital on July 12th. Later on, people said this soldier had been ordered to halt and surrender, but he decided to run instead. People also said that a girl in Gettysburg carried his photograph in her apron pocket. He was Jack Skelly, and she was Georgia McClellan's younger sister, Jennie Wade.[43]

As they moved into Maryland and Pennsylvania, the Tigers traumatized Northern women more directly. Often, all it took was their appearance at a woman's door. One twenty-one-year-old soldier commented that "the people were afraid of us . . . one of the 7th La . . . went into a house near camp and asked the lady of the house for some milk and bread she told him to take a seat & she would go and get the articles—but says she 'What regt do you belong to?' 'The 7th La.' 'Oh-h and the poor thing fainted.'" Another Louisiana soldier, a private in the same brigade, crossed a mountain gap opposite Gettysburg and went to find something to eat. "Where I stopped," he wrote, "there lived a little Dutch woman, who met me at the gate, crying and wringing her hands, saying all the time: 'Spare me and my children and you shall have anything we have got on the place.' She was the worst scared woman I had ever seen."[44]

Pennsylvania residents may have been fearful because of what they had heard about the Tigers months or even years earlier. The "very name of Louisiana soldier is a horror to me," commented one woman living in the path of the invading army. But they may also have been primed for worry by other soldiers. Confederate cavalry troops who preceded the Louisiana foot soldiers into the North were among many Confederate men who spread word of the Tigers' ruthlessness. On one occasion they warned "that the La tigers would kill, burn & destroy everything & everybody in the country."[45] There may have been many reasons why Pennsylvania women—like Fannie Buehler—shrank at the thought of Louisiana soldiers. But they all boiled down to one fear: that the Tigers were not soldiers at all, but monsters.

For now, though, the Tigers had been kept out of the Borough of Gettysburg, and ordered off with the rest of Jubal Early's command toward York. And Gettysburg women could only speculate on what would happen next. Some of them wondered where experienced military help was when they needed it. "Where is our army," one woman had asked herself, "that they let the enemy scour the country and do as they please?" But people knew there were two sides to having Union soldiers nearby. The Army of the Potomac might thwart enemy raiding, but it might also be looking for a fight. Women wanted their own soldiers to come close, but they were also relieved to think they were nowhere around. Which was safer, they wondered, predatory soldiers or the pandemonium of battle?[46]

The problem was hearing or seeing anything for sure. General Early's soldiers had cut communication lines to the borough. On the night of the 26th, Elizabeth Thorn had watched an orange glow expand into the northeast sky, and had been able to make out railroad cars burning. Confederate men had hauled seventeen cars onto the tracks over Rock Creek, and sent them crashing, one by one, into the creekbed. The bridge went too. The railroad, with all that it implied of news, people, mailbags, food, weapons, and supplies, was gone. The telegraph operator had also hustled himself and his equipment out of town. A newspaper editor complained of knowing "nothing of what is going on in the 'outside world.'"[47]

The isolation broke briefly when Union cavalry appeared on Sunday, the 28th. Borough residents cheered the soldiers, and one woman noted happily that "our Government [is] keeping an eye on us." But on Monday, June 29th, the cavalry rode away. Americans in other parts of the country now knew more than they did. In New York City, for example, people could open their daily papers and read that enemy armies were massing near Gettysburg. In the borough itself, though, residents had to go by guesswork, or what news came in at a gallop. Or they could predict the future with their own eyes. On June 30th, residents saw more enemy soldiers looking at them from Seminary Ridge. They also heard of a "great Southern Army moving this way," and learned through scouts that "a heavy force of our soldiers" was within five miles. Union troops to the south. Enemy troops to the west, north, and east. Gettysburg was a village in a vise. "It begins to look as though we will have a battle soon," said one woman. "We are in great fear."[48]

FLYING THICK

On the 29th of June, Union soldiers of Howard's Eleventh Corps, at the leading edge of the Federal army that Pennsylvanians both hoped for and feared, marched through the town of Emmitsburg, Maryland, just south of the Pennsylvania border. There they passed blackened buildings and houses—ruins of the town that had burned two weeks earlier. They had been moving now, off and on, for eighteen days. They had left Frederick before dawn, after barely any sleep, without supper or breakfast, and had trudged on slippery roads through drizzling rain. In the last two days, some brigades had covered over forty miles. The soldiers reached the outskirts of Emmitsburg before dinnertime, and camped outside the town, in a "wet field." The next morning, the 30th, the corps moved closer in, next to a Catholic academy for girls run by the Sisters of Charity.[49]

Maybe it was the sight of the Sisterhood, with what one soldier called its "tasteful" edifices, or maybe it had to do with the mission of the place—so unlike their mission—or maybe they just remembered later how different it was from the scenes that followed, but soldiers spoke of the school with both awe and yearning. It was vacation week, and the schoolgirls were gone. An Italian priest and one of the sisters gave officers a tour. They visited the chapel, and one of the soldiers took a turn at the organ, and they peeked in at the simple, spare rooms of the students. The sisters gave many of the officers dinner that night, and offered some a clean bed. Nuns also brought food out to enlisted men—"nice, soft bread and sweet milk as long as their supply lasted." The night was serene.[50]

Adam Muenzenberger hoped that he could take communion at the convent, but he was not sure they would be there long enough for that. It had now been six days since he had heard that Ernest had died, and, being up in Maryland, in what he felt was "a civilized country," he was thinking about home more than ever. He knew that Barbara would be having "sad thoughts," and he wanted her prayers. "Ask God," he wrote home, "to protect us and to give us a speedy return." Muenzenberger was "worn out" with marching "like dogs," but he was also optimistic "that it will soon be ended." He took out Barbara's picture—his "dearly beloved picture that I carry in my breast pocket through all my travels"—and kissed it. He also said hello to the "little ones" at home, just two of them now.[51]

General Howard missed his family, too: He didn't know what the Chancellorsville baby looked like, and he worried that his little girl, Gracie, would "forget she is papa's daughter." But in his letters to Lizzie at the end of the month, he actually permitted himself to indulge a feeling he had not allowed himself since April, and that was hope. He hoped that "our troubles will be brought to a crisis before long—and if God wills I may be home before long also," and he hoped that Lizzie would "be able to have a good opinion of the 11th Corps if we are engaged again." The corps, he said, "marches well," and, in what was certainly a soothing observation, he noted that "almost all the officers like to please me & cooperate with alacrity."[52]

Howard's soldiers began to sound more like the men of April, too. The corps had been slightly reorganized since the ides of May, and had taken on new regiments. But more than that, the men were moving north, and entering a world that seemed to lift them, body and soul, into fresh ambition. Weary soldiers celebrated the sight of healthy Maryland farms, and reveled in the rich landscape. The ripening fields, the rolling hills, and the mountains were all freshened by the green glory of early summer. The scenery, one soldier said, "made our very hearts happy."[53]

The landscape matched its bounteous looks with social sustenance. When the corps arrived at Middletown, Maryland, they found a town, for once, that welcomed them. Residents waved American flags, and women fluttered handkerchiefs behind windows. "We have been used for the past 6 months to having *wimin* look sourly at us," commented a soldier from a New York regiment. "But here all is changed. Lovely women smile upon us, waive their handkerchiefs at us and stand by the side of the road with pints of milk to give us to drink & tell us to fight for them & protect them." A staff officer concurred. "You should see [the soldiers] as they come from the village or a neighboring farm house laden with bread and milk and pies," he said. "The whole female population is baking." He thought the warmth of the people—the "soft beams of sympathy" that surrounded them—had brought the corps to life. There was, he said, "a new spirit" in the army. And he imagined that "if we have an engagement here or anywhere north, our soldiers will fight with great courage; it cannot be otherwise."[54]

The growing confidence was enhanced by the certainty that whatever was going to happen was very big and very soon. General George Gordon Meade, who replaced General Hooker as Commander of the Army of the Potomac on the morning of June 28th, had ordered the army to mass near Frederick, then to move north toward the Susquehanna River in Pennsylvania to thwart Lee. By Tuesday, the thirtieth, it was clear that much of Lee's army was concentrating east of the South Mountain range, possibly near Gettysburg. Reports from cavalry, scouts, and civilians, however, continued to be "abundant and conflicting." They revealed the proximity of Lee's army, but little of its intentions.[55]

There was nothing definite, then, on the morning of the first of July that told the ninety-five thousand soldiers of the Army of the Potomac that they might be marching into battle. General Meade ordered John Reynolds' First Corps to move toward Gettysburg, and the Eleventh Corps, the second smallest corps in the Union army with less than nine thousand men, to follow at a "supporting distance." The other five corps would be ready to help out if needed, but ready to turn in other directions if that was where Lee decided to go. General Howard broke the Eleventh Corps into two columns to march north, and they were on their way by nine-thirty.[56]

The temperature was warm, the air was heavy, and the marching seemed slow. The men in General Carl Schurz's 3rd Division had the slightly longer route, but at least the road they took was relatively passable—not deeply rutted or blocked by wagons. The soldiers paused momentarily when the head of the column crossed the state line, and Pennsylvania regiments lowered their colors, beat their drums, and gave a cheer for home ground. Then, abruptly, they paused again. A staff officer who had ridden ahead about six miles heard some firing, a little to his left and front. It sounded like the sort of growl the corps had heard often on its march north next to the mountains—a cavalry fight. He and another officer pursued the sound, but the firing—or whatever it was—stopped. And then, on the way back, they discovered something truly compelling—"several splendid cherry trees laden with ripe cherries." Noises of guns were nothing to them now. They "stopped to eat."[57]

General Carl Schurz rode along not hearing much of anything. So the galloping horseman who emerged from the distance at around ten-thirty came as a surprise. He carried an order from General Howard, who had ridden on ahead. It told Schurz to hurry. It told him the First Corps was fighting the enemy at Gettysburg, and it needed help. Schurz shifted gears. He put his men at the "double-quick" and, with his staff, rode ahead himself. He still heard nothing. But the crisis was confirmed by what he saw. Coming toward him on the Taneytown Road leading out of Gettysburg was a battle's human fallout. Men, women, and children, who "seemed to be in great terror," rushed toward him. One woman, carrying a bundle and tugging a small child, tried to stop Schurz as he rode. She screamed at him. "Hard times at Gettysburg! They are shooting and killing! What will become of us!"[58]

It was not until he had ridden up an incline in the road that he heard it, too. Sound that had been caught in the valley, or under the clouds, or been carried away with the mist and wind, now reached him. It was deep percussion.[59]

As the order to double-quick worked through the troops behind Schurz, the men suddenly knew that what had begun as another day of mud and thirst was materializing into a fight for their lives. This realization, explained one soldier, made everything else—the soreness, the fatigue, the heavy weight of their equipment—irrelevant. They were changed, he said, "as by magic." They were ready and running, and "those who have never experienced the wondrous power of a battle already begun, and toward which one is rapidly marching," could not possibly understand it. Maybe the adrenaline that coursed through their bodies crystallized the visible world, or maybe, years later, this treasured moment was magnified, but whatever happened, everything seemed to come into focus. Nothing, said the same man, "escapes observation; every fence and field, the whole topography of the country, the expression on comrades' faces, the tone of command, all are indelibly stamped on mind and memory."[60]

General Howard claimed he would never lose the certain clarity of his first moments at Gettysburg. Later, other senior officers would dispute his recollections, but Howard did not have a doubt about what he did. As he rode toward the borough, he met an officer from the First Corps telling him to bring his men up to town. Howard considered the battle in progress, and then, with his staff, looked for a place to put his men. He found a good one. It was the northern end of Cemetery Ridge, on the hill. It stood above the town, looked over to the ridge to the west, and down upon the valley where the men were fighting. He decided that this was the place for his command—it was "the best defensive position within sight."[61]

While he waited for his troops to come to town, Howard looked for orders from General Reynolds, and found a balcony up above a store to survey the battlefield. Things seemed to be going reasonably well—some Confederate prisoners were being led into town. And there, cantering in from the field, was word from Reynolds. But the young officer delivered hard, disconcerting news—the general had been wounded. A few minutes later, another messenger: General Reynolds was dead. Oliver Otis Howard, who would now assume control of the field of battle for the Federal army, was astounded.[62] He had prayed often for another chance to show what he could do, and now here it was.

Adam Muenzenberger, along with the rest of the 26th Wisconsin regiment, in the 2nd Brigade of the 3rd Division in the Eleventh Corps, entered the Borough of Gettysburg not long after twelve-thirty in the afternoon. The men had been caught in downpours, and they dripped water and sweat. Some of them had no shoes on. And they were famished. *"Wir waren nass wie die Katzen, hungrig wie die Woelfe,"* remembered a sergeant in Muenzenberger's regiment: "We were wet as cats, hungry as wolves." But they would have to eat on the run. As soon as they came into the southern edge of the town, they were ordered north into the fight. Pushing forward along the streets, some of the soldiers threaded themselves through a channel of hands. Women and children passed them cakes and bread with apple butter, and offered them water. The running men ate, drank, and flung the tin cups back. "Courage, ladies," one of the soldiers shouted, "we'll drive the rebs!"[63]

It was after two-thirty in the afternoon when General Carl Schurz climbed onto a rooftop to get a good look at the battle in progress. Schurz had taken control of the Eleventh Corps on the field when Howard assumed command of all Union forces, and he had two divisions—5000 to 6000 men—fighting in front of him. (Howard had kept one division in reserve on Cemetery Hill.) What Schurz saw concerned him. Over on the left, enemy fire had expanded, and Confederates were attacking the gap between the First and Eleventh corps. It was far from ideal ground, these fields north of Gettysburg. Unlike Chancellorsville, it was open and difficult to stage surprises, but it was almost too open—too many fields, not enough walls or embankments, not enough protection.[64]

Schurz looked to the place where he had sent General Francis Barlow's men. Having been informed that even more Confederate troops were closing in on Gettysburg from the north and east, he had ordered General Barlow to take his division and to "refuse" his right wing, to double it back and use it to repel an attack from the side. Schurz was still smarting from the flank attack in May, and he was not anxious to see another one. It is unclear how good the visibility was from the housetop, and how much the smoke obscured the positions of the men. But one thing was obvious to Schurz. Barlow was not there.[65]

General Barlow had not connected with the corps' other division, and was not forming a tight line of men, ready to take an assault from the right. He had instead pushed his men far forward, posting some of them onto and in front of a knoll. Seeing his men exposed and endangered, Schurz made a quick decision to send Wladimir Krzyzanowski's brigade, including Adam Muenzenberger, to help close the gap before it was too late.[66]

But it was already too late.

It is hard to know what General Barlow had been thinking. Possibly he had imagined that by pulling out so far he could stage a flank attack himself, on the left, against the enemy surging in, or perhaps he had seen the knoll as a good defensive position, a fine place for his artillery. But he had been given no orders to place his men where he did, and now one of his brigades—nine hundred men or so—were strung out by the knoll near a creekbed, in front of some trees.[67]

The soldiers positioned on the knoll must have carried with them a variety of emotions. Two months earlier, in a different, much deeper set of woods in Virginia, it had been this brigade, with many of the same German soldiers, under this same German officer, Colonel Leopold von Gilsa, which had been attacked first by Stonewall Jackson's soldiers. Since that terrible time at Chancellorsville, some things had changed. General Barlow, for one thing, had taken command of the division. The boyish-looking Yankee, the Massachusetts blue blood who felt nothing but disdain for "Dutchmen," would later say that he had been "seduced" by General Howard into taking the command. But Barlow had tried to bring the German brigade up to his standards. Seeking to devote himself "particularly" to its many deficiencies, he had even moved the men's camp in early June "so as to bring them all under my immediate eye."[68]

Among the men Barlow put under particular surveillance was the brigade commander himself, Colonel von Gilsa. Von Gilsa did not meet the general's standards of propriety and discipline, and even as they marched toward Gettysburg at the end of June, Barlow (apparently with Howard's support) had had the colonel arrested for being too lax and for disobeying a marching order. Von Gilsa's insubordination, such as it was, may have been as much directed at Howard as Barlow. On June 28th, the colonel had had his staff officers toast General Meade with a pail full of whiskey, and at least one officer became inebriated. Barlow had reinstated von Gilsa, and given him his sword back, only as they closed in on Gettysburg and been within earshot of the battle. And now Barlow had ordered von Gilsa to the knoll.[69]

All of the men in the Eleventh Corps wanted a glorious moment. The long marches, the weeks of feeling like a pack mule, and even the rising confidence had not put enough distance between them and ignominy. Many German-American soldiers had felt their Yankee commander had exposed them at Chancellorsville. *"Er ist ein Yankee, und darum wollte er uns hinschlachten lassen, weil wir meistens lauter Deutsche sind,"* one soldier in the corps had written. They had been throwaway men to the Yankee Howard, he said, who was willing to have them killed, because most of them were Germans.[70] All of the men in the Eleventh Corps sought an honorable day at Gettysburg, then, but certainly immigrant soldiers, and certainly von Gilsa's men out on the knoll, wanted it especially.

Von Gilsa's soldiers had to have reassured themselves, though, by contemplating the odds. How many times could military history repeat itself? How many times would they be positioned at the point of an attack? But the answer came soon enough: at least once more. The Confederates burst upon them so quickly that they did not even have much of an opportunity to ponder the vagaries of fate or, worse, its perversities. Shortly after three o'clock in the afternoon, out of the woods and through the creekbed, came Confederate general Jubal Early's division—another set of screaming men.

General Barlow, who himself was severely injured in this attack, would later say that the Germans made "no fight at all," and that the attack had barely begun when his men "began to run." He would also say that he had an "admirable position," that he had "formed as directed," and that when the enemy attacked, he should have been able to hold "the place easily." Barlow would say all of this, but not everybody agreed with him. Other men—from both armies—would assert that the men near the knoll struggled hard before they retreated. One soldier described the fight as "obstinate," and another, a Confederate private who assailed the Eleventh Corps, claimed that they "stood firm" and "were harder to drive than we had ever known them before." One of Barlow's regiments—of Pennsylvania Germans—lost almost half its men in its effort to hold the enemy back.[71]

The Union troops may have been hard to drive then, but it was not impossible to do so. Krzyzanowski's brigade had been sent over to extend Barlow's line, but by the time it got there Barlow's men were already in retreat, and Confederates were renewing the attack. The soldiers charged and resisted charges through the wheatfields, flattening the grain with bodies. They could read the fine print on each others' battle flags and see enemy eyes close up as they tore at each other. At the same time, bullets hummed "like infuriated bees" above them, into them. And the Eleventh Corps continued to fall back. A Confederate private described what he saw as they did so: "I ran down to a plank fence and the Yankees were running across an old field and looked to be as thick as you ever saw black birds fly."[72]

They weren't all flying. Many of them, including Germans, remained stubborn. The 75th Pennsylvania, in Krzyzanowski's brigade, held out after other regiments, including Muenzenberger's 26th Wisconsin, had fallen back. These immigrant soldiers from Philadelphia (some of whom had cut their military teeth in Europe) fought through bullets "as thick as hail" and were killed by the score. Over 100 of the 185 men who engaged with the enemy were shot. Where had the men of the neighboring brigade gone, and left them to hold the line against the enemy? One German officer had an answer. It hadn't been the generals this time—it certainly hadn't been Howard. But it came about as close to Howard as a man could. It was the non-German soldiers in the brigade of Adelbert Ames—another disdainful New Englander—who had left them in the lurch. Ames' men, said the officer, were "ashamed after the Battle of Chancellorsville . . . to fight any longer next to or with the Dutchmen."[73]

As the lines of the Eleventh and First corps collapsed, every Union commander clamored for help, and hardly anybody got any. General Howard sent word repeatedly to General Henry Slocum of the Twelfth Corps to move up to Gettysburg as soon as possible. General Abner Doubleday, in command of the embattled First Corps, asked Howard to detach more men, and Howard told him to try to "hold out" longer. General Schurz sent several appeals to Howard asking for more troops to fend off the attack on the right, or, as things deteriorated, to at least cover a retreat. Howard eventually detached Charles Coster's brigade from the division at the cemetery. The fresh troops came through town in good order, got into position northeast of the borough, and were suddenly swamped.[74]

Coster's men—which included another regiment of Pennsylvania Germans—were impressed by the Confederate soldiers who attacked them just north of town. They noticed how solid their line was, and how neat the colors of the battle flags were as they moved. They could see that they were a brigade of North Carolina men. Some of them, that is. The others were a brigade of Louisiana men—Harry Hays' Tigers. The Germans fired at the Tigers. The Louisiana soldiers stuttered for a minute, then moved in. The enemies went at each other with guns, with bayonets, and—in the attempt to capture and evade capture—with their fast feet.[75]

Nothing in their tour through Pennsylvania had diminished the cockiness of these Tigers. They were fresh from their rout at Winchester, Virginia, where they had taken men by surprise and where their fellow Louisianians had helped kill a Gettysburg sweetheart. They had crossed the Potomac River on the 23rd of June to the tune of "Dixie" and been amused by Pennsylvanians who trembled in their presence. They had burned some buildings, taken pride in putting the torch to the property of abolitionist Thaddeus Stevens, and gone on to Gettysburg on the 26th. There they had captured some local militia, procured rations of whiskey, bivouacked outside of town, and got drunk.

Just a few days ago they had visited York, where some of the men saw "girls." Now here they were, at a little after three P.M. on July first, back near Gettysburg and facing what one of them thought was "the prettiest sight I ever saw": Yankees in retreat. They charged into what was left of those Yankees and captured men by the dozens.[76]

It was a little after four o'clock when Howard ordered what was already happening, the retreat of the Eleventh Corps and the First Corps to Cemetery Hill. Thousands of soldiers on foot and on horseback, as well as ambulances and caissons, poured into the borough's maze. They streamed into small streets and flooded into bigger ones. Most of them made it to Cemetery Hill in good order. But others carried their fight and their pursuit through gardens, over fences, into houses, into alleys that went nowhere, under the direction of no one. Union soldiers dodged bullets, fired back, and escaped the Confederates on their tails. Some of them slid into barns or sheds, or took refuge in cellars, closets, or kitchens.[77]

Or took refuge in woodsheds or pigpens. It had been a long road from Chancellorsville to Gettysburg for General Alexander Schimmelfennig, and it was hard to know, by the end of the day on the first of July, how far he had really come. Chancellorsville had humiliated and angered him. Now, having taken command of the 3rd Division for Carl Schurz at Gettysburg, he had supervised another retreat. Schimmelfennig had managed this retreat as adeptly as anyone directing a maelstrom could have. Just as at Chancellorsville, his troops withdrew not running but fighting, and the men had taken repeated stands—firing, rallying, and firing again as waves of enemy men crested and broke over them. He himself had stayed close to the Confederate enemy, directing his troops as they headed to the heights south of town.[78]

But what people remembered most about General Schimmelfennig are the events that followed. He had waited north of town until most of his troops had escaped into the borough, and then had himself galloped toward Cemetery Hill. He charged down Washington Street and, with the hill sighted ahead, found an alley that promised a quick path to the heights. But it was a blind alley, blocked in both directions by Confederates. Schimmelfennig dismounted and tried to climb a fence. Caught on the top rail, he was hit in the head with a gun butt and dropped to the other side, acting stunned. The men who followed him, seeing a man in an old cavalry coat instead of a general's uniform, and pressed by other opportunities, did not climb after him. Schimmelfennig then made for the best shelter he could see, a wooden sewer culvert, and hid inside. When it was dark he emerged and found another space, better than a sewer but not much. Some said it was a gap between a woodpile and a swill barrel; others called it a woodshed; some said it was a pigpen. Whatever it was, it hid him from the Confederates who had taken over the town. He could hear enemy men around him—talking in Southern accents. What he could not hear yet—it was way too soon—was the public that made sport of him once again.[79]

Indeed, most men in the Eleventh Corps were probably too busy trying to survive and escape to worry about people's opinions. But one German staff officer was deeply chagrined, not by what he had done personally, but by what the corps would now have to endure. "Think of it," he wrote. "It was a northern village. I had ridden up and down its streets from one end to the other three times that day and everywhere there were manifestations of joy; handkerchiefs were waving everywhere, and ladies stood in the streets offering refreshments to the soldiers as they passed. It seemed so awful to march back through those same streets whipped and beaten. It was the most humiliating step I ever took. . . . I could not at once make up my mind to go. I stood in the middle of the street and saw the rebels coming; they didn't then fire at me; my first impulse was to stay there and let them fire and hit me if they could."[80]

The king of humiliation, though, was the general on the hill. Up by the cemetery where he had been since midafternoon, Otis Howard directed the tumult below him partly by instinct, partly by report, and partly by what he could see through the acrid haze. Late in the afternoon a rainbow came and went over a small hill to the east, and the gunsmoke cleared a little, just enough to unveil the unhappy situation. Seeing the retreat was bad enough; feeling its repercussions was, for Howard, even worse.[81] And he had hard news coming. Around four-thirty that afternoon, just when the retreat was at flood stage, word came from General Meade that Howard, who had commanded all the Union troops at Gettysburg for almost five hours, was to defer to General Winfield Hancock. Hancock was junior to Howard in rank. This was insult enough, but the salt in the wound was the way the soldiers rejoiced in Hancock's arrival—how they cheered the clean-pressed, statuesque general. All Howard could do was to handle the transition gracefully and protest privately, writing immediately to Meade that Hancock's arrival "mortified me and will disgrace me," and requesting an explanation.[82] The question hanging over Howard was an obvious one: Was this Chancellorsville all over again? Were telegraph operators even now tapping word around the country of the corps' cowardice and of his own incompetence?

While Howard nursed his humiliation, many of the soldiers on Cemetery Hill—First and Eleventh corps both—counted themselves lucky to be alive. Howard's soldiers were only at half strength, now—and, seeking to conserve what stamina was left, many of them wrapped themselves in coats and blankets and lay down on graves.[83]

Adam Muenzenberger might have given his right arm for a nice cemetery plot to sleep in, or even a sewer or a swill barrel. He had been taken prisoner. We do not know how he gave himself up or got caught. Had he not run fast enough in the grain fields? Had he, like so many others—and there were 1400 men in the Eleventh Corps taken—been trapped in the town's labyrinth? Perhaps, like other men, he had had a gun leveled at him, and maybe he, too, had heard an enemy soldier shout, "Throw down your gun; surrender," or "Halt, you Yankee sons of bitches!" All we know is that, suddenly, Muenzenberger was on the losing side of his long battle to be home again. That night he was taken to a farm field, behind Confederate lines. He had some friends with him, at least. Asmus Holtz and John Nachtsheim must have given him some comfort in this hostile world, where all he could see was enemy guards and all he could hear was enemy music. At least he could keep some of his German community with him, and pray, like other prisoners, for victory and parole.[84]

Just below the cemetery, on the southeast side of town, Louisiana men occupied the town. Those who were not on guard duty made themselves at home. Many of the Tigers were angry. They had not been allowed to push up Cemetery Hill that afternoon and attack, and perhaps finish off, the re-forming enemy. But there were plenty of ways to avenge their irritation. They could be ungenerous to civilians—refusing to allow them to bury men who lay dead on sidewalks—in one case a decapitated soldier. They could also entertain themselves at the borough's expense. Some of them ransacked a pantry and a cellar, and made themselves a meal. They took turns eating and going to the front windows, and shooting, here and there. Some of them took their skirmishing outside, where they ran through people's gardens and behind houses. When it came time to sleep, they went to bed on the streets, their guns in their arms.[85]

The Tigers were brash, and they were alert, but they did not know everything. They did not know what a woman named Catherine Garlach discovered when she went out at night to feed her pigs. Mrs. Garlach, at home with her four children, waited until after dark before going outside. She took the path to the stable as she always did, past the long woodpiles. The voice she heard had to have startled her: "Be quiet and do not say anything." It was General Schimmelfennig. All around them Confederate soldiers were patrolling, skirmishing, and making themselves comfortable. But Schimmelfennig had an ally now, for Mrs. Garlach wanted to keep her secret.[86]

Up at the cemetery gatehouse late at night on July first, Elizabeth Thorn played host. Sometime in the afternoon, a Union soldier asked her if she would cook supper for General Howard. She was willing, she said, but it would not be easy. She had given away all her bread to the men who had flown past her earlier that day, and all she could really offer was dough cakes, and whatever else she had. It was "good enough for war times," the soldier said. So Thorn made up dough cakes and pan cakes, apple butter, coffee and cooked pieces of meat. And then she waited. And waited. Her guests were late. She finally served General Howard and other generals around midnight. She was awed by her company—"sort of taken back"—as she put it, and did not speak to them. But she was pleased and proud.[87]

Union generals did more than eat that night at Elizabeth Thorn's gatehouse; they talked. Carl Schurz remembered how six or seven of them sat on the floor, illuminated by a single candle stuck in a bottle on top of a barrel. They discussed "what might have been," and they considered what could be, and how they hoped to keep the fight on the high ground. As the night wore on, even Otis Howard regained some optimism. He took comfort in the arrival of the long-looked-for Twelfth Corps, which had come up to Gettysburg from the south, bayonets glistening in the night light. Other corps were on their way, too, and the hillsides were alive with soldiers chopping, picking, shoveling, and positioning themselves. Then, around three o'clock in the morning, General Meade himself made his way to Cemetery Hill. He and Howard inspected the army's position in the moonlight, and Meade confirmed the hill and the ridge as a good place to fight, and ordered the entire army to concentrate there. He also offered balm to his hurt subordinate. "The first [thing] he said to me," commented Howard, was that "he was very sorry to have seemed to cast any discredit upon me; he had no blame to affix." So perhaps this wasn't Chancellorsville after all.[88]

Perhaps it wasn't Chancellorsville, but it also wasn't over. Union soldiers were not the only men animating the hills and ridges around Gettysburg, and Union troops were not the only ones hastening through the night on dim-lit roads. General Lee was marching his entire army in. Meeting late at night with his lieutenants, the Confederate general seemed anxious and impatient. He was determined to stay on the offensive and attack the Federal army as soon as possible. And in Confederate camps outside of Gettysburg many Southern soldiers expressed a "general euphoria" over the afternoon's victory, and reiterated their contempt for what seemed to be a constantly beatable foe.[89]

5

✶✶

BOLD ACTS

ACT ONE
Domestic Violence

To the people of Gettysburg, it must have seemed as if Mars himself had materialized. On the night of June 30, 1863, the borough became ringed with military light. To the west, constellations flickered in the dark mass of South Mountain. They were harmless campfires—they cooked meat, heated coffee, kept cold men warm—but everybody knew they were harbingers of destruction. Closer by, Union cavalrymen had lit fires, too, and in the fields and gardens surrounding the town, their orange light silhouetted the shapes of soldiers. One woman could hear some of these men singing the "Star Spangled Banner." And she could see some of them praying, asking the Heavenly Father for his help.[1]

Harriet Bayly remembered that the last day of June began with a feeling of bad weather. All around her, she said, the air was "charged." The neighbors near her farm north of town were all asking the same questions: "What was going to happen?" and "What will we do if the worst should happen?" and she felt as she did before a storm bore down. The fact that the sun was out the next morning when she woke up did not quiet her fears. The new day seemed more dead than alive. Even the barnyards were quiet. "I could not hear a dog bark or a rooster crow; even the birds did not sing," she said. "It was an awful stillness."[2]

There was a bare-topped hill near her house that had a view, and after she had done her morning chores, she decided to climb it. When she got on top she found other friends, but nothing that she didn't see every day. One of her neighbors suggested that they take a walk farther on. They had gone about a mile when they encountered some Union soldiers—pickets. The men were dusty and clearly tired, and their horses had their heads down.

Harriet Bayly kept walking. Now the whole world seemed becalmed, and she talked to her friend in whispers, even though there seemed to be no one around, for miles, to hear anything.

What happened next, suddenly, came from her right. It may have been the sound of air sucking, or the field shaking, or her ears in pain. But it was un-mistakable: a cannon blast. And, just as suddenly, her world was remade. "While I watched," she said, "it seemed to me tens of thousands of men, as if by magic, rose from the earth. There I stood midway between the two armies; where an instant before there had been fields and woods and the peacefulness of the Sabbath day there burst forth shots and horrible yells and more men than could be numbered."

She turned toward home and hurried, working her way through guns and surging Confederate cavalry. Men shouted: "Madam where are the Yankees?" and "How many Yankees are there out there?" and "Madam, you are in a very dangerous position." Around her, the fields smoked with powder and waved with masses of gray-colored men. An American flag that had flown from the top of the hill had been cut down, and its fractured pole lay on the ground.

Soldiers seized her male companion, and she pushed home alone, thinking about her family and worried about her horses. But then, as Harriet Bayly approached her house, a Confederate soldier shouted at her, too, to halt. He had orders, he said, to arrest her. She protested—she needed to speak to her children at least—and he permitted her to go to the top of a hill and wave a hand-kerchief. An anxious son, watching from an attic window, came running out. Quietly, she asked about the horses, and then she told him she would have to go and that he shouldn't worry. But his face told her he could not help it. "Oh!" she said, "how woe-begone he did look!"[3]

What, we wonder, went through Bayly's mind when she went off with her enemy "escort"? Did she worry that she had been too outspoken an abolition-ist and this is what happened to women who were not shy about their opin-ions? Did she wonder that she was taken for a spy because she had been walking outside, and had spoken to Union soldiers? Or was she baffled, be-cause in most wars in America, white women were neither suspect nor prey?

Conjecture about wars and their boundaries would soon become com-monplace in Gettysburg. While Harriet Bayly was released soon after she was seized—the soldier may have quickly realized his mistake—she and other women were nevertheless caught in a bewildering world. Union soldiers ca-reened back into town during their retreat on July first, and took borough houses as safe havens and shooting sites. Soon afterward, Confederate men commandeered houses and farms. Residents looked around them and wondered what battles had become. It was one thing, it seemed, for a woman to stand on a street corner, to press cakes into a man's palm, and to sing inspirationally. It was one thing, too, to fill water buckets and to wish men success as they marched by to their grim or glorious ends. But it was another thing to see the struggle come back. More than men were hurt when the fight entered gardens and porches, and when shells shattered kitchens and scattered feathers from beds. As the battle assumed a scope and a shape few people expected, common beliefs about the perimeter of war suffered serious injury.

Expectation and convention, of course, were not the only things shattered in Gettysburg in the summer of 1863. Civilian women—like Georgia McClellan, Harriet Bayly, and Elizabeth Thorn—became real victims of the battle's physical and emotional havoc. At the same time, however, women actively entered into the conflict, and did their best to manage the situation. They exposed themselves to fire to support soldiers, and subtly and not so subtly resisted the invaders. Before the battle, women like Fannie Buehler and girls like Sadie Bushman had been handed conflicting opinions of their capabilities, and been repeatedly reminded that they were best suited to serve from the homefront. Now, all of a sudden, they were called on to deploy domestic skills in a war zone, and to locate strength they did not know they had.

"Why do you come to town to have a fight? There are some old fields out there. Why don't you go out there?" demanded one woman, as soldiers pushed through Gettysburg and as bullets zipped by civilian heads.[4] Battlefield was a word to her, and certainly to almost everyone else, that signified redundancy. Battles *were* fields, separate arenas of violence, outside habitation. Out beyond the borough, people who heard guns firing couldn't believe their ears: The battle's soldiers and the town's people were sharing the same ground. Rumors circulated. One girl heard that thirty women and children were killed. "Whether that is true or not," she said, "it is fearful to think of their being in the town during the fighting." Another girl fretted that her family was in danger but was convinced otherwise. "[People] assured me that in war the rule was, always to allow helpless and innocent citizens to get out of a place, and never to destroy them. I then felt comforted. . . ."[5]

Union officers had indeed considered these "rules" and had urged people away from the west side of Gettysburg when fighting encroached on the town. General Howard, for one, had been as concerned about civilians as any commander. But Howard had also designated Cemetery Hill on the south side of town as his defensive base, and posted the rest of his corps north of town, where his soldiers had no choice but to implicate streets and houses in a retreat. Howard knew the town was not free and clear of civilians—many had left, certainly, but there were plenty around—people who had helped him with directions, people who had helped him navigate the town and observe the battle, and people—women especially—who had cheered him on. Either he was blind to civilian concerns in the heat of this emergency or, more likely, he considered the means and the ends. This fight, he hoped, was making the North safe for citizens in general, and if one borough had to suffer, so be it. Howard's choice of Cemetery Hill would eventually be the subject of serious debate. But it would not be because it was a poor place to stage a battle, so close to inhabited houses. A number of senior officers would lay claim to choosing Cemetery Hill as the Federal army's key position because it was an excellent strategic location.[6]

If General Howard selected Cemetery Hill despite its proximity to civilian Gettysburg, his soldiers, as well as First Corps troops, sought domestic sites—cellars, attics, barns, and sheds, in part *because* they were civilian and presumably safer. And Confederate soldiers pursued them into those spaces because what mattered at the moment was killing and capture, not some social dictates that seemed looser and more blurred, south and north, as this war went on.

So Gettysburg houses were opened for army business, and over the next forty-eight hours, as armies enveloped the town and continued to batter each other, the business was brutal. In one home, bullets punctured a wall by a sleeping baby. While a girl stood in another house, a shell burst in, bounced against the interior, and exited through a window. A different shell hit a family's breakfast room, made a missile of the family clock, and turned eating forks into shrapnel. It just spared the family. Army horses walked through one residence; soldiers made a charge through another. All around the western and southern parts of town, family homes were hit by shells and used as shields. One Confederate cavalry officer, observing how soldiers carried combat into parlors and dining rooms and how shells burst into bedrooms, was amazed. "It was the first time," he commented, "I had seen warfare carried on in this way."[7]

When the Civil War descended upon Gettysburg, then, it brought disbelief. At first, however, it produced simple fear. When Union and Confederate soldiers burst into the borough on the afternoon of July first, residents were as distraught as they were bewildered. Where would civilians go to be safe? How would they not be killed? How would they keep children from being hit? "What to do or where to go, I did not know," remembered one woman. "People were running here and there, screaming that the town would be shelled." How frightened we were, she said, "no one can imagine." Another woman on the western side of town ran in desperation, looking for safe passage. "Hurriedly I gathered my children together," she recalled. "But the shot and shell were falling so thick and fast that we started to our own home again, but found that hope must be given up." She finally took refuge in a bank vault.[8]

Others took shelter at home and wondered if they would die there. "I thought surely we would all be killed in our cellars," wrote one woman, and when, later on in the battle, a shell scattered in her basement, she remained alive, but vindicated. Houses and cellars that were not subjected to enemy shells were prey to the enemy himself. A set of "bad looking" Confederates robbed one family at gunpoint. In another house, a "fierce [*sic*] looking fellow came into the cellar with his gun pointed." A girl, facing his gun barrel, did what she supposed a soldier would do, and "immediately screamed we'll surrender." "I never felt such agony in my life," she said.[9]

Heart-stopping terror was one thing; shock was something else. Women and girls saw for the first time what soldiers could do to each other. Forty-one-year-old Mary McAllister, a "spinster," encountered her first battle horror as a red-and-white horse, when a wounded soldier rode by her house, his leaking blood staining the animal's hide. She helped get him inside the house, she remembered later, but "didn't know what in the world to do." She did not know what to do, either, with injured men in a church. The soldiers lay in pews, their amputated arms and legs piled up outside the windows. A young boy, with seven of his fingers nearly gone, asked her for some assistance. "Lady," he said, "would you do something for me?" A surgeon had his own ideas, however. "What is the use doing anything for them?" Mary heard him say, and he "took his knife and cut off the fingers and they dropped down." "I was," she recalled, "so sorry."[10]

She was not only sorry; she was overwhelmed. When a shell struck the roof of the church, she headed home. The Union retreat was at flood tide, however, and the street outside was a stream of pushing soldiers. She ventured into it, and was carried away, "as high up as Buehler's Drug Store before I got across the street." If she was anticipating a sanctuary at home, she was in for another surprise. Her door was "standing open" and her steps were coated with blood.[11]

Crossing the river of soldiers, Mary McAllister almost "forgot the horror in the fright." Others, though, just couldn't let the horror go. "Can we endure the spectacle?" one woman would wonder a few days later. Most of them would endure it, but could not obliterate it. For a lifetime, in fact, images of that afternoon rose unbidden in their minds. People would remember how soldiers simply came apart—one shell knocking the legs off a man; another taking away the top of a skull; a third, blasting away a soldier's head. What shells and shot did not do then and there, surgeons accomplished later.[12]

When Confederate soldiers took over most of the town, as they had by that evening, shock began to transfigure into dread. In the moonlight that night, one woman watched enemy men go into a neighbor's house, take out its contents, put them in a wagon, and drive away. Many families spent the night clustered with neighbors, some of them—the wealthier ones—in dry, well-provisioned cellars, but others in bare basements—muddy, bloody, and wet. Other women and their children tried to sleep on floors, to be out of the way of any gunshot or flying window glass. One woman listened to enemy men on the streets outside boast that it was all theirs now. Another worried that things were going terribly wrong. She summed it up: The rebels, she said, have "possession of us."[13]

Confederate soldiers, including the Louisiana Tigers, did indeed have possession, and they were there for the duration. They occupied most of Gettysburg and held sway over much of the area to the north and west and east. Out at the Bayly farm, the enemy "literally swarmed over this whole place." In the borough, houses and their inhabitants felt the effects of both armies. Elizabeth Thorn's gatehouse, at the edge of Cemetery Hill, was Union territory—Howard territory. Nearby, Georgia McClellan, with her newborn baby and her barely healed body, was in no-man's-land, a skirmisher's playground. A few streets to the north, Sadie Bushman's house was exposed to small-arms fire. Deeper in town, Fannie Buehler was better protected from guns, but prey to Confederate men, and they banged on her door whenever they pleased.[14]

ACT TWO
STRANGE COMPANY

Inside Gettysburg's embattled houses and on its surrounding farms, wartime society took new shape. For a few intense days—and sometimes even longer—the Union men who were hidden or wounded and the white women who protected and fed them became close comrades in arms. Fannie Buehler, for instance, made close allies of two Eleventh Corps soldiers who had been assigned to care for the wounded in her house, and to cook. One became a "good friend," the other "kept us all in good humor." Strangers in life, they became intimates in this emergency.[15]

The battle forced not only the association of Union soldiers and Union women, though; it also brought together less sympathetic sorts. White Gettysburg women, many of whom were alone with children, shared the borough with masses of enemy men. They had feared the strange, sweaty Confederates when they had first come to town, and continued to worry about where an enemy soldier's anger might turn in the heat of the battle or in an unhappy aftermath. But some of these women found that they were not simply helpless in the face of gun-bearing men. They could use their domestic expertise as a way to achieve limited control over the occupation. They could also rely on their "femaleness" to soften the hand of the enemy. They discovered that Confederate soldiers were sometimes willing and eager to turn their anger in one direction and their civility in another, and that jointly they could mitigate the battle's horror.

Women in occupied Gettysburg sometimes used their stoves to win over enemy soldiers. Cooking for Confederates helped "humanize" the relationship for both parties, and to some degree it served to protect family property. Wartime ideology generally charged armies or local militia with safeguarding houses from the scourges of enemy troops. But with many men gone, it was up to Gettysburg women to guard actual property. Cooking became their currency, and it helped to establish a contract of sorts, by which residences and farms were sometimes made safer from looting. Several households served cooked food to ensure the security of their horses. Harriet Bayly protected full-grown, unbroken, unshod colts on the farm by making enemy men a good dinner.[16]

Besides limiting possible depredation, cooking also earned local women the right to speak freely with enemy soldiers. Over meals, Gettysburg women and Confederate invaders conferred about the relative positions of the armies, the merits of certain fighting units, the likelihood of a next engagement. The soldiers were optimistic about who might prevail—they would, of course; their hosts were similarly confident about who might defeat them. They agreed, cordially, to disagree. When Confederate general Ewell visited one house, and shared refreshments with the family, the women "very freely gave them our opinion on the war." The visiting enemy officers "were not at all offended but said if our men had half the spirit [we did] they would fight better."[17]

Out on her farm in occupied territory, Harriet Bayly took on the role of innkeeper, doling out bread and soup to Confederates, and coolly engaging in controversial talk. "They were not rude to us," recalled Bayly. "They knew we were enemies and they talked their slavery and their secession notions and they found out before long that I was an abolitionist; for if they felt no shame in buying and selling and owning human beings why should I be ashamed of not doing it? So I stuck to my colors." Earlier, when she had been out traversing a battlefield, Confederate invaders had taken her prisoner; now, while she did domestic work and served food, her political ardor was as easily swallowed as her soup.[18]

General Lee may have helped these conversations along with his pronouncements about army deportment. On June 27th, just a day after his soldiers had first entered Gettysburg, he issued "General Orders No. 73." "It must be remembered," he said famously, "that we make war only upon armed men, and that we cannot take vengeance for the wrongs our people have suffered without lowering ourselves." The army has had an "unsullied" reputation, he said. His soldiers had a duty to "civilization and Christianity," even in an enemy country, and acts of barbarity and outrage against "the unarmed and defenseless" would be a "disgrace" of the highest magnitude.[19]

Confederate soldiers who bargained with these white families may have been listening to Lee. Just as likely, however, they were responding to more personal needs: a longing for their families, a desire to be fed and cared for. Their "hosts," while eager to guarantee safety, also acted out of human sympathy. They considered the sorrowful Confederate faces that came to their doors asking for food and they imagined their own sons. Sadie Bushman's mother could not withhold her cherry pie from hungry soldiers, not to mention her potatoes, beans, and bread. "Somehow my heart ached for every mother's son of them," she said. Another girl confessed to similar sympathies, and conspired with her siblings and her mother to feed enemy soldiers. They waited until their father, who had "bitter" feelings against the Confederates, was out of sight, and then brought fish out of brine to cook. The children could not bear to hear the Southern boys beg for food, and their mother could not bear to see them eat fish raw, for "those poor fellows were somebodies' sons."[20]

Some older women treated them like "sons," too, by asking them to help out with chores. One woman asked Confederate soldiers to round up chickens. Another needed some grass cut. "She asked two young men in gray," recalled a friend of hers, "if they would cut some grass for some colts or young cattle tied up in the barn. The shells were falling all around at the time. Laughing they said yes they would try although they never [had] in their lives. They got the scythe and cut some grass." Harriet Bayly's family took "kinship" one step further. When a young deserter begged to be taken in and protected at the farm, he passed "as one of the boys of the household." The young Confederate was put to work with the rest of the family picking cherries, and his disguise was so effective he broke off branches and threw them down to his former comrades as they walked beneath the fruit trees.[21]

Some Gettysburg mothers saw sons in enemy soldiers, and some Confederate soldiers found "families" too. One surgeon admitted to missing his children, and asked a little Gettysburg girl to sit on his knee for a minute. Another, a mortally injured Confederate drummer boy, needed a "mother," and a young local woman was sent to help him. It was not the only Southern soldier she comforted. A cousin reported that she took care of "more than one dying boy . . . as he breathed his last, thinking his own mother was there."[22]

So these enemies occasionally reached out to each other to diminish the battle's savagery. And some of them went beyond sympathy. It did not take a large leap for a few young white women, however loyal, to look at the strapping men around them and to consider flirtation. In a house east of the borough, on July 2nd, two young Confederate soldiers knocked on the door for some milk, and they found sociable company as well. They "had fun with the girls," described an older witness, and "asked them if all Pennsylvania girls were so fat and said they were coming back here for wives." In a different occupied house, a young girl bubbled with excitement over the "visit" of "handsome" Confederate officers. Readily dismissing the battle's sober realities, she could barely contain her enthusiasm: "Our house & yard was filled with wounded that night & Gen. Ewell & staff took tea with us!!" she exuded. "They were all very polite and kind, I sat at the head of the table & gave them their coffee so I had a fine opportunity to see them all. With a few I was completely captivated. . . ."[23]

Loyalty did not yield completely to sexual appeal, however. On July 2nd, a "number of Rebels" entered a Gettysburg yard and found a young girl at the house named Julia. They begged her to sing for them. Julia, being "very patriotic," agreed to do so, but only Union songs, so that the Union soldiers might hear her "and be cheered." The Confederate soldiers returned the favor and entertained her with Southern songs—an enemies' duet. Another Gettysburg girl, nineteen years old, also mixed loyalty with pleasure by socializing with an enemy soldier who was "winning in his manners." They got to talking, and she mentioned she and her friends might like to sing some patriotic songs. He, of course, preferred "the Bonny Blue Flag," explaining that it was "a song of the South." The girls said it was unfamiliar, so he tried to teach it to them. But they were refractory, even "very dumb," and for some reason could not learn it.[24]

In this tenuous courtship of enemies, these young white women tended to stay true to social class. Girls of some education and property were most entranced by enemy men, particularly officers, who seemed tutored and well-bred—who had "manners." Romance, such as it was, did not easily extend to enlisted men. The Tigers, with their reputation for lower-class rowdyism and their "ethnic" taint, were especially suspect. The girl who struggled to learn the "Bonny Blue Flag" was typically prejudiced against the Louisiana troops. As she grew more intimate and bold with her music "tutor," she confessed that, present company obviously excepted, she didn't really like some of the Confederate troops—most particularly "Louisiana Tigers." Imagine her surprise, then, when "her" soldier opened his shirt to reveal the Tiger's badge. The power of attraction here trumped her prejudices—either that, or she discovered that the Tigers were savage solely by reputation.[25]

Local girls not only limited flirtation to acceptable enemies; they also stood aloof from certain Union soldiers who sought social acquaintance. German-American soldiers from the Eleventh Corps, some of whom took refuge or assisted the wounded in civilian houses, did not see much flirting. The very act of hiding, of course, carried an unmanly stamp, and several women in town commented on the corps' rapid retreat on July first. But it was clear the men's foreignness dampened romance as well. Julie, the young girl who had engaged enemy soldiers in a singing contest, captivated a German-American soldier, known as George. He had hidden in Julie's barn and was "in love" with her, reported a member of the family. Everybody found him lovable, too, but silly. In heavily accented English, George allegedly pledged his loyalty: "Now, Yulie, you say Chorge no more drink, and Chorge no more drink." Soldier George was perhaps his own worst enemy. "He would also repeat the saying that was common among the Germans of the Eleventh Corps," reported Julie's sister: "I fights mit Sigel, but I runs mit Howard."[26]

The romantic occupation of Gettysburg, not to mention the surrogate families that evolved, were also limited to some degree to people with property. Women with little food to spare, or no supplies to negotiate with, probably had little bargaining power. Furthermore, the bantering and the flirting and the exchanging were, like the military contest itself, limited to white people. No black family sought to socialize with Confederates or dared to trade cooking for safety. Negotiations, and all the ways they relieved the battle's brutality, were exclusive. This limited détente was a foretaste, in a sense, of the future. Years later, many white Confederate and Union veterans forgot some of the animosity of the Civil War, forgot the contentious and repugnant history of slavery, and forgave each other in what one historian has called a "Romance of Reunion."[27] In the occupied houses of Gettysburg, the groundwork for sympathetic "sexual" attraction and mutual respect was already laid out.

ACT THREE
"Dis is Unser!"

Union and Confederate soldiers may have occasionally disarmed themselves among women in and around the borough, but on Cemetery Hill and Cemetery Ridge they went about their work with less cordiality. By the early morning of July 2nd, most, but not all, of seven Union army corps were already at Gettysburg, and the position of Union troops, from Cemetery Hill, then south along the ridge to the Round Tops, had already assumed the shape that would become legendary: the fish hook. General Howard's men helped anchor the northern end of that hook. And General Howard's men had to hang on to it.

If Union troops let that hill go to the enemy, the entire position would be compromised. Carl Schurz had awoken to this worry. All night long, Meade's soldiers had been moving up to Gettysburg and digging in, but he could tell by what he saw in the valley around him that it was still not enough. The Confederates were not out in the open, ready to be counted, but the dark woods that held them were not inviolate, and he knew by the light that glinted off bayonets that enemy soldiers were there by the thousands—probably Lee's whole army. He could also look in several directions and see Confederate artillery against the green fields, prepared for grim business.[28]

With the rising sun at their backs, General Meade and General Howard surveyed the field from Cemetery Hill. Meade, who was wearing spectacles and a black felt hat, knew that his position needed "strengthening and extension," and he contemplated his action against Lee. It was, said Howard, "plan against plan, move against move." Then Meade turned, rode back to the cemetery gate, and began to re-form his lines.[29]

Lee himself, headquartered on Seminary Ridge, was ready to go to work. He and General James Longstreet, his second in command, had discussed the Confederate position late on July first. Longstreet wanted the army to maneuver to some good ground between Gettysburg and Washington, and force a fight at an advantage. But Lee did not want to do that. He felt that a general battle was "unavoidable." He could not now pull back through the mountains with his huge trains, and even though he did not have the cavalry that he needed, and even though the Federal army had a good position, his men had had success thus far. He would not withdraw. He would stay at Gettysburg, he said, where "I am going to whip them or they are going to whip me." But he wondered where and how to make a move. What he didn't wonder about was when. He knew he did not want to wait until Meade's army was at full strength. "If the enemy is there tomorrow," he told General Longstreet, "we will attack him."[30]

This was what Carl Schurz worried about—what all the men on Cemetery Hill worried about—as they awakened on the morning of July second. And they could only hope that an attack would come after they had brought all their men to Gettysburg. General Meade had said that he expected 95,000 troops at his command by the end of the day. Urging the time forward, soldiers listened for ominous sounds. They heard the occasional cracking of musketry—skirmishers were active in the meadows and cornfields—and now and then the isolated pounding of a cannon. But they heard nothing large or menacing. The armies were sensing each other, snarling, showing their teeth. Schurz likened them to chained watchdogs.[31]

The time went by—first the hours of forenoon, then the hours of early afternoon—the Union army gaining men, gaining ground. The day was hot, clear, and very still. Skirmishers kept up their probing and sensing, sending up thin snakes of smoke when they fired. One observer took his spyglass to survey the scene and saw men stretched "lazily on the ground in line of battle, horses attached to the caissons, batteries unlimbered and gunners resting on their guns." Everyone was slack and alert at the same time. "The thunderbolts," he said, "were shut up."[32]

The thing they feared blew up around four o'clock. It happened very fast, very hard. Soldiers of the Eleventh Corps on Cemetery Hill saw sudden smoke opposite them on Seminary Ridge—Confederate batteries—and then, above them, the sky began to pour metal. The firing came from the west and from a hill to the east. The noise, one man said, was "wild, hideous," and sickeningly diverse: the "low buzz of round shot, the whizzing of elongated bolts, the stunning explosion of shells." In the cemetery, headstones smashed and became projectiles, and iron fences shattered and bent. Horses were hit, and they screamed. Men exploded, and their flesh flew. A lot of the shells fell short and some went too far, but enough were deathly perfect in their flight. The batteries on Cemetery Hill responded.[33]

They thought they were being softened up, readied for infantry moving in for the kill, but nobody—at least nobody just then—attacked. They did not know that Lee had decided it was the high ground on the Union left flank, along the Emmitsburg Road, that held the best hope of success. If Lee's men could swallow that flank, capture the elevation, blast down the Union line, get to the rear, get the wagon trains, take the reserve artillery and ammunition, and command the way back to Washington, then maybe the battle—maybe more than the battle—would be done.[34]

The Confederate assault began on the Union left around four-thirty—much later than Lee had hoped. Eleventh Corps soldiers couldn't see down the ridge, over by the rocky hills—only the white smoke that puffed up, too cheerfully. But they could make out musketry fire, and occasional cheers, and they could make out the Rebel Yell—the signature shriek of the advancing enemy. That sound carried well. Then they heard an explosive, massive noise, what one man called "the falling of giant trees in a forest, carrying down everything." It was General Daniel Sickles, who had pushed his Union Third Corps forward of its assigned position on Cemetery Ridge, being hit hard.[35]

When troops posted on Culp's Hill and Cemetery Hill were ordered to other parts of the line as reinforcements, men of the Eleventh Corps knew they were all in trouble. The sounds of the battle were coming closer, too, along the ridge. A little after six o'clock, an artillery captain came riding over with bad news: The enemy had overrun Sickles' corps in a peach orchard, and "unless the rebels were beaten back at once," they would attack the men on Cemetery Hill in the rear and take them all "prisoners in half an hour." "Everywhere is confusion, everything seems to be going against us," bemoaned a Massachusetts soldier. The end, he felt, was "imminent."[36]

But it was not. Over on Little Round Top, Federal soldiers in the Fifth Corps, including the 20th Maine Regiment, bravely chased attackers back, and along the Emmitsburg Road, Union troops survived bloody back-and-forth battles through a wheatfield, an orchard, and a tract of woods. They received reinforcements just as Confederate attackers ran out of support.[37]

It seemed to many Union soldiers on Cemetery Hill that Lee's whole army had been thrown into the assault on the left. And that is why when the fight was over by the Round Tops and on the ridge, and the Confederates were finally driven back, it felt like the interminable day was done. But what seemed was not what was. Not all Confederate soldiers had been put to use in the afternoon's attack. Some of them, including General Early's division, had spent the afternoon waiting. General Hays' brigade—of Louisiana Tigers—had been waiting. And, as the dark enveloped them, they counted down the minutes to begin their own attack against the men on East Cemetery Hill.[38]

The fierce meeting that was to take place that night was marked by some symmetry. Both Louisiana Tigers and the Union army's Eleventh Corps were "outsiders," known for their foreignness, and criticized for their lack of manly qualities. In the case of the Eleventh Corps, "ethnicity" had enhanced the soldiers' reputation as cowards; in the case of the Confederate soldiers, it gave them a name for rapacity. Up to a third of Louisiana troops had been born in Ireland, with a smaller proportion from Germany. Irish immigrants in the Civil War era were frequently castigated for their crudeness—even savagery— and they were seen as "incapable of being true American men." (Gettysburg women certainly entertained such stereotypes, and now anticipated wild behavior from the Louisiana troops that commanded the town.)[39]

So people tended to see the worst in the Tigers just as they tended to see the worst in the Eleventh Corps. Pennsylvania would not be the first time that Lee's Louisiana soldiers and German immigrant soldiers would meet, either, nor the first time that their reputations would take on a life of their own. Ruffian and coward, predator and prey had come to blows in Virginia in early June 1862, when Tigers had trounced German troops in the Shenandoah Valley. And late on the afternoon of May 2, 1863, exactly two months earlier, a brigade of Louisiana men had helped Stonewall Jackson surprise the Eleventh Corps in the woods in the Wilderness.[40]

General Hays' Tigers had spent most of July 2nd crouched in a low trough of ground northeast of the cemetery, edgy and impatient. Some of the soldiers had been angered the night before when they had not been permitted to push forward and occupy these hills, the hills now studded with Union batteries. In the morning, though, they had been lined up behind a low ridge, and, along with Isaac Avery's brigade of North Carolina men, were told to be ready to spring forward and take the high ground. It would be an attack coordinated with two others, one on Culp's Hill, half a mile to the southeast, the other on the northwest side of Cemetery Hill. But now the long day had passed and they had not done anything but lie still and get hot and stiff. Finally, though, when the light was nearly gone, the assault over on Culp's Hill had begun, and their order, too, had come.[41]

One of the Eleventh Corps gunners was cleaning his weapons and cooling them down when he noticed something in a farm meadow—a line of men forming, gray in the gray light. Soldiers positioned below him saw it too—a line of men, with another behind it, "creeping up" from a ravine. The two brigades, the North Carolinians and the Tigers, soon made no secret of their intentions. "The Louisiana men," said General Howard, let out a cry, "shrill and ominous." And then they "came on with a rush." The batteries on the hill belched out shot to stop them.[42]

It might have taken a moment at first to make out the attacking soldiers, but when they leered out of the gloom and drove hell-bent through the Union line, nobody could mistake them. Nor could anyone mistake how the past continued to repeat itself. Once again General Jubal Early's men struck the soldiers who, of all soldiers in the last demoralizing months, had had enough. Von Gilsa's brigade had been through hell in Virginia, and had been overwhelmed, in part by these same men, just yesterday. Now here they were again. Facing bayonets and clubs wielded by the Confederates in "full-throated fury," some of the men gave up. Soon enough Confederate soldiers crested the hill and rushed at the Union batteries, the nerve center of the Union position.[43]

The furious drama that opened that night contained a familiar cast, then. It featured the Union immigrant men who had been among the "cowards" of Chancellorsville, and the "retreaters" of the day before, and it featured the Confederate immigrants who had hoped to finish them off earlier. And now, as the Tigers swept into and over the Eleventh Corps guns on Cemetery Hill, and proceeded to capture batteries, it would be hard to imagine anything other than the same closing scene. But it did not happen. The other Confederate attack on Cemetery Hill—from the northwest—never materialized. Neither did reinforcements from the east. General Carl Schurz, on the other hand, double-quicked infantry regiments into the fray, and other fresh Eleventh Corps regiments poured into the battle, too. Even some of the German soldiers who had taken flight earlier rallied and fought back. The muzzles of the cannon illuminated the ghoulish nighttime struggle, revealing the "desperate daring" that was, according to one soldier, "hardly equalled." Union gunners at the center of the infiltration used whatever was heavy and hard to do damage and to defend their position: fence rails, handspikes, pistols, battery rammers. And the Confederates were fierce. One of them—an officer—flailed his sword as he stood on top of one of the guns. "This battery is ours!" he cried out.[44]

It was a German artilleryman who replied. "No," he shouted back, "Dis battery is *unser*." And he swung a sponge-staff and bowled the officer to the ground. Another man remembered the moment differently: A Louisiana Tiger jumped on the gun. "I demand the surrender of the gun," he said. A big German had words for him. "I teaches ye how to surrender," he answered, and he delivered a handspike into his skull.[45]

Eleventh Corps infantrymen charged against the invaders with their bayonets—and began knocking them down Cemetery Hill. They got help from Second Corps soldiers, with *their* bayonets, and together they finished the repulse. The position on the hill held.

Many of these men would later say that this was the place where Gettysburg could have been lost. Get through the guns, commandeer the hill, and the Union position along the ridge becomes the fishhook that got away. It was, commented a Union army private, "where the battle of Gettysburg came nearer being lost than at any other point or time." General Schurz agreed. It might have been, he said, "the fate of the battle."[46]

There had been many other points in contention that day, of course. All along Cemetery Ridge there had been violations of the line, and places where Union soldiers stood close to losing strategic ground. There had been Little Round Top, where Strong Vincent's brigade, including Col. Joshua Chamberlain's men, had held off wave after wave of Confederate attackers. On Culp's Hill, too, a Union brigade commander, General George Greene, had valiantly held off a division of General Ewell's men when it had exploded toward him just before the attack on East Cemetery Hill.[47]

There were several places and multiple times that day that the battle might have twisted toward the Confederates. But to German soldiers of Howard's corps, Cemetery Hill had been the vital point. And it had been the Eleventh's hour. The Tigers, the fearsome shock troops of the enemy, had, as one soldier put it, "charged the heights of Gettysburg," and they had been broken. These were the individuals, people said, who were so beastly in life they used knives as toothpicks, and who were so ruthless in battle they used rocks as readily as guns. And here they had gone down, proving that they were not tigers after all, but men.[48]

ACT FOUR
Crossfire

On Cemetery Hill on the night of July second, where men of the Eleventh Corps had a moment, finally, to savor something akin to success, soldiers with lanterns made their way over the fighting ground, looking for fallen men they might yet save. Down in the town, residents who had lived through the day's "awfulness" listened to horses scream and men suffer. "We could hear shrieks and groans of the wounded out towards the Cemetary [*sic*]," said one woman. It was "heart rending very sad." "Hundreds of souls," said another, were "ushered" unto God. At Fannie Buehler's house, the sounds of the battle had been so bad that she and her company had covered their ears. Her two-year-old son, too young to translate the sounds of shells into something fearful, commented that the missiles reminded him of goose wings whistling. "Birdies," he said. Georgia McClellan, up on Cemetery Hill, had been unable to escape, prisoner to both her mending body and to the battle. Nearby, the Thorn family had been ordered by General Howard to leave the gatehouse on the morning of July second, and, with shells exploding behind them, they had evacuated. Elizabeth Thorn and her father then made the mistake of returning home at midnight to check on their "fat hogs" and to retrieve bedding. They found the gatehouse surrounded by dead and wounded men, heard soldiers crying to their wives to come and wet their tongues, became overwhelmed, and left again.[49]

During the active fighting, women in Gettysburg came to know the fury of battle. They also came to know enemy anger. For every moment of amity that arose between Confederate men and Gettysburg women, in fact, and for every flirtatious or courteous encounter or negotiated exchange, there were hours of sustained hostility. Ultimately, the town was a battlefield, and civilians and soldiers, with all their sociable impulses, could not imagine it away. Confederate soldiers who talked about protecting women were in town for other reasons, and their roles as surrogates only went so far. "I think the people of this place are very kind," one woman overheard a soldier say when he first arrived in town, "considering we came here to kill off their husbands and sons."[50]

Confederate soldiers not only asked favors and worked bargains, then; they also walked into houses and used force or the threat of force to make women obey and serve them, or, if not obey, to keep quiet. Many of them demanded domestic work without promising anything in return, and in many households, that is what they got. But the soldiers also met resistance. Sometimes using subterfuge, sometimes simply refusing compliance, and occasionally twisting chivalric assumptions to their advantage, women stood up to these invaders. They became outspoken and obstructive. They refused to remain in their homes. Determined to assist Union soldiers, a number of women summoned physical courage, opened their doors, exposed themselves to crossfire, and walked out.

While Confederate occupiers found a relatively cordial reception among some residents, in many households they met nothing but frozen hostility. One woman considered interacting with invaders to be nothing short of blasphemy. Even though she served food to a general and his staff, she could barely talk about it: "How dare a patriot heart beat a welcome to a traitor, however much that is noble may be there! This one foul stain mars it all." Other residents concurred. When Confederate men came knocking on doors and asking for something to eat, in fact, it was often nothing short of a gun, nothing short of the fear of having a house ransacked or burned down or of being personally hurt, that produced food and supplies.[51]

Many soldiers, for their part, made no pretense of chivalry. They broke into houses with axes, ripped down doors, carried off anything and everything. They foraged in household cupboards and looted family food, and searched through bedrooms. They ripped limbs away from fruit trees, butchered family animals, and left behind bloody skins and hooves. They searched people. A group of enemy soldiers pulled one blind man out of bed, unwound his bandages, and looked him over for money.[52]

The occupying soldiers took what they needed, and to some extent they did what they wanted, out of spite and revenge. In one house outside of town they carried family pictures out to the woods, fed army horses out of doughtrays, and mixed flour in bureau drawers. Then they got a jar of black cherries—it looked like blood—poured the mess down the stairs, then poured chaff over it. On the wall they smeared the words, "Done in retaliation for what was done in the South." In another house they took silk dresses out, dragged them through mud, stomped on them and hung them on a fence. They "tore and broke everything to pieces." In a different family home, Confederate soldiers worked with flour. They mixed it with water, added feathers from a bed, and threw their concoction over walls and furniture.[53]

Confederate soldiers vented their anger not only on property but on people as well. They threatened repeatedly to shell the town, and their cockiness lent credence to their threats. Out at Harriet Bayly's farm, on July 2nd, Lee's soldiers radiated confidence when they came asking for bread and apple butter. "I told you so," they said to the family, "didn't I tell you that we would whip the Yanks." In town, Confederate occupiers were similarly boastful. One woman heard that the Union had the "best position, but cannot hold it much longer." The rebels, she said, "do so much bragging that we do not know how much to believe."[54] The problem was that no one could really be sure where war's brutality would stop when it came to civilians. There were some husbands missing, taken as suspects or combatants. Who or what was next? And it was hard to know, too, how victory or defeat affected a man's comportment. Did success mean that a Confederate soldier got uglier or that he became more circumspect?

Confederate occupiers, with their weapons and their numbers, could keep women guessing, and on edge. There were some things, like physical assault, that they may not have perpetrated on local white women—General Lee with his ideas about limited war may have helped see to that. But that did not mean that women did not feel threatened. Or that they did not hear that assault happened. Just west of Carlisle, according to a Lancaster newspaper on July second, a "Miss Worst" was raped by Confederate soldiers.[55]

If Confederate soldiers did not make (obvious) physical demands on white women of the borough, they did force women's accommodation in other ways. They demanded cooking, and women complied. Under the stern eye of the enemy, women baked bread, made cake, brought out pies, cooked chickens, and broiled fish. East of town, a middle-aged woman on a farm opened her door to a soldier on July second. By the way he was dressed, she was sure that he was a Louisiana Tiger. He told her that "General Lee had said that they should ask for food and if they would not give it they should demand it and that was what he was going to do." She fed him ham. He ate some of it and then insulted her. The bread, he complained, was not fit to eat. "Madam," he said, "I can go into any cabin in Virginia, poor and desolate as it is, from Winchester to Richmond, with not a fence standing, and get a better dinner than this."[56]

Cooking was one thing Confederate soldiers made women do. Shutting their mouths was another. There had been pointed talk before the Civil War about Northern women who were bold and outspoken, and who did not know the proper bounds of feminine behavior. The abolition and women's rights movements had produced many of these "Amazons," and passive Northern men had allowed them to multiply. White women in the South, where patriarchal customs had more clout, were seen as relatively decorous and subservient. When Confederate men came to Gettysburg, they could tap into these social discussions, and they could offer some useful lessons. They could defeat Yankee men on the field, of course, and reveal their weakness. But they could also make Yankee women serve and obey, and know their proper place.[57]

To some extent, of course, Confederate soldiers could "subdue" Pennsylvania women just by entering Northern homeland. They had had this effect on Fannie Buehler. This Gettysburg woman had sent the most outspoken woman in her family away as the invaders approached. Her mother's opinions on politics and the war would, Fannie felt, put everyone in danger, and Fannie did not want her to single-handedly test wartime rules. Fannie would see to it that in the invasion her household would exhibit a more conservative and restrained femininity.

Other Gettysburg women shared Fannie Buehler's concern. The mother of one twenty-year-old woman was horrified when her daughter seemed unable or unwilling to withhold her opinions. The family's house, just west of Seminary Ridge, was commandeered by Confederates, and the occupation made the young woman "very angry." When an enemy soldier asked her if she had "any friends in the Army," she replied, "Yes a brother in the Artillery no doubt fighting against you." The enemy soldier responded, "How I would like to capture him." And she let him have it. "It would take braver blood than you have to capture a brother of mine." Her mother was aghast. "Hush," she said, "They might kill you."[58]

Another woman refused to hush and was reprimanded. When Confederate soldiers began to take her well water, she went over to the pump and told them, "Boys I would not waste the water, we do not know how long this may last and all of us need it." One of the men looked at her. "If you say much old lady we will take your well up." Mary McAllister endured a similar rebuke when she attempted to save a barrel of molasses. "Don't knock that barrel over, it is mine," she told enemy soldiers. That was enough female opinion for them. "You damn old b–," they said to her, "Go to the house." She also tried to order Confederate men out of her house, and in doing so, said one soldier, "got a little lippy." Out to the west of town, a young girl said too much, and then too little. When Confederate soldiers began to light her furniture on fire—her house had been used by Union sharpshooters—she leaped out of the cellar and tried to smother the flames. She then got mad. She told them that her mother, who was no longer living, had been a Southern woman and that she "would blush for her parentage" if these men torched the house. One of the soldiers offered her a deal. If she would attest to her Southern loyalty by "hurrahing for the Southern Confederacy," he would "see what could be done." The girl, though, refused to speak disloyally. She was then told to "get out or . . . burn with it." Faced with a choice between a house on fire and a field full of shooting soldiers, she and an aunt chose the field, and ran.[59]

The Confederate occupation of Gettysburg, then, is partly a story of women subdued and censured. But it is also a story of women's resistance. Women struck at Confederate enemies any way they could, by using domestic "weapons," by drawing on conventional assumptions about women's skills and weakness, by using the cover of their youthfulness or old age, or by simply saying "no."

Some Gettysburg women protested the presence of invasion with their cooking. The family that entertained Confederate general Richard Ewell did not bother with delicacies or hospitality; they gave him "plain fare but no welcome." The woman who handed the "Louisiana Tiger" some tough ham wanted to give him a second-rate supper. She could have served him a better meal with the chickens she had hidden.[60] Since it was hard for the intruder to distinguish between this woman's cooking skill and her noncompliance, all she had to endure was his insult.

Women who did prepare good meals for Confederate soldiers may have had two motives in mind: mollifying invader anger and slowing the invading army. When Harriet Bayly and her family chased down their chickens and served them up as soup, they did so not only because they felt they had to, but because they hoped to encourage desertion from the Confederate ranks and to silence as many guns as possible. When they saw the same soldiers appear at consecutive mealtimes, even as fighting was in progress, they had a sense that their strategy worked.[61]

Confederate soldiers, though, were sometimes wary of Pennsylvania cooking, knowing what could result from a hostile woman in the kitchen. When some Southern troops entered Pennsylvania, in fact, they heard a rumor, strengthened by the sight of a house burning, that there had been an attempted poisoning. Gettysburg women, in return, were angered by the assumption that they might use poison. One resident who had labored over a supper for Confederate soldiers noticed that the men were reluctant to eat. "You're afraid I'm trying to poison you? How could you think that?" she asked them. "Do you suppose I would work over you as I've done this afternoon and then try to kill you?" When she ate some of the bread herself and drank some of her own coffee, the Confederate men joined in as well. Mary McAllister's sister would not go this far. Two men entered her house, asked for something to eat, and she complied. She brought out a pie that she had made and offered it to the men. Putting it down for them, with a knife, she said: "Now you cut it the best way you can." One of the soldiers cut it, but hesitated, and said: "You eat a piece." She replied, "Do you think it is poison? The women here don't poison people." They both refused to try the pie.[62]

Gettysburg women used domesticity to limit the actions of their enemies but worked within the "rules" of civilized warfare. They had other "female" ways of assisting Union soldiers and resisting the invaders. Older girls and women put their status as noncombatants and their "defenselessness" to good use. Mary McAllister skillfully employed the shield of her sex when a Union officer asked her to hide his diary from Confederate soldiers—he was fearful of being taken prisoner. Mary did not know at first "where to put it." But she had an idea: "I opened my dress and put it in my dress." The officer was satisfied. "That's the place," he said. "They will not get it there." Catherine Garlach, General Schimmelfennig's protector, also appealed to gender codes to limit Confederate actions. Accosting an enemy soldier who had pushed into her house and was climbing her stairs, she "caught him by the coat . . . and asked him what he was doing there." He replied that the house would be used for sharpshooters. "You can't go up there," she said, without releasing her grip. "You will draw fire on this house full of defenseless women and children." She prevailed.[63]

Confederate soldiers, of course, could call women's bluff. The young woman who harangued enemy soldiers about setting fire to her house, and claimed that they were a disgrace to Southern manhood, also tried to shame them by referring to herself and her aunt as "defenceless females" who were being thrown out "in the midst of a battle." Soldiers did not appreciate her protests, or did not believe her, and they brought out the torch.[64]

Women and girls occasionally had better luck using simple and authoritative rebuffs than trying to play to a tenuous chivalry. One young girl, faced with soldiers who wanted something to eat with their biscuits, told them, "If you are hungry you can eat them as they are." Another, a fourteen-year-old girl, told a soldier who wanted his canteen filled with water that the well was "within sight," and "he didn't look like a cripple." An older woman confronted soldiers who demanded that she finish baking bread for them. "There is the stove," she told them, "put it on and bake it." The next day a young man came in and asked her if she would cook some bacon and onions for his officer who was asleep in the barn. She was even more emphatic. "You can cook and there is the stove," she told him, "fry it yourself." He did.[65]

Perhaps their age helped older women dictate to youthful soldiers and youthful officers, or perhaps these women were more comfortable issuing commands or refusing orders than most people acknowledged. Whatever the reason, women protecting the houses in Gettysburg and advocating for hurt and dying men could be fearsome. "You can't take this last cow!" one woman asserted, as she shook her fist in the face of an enemy soldier. Harriet Bayly similarly "rose up in . . . wrath" when she discovered that Confederate men had been ignoring suffering wounded men on the first day's battlefield. "Is it possible that none of you will bring water to these poor fellows?" An officer heard her angry protest and sent men on horseback to fill canteens. Fannie Buehler, who had gone to great pains to remove her obstreperous mother from her household before the invasion, found that she herself was growing more outspoken. As she was finishing a meal after the first day's fight, her doorbell rang "violently." Fannie, who had a house full of wounded men, "having no fear," opened the door to Confederate men who "accosted" her and demanded a search of her house. She "appeared very bold on this occasion" and insisted on leading the tour herself.[66]

Women and girls grew bold at the Battle of Gettysburg by speaking out and telling enemy men what they needed and when soldiers had stepped out of line. They also grew bold with physical courage. Even as the battle's thunder amplified, and as men continued to kill and die, they saw the strengthening of "nerve." It was, said one woman, nothing compared with General Howard. She had heard that he sat on a tombstone reading calmly when a shell burst next to him, and he did not divert his eyes from his message. It was nothing like that. And yet it was. As she put it, there was "a calming effect such terrific scenes and emergencies, resulting from the contending powers of right and wrong, do have upon humanity." Every new shell, she said, "imparted renewed vigor and fortitude to our patriotism."[67]

Women applied their physical fortitude to many tasks, including what Fannie Buehler called "women's work": caring for wounded men, feeding soldiers, sheltering their own children. In the process, they left the protection of cellars and houses. Fannie explained that she would have been comfortable in her commodious cellar, but that she "never before lived under ground and did not propose doing so then."[68]

Nine-year-old Sadie Bushman knew something about experiencing a battle above ground. As she remembered it, on the day the armies first converged on the borough, her mother announced that "they are going to shell the town," and they "must all get away." Sadie was ordered to take a younger brother to the safety of her grandparents' house, two miles out of town. Her parents would follow with other children. No sooner had the children reached the street, however, than Sadie and her brother were swept up by people fleeing the shooting, and separated from the rest of the family. They were about "halfway" to their grandparents' farm when they were startled by a "blinding flash." A Union officer seized the children, remarked on their narrow escape, and helped them the rest of the way.[69]

But the farm offered no refuge. "Things were almost as bad there," Sadie recalled. The house had become a makeshift hospital and the yard was an operating theater. Just as Sadie reached the safety of the house, in fact, Union soldiers arrived, bearing a man with his leg "terribly shot." And the shock did not stop there. The surgeon needed help. He "turned to me and asked me if I could hold a cup of water to the poor man's mouth while the leg was being taken off," Sadie said. "Terribly frightened," she complied. And the sight of the procedure was indelible. "They laid the leg over a carpenter's horse," she recalled, and "I had to see the whole operation, and I can remember every cut as plainly to-day as I saw it then." But she did not faint, or vomit, or run away. I had "more fear" of the surgeon than of the mangled man, said Sadie. "How I accomplished it I do not know, but I stood there." As Sadie recalled, she not only stood there, but she stayed, for "the most fearful two weeks I ever knew," all the while helping the doctor help the soldiers. When her father finally found her he brought her home, but within a few days she was out again, working "day and night sometimes" to assist the wounded. She was so small she could not reach up to the sick men, to do what nurses must have done—wash a sweaty face, change a dressing, spoon some broth into mouths. And so she climbed onto the beds to care for her patients.[70]

Sadie Bushman may have been the youngest girl in Gettysburg to leave home and take part in the battle's bloody work, but she was by no means the only girl or woman to use her "nerve." Others also worked openly and actively to help soldiers. One woman left her house, ran across streets "as fast as I could" to find bread, even as sharpshooters' bullets hissed and shrieked past her. Confederate soldiers lying in nearby alleys screamed and laughed at the sight of her exposure. Other women got into the thick of a fight. One stepped between a Confederate officer who had drawn his revolver and a Union colonel who refused to relinquish his sword, and begged them to both cool down. Another, a sixteen-year-old girl, could not stomach the sight of Union soldiers being shot by Confederate pickets at a Gettysburg intersection. She stationed herself where Union men could see her and shouted out a warning, "Look Out! Pickets below! They'll fire on you!" The men she alarmed made their way through with "flying dashes." Enemy riflemen, realizing her effectiveness, "turned their guns on her." Bullets zinged the door where she stood, but for half an hour she sent out her cries until Union pickets took over her work.[71]

Elizabeth Thorn also openly assisted soldiers. On July first, before she did women's work serving dinner to generals, and while the battle was in its early fury, a Union soldier with "straps on his shoulders" came to the gatehouse and asked her if there was a man available. He needed someone, he said, to point out the roads, to show where they led. She could not send her children and she could not send her father, since he was sick and spoke only German. She offered herself. The officer said there must be a man somewhere, and she offered herself again. He hesitated. There was, he asserted, "too much danger for a woman," and he wondered if she would be afraid. Thorn convinced him that she was not afraid, and told him that there was no choice—either she went and exposed herself to artillery fire or a slip of a boy or a sick old man would have to go. She went, convincing herself to head outside with a falsehood—by saying there was as much danger inside as outside.[72]

She was wearing, she said, a gingham apron, which she put over her head to shield the blaze of the sun. She traveled with the soldier down into flax, oat, and wheat fields, until the hill she called home, now bristling with batteries, loomed above her. Soldiers seemed astounded at her appearance, and one of them asked if it had come to it that women were now in the army. But the officer assured them that even though Elizabeth Thorn walked into a battlefield, the world as they knew it was still intact. They assented then, and a regimental band struck up a little piece for her, and the men cheered. When the party reached a point where they could oversee the town, Thorn pointed out the roads to York, Carlisle, and Hanover. The officer, as she remembered it, kept "his horse between her and the rebel fire to shield her from danger." And soon enough she was back home, her tour of military duty over. Then she moved back into doing what women in wartime were supposed to do. The same officer who had escorted her into the battlefield later knocked on her door and asked if she would please make supper for General Howard.

ACT FIVE
WHEN THE BATTLE HIT HOME

In their work, indoors and out, women like Elizabeth Thorn engaged physically in the Battle of Gettysburg. They assisted men who were healthy and fighting and men who were injured. They actively brokered with enemy soldiers to make the embattled town habitable, and to protect their homes. In pressured settings, and in households freighted with anxiety, they became "sweethearts" and "mothers." Still others confronted the enemy men in their midst, employing common assumptions and agreed-upon rules about women and war to obstructive ends. Not simply victims of the battle, they became agents of protest and opposition.

In some cases, however, women's efforts to take control of their lives in this crisis, to be actively and positively involved, failed. Most women were not simply victims of the battle, but a few of them undeniably were. To different degrees, Harriet Bayly and Georgia McClellan found themselves on the receiving end of brutality.

There could never have been a picture of Harriet Bayly's battle wounds, but that did not mean she was not hurt. She had gone to great lengths to establish battlefield cordiality—cooking, feeding, and caring—but it only gained her so much. It did not protect her animals. The Bayly family had tried to ride horses away to safety before the battle, and when that had not worked, they rigged up a hiding place. They led the three family horses into a room beneath the barn that they used to stable the sheep. Spreading straw on the floor to prevent the telltale knocking of hooves, they then piled cut hay against the door. And it worked. Confederate soldiers had surrounded the farm, come and gone as they pleased, slaughtered sheep, stolen their cows, demanded food, and at the close of the third of July, the horses were still there. Chestnut-colored Nellie, Harriet's link to her dead daughter, was safe.[73]

It was a brother-in-law who made the mistake. It was late, the sun was nearly down, and there did not seem to be any enemy men around. A certain casualness must have crept in then, a relaxing of the guard, and he took a bundle of hay and went openly toward the outside door. Where the soldier came from, no one could tell.

"We were under their rule," Harriet said simply. "We felt badly enough about them all, but when that soldier led out Nellie—well, I can hardly tell it." She called to mind the morning when her daughter had been given the young horse and had named it. "Our hearts were yet sore," she said, so "it was not easy to see her 'Nellie' taken away. We all cried and I pleaded hard with the man to leave her."

"She was our dead child's pet," I said, "and you can have anything on the farm if you will not take her."

"At last he threw me the rein, saying, 'Madam, if you have a parlor lock her in it, for you will lose her if you don't.'"

Harriet Bayly and her family then petted Nellie, and it is easy to picture them crowded in gratitude, rubbing Nellie's forehead and her soft muzzle, and reaching around her neck. Nellie, the swift and gentle horse, whom Jane Ann had named when she was a "bit of a girl," was spared.

It is easy to picture this, but much harder to imagine the family's despair when the soldier returned only a minute or so later. He said that he was sorry and he hated it all too, but he had to take her away after all. And he did. "That was," said Harriet, "the last we ever saw of Nellie."

Georgia McClellan had invisible wounds, too, and they were deep. She and her newborn baby had spent most of the first days of July in bed in her house just within Union lines, on East Cemetery Hill. Almost equidistant between General Howard's earthworks and a nest of Confederate sharpshooters to the north, the house was caught repeatedly in crossfire. Georgia had seen something of the first day's fight—soldiers and ammunition wagons in wheatfields, and smoke from the guns. And that night she had heard the hurt men all around her crying for "help, Mother, and God." It had been a "horror."[74]

Georgia's sister Jennie, who, along with the rest of the family, had based herself in Georgia's two-family house, made the best of the battle's chaos. She drenched her skirt carrying water to thirsty soldiers, she baked for men who came hungry to the door, and she wrapped soldiers' wounds. At night, on July first, when the men's crying grew too pitiful to bear, Jennie got down on her hands and knees—she did not want to be hit by stray gunfire—and crawled outside to deliver water.[75]

On July second, a ten-pound shell crashed through the upstairs of Georgia McClellan's house and lodged in a wall. Confederate batteries continued to take aim at Cemetery Hill, and the house remained targeted by sharpshooters. Jennie Wade and her mother handed out all the bread they had and started the yeast for more. Sometime during the day, Jennie fainted. Georgia continued to lie in bed. In the early evening, not far away, Louisiana Tigers tried to take the lines of the Eleventh Corps and failed. More men shot at each other, more cannons fired, and, well into the night, more men cried out loud.[76]

On the morning of July third, Union soldiers, attempting to take back a position on Culp's Hill they had lost the night before, sounded their guns early. Jennie Wade and her brother went outside to get wood to fire the oven. The women ate bread, butter, and applesauce for breakfast, and then Jennie read aloud from the Book of Psalms. Something about the reading, though, irritated Georgia, and she asked Jennie to stop. Nobody could do anything to quiet the battle, however, and just about the time Georgia hushed her sister, rifle fire hit the side of the house, shattering all the windows. One of the bullets hit the bedpost where Georgia lay. Her mother touched it—still warm. The Wade women had thought the west side of the house was dangerous and they had moved the bed to face the north. The bullet came from the north.[77]

Then it was about eight o'clock in the morning. In the room next to Georgia, Jennie began to mix up dough. Commenting on the firing outside, she said that she hoped if anyone was killed, it would be her and not her sister with the new baby. Then it was about eight-thirty. North of the house, a soldier, probably positioned dozens of yards away, took his loaded rifle and hoisted it to his shoulder. Maybe it had been his bullet that had gone astray on the first shot, and he wanted a different angle. Maybe he thought that this was the shot that would really finish off the sharpshooter that seemed to be using the brick house. And he fired. His bullet did have a different trajectory this time. It shot down the street, flew across the threshold of the McClellan house and through the front door. Then it pushed through an interior door. It had enough velocity, still, to enter the back of the twenty-year-old girl who was working dough, and to penetrate her chest. It stopped only at the breast of her corset, just in front of her broken heart. Jennie made no sound when she died, only when she fell. Georgia screamed. Some German soldiers came from outside to help—Eleventh Corps men.[78]

In Gettysburg, the theater of war had widened.

6

★★

THE WIDE EYE OF THE STORM

IN LATE MORNING ON the third of July, less than a mile from where the Wade family nursed its new grief, Union soldiers on Cemetery Ridge took in the heat and waited. They were veterans of two days' battle now, and their bodies had been alternately shocked and spent. Some of them had not eaten since the shooting began, and the warm water in their canteens only augmented their thirst. Their wool uniforms, too, took the sweat and the dirt and the smell from their bodies and gave it back to them with itch. Mocking the men's discomfort, the sun doubled itself on muskets and bayonets, and made mirrors of brass guns. Down on the Emmitsburg Road, at around ten o'clock in the morning, skirmishers set a big barn and house on fire and fueled the hot look of misery.[1]

Some of the men fainted in the heat, but others slept through it, exhausted. They had spent the evening in a midsummer's nightmare, sharing the ground with the dead and the dying, most of them unable to escape the sounds of pain that emanated from the fields. The night's lights had added to the haunting. Lanterns had been hung on tree branches to illuminate surgeons' work, and been carried by orderlies through fields to find men who still had a chance. Skirmishers, too, had sparked repeatedly into the darkness. But now, on Friday, there was no room for tiredness, as the soldiers shifted once again from aftermath to expectation. Both armies had lost a lot of men, but nobody had pulled away. Union soldiers could look across to Seminary Ridge and see a long line of enemy batteries, a certain sign that something else was coming.[2]

General George Meade, commander of the Army of the Potomac, sat down to some stewed chicken and warm toast at around eleven o'clock, and then lit a cigar. Just north of him, on Cemetery Hill, the noise of firing had lessened a little after ten-thirty, when a fight on Culp's Hill over some breastworks had finally resolved to Federal advantage. The relative quiet that followed reminded

General Carl Schurz of the kind of languid mornings people knew in peacetime, and he almost expected church bells to ring out, calling families to service. He thought the calm made them all nervous, however. "There was," he said, "something ominous, something uncanny in these strange, unexpected hours of profound silence." He wondered if they had all reached the point where they needed the thundering of cannon as a comfort.[3]

Confederate infantrymen on Seminary Ridge at least knew what the battle's next move was, and in the early afternoon they were waiting to make it. General Lee had ordered nine brigades, under Generals George Pickett, James Pettigrew, and Isaac Trimble, to cross the fields to the east and make an assault on the Federal center on Cemetery Ridge. Massive artillery fire would weaken the Union position first. As they waited to make their move, a few of the soldiers passed the time eating corn cakes. Others dozed. One man, who began to daydream, pictured what the afternoon might look like without the war. Like General Schurz on the opposing ridge, he translated the day's languor into pastoral work, and pictured his fellow soldiers as harvesters, resting in the noonday shade. The fantasy could not have lasted long. He knew what kind of harvesting they would be doing that day, and he also knew, certainly, that there would be a moment soon when they would all have to do something brave and rash, and maybe live honorably, but just as likely die, or suffer. Did the time fly by, then, we wonder, or did it crawl?[4]

Years later, long after the war was over, some of these men would come back to walk this land again. They would savor every inch of ground, examine and contemplate their action on each rise, each declivity. Millions of others, too, people who never fought here, but who identified with these soldiers just the same, would study the place in detail, sometimes lamenting the day's outcome, sometimes celebrating it. They would talk about how the armies' fortunes took a turn here, how confidence shifted sides, and how the war began to be lost, or won.

The moment before the artillery barrage began, which was two hours before 12,000 men began to charge across the fields, held special poignancy for Confederates and their many champions. William Faulkner was one Southern writer who captured the irrevocable momentum of that afternoon, and his words, summing up how a whole generation was held in thrall by the memory of that day, are cited over and over again. "For every Southern boy fourteen years old, not once but whenever he wants it," Faulkner wrote in *Intruder in the Dust*, "there is the instant when it's still not yet two o'clock on that July afternoon in 1863, . . . and it's all in the balance, it hasn't happened yet, it hasn't even begun yet, it not only hasn't begun yet, but there is still time for it not to begin against that position and those circumstances . . . that moment doesn't need even a fourteen-year-old boy to think *This time. Maybe this time* with all this much to lose and all this much to gain. . . ."[5]

Pickett's Charge, as it would be called, would ultimately assume immense importance in American history. Few of those who would later contemplate that day, however—the soldiers, the historians, the armchair readers—would pay much heed to the civilian dimensions of the battlefield. The property the men traversed or defended, the fences they ducked behind or scrambled over, the houses they shot through or that shielded them, were mostly relegated to backdrop. Sometimes people focused on the details of the topography, especially the way it impeded or aided the action, but by and large they granted the setting little significance. Most chroniclers missed and dismissed the human context of the place, and, especially, they missed its ironic meaning.

It was not that the farms or outbuildings on the Confederate left flank, where Pickett's charge intensified, were particularly unusual, or that their inhabitants were conspicuous. Nobody shouted at the soldiers, or waved handkerchiefs, or showed flags. The properties on the northwestern end of Cemetery Ridge were largely empty. The men and women and children who lived there had left some time before, fearful of what the armies might bring and, worse, what they might take away.

But if the social landscape of Pickett's Charge was not obvious, it was also not insignificant. Many of the people who lived on the ridgeland just south of Gettysburg were African Americans, and here, between battle lines, stood their houses and barns. Underfoot were some of the fields that they tilled and planted, that even now sent up tender rows of wheat and barley. This was the land that some of them owned, that their children tramped on their way to school, that bore a history of their labor, their wary survival, and their success. These free black people knew this soil, this red, granite-flecked dirt, this land that on July 3, 1863, was perhaps the most contested acreage in the world, better than anyone.

By all accounts, Abraham and Elizabeth Brian and their children Francis and William, and Mag and Alf Palm and their daughter Josephine, and all their friends and neighbors, had moved away from Cemetery Hill by the first days of July. We do not know when they left, or where most of them went, but we do know why they departed. The threat that rode north into Pennsylvania at the end of June, that shot and chased down dark-skinned people, that sent refugees along dusty roads and over wide rivers, had moved east. Every African American in the path of the Southern invaders—every man, every woman, and every young girl and boy—was susceptible to capture. And once the kidnapping began, no black Pennsylvanian, born free or born enslaved, knew when or if it would stop.

THE TERROR

Confederate cavalry, with General Albert Jenkins in charge, had pushed into the Cumberland Valley of Pennsylvania in the middle of June, and this invading force, the leading edge of the Confederate advance, began looting and scavenging supplies immediately. The troopers also wasted no time in targeting "contraband"—black refugees from northern Virginia and Maryland, as well as local civilians. On Monday morning, June 15th, a young white woman in Chambersburg, Pennsylvania, named Rachel Cormany, watched black women and men fly by her house, claiming the enemy was "on their heels." The fugitives' horses were moving so fast that Cormany noticed some peoples' hats had come off, that others had lost their coats, and that the wind was peeling off the covers of wagons. One woman in flight, astride her horse, was "going what she could."[6]

It was late that night when the threat materialized in Chambersburg. Just before midnight, residents heard a hard pounding of hooves and went to their windows. About 1500 horsemen were thundering down the street. They were "hard looking" soldiers, with matted hair down to their shoulders, beards down to their waists, and hats garish with feathers and plumes. One of their officers stopped and demanded the "mayaw of this town." A gun went off. The soldiers went into a frenzy, claiming that they would turn Chambersburg into a waste of ashes if anybody fired again.[7]

Rachel Cormany, who was at home with her young daughter, went to bed after the cavalry first passed through. When she woke up the following morning, the town seemed "quiet," and she wondered if the invaders had moved on. But the next thing she knew, soldiers appeared and began to chase black women and children, "driving them off by droves." She saw people seized who had grown up in Chambersburg and listened as a woman begged for her children to be spared, in vain. "It is a query," Cormany wrote, "what they want with those little babies—whole families were taken." She noticed, as they moved past her like "cattle," that "nearly all hung their heads."[8]

The troopers hunted in the houses and barns of Chambersburg through that day and the next—searching for men's clothing and food, for horses, hay, oats, and for more people. One resident saw the horsemen hunting in the fields, "scouring" the wheat for signs of humans, running them down. "The cavalrymen," he noted, "rode in search of their prey, and many were caught—some after a desperate chase and being fired at."[9]

On June 17th, when Jenkins' men left the Chambersburg area, they took with them the people they had kidnapped. One witness estimated thirty to forty African Americans were seized; another counted fifty, and a third, five times that many. Some of the youngest captives were strapped on the backs of horses, mounted close to their abductors. Others were put in wagons. And some men were secured in a time-honored method. According to one newspaper reporter, the male captives were "bound with ropes." And according to another journalist, "The stronger and more refractory ones were tied together, making somewhat of an extemporized coffle-gang."[10]

Chambersburg was not the only town to feel the brutality. Other border towns in Pennsylvania—McConnellsburg, Mercersburg, Greencastle—also suffered the early thrust of the invasion, and the stories of observers were the same: stolen people driven through town with animals and goods. Horsemen from the South carried their human booty with them—with their "sad countenances"—as they ferreted through farms and houses. They came into neighborhoods, shouted, brandished weapons, made speeches and threats, searched, and left. Then they came back again. The horsemen took people in the middle of the night, and flagrantly, in sunlight. One woman in Mercersburg—"poor old Eliza, and her little boy"—hid out in the grain fields during the day, and crept in at night to get something to eat. Such desperate measures saved Eliza, but nothing could save her daughter, Jane, who, with her two children, "was captured and taken back to Virginia."[11]

The terror went on for days, as the raiding parties cleaned out the southern tier of central Pennsylvania, returned below the Mason-Dixon line, and then went back for more. One Confederate cavalryman in Jenkins' brigade described the routine in his diary. On the 16th of June, he noted, "Boys [were] capturing negroes and horses." On the 17th, he rode until midnight, back into Maryland. On the 20th, he returned North for more "plunder." In some neighborhoods, this kind of marauding kept up as long as Lee was in Pennsylvania. A pastor from Mercersburg described the repeated atrocities as a macabre carousel. On June 19th, he noted, the Confederates rode through with horses, immense numbers of cattle, "and negroes." A week later, he described horsemen passing and repassing, "our colored persons with them, to be sold into slavery." One day they came and abducted "a dozen colored persons, mostly contrabands, women and children." Later, on July 1st, a group of men took "6 or 7 of our free people of color."[12] Another witness was certain that the soldiers did not distinguish between the free-born and the formerly enslaved. "They claimed all these negroes as Virginia slaves," he reported, "but I was positively assured that two or three were born and raised in this neighborhood. One, Sam Brooks, split many a cord of wood for me."[13]

In the eyes of some of these white observers, the hunt for African Americans represented humanity at its worst. Rachel Cormany, the young mother in Chambersburg, claimed that "it grated on our hearts to have to sit quietly &

look at such brutal deeds." One of the Mercersburg witnesses said that it was "the worst spectacle I ever saw in this war" and "a most pitiful sight, sufficient to settle the slavery question for every humane mind." Another man found the kidnapping "revolting."[14]

Above all, these white Pennsylvania residents could not understand why enemy depredation extended to noncombatants, particularly women and children. Some of them said they expected other sorts of Confederate raiding. The taking of horses and cattle and even the pillaging of houses, they believed, was an unfortunate but inescapable consequence of this war. One man listened sympathetically to a Confederate officer as he rationalized the conduct of his troops: "You have only a little taste of what you have done to our people in the South," commented the soldier. "Your army destroyed all the fences, burnt towns, turned poor women out of house and home, broke pianos, furniture, old family pictures, and committed every act of vandalism. I thank God that the hour has come when this war will be fought out on Pennsylvania soil." And his listener concurred: "If this charge is true, I must confess we deserve punishment in the North." Another Pennsylvanian agreed that the taking of horses, cattle, and other things was "within the rules of war."[15]

But these residents recoiled at the taking of people, and the way that their towns had become sites of slave hunts, and, worst of all, that free families—families they had known all their lives—were abducted. They protested that what they were witnessing was shocking in a country like America—purportedly civilized and Christian. They also argued that the "carrying away of free negroes" decisively undermined Confederate assertions that the war was not about sustaining slavery. "This feature of the war," commented one man, "indicated the object for which it was waged, to establish a government founded upon human slavery."[16]

White Pennsylvanians occasionally did more than condemn or report the taking of black civilians; they interceded. In Chambersburg, a resident named Jacob Hoke used a friend who "had influence with Jenkins" to bring about the release of two captives. And in Greencastle on June 16th, a group of residents, some armed with revolvers, surrounded Confederate wagons en route to Virginia with thirty to forty women and children. The local citizens cut the horses loose, seized the Confederate guards and released the prisoners. When one of the Confederates demanded $50,000 for lost "property," several residents demurred, remarking that they did not work in the slave trade. They also prepared themselves for what they were told would happen next: the torching of the town. (It did not occur).[17]

The majority of African Americans taken, it appears, were women and children. Men were not given a reprieve in these raids; many were simply not at home. Just as white civilian men had evacuated as the enemy approached, black men had left as well, and likely for the same reasons—to help hide livestock and possessions or to avoid being seized. These men had mistakenly assumed that they, not their families, would be targets of Confederate brutality, and had left "thinking the women & children would not be disturbed." Some men of color were not present in Chambersburg in 1863 for another reason as well. They were away from home fighting for the Union in South Carolina. As soldiers in the Massachusetts Fifty-fourth Volunteer Infantry, they were one month away from assailing Fort Wagner outside of Charleston harbor.[18]

The witnesses who described the preponderance of black women and children among the captives in 1863 were silent on the subject that had to have weighed heavily on women's minds: sexual assault. Many white Pennsylvania women had anticipated an invasion of male soldiers with panic and dread, fearing what they called "outlandish things which would be done," and worrying about whether or not Confederate soldiers "would molest the women."[19] What more, we must ask, did black women fear? And after some of them had encountered Confederate soldiers, and been carried away from their homes, what did they endure? Given the fact that soldiers in both armies apparently subjected black women to sexual assault throughout the course of the war, including rape on occasion, it would have been extraordinary indeed if sexual violence did not play a part in the ordeals of these women and girls in 1863.[20]

For their part, soldiers from the South left a slim record of these forays into Pennsylvania. One surviving letter, however, suggests that the men engaged in seizing black civilians had no uniform attitude toward the kidnapping. Written by a Confederate officer named William Christian to his family, and found on the Gettysburg battlefield, the letter describes the man's misgivings about capturing black residents. "We took a lot of negroes yesterday," Christian wrote from Greenwood, Pennsylvania, en route to Gettysburg on the 28th of June. "I was offered my choice, but as I could not get them back home I would not take them. In fact, my humanity revolted at taking the poor devils away from their homes. They were so scared that I turned them all loose." Christian, who had been trained as a physician in Philadelphia, served as colonel of a Virginia infantry regiment. His reluctance to take captives home seemed tied as much to the logistics of transport as to compassion.[21]

Witness reports suggest that Christian's sensibilities, however compromised, were not widely shared. In Chambersburg, Rachel Cormany recorded a soldier's gruff response to a kidnapped woman who pleaded for her children. "All the sympathy she received from him," said Cormany, "was a rough 'March along'— at which she would quicken her pace again." In another town, a white resident asked a soldier guarding wagons filled with captured (and free) black Americans how he could participate in such despicable acts: "Do you not feel bad and mean in such an occupation?" The soldier replied that "he felt very comfortable." A judge in the same town asked one of the invaders if "they took free negroes." "Yes," he replied, "and we will take you too if you do not shut up!"[22]

The seizing of people of color was carried out most obviously by Confederate cavalry who operated in the southern Pennsylvania borderland, west of Gettysburg. Jenkins' troopers may have provoked particular public comment and outrage because they represented the first Confederate intrusion into Pennsylvania. But John Imboden's cavalry brigade and J. E. B. Stuart's cavalry corps also apparently seized African Americans in Pennsylvania.[23]

Confederate infantrymen and senior infantry commanders were involved as well. Newspaper and civilian records point to soldiers from Ewell's corps, Hill's corps, and Longstreet's corps taking African Americans during the invasion. Military records also point to Longstreet himself. The corps commander, Robert E. Lee's right-hand man, instructed General Pickett, who was in Chambersburg, to carry with him "captured contrabands" on the way to Gettysburg. Longstreet may have been carrying out something of a tradition. When Stonewall Jackson defeated Federal troops at Harper's Ferry in the fall of 1862, he ordered the seizure of hundreds of "contrabands." Whether the Confederate army was more careful about differentiating runaway slaves from free people in the fall of 1862 than the summer of 1863 is hard to know. According to one historian, it is not necessarily a relevant distinction. "Slave-catching," he has argued, whether directed at free or formerly enslaved people, was "in no way a military activity." Regardless of its standing in Confederate army policy, kidnapping was clearly sanctioned at the highest Confederate levels. According to another scholar, it was a practice intended to avenge the Emancipation Proclamation, the arming of black soldiers, and Northern depredations in the South.[24]

The subject of Confederate (and Union) army comportment was a compelling topic for white civilians caught in the invasion. During lulls in raids and active fighting, Confederate soldiers and Pennsylvanians sometimes not only debated the cause and course of the war, but discussed which army bore the responsibility for widening the war's parameters. African American civilians may have cared something about whether Union or Confederate men had initiated "hard war," but hardly took part in these conversations. They also did not need to debate the war's meaning. The issue of whether slavery was or was not the heartbeat of the rebellion, or whether racial hatred infused the conduct of the war, was not something discussible, the way it was for white residents. These people of color were living—and fleeing—witnesses to the way race and slavery mattered. A white teacher, who met refugees on the road to Carlisle, Pennsylvania, heard firsthand what the invasion meant to black families. One fugitive was covered with dust and "very nearly dead" with exhaustion—he had traveled north forty miles from his home. He told the teacher that what he feared most was "de Rebels kotchin' us an' takin' our chill'en fum us an' sellin' em to de drivahs an' we wud nevah see dem ag'in."[25]

The news of human hunting in Pennsylvania rippled beyond the first epicenters of terror, and, in the last weeks of June 1863, waves of black families moved northward. People were up before daylight, threading themselves through grain fields or moving hurriedly along dirt roads. Some people were too old to go, but they fled anyway. Others were "poor people completely worn out, carrying their families on their backs." One woman held her two children from the Cumberland Valley all the way to Philadelphia, alternating who had to walk and who got lifted. Her shoes were worn away. Sick people went. One man with smallpox left home. A fatally ill girl evacuated, too, and then lay dying—but free—in a Harrisburg church.[26]

Some people of color took flight the way fugitives from slavery had always traveled through Pennsylvania—by using the routes of the Underground Railroad. The refugees heading toward Harrisburg told the white teacher who met them on the road that they had been advised "to keep yo 'ise wide op'n to dat big mounting on de lef' han' side all de way to de ribber." Many black fugitives, of course, had no question about the way. They had been sheltering escapees and pointing them in this direction for decades, probably never imagining that they, too, would be getting up before dawn, hiding under the height of corn stalks, and working their way from one safe house to the next.[27]

White travelers to the borderland of central Pennsylvania reported that by the last days of June 1863 there was scarcely a "negro left" in the area. A newspaper correspondent measured the evacuation by the services that seemed to be missing. There were no cooks left in kitchens, no barbers to be seen. "At Mechanicsburg yesterday we made a dinner of peanuts," he noted, "the hotel proprietor declaring that his assistants had vanished. At York the same story was told, and at Carlisle there was no variation."[28]

Many of the refugees moved east across the state to the sanctuary of Philadelphia, where ministers mobilized congregations, communities opened their meetinghouses, and residents offered the protection of their private homes. Many of those on the run, though, sought refuge across the Susquehanna River in Harrisburg, the state capital. Nearly 2000 people congregated in the city's parks, took shelter in churches, and crowded into the courthouse. The governor offered homeless families rations of meat and crackers. Safety on the road and in these cities, however, was a relative thing. One witness remarked that African Americans found "no shelter from white citizens." Another claimed that Union soldiers were given to scaring fugitives as they passed by on the way north. In Harrisburg itself, some residents commiserated with the congregating refugees, but others were unwelcoming. "It would be better for the contraband to stay where he is at all hazards," warned one Harrisburg newspaper, "than run the gauntlet of prejudice, the downright hatred . . . which he finds at his every step northward." Rather than calling on Harrisburg residents to put aside their prejudice and to embrace something akin to compassion, this paper called on refugees to stay away—even while admitting they were "in danger of capture."[29]

The terror that African Americans felt was not only the fear of being stolen south, but the deep concern that this was only the beginning—that if the Confederates were successful, who knew what dark age might ensue. A New York newspaper put the meaning of a Confederate victory in Pennsylvania succinctly to its African American readers: "Our life, our liberty, our country, our religious privileges, our family, OUR ALL is at stake." And so, people fled. Many of them were successful at avoiding capture, but some were not, and those who were caught did everything in their power not to be dragged away. Some of them pleaded and cried. Others tried to wrestle free. Two African American civilians fought back personally against their captors, one of them winning the struggle, the other losing. The first man took a gun from the soldier guarding him, shot him, and ran. The second man refused "to go over the river" with the Confederate army when it retreated into Virginia. So soldiers settled things with him. They slashed his chest and abdomen, cut off his genitals, and poured turpentine on the lacerations. A Vermont soldier saw him as he lay in a barn near the Potomac River, "grinding his teeth & foaming at the mouth."[30]

THE BLACK COMMUNITY UNDER SIEGE

As the crisis in Pennsylvania shifted from cavalry and infantry incursions to an impending battle by the end of June, and as the armies began to move toward a specific location, black residents in the Gettysburg area evacuated in earnest. One day late in the month, the AME bishop arrived at the quarterly meeting in the borough. He spoke, wrote a witness, "kindly and courageously." The congregation then sang, joining together in "The Year of Jubilee Has Come." But word of enemy soldiers suddenly worked its way through the church. Almost as an act of magic, the singing stopped, and "in a moment bishop and people had disappeared."[31]

Some white residents dutifully noted black flight from the border country, and variously expressed their amusement, annoyance, or sympathy. They also tended to describe black fugitives as mass victims. African Americans were a "flock of sheep," or a herd of "buffalo before a prairie fire," or a "crowd" in consternation. Most white people did not have the time or interest to consider individual responses to the invasion—to note, for instance, the differences between the poor folk who fled with every possession and property and business owners. Nor did they consider the different concerns of black men and women, or the dissimilarities between the people who fled and the people who remained.[32]

Neither, of course, did black people have the time then, nor the wherewithal or interest afterward, to communicate their own distinctively painful experiences. Lloyd Watts, an indefatigable note-taker, left no obvious record of his battle days, for example. Yet from piecemeal evidence, we do know something of what different people endured. We know that Owen Robinson, the confectioner who had worked so hard for progress in the black community, and whose church had cared for "brethren" in bondage, tried to quickly remove himself and his family from the border. It mattered little to him that he had papers that spoke of his legal freedom or described him in detail. He had certainly heard that these Southern soldiers did not care about documents. So Robinson gathered together his large family. He gave his pigs to white people to care for, he left his business to good or bad fortune, and he got away.[33]

Abraham and Elizabeth Brian were forced to leave their twelve-acre farm south of Cemetery Hill, and their tenant house, and their property in town. In the spring of 1863, the family, including the boys Francis and William, had all turned their backs to rising rumors. They had tilled their soil, planted wheat and barley, and put in a vegetable garden. But ultimately they abandoned it all. Lucky thing for them, too. Their farm would not simply be in the environs of the fighting, or within earshot. It would be smack in the middle of the Confederate left flank as it fired and charged and was forced back on the third of July. The Brian family fences would serve in Union breastworks, their vegetables and wheat would feed Union men, and their small, white, one-and-a-half-story house would stand inside the bloody whirlwind, give soldiers shelter, and withstand shot and shell. A century and a half later, it would still be there.[34]

The small white house that the Palm family had rented from the Brians—more like a shack, really—at the west end of the farm, on the Emmitsburg Road, was hit hard by the charge. Mag Palm did not stay around to see it blasted, nor did she risk her freedom and that of her daughter, Josephine. Like her black neighbors, she got out of the way. While some residents said later that Mag helped warn families about enemy soldiers, and others suggested that she spent the battle on the borough's streets, unbothered by the danger and even "impertinent" to enemy men, what is certain is that Mag knew what kidnapping felt like. She knew what it meant to be a short distance from slavery. It is likely, then, that if Mag made a show of bravado in town, she also knew when and how to leave.[35]

Randolph Johnston, of course, had wanted to stay. Ignoring public opinion that claimed that black men with guns were likely to "bring upon us terrible calamities," and newspapers that urged men of color to remain "in their proper places," Johnston, captain of his "colored company," had continued to prepare men to fight. Local lawyer David Wills telegraphed Governor Curtin and declared the readiness of the sixty emergency volunteers, but Wills wondered if they would "be accepted." The answer was no. The governor telegraphed him back that for this crisis "we have no authority to enlist colored men"—they would have to get permission from the War Department. By then, of course, it would be too late. Pennsylvania would begin to train African Americans for service in the regular Federal army, but not in time for this invasion—the first recruits entered camp near Philadelphia on June 26th, the day Confederate soldiers first marched into Gettysburg.[36]

Johnston's volunteers may have disassembled under the burden of discouraging word from white officials. But it is just as likely that the soldiers regrouped or worked individually to help defend their homeland. In Harrisburg, in late June, two companies of African Americans, including refugees from the borderland, were armed and equipped to help defend the capital. Once again, however, they were prohibited from active duty. The same fears that had kept men of color out of the army for so long, and that still kept many soldiers away from combat, surfaced at the point of the invasion. Black men, armed, drilled, and willing to fight, were ordered to work on entrenchments. Even then, it seems, they had to keep an eye out for harassment. Union soldiers stationed at Harrisburg sometimes taunted male refugees who congregated at the capital, and worse. One newspaper reported that a "fugitive slave" who had worked on the fortifications was shot in the chest, "unprovoked." Another was "rounded up and forced to work and then beaten when he resisted." In York, Pennsylvania, black men faced similar coercion, and expressed similar resistance. On June 23rd, a "squad of soldiers" came into town and rounded up "able bodied darkies" to work on entrenchments. Some men were pulled out of their beds. A reporter described the men's reaction to this forced labor as "great consternation."[37]

Most African American men in Pennsylvania were denied the opportunity to fight the Confederates with weapons. But not all of them. One company of black men helped hold back invading soldiers, and their efforts, considered one of the first military engagements in the war by men of color, is still overlooked. The site of the action was the Columbia–Wrightsville bridge, a span a mile and a quarter long over the Susquehanna River. Before word had come of the Army of the Potomac's move north from Virginia, General Lee and corps commander Richard Ewell had envisioned taking Harrisburg from the east and south. The bridge over the Susquehanna River—twenty-five miles southeast of the capital—was key. On June 28th, an emergency Pennsylvania militia unit and a company of African American men recruited from the area—numbering at least fifty—attempted to hold the bridge against 2500 seasoned Confederate troops (including artillery), until the bridge could be destroyed. "The negros," commented one observer, "did nobly." The officer in command of the militia had even more to say. "When the fight commenced," he reported, the black company "took their guns and stood up to their work bravely. They fell back only when ordered to do so." One of the black volunteers paid the ultimate price for this work: His head was "taken off by a shell." As one historian has pointed out, this man—no one knows his name—was only the third Northern soldier killed in the Gettysburg campaign.[38]

The different histories of the Columbia Bridge volunteers, of Randolph Johnston, of Owen Robinson, and of the Brian and Palm families speak to the multiple dimensions of black civilian experience during the Gettysburg episode of the Civil War. Some of these people sought to fight the invaders, while others thought the better part of valor was to protect their independence. Some of those who left made away with every possession and treasure they owned on their backs. Others abandoned good-sized farms and paying jobs. For all their differences, however, these people did face common enemies. The invasion was a great equalizer for black families in southern Pennsylvania, underscoring for everybody the fragility of freedom.

THE MOMENT OF "ALMOST"

The Battle of Gettysburg is not only a story of black evacuation, but also a tale of people who remained at home, sometimes protected, often not, and of hiding, near misses, and capture. Most African Americans had left the borough by July first, but not all of them. One white woman who remained in Gettysburg for the three-day battle explained that some black residents "were obliged to stay at home." What were the circumstances that kept people of color in town, when all the news and rumor coming north spoke of impending terror? Was it that a family could not bear to give up its property, its livestock, or its hard-earned home? More likely, it seems, some black women and men did not leave Gettysburg because they could not. This happened, apparently, to a man called "Jack." Jack was "bow-legged," and when he pictured the velocity and power of enemy soldiers on horseback, and compared it with his own hampered running, he was too doubtful. According to a white man who knew him, Jack "didn't have any confidence in his ability to outrun the raiders," and he was forced to stay.[39]

White friends and employers may have convinced some African American residents to stay by promising to protect them. One Gettysburg woman told a widow and her daughter to come to her house; she had a loft over the kitchen, and once she had taken the ladder away, "they would be safe." The women took her at her word and climbed into the loft on June 26th, when General Early's soldiers came marching through. Another white family, four miles north of town, led its two black servants to a crawl space underneath a porch. They replaced the stones around the porch and hung some sacks over the wall to hide the hole, "so it wouldn't look as if it had been disturbed."[40]

The decision to stay—especially when it involved an employer—was not necessarily freely made. Like so much in life, part of what determined whether or not a person could be safe or secure depended on wealth and means. People dependent on employers may not have felt free to go. Paid work, especially for women, was to be found through white families, and in this emergency these families wanted help. Not threatened in the same way themselves, they "offered" their employees safety and job security at the same time.

In the end, though, some black women and men decided that faith in white protection, loyalty to their white friends and employers, and the security of their jobs were not as strong as the refuge of a black community far away from the border. So they stood firm, said no, or simply left. The two women in the loft, for example, just couldn't bear the anxiety. After one fearful night with no rest, they took off the next day, the daughter confessing that "she couldn't be paid to put in such another night, that she heard soldiers walking around— that they surely knew who was on that loft." Surely, too, this mother and daughter must have wondered if their protectors might be threatened or pressured into giving them up. West of Gettysburg, soldiers threatened to torch houses that held "contraband."[41]

Fannie Buehler discovered the limits of loyalty. Like other white residents of Gettysburg, Buehler had counted on black workers to carry her through the crisis. She had credibility too, among the black community. She occasionally attended the AME church, and her husband David was a "black Republican"—Lincoln's kind. When a Confederate invasion seemed imminent, and it was clear that her husband might evacuate, Fannie tried to hold on to her domestic help. They had other intentions, however. One of them left in early June "from fear" of abduction. But the other, Buehler said, "I thought I had captured, for she promised to stand by me, and I promised to protect her, yet when she saw the Rebels she fled I know not whither, as I never saw her afterwards." Some of these black residents, therefore, faced two sorts of capture— one by armed Confederate hunters, and the other by families they knew and worked for, and whose pleas and needs had to be weighed against the threat to their own freedom.[42]

While Fannie Buehler could not persuade the African American girls who worked for her to stay, other employers convinced, coerced, or "captured" more successfully. A white farmer who employed a black laborer named "Isaac" grew tired of leaving Gettysburg with every report of a raid. At the end of June 1863, he was warned yet again of an invasion, but he decided to remain at home, with his employee. "We won't run no more," he said to Isaac. And Isaac stayed. So did a twenty-year-old "servantmaid" who worked for a white woman with two small children. And at the Globe Hotel, black help was also kept on. Even as the first units of the Confederate army came into town on June 26th, even after they began playing "Dixie" and other "enemy" airs to the public from the town square, and even as men in gray combed the streets, black employees at the Globe Hotel worked into the night hiding hotel foodstuffs, and digging a trench in the garden to bury bottles of liquor.[43]

So on July first, when soldiers of both armies converged on Gettysburg and began to bloody each other in earnest, some African American residents were still around. The lucky ones—though luck was a relative term those days—became invisible. They blended into woods and hillsides, and tried to hide where no one, not even predatory soldiers, would think of looking. The man named Isaac, charged with hiding his employer's seven horses plus a wagon loaded with provisions and grain, found an old road in the woods. There he hid throughout the battle, "fearin'" and "tremblin'" as the artillery bellowed "continuous thunder" and as the woods filled with "black smoke." "We didn't have no feelin'," he said, "for shuttin' our eyes." One woman secreted herself in a church belfry, and another, during the heat of the fight on the first day, went down into a cellar and discovered she was the only dark-skinned person there. She concealed herself in a deep corner. Jack, the bowlegged man who could not run far or fast, found a haystack and, crawling beneath the fetid weight, stayed motionless and hungry for days. A man who knew him said he "almost starved."[44]

While a few men and women sought to blend into the Gettysburg landscape, others tried to avoid notice with another ploy. They drew perhaps on hard years of experience in slave country, where they had deceived overseers or owners. Instead of rendering themselves invisible, they made themselves undesirable. They were, according to one white observer, "at the shortest notice suddenly transformed into limping, halting, and apparently worthless specimens of humanity."[45]

The work asked of some black women during the Battle of Gettysburg brought them almost face-to-face with the enemy. In occupied areas of the borough, where Confederate soldiers sometimes offered a modicum of protection in exchange for cooked food, black women became vital to the negotiations. The two "servants" who were hidden beneath a porch and blocked in with stones were asked to come out at regular intervals and cook for Confederate soldiers. The family posted a guard to hide them when soldiers appeared, but as soon as they left "those colored people had plenty to do, cooking." At one meal, thirteen soldiers came inside to eat. The family attributed Confederate forbearance to the cooking. "No wonder," a son commented, "the men were good to us."[46]

The young "servantmaid" came close to disclosure several times. The battle drove her from house to house with her employer's family, and she dodged shells and soldiers both. In one house, she was so close to the shooting she could hear the action of guns. "We were inside the Rebel lines," she said, "and the soldiers were all the time running in and out of the house. You'd hear 'em load their guns—clicky-click, and push 'em out the windows and fire. We didn't know what they was goin' to do with us." Later on, she, too, was called on to cook for a sick Confederate officer, after a white resident had secured a promise of protection. Her fear of abduction was then compounded by complete fatigue. "We stayed up all night doin' nothin' but cook and bake for the Rebels," she explained, "By morning we were pretty near dead."[47]

For some black residents of Gettysburg, working to the point of exhaustion, hiding in trepidation, and taking flight from captors was the least of it. Some people had to defend themselves against seizure. On July first, most Confederate soldiers absorbed themselves with combat, engaging Federal troops and sending them retreating toward Cemetery Hill. But a few soldiers, it seems, had more on their minds than warfare against armed men, and they began to round up and take black civilians.

The "servantmaid" was nearly captured. Taking flight with her widowed employer and two children, the young woman crossed a field to find herself at a house swarming with Confederate soldiers. They stopped her, and turned to the white woman who was with her: "Hey, what you doin' with her?" they demanded. "She's got to go along with us." But her employer stood her ground. "You don't know what you're talkin' about," she retorted, and kept her nursemaid with her. The imperious mother was certainly aware of the double standard of army conduct. While her black nursemaid was eyed as seizable "contraband," she could stand up to a soldier because she was a genteel white woman, pleading for her "family." The Confederate high command, having exhorted its invading soldiers to treat (white) Pennsylvania civilians with some respect, may have inadvertently protected some black women as well.[48]

But other African Americans in Gettysburg had no such intercessors. A boy in town would never forget what he says he witnessed on the first of July. He saw "a number of colored people" corralled together and marched away from the borough. They passed by his house "crying and moaning" and he could see his family's washerwoman among them. She called out to him, "Good-by; we are going back to slavery." But "Old Liz" escaped. Just in front of the Lutheran Church in Gettysburg, she took advantage of the chaos and the crowds of soldiers and civilians and bolted. She waited out the battle days hidden in the church, hungry and thirsty. After the Confederates had retreated she found the family and gave them the good news. "Thank God," she said, "I's alive yet."[49]

These witnesses leave us with more questions than answers. Were seizures in Gettysburg itself widespread or singular events? Does the paucity of witnesses in and around the borough suggest that there was little to observe or does it simply reflect the confusion and tumult of the battle? Even where there is a plethora of evidence, west of Gettysburg especially, uncertainties remain. One historian estimates that "at least several hundred" African Americans were taken from Pennsylvania. Where were these captives sent, what did they undergo, and for how long? We can tell from scraps of evidence, from references in military reports and prison records, from written recollections, and from poignant queries, that some people carried away from Pennsylvania were imprisoned in the South, some were sold to slave traders, and some were reclaimed by owners. We know, too, that some were lost to their families, for years.[50] But a more complete account of black civilians rounded up during the Gettysburg campaign—including the details of children strapped on horses, men tied in coffles, girls and women carried captive through the countryside, and including the details of black people who refused "to go over the river," and who might have suffered as one man did—may be forever gone.

The houses and shacks that stood on the north end of Cemetery Ridge on the third of July were wooden testaments to this experience. Their emptiness spoke to this story. To soldiers on the two opposing ridges that afternoon, and to the many, many people who honored them later, however, they were structures to take aim at, to take shelter behind, or to simply shoot past.

The shooting that day, or at least the signal that opened it, began at approximately one o'clock in the afternoon. Confederate and Union soldiers on either side of Abraham Brian's house, and all along the ridges south of Gettysburg, were jolted alert by the firing of two cannons. Within minutes, Confederate batteries on Seminary Ridge boomed murder, and batteries on Cemetery Ridge boomed back.[51]

One woman in Gettysburg challenged the world to ever produce such a horrible overpowering sound. Such cannonading, she said, "no one ever heard." "Nothing," she added, "can be compared to it," and no one "can form any idea of how terrible it is." Another woman sat under the sounds like "heavens and earth . . . crashing together" and suffered for the human damage that she imagined. With each spinning shell and each explosion, she said, "human beings were hurried, through excruciating pain, into another world." She almost wished that instead of seeing the misery that would follow, she "would be taken away" by God.[52]

In the borough, even a deaf man experienced the strength of the firing. He could feel the vibrations, and from his cellar post could tell the people he was with the severity of the hits. "That was a heavy one," he would sign with his fingers. Two women in another basement listened to the roar and tried to interpret it. "Their side!" they would shout out, when Confederate guns blasted. "Our side!" they would exclaim again, when Union guns responded. "Their side—our side! Their side—our side!" And when the Union guns stopped, they were disconsolate. "Oh," they said, "we've been stopped!" And when they resumed firing, they were elated. "There it is again!" But soon enough the Union guns stopped for real. No one in town knew it, but the men were holding their fire.[53]

Up on Cemetery Hill, an Eleventh Corps soldier could have sworn the artillery duel lasted an "age" rather than two hours. It had to be measured, he said, not in minutes, but in the "amount of nervous suffering and mental agony." There was no place to rest. If you lay on the ground with your hands over your ears, he explained, the ground would shake. If you lay on your back with your face to the sky, the sky was black with missiles and fragments. If you looked into the cemetery all you saw were streaks of fire that came your way and sulfurous smoke that coated you with soot. If you lifted your head above a rock wall toward the Confederate line, the cannonballs would take you down. You were drenched with sweat; your uniform was wet with your nerves. Yet this soldier was luckier than a friend of his who survived the bombardment. He was so shaken by the artillery that his teeth began to get loose, and, within the next few days, almost all of them fell out.[54]

Around three o'clock the cannonade stopped, and then the Confederate attack column—12,000 men—emerged from the woods. It stretched for nearly a mile. The flags were flying and the men were trimly neat, almost like a dress parade. Some of them, on the left, were pointed at Cemetery Hill. The Eleventh Corps soldier was alarmed: "We looked one another in the face, examined our muskets and said, 'Now we are in it for sure.'"[55]

But they were not. The soldiers on the Confederate left and right wheeled together, shrunk to half as long and twice as deep, and concentrated on some trees at the top of the ridge. The left of the Confederate line—under General Pettigrew—took fifteen minutes to get through the fields to the Emmitsburg Road. Under artillery and musketry fire from Federal troops, the men were momentarily caught up and delayed by sturdy farm fences, but they scrambled over them and moved up the shallow hill, some of them past Mag Palm's damaged house. They began to double-quick at the incline and pointed toward the trees, even as the fire intensified. Some attacking soldiers took shelter in Abraham Brian's barn. Union soldiers surrounded them. Just to the south, other Confederate troops, under General Pickett, roared up to Cemetery Ridge, even while being taken down like "nine pins." About a hundred Confederate men, led on foot by General Lewis Armistead, found a gap in the Union line at an angle, and pushed over a rock wall. Within minutes, however, they were enveloped by rifle fire. Fatal blasts from Union artillery toward the Confederate right helped finish the fight. The charge was over.[56]

Carl Schurz recognized its finality and the Union victory when he saw "huge swarms of men in utter disorder hurrying back the way they had come." Confederate troops went back and back, past the Emmitsburg Road, past Seminary Ridge, back to their camps. There was almost no one left in charge—they were either dead or injured, and the men did just what they wanted, which was to leave a scene of disaster. The area where the charge had concentrated was not just littered with bodies and wounded men; it was layered with them. Almost 9000 men were casualties in the charge and the repulse.[57]

After the Civil War ended, Pickett's Charge would be seen as the height of Confederate hopes. The point on the wall on Cemetery Ridge where soldiers briefly penetrated the Union line would become known as the High Water Mark. The Confederate veterans who returned to the site, the citizens they fought for, and the millions of Americans who later honored their memory would treasure that place and that moment in time. Like William Faulkner, they would try to imagine how it might have been otherwise, had the soldiers made it, and to picture, over and over, how close they came. They would repeat one word as a kind of mantra: *Almost.*

It has been harder over the years to hear the other people: the children who were breathing relief from under porches, the women blending into the black of cellars, the men struggling to breathe at the bottom of haystacks. Who were, perhaps, imagining how it might have been had the invading army succeeded. Who were also thinking, *Almost.*

And it is hardest of all to hear the voices of the men and the women and the children who were already in wagons or in coffles, being driven away from Pennsylvania, who were also certainly thinking, Almost. *Almost* free.

☆ PART THREE ☆

7

★

THE AFTERMATH

THERE ARE USUALLY TWO parts to a battle: the first part where soldiers lock each other in struggle, and the second part, the aftermath, where soldiers die slowly or heal, and where the damaged world is made whole. There is no clear end to this second stage—if in fact there is an end—and it is always of less account. The public hungers for details of mortal combat, but turns its back on stories of chronic pain and slow recovery, on military retreat or imprisonment, on ravaged battle sites, and on tired, used-up people. So, too, at Gettysburg, everything after the third of July was relegated to anticlimax.

Yet human struggle persisted at Gettysburg. Wounded soldiers fought for life, and borough women and visiting medical professionals fought alongside them. Just as there had been drama and urgency on the battlefield, with life at stake, there were now crises over shelter, sustenance, and treatment, with life at stake. Soldiers who had displayed courage under fire now displayed courage as life ebbed away. And women who had just endured trauma of unbelievable magnitude now rose to a different, no less demanding, occasion.

There was not only curing and healing to do in Gettysburg; there was physical reconstruction. After the armies had marched away, and the press had panted after them, borough residents scrambled to make their houses, their streets, their farms, and their fields workable once more. Some of the hardest, most thankless tasks in the battle's wake fell to women and to the poor. Local and visiting African Americans were among those who coped with the battle's grimmest residue. And it was more than a matter of cleaning up. Gettysburg not only hosted a battle and coped with massive numbers of wounded men; it also staged a big commemoration ceremony the following November. Over the space of five months, this borough of 2400 residents dealt with tens of thousands of needy, anxious people. For a small town, it was a tall order.

145

The labor that these people performed throughout the summer and fall of 1863 would eventually be forgotten in the annals of Gettysburg, as the public came to believe in the "Battle" as a limited event featuring army combat. Before this civilian toil was generally dismissed, however, it briefly attracted the attention of the press. In a wave of attacks distinctly reminiscent of the aftermath of Chancellorsville, a number of journalists sharply criticized Gettysburg citizens for their behavior in the invasion. New York newspapers, which led the fault-finding, made it very clear that, as hard as some people had worked, others had simply not measured up. The criticism not only exposed reigning ideas about ideal civilian behavior but also revealed political and economic prejudice. And ethnic intolerance. Many of the attacks centered on Gettysburg's "Dutch" population. After the Battle of Chancellorsville, national newspapers had targeted German-American soldiers. Now they went after immigrant residents. These people, it seems, just couldn't win.

IT BEGGARED ALL DESCRIPTION

The aftermath of the Battle of Gettysburg followed the repulse of Pickett's Charge on July 3rd, when General Meade decided he did not have the resources to launch a quick counterattack, and when General Lee made the decision that he needed to move his army back to Virginia as soon as he could. Lee stayed up late that night planning his retreat, and early the next day, a rainy 4th of July, he put it in motion. He sent ambulances and wagons of equipment out before the infantry—seventeen miles of them, according to one witness. He also sent a wagon train of loot—a "train of plunder"—that General Ewell had captured in his raiding. Somewhere in this massive snake of soldiers were nine white civilian men from the Gettysburg area, including government officials, men accused of spying, and men who had simply looked suspicious. And, unless they had already been driven back into slave country, somewhere amid this defeated army were captured African Americans.[1]

The Confederates also marched away thousands of military prisoners of war, many of them soldiers of the Eleventh Corps of the Army of the Potomac, captured on the first day of July. Among the prisoners were Adam Muenzenberger and his two friends from Wisconsin, and Bernhard Domschcke, the anti-slavery editor from Milwaukee—a captain in Muenzenberger's regiment. Many of these men held out hope that they would be exchanged or that the battle had been so decisive that it would end the war. They prayed, too, that the Union army would attack the Confederate army on its withdrawal from Gettysburg and "free us." This was their hope, Domschcke said, but he knew it was "a grasp at a straw."[2]

The prisoners' prayers were partly realized. General Meade's army did move out of the borough to pursue General Lee. Pursuit, however, may be too energetic a word to describe the army's cautious, awkward trailing of the enemy. The chase was marred by everything from the wet weather, to the relatively expeditious maneuvering of Lee, to Meade's misjudgments. The Eleventh Corps pulled away from Cemetery Hill on the 5th of July, ordered to march south. Many of its soldiers were shoeless, most were hungry, and all were exhausted. Otis Howard was utterly drained. He was, he wrote home, "much worn," "fatigued," and "pretty well tired out." He "longed for rest." At the same time, Howard thought they were—hoped they were—about to fight Lee's army again. They would catch the Confederates before they got across the Potomac. "We must have one more trial," he wrote Lizzie in Maine. "God grant us success in this next battle." But it did not happen. On the night of July 12th, after they had closed in on Lee near the river, Meade convened his corps commanders to discuss the wisdom of an attack. Howard voted to attack. Most of the others thought the time was not right. They waited through the next day, which proved to be one day too long. Lee crossed the Potomac near Williamsport, Maryland, on the night of July 13th. "The enemy has got away from us again," Howard wrote home.[3] The invasion, the battle, the retreat, the pursuit, were finished.

In Gettysburg, the news of the withdrawal came uncertainly at first, and relief rose in increments. Some residents suspected the enemy's retreat when they heard whispered orders outside their front doors, or saw soldiers being prodded awake. But they believed it for sure when they watched soldiers leave en masse, not by dozens or hundreds, but mile after mile after mile. One woman in town had never seen "such a going sight," as the long army and its wagon train weaved its way through the western hills.[4]

The 4th of July was almost liberation day, but not quite. A parade of Union troops ignored the rain and marched down in triumph through the borough, cheering residents with their fife and drum. People exchanged greetings and prayers. The Confederate army still clung to some of its positions on Seminary Ridge through the day, however, and sharpshooters harassed targets in town.[5]

By the 5th of July, people began to breathe more freely. For a few residents, though, celebration was too much to ask. They were "too sad" or worn out. Harriet Bayly was spent. "When it was all over and the last one of the enemy had gone the feeling of relief was great," Harriet said, "but I was too tired to enjoy it." "For weeks," she explained, "I wanted to do nothing but sleep."[6] Nobody commented publicly on the emotions at Georgia McClellan's house, but nobody needed to. It was easy to imagine Georgia's raw feelings when her sister

Jennie was wrapped for burial in a childhood quilt; or her mother's state of mind when she was asked to bake the bread that Jennie had begun but never finished; or the family's grief as it gathered on July 4th to deposit Jennie in a "hole in the garden." Some of the mourners could still see the signs of her fatal labor—the place where the bullet had penetrated her chest; the dough dried on her hands; the flour still whitening her clothes. Georgia McClellan may have indulged her suffering then, but soon afterward she turned to other people's pain. The next week, she handed her baby to her mother and walked down to the courthouse to help the wounded.[7]

Georgia McClellan's willingness to part with a newborn baby to work with injured soldiers speaks to the critical exigencies of the aftermath. The scene in field hospitals, in churches, sheds, barns, parlors, and bedrooms represented trauma at its most urgent and horrific. And there were not only human bodies to heal in Gettysburg, of course; there was the place itself. The battle's cyclone had lifted a neat and ordered town and left behind a twisted and gory shambles. Evergreen Cemetery, the pride of the borough, was a wreck. The "city of the dead" was littered with the detritus of the army and the remains of the fight—shot and shell had scattered everywhere, smashing iron railings and ornaments. General Howard had tried to protect tombstones, but he could do nothing about the battle soot. Or the force of the violence. A marble lamb lay on a broken gun carriage, where it had been flung by a blast. People did not mention urine or excrement, but it was there nonetheless—the sharp smells of Howard's men mingling with the scent of summer flowers.[8]

The desolation went beyond Cemetery Hill to every barn and house, every yard and garden, every orchard and every crop in the armies' paths. Some would say the destruction carried for five or six miles—that was how far the pillaged houses and damaged property extended. Harriet Bayly believed "that at least twenty miles of country lying close around the town were taken up by the manifold and murderous agents of the fight: men, horses, cannon, wagons, ambulances and hospitals." Still other observers would say it was nothing less than "forty square miles." Most people did not argue about the parameters of the damage, but insisted that its horror was what mattered. One observer claimed that Gettysburg during the first two weeks of July "beggar[ed] description."[9]

Symptomatic of the disorder were fenceless fields. Rock walls had gone into breastworks, fence rails into fortifications or fuel. After the battle, said one resident, fence posts stood lonely "here and there . . . like sentinels on guard." With no enclosures, animals of all kinds—sheep, cows, horses, and most of all hogs—roamed the countryside, rooting up and feeding on bodies, getting into gardens and crops. People had depended on these animals. They represented their food, their daily milk, their harvests, and their conveyances. Some of them had been family pets.[10] One boy remembered how his "old cow that had been in the family for years" had disappeared during the battle. He had seen sure signs—cow hides and cow heads littering the fields—that she was gone for good. But at dinnertime one night in July, the family heard a "bellowing" in the street. "There stood our dear old cow," the boy remembered. She had bullet holes in her neck and side, but had survived. "She looked," he added, "about as happy as it is possible for a cow to look at being home again."[11]

Gettysburg residents lived among ruins, and they went hungry. One family came home and found its fat hogs had become nothing more than scattered pigs' feet. Another woman fed her family of eight a quart of beans. For the first few days after the battle, the people of the borough and the wounded men that were now their neighbors and housemates had little to eat. Only when trains were back in service, and when farmers from the uninjured countryside made their way to the town square, and when goods from charity groups worked their way into kitchens and onto cookstoves, could people actually make a decent meal. It is a wonder, of course, that residents could muster any hunger. They lived under a blanket of fly-filled and fetid air produced by 8000 dead men, 5000 putrifying horses and mules, and mounds of army refuse. They lived, too, with the fear that emanating from this rot were fatal gasses, ready to carry them away as surely as soldiers' bullets. They closed their windows, then, and encased themselves in stultifying heat. They had heard what might happen if they exposed themselves to the foul air. One set of visitors "from a pure atmosphere" had come to the borough after the battle. They breathed the local air, "were poisoned and went home and died."[12]

People held peppermint and pennyroyal oil to their faces when they did go out, and attempted to clean the place up. They spread disinfecting chloride of lime on the streets, whitening the dust, the mud, and the dried blood. They poured kerosene on the bodies of horses and mules, and added the acrid smell of cremation to the stench of decay. They could not reach all of the animals, though. Some of the horses were so close to houses or fruit trees that homeowners had to leave them to rot, their gaping stomachs open to predators, their leathered skin tight over their ribs, their teeth protruding in what appeared to be agonal pain.[13]

And yet, after a few days, some residents adjusted to the horror. One woman and her sister managed to walk over the battlefield, indifferently noting parts of bodies protruding from the ground. The sister even picked up a dried hand and brought it home as a "relic." Her family agreed there was nothing "repulsive" about the hand, and "remarked on the smallness of the fingers." They determined that "it must have belonged to a very young soldier or a Southerner who had never worked with his hands." Other residents, though, did not tolerate the battle's human residue so easily. A farmer's son, nineteen at the time of the battle, would remember until old age the sight of a dead soldier hanging by his belt in a tree, and, worse, what he and his father discovered. It was another soldier, dead for four days at least, leaning against a tree. When the two men tried to move him to a grave, his "scalp slipped right off." "That was awful, wasn't it?" he said. A young woman stored another set of ghastly memories. After the battle, she began to be sick from some well water. When officials fished in the well, they pulled up a wrist and a thumb. "There was a lot of gaggin' done among 'em," she said. She knew of another well, too—"half-filled with dead soldiers." "Those," she added, "was rough times—rough times."[14]

The Battle of Gettysburg spared no one in the borough. It brought universal hardship and suffering, and it dislocated everyone's family and everyone's life. Dealing with the battle's human fallout, however, was work not universally shared. Most soldiers did not share it. They moved on, pursuing other soldiers, staging other celebrated battles. White civilian men and boys focused on rebuilding their workaday lives and family homes and farms. It was not "their" job to remedy injured men. One man, in fact, thinking back to the days in the battle's aftermath, remembered the field hospital that he had occasionally visited. "I do not remember what the attraction was," he commented.[15]

It was the women of Gettysburg who shouldered the work of nursing. They had sacrificed their sons, their brothers, their husbands to the cause, and done double work on the homefront, but now, after a battle had deposited over 20,000 injured men in their town, they were expected to do more. The caring of the wounded, as Fannie Buehler put it, was "women's work." "Our Union men" said Fannie, "had, with God's help, driven the enemy back from our homes in the North. It remained for us to do our part as nobly and as well."[16]

To be sure, these women would have plenty of help. Nuns came in from nearby Emmitsburg. Medical volunteers rode in on trains, including men and women from the Christian and Sanitary Commissions who set up operations first in the borough and then, by mid-July, in a nearby hospital camp. Parents and sisters and wives of injured men also arrived at Gettysburg to support their soldiers. Thousands of caretakers thus converged on Gettysburg to help out and to supervise, but women of the borough, from the moment the first bullet found its human mark to the cold days in November when men were finally taken away in trains, were vital to the endeavor.[17]

And that endeavor meant round-the-clock toil. One Gettysburg woman described battletime caretaking as "do or die" labor; others felt that they came perilously close to dying. Up day and night during the first days of July, they had cooked what little food or flour they had left. They had pumped water until their hands grew raw and baked bread until they blistered, and now they catered to the wounded, contended with other caregivers, and managed their own families and houses and farms. They slept fitfully. They became sick. A few became "chronic invalids." One woman reportedly exhausted herself baking 135 loaves of bread in an oven in her yard during the battle, even as minié balls flew around her. Another woman was said to have dressed 116 wounds in one afternoon, including nine limb stumps, with no surgeon to help or supervise. She also served twelve buckets of coffee and twelve buckets of soup. Within a week after the battle she was said to be "hovering between life and death in an epileptic state that left little hope of her recovery." Another woman had seemed "well" until she entered the post-battle fray, and six months later she was dead. A friend of hers explained that "she has declined since the battle, after which she worked harder than she should have done."[18]

Most women were not mortally injured by their efforts during and after the battle, of course, but nevertheless claimed to be close to collapse. Even Fannie Buehler, so proud of the "women's" work she and others had performed, acknowledged that she was pushed beyond what she wanted to do. "About the latter part of July," she wrote later, "my health broke down and the doctor said I must take a rest." She was not allowed to relax. "One day during this rest, an Orderly appeared at the door and begged I would take in his Colonel, who was mortally wounded, and could not live many weeks." Fannie tried to say no. "I begged him to find another place for his Colonel . . . for I did not feel quite strong enough for the undertaking." She was convinced otherwise, however, and "consented."[19] Civilian women like Fannie gave willingly of their flagging energy, but also saw themselves as casualties of the aftermath.

White women were not the only residents engaged in bringing order and health back to the borough. People of color also coped with the shambles around them. That is, if they had the wherewithal to return. Some African Americans, according to one historian, left the Gettysburg area for good. They had hurriedly bundled together their worldly goods and they had cleared out. All the accumulated years, the friends, the ties of their jobs, the community of the church, everything that had shaped their lives in the borderland became part of their past. Perhaps they made a home in the communities that took them in during the invasion, or in the cities where they had found work. Or possibly they kept moving. Refugees who had had an actual investment in Gettysburg, who had houses or land, were the ones who tended to return to the borough to deal with what the armies had left them.[20]

And what they had to deal with wasn't pretty. Although, as one black woman put it, "the place was rid out," and "we were free souls then," freedom from want and shelter were still at stake. Unlike white residents who had sometimes bartered cooking or conversation for household protection during the battle, most black property owners had been forced to leave their homes to the vagaries of combat. And, as it happened, many of their homes were either in the direct line of fire or in the sphere of occupation. The people who lived near Cemetery Hill probably had it worst. Abraham and Elizabeth Brian came home to a house that had been stripped of its siding and beaten by the bullets and shells of Pickett's Charge. Not far from the Brians, an African American widow named Sophia Devan lost doors, roofing, gardens, fences, beds, bedding, crockery, clocks, chairs, and tables. Unable to sleep, eat, or sit, she had to leave home again, and didn't come back for a year. The house where Mag Palm had lived had served the Union well—it had sheltered soldiers, and been blasted by artillery and infantry fire. It had been so much in the path of the Confederate assault column, in fact, that it was essentially destroyed. Abraham Brian, who later sought some compensation for damages, claimed the tenant house as a total loss.[21]

The black community went to work. Women and men rehabilitated their own homes and they helped white people repair theirs. Some women took temporary jobs with the army. Quartermaster records suggest that black women of the borough took in the blood-soaked, bullet-torn clothing left on the field and washed it, sewed it, and sent it back for more soldiers to fight in. Other women of color helped with the wounded. One newspaper correspondent noted how Lydia Smith, a "poor" African American woman, had borrowed a wagon and a horse and had brought clothing and food down to Gettysburg's hospitals, where she distributed them personally. Some of her recipients were wounded Confederates. "This is quite a commentary," remarked the reporter, "upon Gen. Lee's army of kidnappers and horse thieves who came here and fell wounded in their bold attempt to kidnap and carry off these free people of color."[22]

Black men, some local and some employed from outside the borough, helped rebuild railroads. They also worked in kitchens at the hospitals. A nurse at a Sanitary Commission hospital near the terminus of the trains noted black men in a camp "working for the government on the railroad." She was struck by their prayer meetings, their singing, and the way they expressed kindness to their white visitors and to "Massa Lincoln." She was also struck by their destitution. "Very little care was taken of these poor men," she commented. The Sanitary Commission offered to help some of those who became sick, and one of the volunteer nurses took matters into her own hands, purchasing bright cloth and sewing handkerchiefs that were handed out after their prayer meeting. "When the distribution was over, each man tied his head up in his handkerchief, and sang one more hymn, thanking and blessing the white people."[23]

These white women were not only pleased to note black gratitude, but also black compliance—or they thought it was compliance. In Sanitary Commission kitchens, women felt that they "rather reigned" over black men who cooked huge kettles of soup and coffee "under our direction." The men may have seen things differently. They assisted with the cooking, but they made the kind of noise they wanted while they worked. They "sang at the tops of their voices all day," remarked the white volunteer, and their singing, in contrast to the cooking, was "not under our direction." And the songs they sang may have been distinctly ironic. One of them went "O darkies, hab you seen my massa?"[24]

If black men in hospital kitchens raised their voices, other African Americans who helped restore Gettysburg were less noticeable. Certainly the white press helped all people of color achieve a low profile by ignoring their concerns and activities, but the invisibility of black residents may also have reflected their relatively seamless re-entry into Gettysburg life. This stood in marked contrast to communities farther north, where the continued presence of refugees provoked white concern. Newspaper editors in Harrisburg, for example, admitted that refugees had been invaluable in preparing the city's defenses, but now insisted they threatened public safety. Even more disturbing was the fact that some of the men were still armed. "In the name of the public peace and order," cried a Democratic newspaper, "we ask the authorities why this is permitted?" Editors feared "riots and bloodshed." City police took action on July 9th. They "collected" 300 "contraband" refugees and put them on an afternoon train. "The removal of these negroes," asserted the paper, "is a wise measure." Black men remained in the city at their peril. Soldiers bayoneted one African American when he refused to unload freight cars for them. Another white soldier "deliberately" shot a sixteen-year-old black boy in the spine—he had been a fugitive slave who had labored on the city's fortifications.[25] Black civilians had been necessary for the defense of the capital but now that the crisis had passed, it was time for them to go. And if they did not leave, no one could guarantee their safety.

DIGGING SACRED GROUND

If there were usually two parts to a battle—fight and recovery—in Gettysburg there were three: fight, recovery, and remembrance. White women and black residents of the borough area not only took part in rebuilding after the battle; they also served as part of the workforce that helped sanctify and honor the dead. At the dedication of the Soldier's National Cemetery in November, Gettysburg once again played host to thousands of visitors and attracted a national audience. And, once again, a cast of local people made the event possible. And later, when the moment skyrocketed to fame, they disappeared from view.

The 19th of November 1863, the day that a retired congressman and an American president praised fallen Union soldiers and told the world what the Battle of Gettysburg signified, would ultimately be known for the president's three-minute speech. But "The Gettysburg Address," like the battle it honored, was actually an event of long duration, involving women and men in some of the grisliest work imaginable. The procession, the prayers, and the speakers on that autumn day would recognize soldiers who had fought and died four months earlier, and who had been neatly buried. But before they became the honored dead they had been the awful dead—decayed, bloated, partially buried. The effort to dignify the Union dead had begun in the middle of the battle itself, when soldiers, army prisoners, and borough residents sought to cover bodies and, if they could and if they knew, to identify them.

Up on Cemetery Hill this work had begun when Elizabeth Thorn and her father, John Möser, had walked home after the battle. Even before they had reached their shattered gatehouse, Thorn said, the president of Evergreen Cemetery met them and tried to hurry them along. "There is more work for you than you are able to do," he announced. It was an understatement. Under the blanket of "foul air," Thorn, burdened by pregnancy, began the grim work. She and her father measured off and dug close to a hundred graves, in order to give some soldiers a cemetery home.[26]

The grave-digging left its mark. "You may know how I felt," Thorn said, "my husband in the army, my father an aged man." Desperate for help, she telegraphed friends to come and assist her, and told them she would pay. Two arrived. One immediately got "deathly sick and left"; the other "went away very sick" after five days. Back again with just her father, working "harder" than ever, and poorer, too, after paying her helpers' wages, Elizabeth Thorn was driven by "only excitement." Later on, she would look back on these trials and believe she never recovered from them. "From that time on," Thorn said, her own health failed, and her "dear little baby," born the following fall, "was not very strong." "Those hard days," she said, "always told on my life."[27]

Elizabeth Thorn helped put soldiers into the ground. A black man named Basil Biggs helped take soldiers out. It was in July, not long after the battle, that town leaders in Gettysburg came up with the idea that there should be a place where dead Union soldiers could, as the governor later put it, be "honorably interred." They argued extensively about whether that place should use Evergreen

Cemetery land and be managed by the local officials or whether it should be something quite distinct. The independents won. It would be a separate cemetery, dedicated to the Union dead, run by the states whose men had fought at the battle. It would be professionally designed and ceremonially consecrated. And it would involve moving a lot of soldiers. Bodies of Union soldiers lay all over Gettysburg, some carefully buried, others lying helter-skelter under fields, under leaves, and in the woods.[28]

The man who got the job of moving the remains bid a little over a dollar and a half per body. His disinterment team included a number of black laborers, forty-four-year-old Basil Biggs among them. Biggs hadn't lived long in Pennsylvania. He had moved his family from Maryland five years earlier for the sake of his children's schooling. But he had already made a name for himself as an enterprising farmer and energetic "agent" of the Underground Railroad. He had known where to send his family when Lee entered Pennsylvania, and found them safe passage to a place up near the Susquehanna River. But as savvy as he was, he almost missed saving himself. When Confederate cavalry penetrated the Borough of Gettysburg to the west, Biggs emerged on a borrowed horse on the east of town and fled toward York. He returned to find his rented farm had been used as a Confederate hospital and it had been wrecked. Everything he owned, from his cows and pigs, to his growing wheat and oats, to his carpets, beds, and chairs, to his jams and jellies, had been eaten up, beat up, or taken away. Which is probably why he took a job handling dead men.[29]

By November 19, 1863, when Edward Everett and Abraham Lincoln spoke to the throngs at Gettysburg, Basil Biggs and company had reburied close to a thousand men. They would not finish their work—which amounted to more than 3500 corpses—until the middle of March 1864, four months after the visiting dignitaries had sanctified the ground.[30]

The reburial work moved decorously. The men picked up coffins at the railway station, brought them to the original burial site, and, under the supervision of a man named Samuel Weaver, took their time to inspect and remove the remains. Biggs and another man then used their horse teams to take the coffins to the new cemetery for reburial. They found soldiers everywhere, in every condition. Some of them were in trenches, side by side. Some of them had been deposited in clay, or in wet soil, and still looked like men. Others— particularly those who had been buried in sandy soil—were nearly gone. The bodies of men who had fought north of town on the first day—mostly First and Eleventh Corps soldiers—had disintegrated. That battlefield had fallen early on into Confederate hands. When the first burial squads got to them on Monday, July 6th, the men were already unrecognizable. And when Basil Biggs and other workers found them months later, they were nothing but bones.[31]

Samuel Weaver's team did more than move bodies and dirt. It sometimes succeeded in comforting the bereaved. The men not only unearthed corpses, clothes, and blankets, but personal belongings the soldiers had carried: tiny diaries, and letters and Testaments—all too precious, it seems, to have been left behind in the headlong rush. They also found combs, mirrors, and money, and knives, pipes, and many pencils. What were soldiers doing with pencils? Capturing a moment amid the anguished waiting? Preparing to send a note home if they were badly wounded? The team also found photographs of young women, mostly ambrotypes. All of these were vital clues that helped match the unknown to names. "Words would fail to describe," wrote one Gettysburg resident, "the grateful relief that this work has brought to many a sorrowing household!"[32]

Thanks to the efforts of photographers, it is possible to picture the men at their melancholy labor. A cameraman caught up with the disinterment squad in nearby Hanover, Pennsylvania, unearthing men there. We can see two workers, perhaps Basil Biggs himself, holding the remains of a soldier. Samuel Weaver takes notes. The photograph reveals particulars of the job—it tells us what sorts of tools the men used, what they wore, and what sort of person was assigned what part of the dirty work. What it does not tell us, of course, is what these men did with their emotions as they sorted through people— whether they grew inured to the dead and learned to work mechanically, or whether the smell and the sight of humans turned from flesh to dust exacted a lasting psychological toll."[33]

Men like Basil Biggs and Samuel Weaver made the dedication of the Soldier's National Cemetery possible. So did women like Elizabeth Thorn and her father, who helped transform the ruins of Evergreen Cemetery, where the dignitaries spoke, into a place of order. So did the men who rebuilt the railroad after the battle, allowing visitors to ride to the site. And, as the date for the cemetery dedication drew close, other women and men moved into action, decorating the borough, organizing the ceremony, readying accommodations. Practically every resident, no matter how well-to-do, had a part to play. Prominent white women were not permitted to walk or ride in the procession, but they were offered good seats near the speaker's stand, and they were expected to be generous hosts. The wife of a local bank officer was told to plan dinner for the vice president of the United States, the governor of Maine, and the secretary of the navy. None of these men showed up, but the late General John Reynolds' brother did come to eat "turkey, plum pudding, peaches, pickels, sweet potatoes, onions, apples." This young woman had the money to host distinguished visitors, but she did not do her entertaining alone. Invisible to almost everyone at Gettysburg's momentous occasion were the black women who worked behind the scenes to cook the turkeys, shake out the rugs, wash the floors, watch the babies, steam the puddings. This woman acknowledged to her mother how she survived the whirlwind of the Gettysburg Address: "I got a colored woman to come and help for two days."[34]

CIVILIAN SACRIFICE:
SHADES OF CHANCELLORSVILLE

It is likely that most of the borough residents who endured or supported Gettysburg's massive events in 1863 did not expect public acknowledgment of their work. But it is also likely that they did not expect to be criticized for it. Barely had battlefield blood been washed away, however, before Gettysburg civilians faced a barrage of condemnation for the way they had handled themselves in the crisis. They were told they were mercenary; that they were unpatriotic; that they were unchivalrous. The reasons for such harsh attacks on civilians who had been so obviously traumatized are many, but it is evident in the language of some of the attackers that Gettysburg was considered a hotbed of "Dutchness," a center of German selfishness and ignorance. Two months earlier, German-American soldiers had felt the cold disdain of the Anglo-American public. Now immigrant civilians, and those who were lumped in with immigrant civilians, felt it too.

The press weighed in on civilian comportment and delivered its first un-flattering judgments by the second week of July. New York papers led the charge, with comments that Gettysburg inhabitants had been stingy and petty. Lorenzo Crounse, of the *New York Times,* asserted that the people of Gettysburg had served in the battle with "craven-hearted meanness," and that they were decidedly "unpatriotic." His accusations, which he repeated again and again, were "fully substantiated": The borough's residents had hurriedly produced claims on the army, and hesitated in giving over goods. They had demanded money for rails that were used for campfires. They had charged exorbitant prices for bread and milk. Crounse's indictment was reprinted widely in national newspapers and echoed by other angry witnesses. One man alleged that Gettysburg people were "some of the most intensely mean persons . . . that the world produces." He recalled how one resident, for instance, who demanded compensation because four bricks had been knocked off his chimney during an artillery barrage. A surgeon on the field likewise asserted that he was not given bread or crackers until the baker had assurances that he would be paid. An artillery officer with the Union army reported that residents with complaints came to him "in shoals."[35]

Gettysburg attackers did not level accusations of stinginess and disloyalty in any arbitrary way. They connected the borough's failings to misguided politics and to ethnic descent. The *New York Times* suggested that uncharitable borough residents had been ambivalent about President Lincoln (he had, in fact, won the borough vote, but barely) and pointed out that Adams County bordered "Copperhead" York County, allegedly full of Southern sympathizers. More emphatically, critics charged that Gettysburg's avarice was tied to its German-American population, "known" for its disloyalty and cowardice. It was certainly no accident that Lorenzo Crounse, the reporter who let loose the reports about Gettysburg's "miserliness," was one of the men who had publicly accused German Americans of "unsoldierly" behavior at Chancellorsville.[36]

Not only did reporters contribute to negative sentiment, but medical personnel also published comments about Gettysburg's Germans. One hospital worker described local farmers as "evil beasts." Native-born soldiers, both Confederate and Union, sometimes added their opinions to the ethnic poison. Their remarks, occasionally picked up by the press, often mixed in gender rebukes. They described German women and girls as coarse, "hard featured," and ungenerous. One soldier complained that he was charged a dollar for a gallon of milk from a German woman who was "dumpy"; others bemoaned extravagant prices set for bread, sausage, and pies. One national news magazine picked up the complaints and printed a cartoon that depicted a Pennsylvania German selling Susquehanna water for six cents a glass.[37]

The public attacks on the residents of Gettysburg were full of falsehoods, but there was more to the charges than bigoted spite. Nearly half of Adams County people were of German descent, and historians have suggested that many of these people were Democrats who were "lukewarm" about the war. They argue that many Pennsylvania "Dutch" from southern Pennsylvania did not leap to enlist in the Union army, or jump to Governor Curtin's call for emergency volunteers. They were not actively disloyal—emergency troops ultimately contained a good percentage of these Germans—but they were not actively committed to Lincoln's war either. Their large numbers made the relationship between them and non-German Republicans both intense and mean.[38]

Political divisions tied to ethnic tensions may have provoked the unhappy dynamics of Gettysburg's aftermath. So probably did issues of wealth and poverty. And here evidence leads directly to the Evergreen Cemetery gatehouse, and to the family of Elizabeth Thorn. Thorn, her parents, and her children had returned to Gettysburg on Tuesday, July 7th, to find the gatehouse, inside and out, in ruins, and everything surrounded by a deep stink. Seventeen men had been buried in her garden, and thirty-four horses lay rotting in fields nearby, smelling "awful." Her food was gone, too—her garden stripped, her pigs eaten, her beehives broken and robbed of honey, her chickens reduced to a suggestion of feathers. She had also seen some of her furniture on wagons, wheeling away with the Union army. What she had left was a windowless house and featherbeds "from the old country" that were "full of blood and mud." They had been stained, she heard, by six amputated legs.[39]

When she wasn't digging graves in the cemetery, Elizabeth Thorn tried to cope with this disaster. She scrubbed her linens, but in the end the battle blood won, and she threw her bedding away. Her clothing had disappeared, too, and she was forced to wear one heavy dress for weeks. Her family slept in a tent. Sometimes, it was just too much, and one day she sought some help. Seeing a Union officer riding by, she called his attention to her ruined bedding, and asked him if there was any help for civilians like herself. She wondered if she "would ever get any pay for things spoiled like this." She explained that the family's bedclothes were destroyed. The officer had one word for her, spoken "in a very short way." "No!" he said.[40]

Her father, John Möser, was willing to ask, too. On July 2nd, presumably when Union troops were actively engaged on the southern end of Cemetery Ridge, General Howard, occupying Cemetery Hill, was handed a note from Möser protesting the "occupation of this cimetry Ground and the destruction of my private property by your Army." The author, one "John Moeser, Sexton," described his losses as 5000 pounds of hay, $25 worth of grass, 25 baskets of potatoes, $15 worth of "sundry greens," and a milk cow. He was, he said, "a poor man."[41]

Möser had seen his family suffer enough to ask a busy general in the middle of a deadly battle for some help. There had to be some limits, he believed, to what a family could be forced to give up. But Möser did not get the response he sought. Instead he got, or rather the town got, huge publicity. Stories about his note spread quickly, and his request became a lightning rod for accusations and rebuttals about Gettysburg's loyalty and patriotism.[42]

Why had John Möser sent the note? Was this politics again? Was Möser, unlike his son-in-law Peter Thorn, a Democrat who had had enough of this long war? Did his German-ness have something to do with it? Maybe he was aware of the controversy that swirled around Howard's Eleventh Corps. Maybe he knew what the German press had been saying about General Howard since Chancellorsville—that the general was willing to submit his men, but not himself, to humiliation, and that he had sacrificed his "foreign" soldiers. Perhaps Möser was speaking for his family in requesting some compensation, but perhaps he was also speaking on behalf of German Americans everywhere.

Most likely what compelled Elizabeth Thorn's father to write the note was just what he said motivated him: destitution. Möser had made it clear that he was a poor man. His plea thus points to an important dimension of civilian contribution in wartime. The extent to which people could "serve" in a battle or aftermath, and the extent to which they would be credited or censured for such service, depended not only on who they were, but on how much they could bear to lose. (The two went hand in hand, of course—some of the poorest people in town were immigrants.) Sacrifice was easiest for those who could afford it. Some families had the resources to rebuild their homes and businesses quickly and the wherewithal to give food, farm animals, and belongings to the armies. Some residents also had the time and the energy to take care of the sick and the injured. People of relative wealth or comfort or position were able to be very "patriotic."

Fannie Buehler did not consider herself wealthy, but she was in a better position than others to give generously of her time and property. She was the wife of a "prominent politician" who was also a lawyer and newspaper editor. Fannie worked selflessly in the battle and during the aftermath, taking in soldiers and nursing and feeding injured men. Fannie also "charged no one for anything they ate or drank, or for any service rendered during this fearful summer." Her sacrifice was real and her exhaustion and her physical pain were measurable. But Fannie's generosity was made tolerable in part by the fact that "there was no lack of provisions in our home"; in fact, she had a pantry and cellar full of hams, flour, butter, coffee, sugar, and vegetables. She had protected her linens and bedding and her "best clothes" by arranging to send them away in a railway car. She had a third floor that could be given over entirely to one wounded officer. She also, of course, was white, and had been able to deal with intruding Confederates by appearing, as she had put it, "very bold." And she did it all without thinking of compensation. Fannie was charitable in part because she believed wholeheartedly in the cause and in what women should give, but also because she could afford to be.[43]

Accusations against Gettysburg and Adams County civilians did not die in 1863; they surfaced occasionally in the years to follow. In 1865, a nationally known reporter for the *Atlantic Monthly* reminded his reading audience that German farmers in the Gettysburg area "did not gain much credit either for courage or patriotism at that time." He specifically criticized one German woman who expressed regret over losing her food, fences, bedding, fields, orchards, and wells. "This poor woman's entire interest in the great battle," he wrote, was "centred in her own losses. That the country lost or gained she did not know nor care, never having once thought of that side of the question." Rich or poor, this reporter suggested, Gettysburg folk had been either with the Union, or against it.[44]

From the beginning, Gettysburg had had its defenders. Within two weeks of the battle a group of clergymen attending the wounded countered the "slanderous and libelous tirade" of *The New York Times*. The men did not defend the rights of poor people to request help from the army; instead, they denied the reports. Of citizens who might have rushed to the army with claims for their losses, they said, "we know nothing." They said they had seen first-hand how grateful Gettysburg residents were to the Union army, and how they had extended themselves, and had "sacrificed their all." These clergy were unable to convince *The New York Times*. "Nobody doubts," responded Lorenzo Crounse, that "the people of Adams County are doing all that their illiberal definition of the term 'patriotism' will allow. . . . But it will take the statements of even more than twenty clergymen to eradicate the experiences and the undeniable facts which came to my knowledge in Gettysburg."[45]

Major General Oliver Otis Howard actually helped still the powerful invective against Gettysburg. A few weeks after the battle, Howard was asked by the president of Evergreen Cemetery to deny that he had ever received a request for payment from a borough resident. The president, David McConaughy (who was also the Thorns' employer), wanted to end the slander. He reminded Howard that he himself had never complained about the "injuries to the Cemetery." He had, in fact, acted "as if wholly unconscious of them—regarding them as nothing as compared with the glorious achievements of our army and the blood with which our brave soldiers consecrated its sod." And he wanted Howard to vindicate the town.[46]

It seems that General Howard tried to do so. According to McConaughy in a letter written decades later, the general set the record straight. He made it clear that the "schedule of the losses of Mrs Thorn" had been "magnified" and he downplayed the assertion that residents had issued demands even before the "Cries of the Wounded had Ceased & the smoke floated from the Field of Battle."[47]

Howard thus quieted the critics. So did Lorenzo Crounse, who eventually retracted his comments. Both men calmed the situation, though, less by sympathizing with aggrieved civilians than by asserting that most Gettysburg people had been large-hearted. They left unanswered the questions that beleaguered residents like the Thorns had brought up themselves. What was a civilian's duty in a battle that went beyond conventional bounds? How were families caught in the crossfire supposed to give if they had little to give—if their strength and their resources were nearly gone? And they left unanswered the question that had hovered over both of the big eastern battles of 1863: When would German immigrants be able to elicit more praise than reproach from the American public?

In the years that followed the Civil War, the borough's "flawed" comportment in the battle receded in popular memory, as the borough itself slipped from historical view. The uncontestable work that civilians did to sustain the armies in combat, to rehabilitate soldiers, to repair the town, to host multitudes, became nothing more than a murmur behind the explosive story of men in combat. For much of the nineteenth and twentieth centuries, what people remembered about Gettysburg was what soldiers did for three days, not what civilians did—or did not do—for three days and for weeks and months beyond.[48]

8
* ** *

THE SEESAW OF HONOR; OR,

How the Pigpen Was Mightier than the Sword

TO SOLDIERS OF THE Eleventh Corps of the Army of the Potomac, the Battle of Gettysburg had been about more than stemming an invasion. It had been an opportunity to thwart popular prejudice and to gain admittance to that circle of men that the public revered almost more than anybody else, the circle of courageous soldiers. German-American troops had reveled in triumphant moments at Gettysburg, and shared in the general glory of the Union victory, but many of them realized soon enough that Pennsylvania in July would not undo Virginia in May. Some soldiers realized, too, that the army would never, ever, be the panacea they sought, that what opposed them was so pervasive and entrenched that it would take decades, not battles, to unseat it.

The trouble was, some men did not have decades. Within months, in fact, Corporal Adam Muenzenberger would be fighting for his life. Within years, General Alexander Schimmelfennig would be struggling for his. Major General Carl Schurz, on the other hand, would carry on his fight well beyond the war, and his search for military honor would continue to place him at odds with his equally long-lived corps commander, Oliver Otis Howard. Both men fought on a shared front, however. Not only did the two of them hope to open the league of courage to new sorts of soldiers; they also sought to open it to men of principle. Both of them believed that in this Civil War it was not physical means, but moral ends, that ultimately mattered.

GOOD-BYE TO THE "HUMBUG"
ADAM MUENZENBERGER

One widely accepted truth of military honor was that to gain and enjoy public respect, a man had to stay out of enemy hands. A soldier who died on the field garnered accolades; in fact, the Union men of Gettysburg who earned the highest praise were the battlefield dead. Men who recovered from their injuries—who were scarred, disabled, or dismembered—were also revered. Then there were the able-bodied men who survived the fight, who enjoyed public applause at least briefly, before they began to argue about which unit and which commander deserved the most credit. At the lower end of the ladder of honor, though, more pitied than esteemed, were the individuals who walked away from battle as prisoners. If the pinnacle of martial manhood was a soldier wielding a gun or a bayonet, the nadir had to have been a soldier stripped of his weapons, herded like a sad or angry animal, taunted by enemies.

And so Adam Muenzenberger, who had once fretted about misleading press reports, and about nativist hatred, and about feeling used, was now on a new road to disregard. And on a new road to physical misery. Suddenly, his priorities shifted. Although he may have still cared about how newspapers reported the work of Schurz's men, and how the "humbug" war played out, by the late summer of 1863 his battles had become elemental: He had to get out of prison and go home. He had to stay alive.

Muenzenberger began his fight for survival on the first of July at Gettysburg, the day he was captured. Many Eleventh Corps prisoners had spent the duration of the battle in a field, guarded and "sneered at" by Confederate soldiers. The lucky ones were given paltry food—in some cases a piece of raw meat, some flour and salt—and nothing to cook it with. Gettysburg's Harriet Bayly, walking back from the battlefields on July 2nd, passed by some of these men north of town. They "swarmed" around her and begged her to take letters for them. She gave them encouragement. They stood "every chance of getting off," she told them.[1]

As the battle progressed, prisoners vacillated between optimism and misery. They knew nothing about army successes or failures, and the thunderous sounds of guns that broke the silence on the third of July only disquieted them further. Prisoner Bernhard Domschcke, a captain in the 26th Wisconsin, commented that the noise, which no one could interpret, "doubled our suffering."[2]

Their unhappiness deepened with the realization that Union victory did not mean freedom, and that they were to march south with the Confederate army. We were being taken, said Domschcke, "away from the land of freedom, to the Hell of treason and barbarism—to Richmond." Once they began their march, Domschcke measured the trip into Southern hell by the expressions of women. On July 5th, women in Fairfield, Pennsylvania, distraught at the sight of thousands of blue-coated prisoners, stood in doorways and sobbed. The soldiers put on a brave face. "We'll soon be back," they said. Farther south, civilian demeanors grew harsh. As the prisoners marched through Maryland, a smiling

The only known extant photograph of Adam Muenzenberger, c. 1862. *Source: www.russscott.com/~rscott/ 26thwis/addmuen.htm.*

Carl Schurz, c. 1863. *Courtesy of Prints and Photographs Division, Library of Congress.*

Alexander Schimmelfennig, c. 1863.
*Courtesy of the United States Army
Military History Institute, Carlisle, PA.*

Oliver Otis Howard, early 1862.
(Howard's right arm was amputated as
the result of a battle injury in June, 1862.)
*Courtesy of Prints and Photographs Division,
Library of Congress.*

This woodshed, owned by the Garlach family of Gettysburg, allegedly served as the refuge of General Alexander Schimmelfennig during the Battle of Gettysburg. Carl Schurz referred to it as a pigsty. *Courtesy of the Adams County Historical Society.*

A view of Gettysburg from Seminary Ridge, August 1863. (Tyson Brothers photograph.) *Courtesy of the Adams County Historical Society, Gettysburg, PA.*

Elizabeth and Peter
Thorn, in the late 1850s.
Courtesy of Brian Kennell.

The Evergreen Cemetery Gatehouse, home of Elizabeth and Peter Thorn and family.
This photograph was taken shortly after the battle. *Courtesy of Brian Kennell.*

"BECAUSE EVERY MAN I ASKED WAS TOO COWARDLY TO COME!" SAID GENERAL HOWARD.

The public story of Elizabeth Thorn during the Battle of Gettysburg changed considerably over the years. In this selection from a 1937 cartoon, published in a Harrisburg paper, Thorn assists General O. O. Howard by pointing out to him local roads. Howard had asked men who were hiding in Thorn's cellar to help him out, but they had "refused to a man." Howard's right arm, which was amputated in 1862, is miraculously intact. *Source: The Harrisburg Evening News, May 28, 1937.*

Georgia Wade McClellan, left, her friend Maria Comfort, center, and her sister Jennie Wade, right, in a photograph taken in 1861. *From the Collections of the Rochester Museum & Science Center, Rochester, NY.*

Mag Palm posed in this photograph with her hands "bound," approximating the way she was tied up by kidnappers in 1858. *Courtesy of the Adams County Historical Society, Gettysburg, PA.*

Lloyd F. A. Watts.
Courtesy of Jean Odom.

This Brady photograph, taken within weeks of the battle, shows the house of Abraham and Elizabeth Brian. The Brian house, which still stands, is located on the northern end of Cemetery Ridge, near the apex of Pickett's Charge. *Courtesy of Prints and Photographs Division, Library of Congress.*

A reinterment team, likely including Gettysburg's Basil Biggs, exhumes a soldier in Hanover, PA. The soldier, who fought in the Gettysburg campaign, will be reburied in the Soldier's National Cemetery in Gettysburg. *Source: Encounter at Hanover: Prelude to Gettysburg* (Hanover Chamber of Commerce, 1963).

African American tourists at the Gettysburg battlefield. Postcard photograph, c. 1910. *Courtesy of Timothy H. Smith.*

The Ku Klux Klan gathers on the Gettysburg battlefield, 1925. *Courtesy of the Gettysburg National Military Park Archives.*

woman "shouted triumphantly" to their Confederate captors: "That is the way to bring them in." In Winchester, Virginia, "aristocratic" women surveyed the procession of prisoners from their verandas and "radiated joy."[3]

The soldiers carried their hope south through the Shenandoah Valley, but it diminished mile by mile. They heard mention of parole, but parole did not happen. They heard talk that they would be liberated, too, just as soon as Meade's army caught up to them. But then they were ferried across the swollen Potomac on flatboats, back into enemy country, and that hope was extinguished. Hungry and tired, some of them surviving on wheat kernels and green apples, they trudged once more through the damaged landscape of Virginia. They passed houses that seemed close to collapse, boarded-up stores and locked businesses, and women who, even if gloating, wore black and looked poor. In Staunton, Virginia, Union officers were put on trains to Richmond. Enlisted men like Adam Muenzenberger kept walking, 130 miles more.[4]

In Richmond, Bernhard Domschcke came to realize the depth and breadth of anti-immigrant prejudice. As an officer, Domschcke was housed in Libby Prison in Richmond, where he may have benefited from preferential treatment. Officers suffered from cold and hunger, but they occasionally sustained themselves with packages of tinned meats or dried fruits sent from home. They also kept up spirits with debating clubs, language classes, minstrel shows, and games of whist. But while the social world of this Richmond prison reaffirmed privilege, it continued to remind German Americans that education, wealth, and rank did not guarantee acceptance. Neither, apparently, did military victory. Americans had "venom" for the Germans at Libby, said Domschcke. They had learned at their "mother's knee an unshakable antipathy for Germans" and this hatred had expanded with the "false" reports of Chancellorsville. German-American prisoners had to endure a "hail" of invective, as disdainful native-born men sank their "teeth of scorn into the 'Dutchman.'" So much for the success of Gettysburg.[5]

At Belle Isle, where Adam Muenzenberger and other enlisted men were taken, German-American soldiers worried less about embedded nativism than simple survival. Belle Isle was an island prison, located at a curve in the James River, and moated by rapids. It was a barren, bleak place, known by the Northern press for its foul conditions. A visiting Union officer reported that he saw men sleeping in holes in the ground "like shallow graves," and prisoners with no pants, in "every state of destitution and misery." Even Richmond officials, who in 1863 governed over a city of unprecedented scarcity, called it the "most wretched place in town." Richmond papers outlined the dilemma as they saw it. They had "thirteen thousand Yankees" on their hands, who, "being naturally greedy, they eat like so many wolves or hyenas," and the city had to choose between the prisoners and "the wives and children of the soldiers in the field." The decision was not a difficult one, and the Yankees went hungry. So very hungry, in fact, that some of the men may have seized dogs to eat. "Belle Island, Richmond's prison for Yankees," claimed a local paper, "poses hazards for dogs, especially those in good flesh. The Yankees eat them."[6]

Rhetoric on the topic of prisons was notoriously hot during the Civil War, and Northern papers did their best to scandalize readers, particularly about Richmond. But had men like Adam Muenzenberger been able to tell a full tale, it is not clear that they would have been any less scathing. Unlike the officers of his corps, who tried to tolerate Richmond life with games or entertainment, Muenzenberger spent many of his prison days truly suffering. He had begun his Belle Isle life as brave and stalwart as ever, with his Wisconsin friends as his shield. He was, he wrote Barbara at the end of August, "hale and hearty," and he and his friends were all "pretty well accustomed to our trials and are resigned to our fate."[7]

Muenzenberger's prison letters were positive and calm, as his letters always were in dire times: after hearing that his children had died, and before a battle. At the same time, however, they suggested foreboding, because he omitted in them a long-standing ritual: He did not ask his wife about her teacup. Since he had been in the army, Adam Muenzenberger had faithfully repeated a request to Barbara. He had wanted her to examine her teacup. "What does your teacup say?" he had wondered on one occasion. "Please give me the news from the teacup and don't omit anything," he had requested at another time. Whether his wife was supposed to study the leaves, the swirling heat, or the tea itself is unclear, but it had become for them either a guide or a talisman. Once, at the end of May, he had asked her if she saw something certain and final. "Does the end come soon?" he had wondered. We do not know whether the soldier meant the end of the war or whether he referred more darkly to his own demise. And we do not know what Barbara Muenzenberger saw in her drink and whether she told him. All we know is that after Gettysburg, after he was marched south and locked up in Virginia, he never mentioned teacups to his wife again.[8]

During September, the prisoner who had been hale and hearty became a man whose life was thinning out. Muenzenberger wrote home that his clothes were "in tatters" and the food he received was "a little too much to starve on and not enough to live on." He was still eating meat—but so little, he said, his youngest child would go hungry on it. The soup he was served was flavored with dirt and flies. His blankets had been "taken away from us by the southerners," and he slept under a tent, on the bare ground. But he was still the man who could muster courage. "I hope," he wrote to his wife, "that you are not worrying about me too much."[9]

By the end of October, though, the cracks in his confidence grew deep. A good hometown friend, John Nachsteim, a fellow German taken at Gettysburg, was carried away to the prison hospital and was probably dead. Muenzenberger had not heard from home in months and, having lost two of his children already that year, did not dare count on the health of the others. He pleaded for news. "Write how my two little darlings are," he begged his wife, "whether or not they are alive." And he asked for help. "Pray for me," he urged. Barbara did pray. So did his seven-year-old daughter. So did his youngest son, who knew nothing more than how to lift his hands. And Barbara begged him, in return mail, to persevere. But in Richmond nobody trusted a language they could not translate, and her encouraging letters, written in German, were sent back to Wisconsin, unread.[10]

In the fall of 1863, the Northern public began to hear more and more about Union soldiers in Richmond. Journalists reported that prison officials had reduced rations. Surgeons who returned north spoke of seeing men covered in vermin and filth. Then, in November, some reporters witnessed the effects of prison life firsthand when they observed exchanged prisoners disembarking in Annapolis. The men, said a *New York Times* reporter, were "so attenuated and unstrung that they looked almost like so many running skeletons." The poet Walt Whitman had a similar response when he encountered prisoners just released from Belle Isle. "Can those be men?" he asked. "Are they not mummified dwindled corpses?"[11]

It was in that same month—November 1863—that Adam Muenzenberger—or the shadow of a man that passed for him—was admitted to the prison hospital. And on December third he died. His death certificate, penned in a Richmond hospital, listed diarrhea as the cause of mortality. But there was a second opinion, too. In penciled script, another hand echoed the soldier himself. He perished, it said, from "want of nourishment." If there is any sort of solace to be drawn from Muenzenberger's death, it is perhaps its timing. In the middle of February 1864, a new Confederate prison in Americus, Georgia, was completed. Designed to relieve the overcrowded misery at Belle Isle, it was said to have superior facilities and to be better able to feed its inmates. Soldiers would also be warmer than they were in winter in Virginia. On February 18th, the first 400 men were transported to the new prison. Andersonville, as it would be called, became synonymous with the Civil War's worst horrors.[12]

THE PIGPEN AND THE SWORD
ALEXANDER SCHIMMELFENNIG

Men like Adam Muenzenberger had hoped that Gettysburg would be the answer to Chancellorsville, that the public would hear of brave work in Pennsylvania and forget about fright in Virginia. Soldiers luckier than the Wisconsin soldier, who emerged from the battle free and intact, felt that they had done the job: They had held their ground tenaciously against superior forces on the first day; they had survived a punishing retreat; they had re-formed and been ready to fight. On July 2nd, they had helped repel a ferocious attack, and both infantrymen and cannoneers had held the Union position on Cemetery Hill. They had been firm and steady.[13]

Many reporters, it seems, agreed with them. In contrast to the disparaging way they spoke of Gettysburg civilians, many newspapermen gave German-American soldiers the benefit of the doubt. The *New York Times,* delighted by the victory in Pennsylvania, applauded the "Gallant Behavior of the Eleventh Army Corps." The effort to turn the corps' right wing on July first, the paper asserted, had "entirely failed." Furthermore, the Eleventh Corps had made a "gallant" charge on Longstreet's corps, capturing no less than a thousand prisoners, and General Howard had raised a rallying cry. "Remember Chancellorsville!" he had shouted, and immediately the men had "rushed into the fight like infuriated demons, and the whole line of the enemy gave way before them." By July 4th, correspondents had more accurate information. The Eleventh Corps still had fought well, that is, "most of it." By July 6th, the corps had only "partially" redeemed Chancellorsville because of the "considerable confusion" it created when it retired through town. But even though the *New York Times* modified its enthusiasm, it and other English-language newspapers credited Howard's soldiers with a strong performance. Reporters used words they had rarely applied to this set of men: "stalwart" and "gallant" and "furious." Their repulses were also "nobly" carried out; their retreats were in "good order."[14]

But if only it were that easy. Rising slowly but emphatically against the press's applause were veterans' voices of disapproval. Caught up in the seesaw of acclaim, soldiers who had fought next to German-American troops at Gettysburg were not going to allow honor to be directed away from themselves. First Corps veterans were especially emphatic and angry in this regard. Many of them blamed the German troops for what they saw as a precipitous retreat on July 1st that left them vulnerable to attack then (and to critique later). Native-born soldiers within the corps also went on the attack, just as they had after Chancellorsville. One soldier boasted to his mother that when German troops had run to safety during the Tigers' nighttime attack on July 2nd, he had managed to "welt" a "dutchman" with his sword. His mother wrote back that by slashing at the immigrant soldier he had done "good service." General Francis Barlow, criticized for recklessly exposing his troops at Gettysburg, again turned on his men. Writing to a friend, he complained that "these Dutch won't fight," and that "they ruin all with whom they come in contact." Barlow's feelings seem to have been widely shared. Men who were reassigned to the corps as reinforcements after Gettysburg balked. And when talk came of breaking up the corps in midsummer, hardly anybody objected. General Howard admitted to General-in-Chief Henry Halleck that sentiment ran so strong against his men that it was now nearly impossible to overcome "existing prejudices in this army against the Eleventh Corps." Carl Schurz concurred. Once again, he said, "the foreign legion" served as "a scapegoat."[15]

Sentiment against the Eleventh Corps was not only strong, but longlasting. Native-born soldiers had the public's ear through much of the nineteenth century, of course, especially as they began to publish their regimental histories and reminiscences. But it was not only soldiers who perpetuated a less-than-flattering picture of German-American troops. The Borough of Gettysburg became home to the "Schimmelfennig story" and local civilians not only passed on accounts of the general in hiding but offered tourists glimpses of what soon became a historic site: the pigpen.

The tale of Alexander Schimmelfennig's escape and hiding became lively sport for the local press almost as soon as he emerged on the 4th of July. One regional newspaper claimed that "it affords us pleasure to announce that [Schimmelfennig] is still on his taps," following his escape "by a dodge worthy of the sharpest Yankee." The paper further revealed that the general had disguised himself with someone else's coat—covering up his general's uniform— and that he had emerged when he heard "Yankee Doodle" being played; then "he thought it safe to come out." The paper quoted someone who facetiously compared Schimmelfennig with the German-American generals Louis Blenker and Franz Sigel. "Te Seekels un te Plenkers ish nudding," this man said, "Schimmelpfennigs te man[!]" Another paper threw Schimmelfennig's experiences into bathetic relief when it positioned its story of the German general next to a report about General Francis Barlow, who had so exposed himself on July 1st that he had been hit six times with musket balls.[16]

Newspaper reporters contributed to the Alexander Schimmelfennig myth, but to a large extent the soldier's story was "owned" by the Garlach family in Gettysburg, especially Catherine Garlach, who discovered the German-American soldier outside her house, and daughter Anna Garlach, age eighteen, who would retell the story later. The Garlachs felt affection for Schimmelfennig and proprietary of the soldier. He was evidently "their" general and they showed visitors "his" shed and culvert. And their stories gave listeners something to smile about. In published accounts at the turn of the century, the Garlachs described the "little general's" crafty hiding and his joyous release. Schimmelfennig, said the family, was greeted by his men with such enthusiasm that they were "ready to pick him up and hug him." Anna Garlach also sought to defend the soldier. "I have heard persons speak of cowardice when referring to General

Schimmelfennig during the battle days," she commented. "I was only a girl then but I could see nothing cowardly in what he did." She could see nothing cowardly, but perhaps her readers could. They could read the word coward three times in her first two paragraphs. They could picture, thanks to her, General Schimmelfennig running from the Confederates, and they could imagine him as he "hurriedly crawled out of sight" through a sewer culvert. They could also imagine her mother intrepidly braving Confederate occupiers to feed the general. And, finally, they could envision him emerging from his cramped space and scuttling away, "walking stiff and cramped like."[17]

Schimmelfennig's story, which helped paint the face of military cowardice at Gettysburg as "Dutch," was buoyed by other witness accounts of German Americans. These, too, stressed the timidity—usually the silly timidity—of immigrant civilians. They are companion pieces in a sense to the popular pictures of German civilian stinginess and disloyalty, and together they represent a vast set of images of German inadequacy at Gettysburg. Even though newspapers like the *New York Times* lauded the battle's immigrant soldiers, it could not compete with the array of reports, accounts, and folktales that diminished all people—military and civilian, women and men—of German descent.

The local Republican press jumped into action just two months after the battle with a front-page story that parodied a German-born Pennsylvanian who had been frightened by the armies. "Ven de Rebbels gum into de Walley, tudder time," this man allegedly remarked, "gimmeny cripes but we was scaret!" A visiting nurse added her two cents to the picture of Adams County "courage." In her published reminiscences of Gettysburg's aftermath, she recalled a "stupid old Dutchman" who, three weeks after the battle, went to the hospital to see the "rebels." The nurse in command asked him why he hadn't seen a rebel before. "Why didn't you take your gun," she asked, "and help to drive them out of town?" "A feller might'er got hit," he replied, to gales of laughter.[18]

Native-born civilians also volunteered immigrant stories. They drew amusing pictures of faint-hearted Germans, who, like African American runaways, cast the storytellers into bold relief. One borough resident recalled a funny "old dutchman" who had attached a rusty bayonet to a broomstick and challenged a Confederate soldier. "Stop rebel I'll shoot you," he said ineffectively. Another remembered a German man who had joined their household in a Gettysburg cellar on July 2nd. "To the amusement of all there," he sat on a barrelhead, and the top fell in. The assembled group pulled him out by his head. "We all laughed." Similar laughs were to be had over at Sadie Bushman's house when a German neighbor, frightened by shooting and shells, was heard to cry out, among other things, "Stop a' shootin still—when them guns belch it skeers us so bad in the cellar still; Ya! Ya! Stop a shootin' General Schimmel's funny boys!"[19]

Some Gettysburg civilians professed sincere appreciation for German-American troops during the battle. At the same time, they frequently praised these men for their sympathetic—even womanly—qualities, rather than for martial abilities. Harriet Bayly labored alongside a German surgeon when she tended injured soldiers on July second. He looked over her work and she in turn praised him for being "as gentle as a woman." In Fannie Buehler's house, two Eleventh Corps soldiers, an Irishman and a German, assisted her with household work. The men were especially helpful with Fannie's two-year-old boy, not to mention washing dishes, paring vegetables, and saying "funny things." Fannie recalled how the German even went on a reconnaissance mission—braving enemy lines—for baker's yeast.[20]

Civilian recollections of frightened and funny Germans, which were occasionally generated by people of earlier German descent,[21] helped bolster the Alexander Schimmelfennig story. There were other tales to be had of course. In the late nineteenth century, Eleventh Corps soldiers—including Generals Schurz and Howard—published accounts of brave immigrant work at Gettysburg and tried to temper the legend. And during his short lifetime, Schimmelfennig himself not only offered the public an alternative military record, but tried to write the history of the war (and certainly the Battle of Gettysburg) as he saw it.

Alexander Schimmelfennig had successfully requested a transfer away from the Eleventh Corps after Gettysburg, and he was sent to South Carolina. There he whittled away at Confederate strongholds around Charleston.[22] If pigpens and woodsheds did not have such appeal, Schimmelfennig might have been known for some of this later service. On February 18, 1865, Confederate troops evacuated Charleston, and General Schimmelfennig was the first Union general to enter the "seat of secession" with his troops. He accepted the city's surrender. He also commanded a quieter victory. On the first of July 1864, he led the 55th Massachusetts volunteer infantry, companion regiment to the legendary 54th, into its first combat action on James Island, South Carolina, where it captured Confederate guns. African American soldiers shouted "Remember Fort Pillow!" in triumph. It was a year to the day the German general had taken refuge in Gettysburg. The following winter, the same troops followed Schimmelfennig into Charleston to a chorus of "John Brown's Body," "Babylon Is Falling," and "The Battle Cry of Freedom."[23]

The German-born general, then, had a military record in the Civil War that offered the public plenty of material for positive narratives: He had been a successful and courageous soldier before Chancellorsville, and after Gettysburg he engaged in military actions with huge symbolic (and corrective) potential. Schimmelfennig hoped to add more to history than his personal record. He planned to publish an account that would, finally, set the story straight: a narrative of German Americans in the Civil War. He left South Carolina in April 1865 because of tuberculosis, and moved to a water-cure establishment near Reading, Pennsylvania, close to his family. And he began to write. But one day in mid-September—it was a Thursday, in the morning—the forty-one-year-old soldier was sitting in a chair, speaking to his wife, Sophie. He drank a glass of water, and put it down on a table next to him—and died. His lungs, a postmortem examination revealed, were almost entirely destroyed. Whatever happened to the manuscript that he was working on is unknown. It was never finished and never found.[24]

The German community closed ranks around the dead general and rallied in his honor. Schimmelfennig's funeral cortege, several city squares in length, featured a German brass band, marching veterans, and members of local German societies. As the procession passed, shopkeepers closed their doors and church bells pealed. Obituaries in the local press praised the general's bravery in revolutionary Germany, his enthusiasm for raising and commanding a regiment at the outbreak of the Civil War, and his participation in "some of the hardest fought battles of the war." They mentioned his historic moment in Charleston. At a meeting in New York the following month, German Americans also raised a glass to Schimmelfennig. They celebrated him for his "devotion to the cause of the Republic, and for his valour on freedom's battlefields." They talked about his "generous heart" and his "eminent abilities." They also mentioned his occupation of Charleston. No one said anything about Gettysburg, pigpens, or woodsheds.[25]

In the borough itself, however, the "pigpen" story had staying power. Long after German-American veterans had died and had taken with them testimony to strong battle performances, Schimmelfennig's refuge endured, continuing to remind the public of courage's ethnic limits. Even after the woodshed itself was removed, the site attracted visitors. And by the end of the twentieth century, borough tours had incorporated the general's story into their walks, and a historical marker identified his hiding place. Schimmelfennig's actions at Gettysburg, especially his "famous sty," were also featured in a locally popular song. By the year 2000, licensed battlefield guides concurred that the story of Schimmelfennig in hiding held "enduring fascination for the public, regardless of the facts."[26]

THE CHARACTER OF COURAGE
CARL SCHURZ

General Carl Schurz lived a long time. He lived long enough to see not only how immigrant soldiers in the Eleventh Corps suffered ongoing slights, but how they enjoyed some vindication of their work—particularly their work at

Chancellorsville—by the end of the nineteenth century. He lived long enough to see German-American soldiers who fought at Gettysburg venerated by sturdy monuments at the military park. And he lived long enough to add to German-American honor with his own memoirs of immigrant courage. But if Schurz was gratified by the way that German Americans were occasionally recognized for their bravery, he also lived long enough to see and regret how courage itself was being recast. Moral courage, which he had championed as much as physical courage, was mattering less and less in Civil War memory. The fight against slavery, which had inspired him and other German-American officers in the army to endure trial upon trial—and slander upon slander—was becoming an unwanted topic of conversation. Increasingly, what many Americans wanted to talk about was how men like Schurz had fought, not why.

Carl Schurz's own career as a field commander ended less than a year after Gettysburg. Shortly after the battle, a number of the senior officers of the Eleventh Corps, tired of fighting Confederates and Union critics both, either sought reassignment or expressed the hope that the corps might be broken up. What happened may have been the next best thing. In late September, the Eleventh Corps was pulled out of the Army of the Potomac and, along with the Twelfth Corps, was sent to the west under the command of General Joseph Hooker, formerly of Chancellorsville. As part of a broad effort to help liberate the Army of the Cumberland, besieged at Chattanooga, Tennessee, the corps served in campaigns at Wauhatchie, at Missionary Ridge, and at Knoxville, and by most accounts acquitted itself creditably.[27]

Most of the corps that is. General Hooker singled out Schurz's friend and subordinate Colonel Friedrich Hecker for rebuke in his 1864 report of the Chattanooga campaign—accusing him of not following orders. Schurz fought back against Hooker's "malicious" comments in a court of inquiry, and while Hecker was cleared, relations between Hooker and Schurz deteriorated. In the spring of 1864, shortly after the Eleventh and Twelfth Corps were consolidated into the Twentieth Corps, again under Hooker, Schurz was ordered to a "Corps of Instruction" near Nashville. He took a leave of absence to campaign for Lincoln, and returned to the army to serve as chief of staff to General Henry Slocum, also a Gettysburg veteran. But in the words of one biographer, it was clear that he had been "shelved."[28]

After the Civil War ended, Carl Schurz remained committed to defending his own record and that of German-American soldiers, particularly against criticism that poured forth from other ex-soldiers in the last quarter of the 1800s. Schurz knew how difficult it would be to eradicate long-entrenched notions, however. "Public opinion," he wrote, "is generally swayed by first impressions, and an injury once done can but rarely be repaired."[29]

But the passage of time was on his side. As the century ended, nativist sentiment shifted. New popular perceptions of German immigrants aligned with
changing perceptions of wartime heroism to soften the image of German-
American soldiers. Toward the turn of the century, the arrival of new immigrants in the United States from Eastern Europe and Asia made "older"
German- and Irish-born residents seem more fully American. New immigrants
seemed to threaten the economic security and social supremacy of the native-
born, while "older" immigrants not only seemed less dangerous, but increasingly "white." German Americans in the mid-nineteenth century had once
been suspect for their "racial" peculiarities, but by the end of the century their
background had become an asset.[30] Carl Schurz himself epitomized the shift.
Whereas at one time he was denigrated as a racial stranger—a "red-bearded
Teuton"—by the time he died he was lauded for his contributions to the white
"race." One eulogizer claimed Schurz to be "the choicest example of that splendid host of Germans who have enriched and strengthened and fertilized our
native stock, to produce that composite creature, the latest result of time, the
blending of all the Caucasian races—the new American."[31]

Not only did changing opinions of older immigrants further some reassessment of German-American soldiers; so did changing ideas about the Civil
War itself. White Northern and Southern reconciliation after Reconstruction
meant that public discussions of sectional division, including rifts over slavery, were less appealing than discussions about the "manhood" that Confederate and Union soldiers had shared. To some extent, every soldier who had
wielded a weapon was a winner, and, as more and more veterans passed away,
those who survived were precious to the public for having served—for simply
"being there."[32] Ethnic differences and sectional differences diminished in significance; longevity was everything.

Broad acknowledgment of all Union veterans' achievements found full expression in the battlefield at Gettysburg. Former soldiers, often with state assistance, sponsored durable records of their battle work in granite, marble,
and bronze. During the 1880s, especially, monument makers went into a
frenzy of chiseling to honor troop positions and maneuvers. Eleventh Corps
veterans recorded their stalwart action north of town and on East Cemetery
Hill, predictably eschewing words like flight or rout. The German troops
demonstrated only fortitude and prudence as they "retired" or "withdrew" on
July first. Regimental markers also did not bear witness to any flight; they
stood forward on the field, unyielding. Veterans took delight in these markers. Schurz and others came to give speeches, often in German, at monument
dedication ceremonies, and German-American tourists arrived at the park,
sometimes by the hundreds, to walk the lines and take in evidence of the
courage of their countrymen.[33]

New written histories offered powerful support to this concrete remembrance. In 1896, Augustus Choate Hamlin, a lieutenant colonel and former surgeon with the Eleventh Corps, published an account of his life in the army, giving German-American soldiers credit in the war from beginning to end. What would have happened to America, he asked, had it not been for resolute German Americans and their followers? Has the country yet recognized their contributions? Or their brave performances in battle? Has it ever truly understood Chancellorsville?[34] Prejudice against the Eleventh Corps, said Hamlin, had gone on too long, "blighting the honor and embittering the life of ten thousand deserving soldiers." The "hootings," the label of "worthless Dutchmen," all the reproaches that became "household words in the land, and linger yet" had done real damage to these men. "In time," he said, "it bends the bravest heart and wrecks the strongest resolution."[35]

Hamlin's history, which Schurz claimed was written with "absolute impartiality," was sweet balm to the former general. So were monuments and markers at Gettysburg that tempered the legends of German cowardice. But as much as Schurz was gratified by some positive acknowledgment, he was deeply troubled by what he saw as the country's social amnesia. When soldiers were honored for simply being there and standing firm, he felt the essence of the war was lost. To him, the Civil War had been about courage in the cause of freedom. The war's despicable atrocities had been committed, as he saw it, in the name of that freedom. At Gettysburg, Schurz had witnessed horrors that he would never forget. He had seen monstrous bodies, "puffed out almost beyond recognition," some with arms raised, some kneeling, some clawing the earth, many in "what must have been a frightful death-struggle." But what stood above such scenes was the reason. The carnage at Gettysburg, Schurz believed, was "an indisputable necessity" in the fight against slavery. It was "imperative" in the struggle for "our cause."[36]

On January 31, 1865, Schurz witnessed the fruits of that victorious cause when he sat in the gallery at the House of Representatives and watched the House pass the Thirteenth Amendment to abolish slavery. While people cheered, shouted, and cried, Carl Schurz sat unable to speak, so full was he of feeling. And after the war, after his beloved Lincoln was gone, Schurz continued to be concerned with social justice. In 1865, he toured the South at the request of President Andrew Johnson and evaluated Johnson's reconstruction policies. Schurz reported widespread cruelty, unfree labor, recalcitrant planters, and the absolute need for more government help. He talked about the necessity of black male suffrage and the possibility of land redistribution. He spoke of a "great social revolution only half accomplished."[37]

After Reconstruction, Schurz turned to politics and policymaking, and energetically renewed his advocacy of German immigrants. He served as senator from Missouri, as Secretary of the Interior, as editor of the *Detroit Post* and *New York Evening Post,* and as a campaigner for civil service reform.[38] Schurz also continued to believe in the importance of courageous principle over courageous performance. In the last great work of his life, his memoirs, finished just before his death in 1906, he had his final say about bravery. He spoke of knowing two officers in the Civil War, one of them a brave man who leaped into danger at the slightest opportunity and who had served the armies of several countries. The other officer was a man whose courage came with a cause, but who did his work methodically. Carl Schurz worried that in America the first soldier was considered more heroic than the second; that bravery—in the name of anything—was becoming sovereign and that virtue was of decreasing value.[39]

Carl Schurz died in 1906, just as the "causeless" Civil War was making its ascendancy. He also passed away before new, deep anti-German sentiment began to grip the country. In 1896, in his defense of the Eleventh Corps at Chancellorsville, Augustus Choate Hamlin had stressed how the "German character" was replete with "martial virtues." "Since the days of the Caesars," he had claimed, "its unquenchable warlike spirit has never been denied or questioned." Two decades later, no one seeking sympathy for these immigrant soldiers would take that slant. In light of German imperialism in Europe, the nativist prejudice that vilified the Eleventh Corps in the mid-1800s became the Germanophobia of the early twentieth century.[40]

Schurz had worried about intensifying German militarism and its effect on German–American relations. In hindsight, of course, he had reason to be concerned. When the United States declared war on Germany in 1917, German Americans faced a lot more than equivocation about their role in the Civil War; they faced serious persecution. They were accused of disloyalty and faced bans on their language, on cultural rituals, and on German music. Place names for towns, parks, and streets were changed. The teaching of German was banned in twenty-six states, German books were burned; German presses were put under surveillance. People of German descent had their property vandalized, and they were beaten for allegedly unpatriotic remarks.[41]

At Gettysburg itself, new sorts of anti-German sentiment found its way into battle histories and battlefield rituals. After the turn of the century, when white veterans of both the Union and Confederacy tried to outdo each other in proffering compliments, Germany became the "bad" example of how wars could be conducted. Blatantly ignoring civilian experience in the Gettysburg campaign, particularly African-American experience, one Memorial Day speaker in 1918 lauded Northern and Southern army comportment at Gettysburg. Neither army, said the speaker, had ever desecrated its enemies the way German armies had in Europe. No churches or hospitals or orchards or homes were "destroyed in the utter and wanton lust of destruction." "Our" soldiers "left no trail of mad mutilation and outrage." He pointed to Confederate markers on the battlefield. They "stand side by side [with Union monuments] and . . . mingle in a common brotherhood of manhood and citizenship."[42]

If selective Civil War memory could help Americans denigrate contemporary Germans, selective popular culture at Gettysburg could also sustain and perpetuate unflattering pictures of German Civil War soldiers. The persistence of Alexander Schimmelfennig's story did not encourage any hatred of German-American soldiers, but it did not encourage respect, either. If Americans wanted to denigrate Germany, and German Americans by association, the story about the man who hid for three days in the pigpen would do the job. As long as Schimmelfennig maintained his celebrity at the site of one of "manhood's" defining moments, German soldiery was seriously undercut.[43]

Anti-German opinion may also have manifested itself in the neglect of an important Civil War study. In 1911, a "definitive" history of German Americans in the Civil War—the history that Alexander Schimmelfennig tried to write, and the history that Schurz and others had pined for—was published in German. Wilhelm Kaufmann's book, produced in Munich just before World War One, remained untranslated for almost a century. Perhaps, as the book's editors suggest, publishers did not have the confidence to bring out a book about German military accomplishments in light of the two world wars, even if these Germans were really Americans, and the war was fought on American soil. Perhaps, though, Kaufmann's work sat untranslated because of a long-standing dynamic. The large Anglo-American Civil War audience had dismissed these men in the 1860s and it *still* did not care much about them. It had, after all, continued to ignore other "ethnic" troops, like the similarly misunderstood Louisiana Tigers. Only in the late twentieth century, in the context of rising enthusiasm for multicultural and "bottom-up" history, were publishers willing to try their luck with stories and studies of immigrant experience in the American Civil War.[44]

It was only at the turn of the twenty-first century, too, that a number of military analysts were willing to write those stories. Gettysburg historians began to warm to the Eleventh Corps. They exonerated them, called them "unlucky" instead of cowardly or inept, and suggested that events on the first of July had very little to do with "ethnic" troops and more to do with Confederate ingenuity or the failure of Yankee generals. Other scholars, in turn, emphasized the ethnic character and identity of Eleventh Corps troops and stressed their distinct competence. As many of these writers admitted, however, ready labels like "Flying Dutchman" did not disappear. Public opinion, as Carl Schurz would say, was still swayed by first impressions.[45]

"UH OH"
OLIVER OTIS HOWARD

If public judgment on German-American performance in the Army of the Potomac warmed slightly, if unevenly, over the twentieth century, it cooled on
the commander of the Eleventh Corps. Opinion on Oliver Otis Howard was
always divided between those who viewed him as a decent, competent, God-
honoring general and those who dismissed him as "Uh Oh Howard," a man
who commanded two of the most famous routs in the Civil War. Had Otis
Howard himself shaped popular memory at Gettysburg—and the major general tried harder than almost anyone else to do so—it might have gone something like this: Howard fought bravely, led "outsiders" kindly, chose the Union
position wisely, did good duty to God, and, above all, when the war was over,
he gave Gettysburg meaning by trying to complete the social revolution of the
Civil War. If Abraham Lincoln left the words "unfinished work" undefined in
his Gettysburg Address, Otis Howard tried to give them specific intent. For
Howard, the unfinished work was the work of black freedom.

Like Carl Schurz, then, Oliver Otis Howard was committed to the war's
ends as much as to its means. Like Schurz, Howard tried to widen the hero's
circle in Civil War memory. Schurz wanted it to include the foreign-born,
Howard wanted it to include Christian soldiers as well. Both men wanted it to
include people of principle.

Howard had many opportunities to shape American memory in his long
life (he died at the age of eighty). He spoke at reunions, dinners, dedications,
memorial ceremonies, and veteran meetings and he published widely. And
certainly he had to have been gratified by the way some people held him in
high regard. During the Civil War itself, he was praised for his work under
Hooker and Sherman in Tennessee in late 1863 and 1864, and the praise translated into promotions. He became Fourth Corps commander in April 1864
and was then promoted—above Hooker—to Commander of the Army of the
Tennessee, and took charge of William T. Sherman's right wing in the famous
march through Georgia and the Carolinas. After the war Howard received the
Congressional Medal of Honor for bravery at the Battle of Fair Oaks outside
of Richmond in 1862, where he had lost his arm.[46]

And Howard was praised for his work at Gettysburg. He was commended
immediately after the battle by the army's high command, and in early 1864,
the United States Congress extended formal thanks to officers of the Army of
the Potomac for the victory in Pennsylvania. Its appreciation went to three
people: General Joseph Hooker, for bringing the army to the edge of battle;
General Meade for carrying the army through to success; and Oliver Otis
Howard, for selecting the Union army's position on Cemetery Hill.[47]

Howard was especially protective of his reputation at Gettysburg. It was his antidote to Chancellorsville, certainly, but he also knew that much of the public viewed it as *the* battle of the war—the turning point, the signal victory in the defeat of the Confederacy. He also valued Gettysburg for the way it was linked in the public mind, thanks to Abraham Lincoln, with the causes he himself so closely embraced—emancipation and freedom. Gettysburg was, in short, the place in Civil War memory where he could legitimately be both a Christian and a soldier. It was the place, he would claim in 1875, where "I have taken special pride."[48]

Gettysburg meant a lot to Otis Howard, but he was aware of how tenuously he held onto honor there. He despised the seesaw of acclaim, the inevitable military judgment that elevated one set of soldiers only at another's expense, but he could not avoid it. Compliments, he knew, engendered resentment, and when he received what he called an "excess of praise, much of it unmerited," shortly after the battle, he knew it would "excite the unkind criticism of some of my brother officers." He was right. Soon he was accused of coveting Meade's place as commander of the army.[49]

It was also only a matter of time before fellow officers raised other serious doubts about his performance at Gettysburg. How competently had he directed the action of the First and Eleventh corps after General Reynolds' death? Why had he sent the Eleventh Corps so far forward on July 1, only to be outflanked, reminiscent of Chancellorsville? Had he ordered a retreat to the cemetery soon enough? And the biggest question of all: Should he have been commended for selection of the Union defensive position on Cemetery Hill? Maybe General Reynolds or General Hancock or even General Buford deserved credit for the choice.[50]

Howard's reputation at Gettysburg depended on a lot more than his performance there, of course. It was also tied to how he was viewed in general by army personnel. And he continued to be dogged by the accusation that he was not tough enough. General Joseph Hooker proved to be one of his sharpest critics. In June 1872, Hooker commented in a newspaper interview that Howard "was always a woman among troops." He went on: "If he [Howard] was not born in petticoats he ought to have been and ought to wear them. He was always taken up with Sunday Schools and the temperance cause. Those things are all very good, you know, but have very little to do with commanding army corps. He would command a prayer meeting with a good deal more ability than he would an army." Why was Hooker, who was full of praise for Howard after Gettysburg, given to such slights later on? Hooker and Howard had always had different cultural styles, but casting slurs on military manhood may have been one of the best ways of avenging insult. In July 1864, after Howard had been made commander of the Army of the Tennessee, Hooker "asked to be relieved." Howard asserted later that Hooker felt the appointment should have been his.[51]

Yet attacks came from veterans of the Eleventh Corps as well, and especially from his old nemesis, Carl Schurz. And sometimes they were an utter surprise to him. Howard believed he had had an agreeable parting with many of the immigrant men in his command. After the summer of 1863, in fact, he still believed that his star and that of German-American soldiers in his command might rise together. When the corps was ordered from the Army of the Potomac to the west, Howard had expressed the hope that the transfer would be a new lease on the corps' life. In the west, he wrote home, "I believe my Corps will be better appreciated." He had been proud of the work of his German troops, and he had little sympathy for other Yankee officers who sought, once again, to be rid of them. In a letter to his wife at the end of July 1863 he noted how New England general Adelbert Ames had "exchanged his Germans." Howard disapproved of Ames' arrogance toward the immigrant soldiers, commenting that Ames "does not have any fancy for German troops [and] is almost uncivil to them." He believed that, despite their difficult months together, immigrant soldiers regarded him with respect and cordiality. "The Germans," he said in late July, "begin to be attached to me."[52]

Howard was not speaking, of course, of German-born soldiers like Alexander Schimmelfennig or Leopold von Gilsa, who were more than happy to be transferred away from him. And he certainly could not have been speaking of Carl Schurz. Schurz and Howard never warmed to each other. Despite their similar social commitments, despite the fact that Schurz also despised the seesaw of honor—that he, too, was tired of soldiers who "were fond of vaunting their own brave deeds at the expense of others"—neither man could extricate himself from the backbiting. Nor could they entirely avoid each other. Even after the war they occasionally crossed paths—in work for the government in Reconstruction, and during the period of Indian Wars, when Howard, alternately Indian chaser and advocate, needed to correspond with Schurz, then Secretary of the Interior. They also occasionally needed to communicate on matters—usually personnel matters—related to corps history.[53]

Throughout the nineteenth century, Schurz and Howard continued to lock horns. Schurz, perhaps avenging decades of insults, helped deliver a brutal attack on Howard late in the century. The German general had served as a consultant on the Augustus Hamlin book that redeemed the Eleventh Corps at Chancellorsville. In December of 1896, Howard had heard rumors that the new history would be the corps'—everybody's—ultimate vindication. This was good news—finally an account that did justice to the long-injured men, collectively. And Howard had an opportunity to deliver his thanks. Just before

Christmas, at a dinner reunion of corps veterans in New York City, Howard moved a standing vote to Colonel Hamlin "for his diligence and success in completing his defense of the 11th corps at Chancellorsville." Howard had ordered multiple copies, but had yet to receive them. He had no clear idea what the book said.[54]

The toast was completed, the dinner was over, and Howard went home with a copy of Hamlin's book. Howard had been shocked before, but never like this. He read how he had cruelly discredited the corps in 1863, and that his slander had been "broadcast over the world." He read resolutions, too, by the "Society of the Officers and Soldiers of said Eleventh Corps," that asserted they had behaved "gallantly and desperately" but that their commanders "sought to conceal their [own] incapacity." He read words, too, that went right for his jugular. When Howard first arrived at the corps, the book said, the men had been pleased by Howard's "open countenance and pleasant manners," but at the same time they were concerned about such an "exhuberant" Christian. They believed that winning in battle came from "audacity, courage and vigilance, and was not deduced from auspices or assisted by incantations."[55]

Howard was "stung." "I thought," he wrote to a friend on Christmas Eve, "I had stood by the 11th Corps with sturdiness and open speech for thirty-three years, and didn't know till I saw this book that [I had been accused] of slandering the Corps. Surely . . . that was not in my heart." What hurt especially was the shot to his religiosity, and the implication that he was not a strong man. "Schurz is the hero, and I am the weakling," lamented Howard. "I do not wish for any more of these embittered recollections." His request at the dinner for "a rising vote" in honor of the book, before he had seen it, made sure that "the mortification is complete."[56]

Howard badly wanted a "lease of life and the strength" to make his rebuttal to his critics.[57] And he got it. So did Carl Schurz. Racing against time and health, and against each other, to some extent, the two men worked on their memoirs nearly simultaneously. The accounts came out within a year of each other, Schurz's in 1907, the year after he died, and Howard's in 1908, the year before he passed away. In his *Reminiscences*, Schurz hit Howard with a few final broadsides, casting doubts on Howard's military leadership and suggesting that Howard, with his "Christian soldier business," never really fit into the company of army men.[58]

Schurz's slights and jabs were nothing new for Howard. But their appearance at the turn of the century, just as he was trying to package his own life and career for posterity, may have been particularly damaging. Howard was now more out of fashion than he had ever been. He had always been something of an anomaly in the army, but back in the middle decades of the 1800s, there were plenty of middle-class men who embraced, as he did, ideals of temperance, self-restraint, and piety. For many educated Northerners, too, heartfelt abolitionism like his was the order of the day. But toward the end of the nineteenth century, Howard's Christian soldier was out of touch with the times. A man's man—exemplified by President Theodore Roosevelt—was increasingly rough and tumble, someone who fought, whether in war, in the West, or in a sporting event, for fighting's sake. Moral purpose, especially when it was associated with civil rights and racial justice, sometimes simply got in the way.[59]

Howard never regretted his Christian dedication, of course, nor his work on behalf of beleaguered communities. Despite a lifelong desire to keep his record "bright" and "unsullied," and despite his deep pride, Otis Howard did not shy away from social controversy. In the war, in an era of intense nativism, he linked himself with immigrants; after the war, in the volatile world of Reconstruction, he championed the needs of African Americans. Later in his army life, when politicians, the public, philanthropists, and Indian tribes themselves all disagreed about the future, he negotiated with Native Americans.[60]

It had been in the aftermath of the Civil War that Howard truly became a lightning rod for public anger. Like Carl Schurz, Howard did not leave the work of the Civil War after Appomattox. As a "practical" abolitionist, who believed in integration and claimed to be free from social prejudice, he had long been convinced that freed persons needed education and employment. Appointed by Andrew Johnson as Commissioner of the Bureau of Refugees, Freedmen and Abandoned Lands, better known as the Freedmen's Bureau, Howard at first promoted nearly revolutionary change in the South. In June 1865, he ordered the Bureau to lease confiscated and abandoned Confederate lands, in forty-acre plots, to ex-slaves. He would try to make freedom real for women and men who had worked the land for generations, but who had never seen the results of their efforts.[61]

The project was short-lived. Andrew Johnson rescinded Howard's order, and Howard, believing that a crippled Freedmen's Bureau was better than no bureau at all, stood by and watched as farms already tilled and planted were returned to their former owners. Criticized now by ex-Confederates for his audacity, and by former abolitionists and freedmen alike for his appeasement of Johnson, he put on emotional armor and persevered. To one angry, unreconstructed planter, he was unrepentant: "I am now struggling for you, and your poor people, black and white." "Your children," he added in closing, "will thank us."[62]

In his work for the Freedmen's Bureau, which lasted into the 1870s, Howard may have done as much as any white Civil War soldier to give purpose to the war, and to make the war's bloodletting amount to something. He was not an especially able administrator, and his success was partial. (One of his best-known efforts was the co-founding in 1867 of Howard University.) And he continued to make many enemies. Representing all the hopes and fears and cataclysmic change of the war—all the ways that the Federal government intruded in lives and all the ways the government failed to help—Howard attracted hostility from all directions. But there were people who appreciated his efforts, if not his results. "Nothing is more convenient than to heap on the Freedmen's Bureau all the evils of that evil day," wrote W. E. B. Du Bois in 1903, but that is "neither sensible or just. Some one had blundered, but that was long before Oliver Howard was born." Sojourner Truth added her voice to those who sympathized. At a particularly difficult time for the Bureau, in 1873, she wrote to Howard and confessed she heard "people saying for you and against you." But, she said, "I speak in behalf of you, knowing what you have done in behalf of my poor race."[63]

Had the country—particularly its government—continued to honor its promises to freedmen in the decades following the Civil War, and had it made social and racial justice a paramount concern in the twentieth century, Oliver Otis Howard might have been better regarded in Civil War history. His military service at Gettysburg might never have earned him accolades, but his social conscience and his work alongside immigrant "outsiders" might have given him the benefit of the doubt. Furthermore, his efforts to complete Lincoln's "unfinished work" might have made him a heroic executor of the freedom that Gettysburg helped win. Even his gentleness and piety might have been forgiven. These "unmanly" means, after all, served powerful ends. But the country did not honor its promises to freedmen and women. And the movement toward Northern and Southern "healing," predicated as it was on diminishing concern for ex-slaves and on increased segregation and violence, helped kill Howard's reputation. People who called to mind the misery of slavery and the painful challenges of black freedom would not—for a long time at least—be the darlings of Civil War memory.[64]

In the late 1990s, a historian reviewing Howard's life saw the career soldier as a metaphor "of much of nineteenth-century American history." Indeed, opinions about Otis Howard, which were often mixed or contradictory, suggest the tensions and conflicts of Civil War–era America. Later opinions about Howard were also linked to conflicting ideas about gender, about equality and inclusivity, and about the Civil War and its legacy. In the early twenty-first century, Howard remains a figure with an uncertain reputation. To some degree, this reflects progressive change. The eclipsing of Oliver Otis Howard is grounded in the fact that the German Americans he led in 1863 are becoming better understood, and in the inevitable tilting of military opinion, Howard has lost ground. His diminished stature also reflects the recognition that African Americans were themselves agents in wartime history, and that the course of the Civil War and Reconstruction was shaped by black men and women as much as by any white men, including Lincoln and Johnson and their appointees.[65]

But it would be a mistake to exaggerate the degree to which immigrants and people of color have achieved recognition in Civil War history, especially in the history of the Battle of Gettysburg. This is evident at the battlefield itself, where monuments and markers speak to German-American courage, but where many Park tours bypass Eleventh Corps lines. The story of Schimmelfennig in hiding is also alive and well, and tales of "Uh Oh Howard" and "Howard's Cowards" continue to amuse. To some degree, the reputations of Otis Howard and German Americans of the Eleventh Corps have held steady since the summer of 1863. These soldiers remain the foils for the "courageous" men who surrounded them at Gettysburg, on all sides.[66]

9

★★★

WOMEN AND REMEMBRANCE

OLIVER OTIS HOWARD WANTED his version of the Battle of Gettysburg to be the one the public remembered, and he would work for this to the end of his long life. He did not worry about being forgotten altogether. As long as historians chronicled military maneuvers, as long as monuments lasted, as long as tourists came to Gettysburg and looked around them, he knew he had a place, for better or for worse, in posterity.

Not many people were interested in, or knew about his wife, Lizzie, who also survived the war. In the spring of 1865, Otis Howard's brother Rowland sent the general a letter from Maine that described how he thought the war had affected the women in Howard's life. Their mother, he said, was a poor woman "whose whole mind & will is often on the point of yielding to the severe pressure of care." Lizzie, he said, had "developed & matured mentally and spiritually under the severe discipline that she has had." But then he added: "I have thought lately that . . . in answering what is the chief End of Man it might be answered To Kill Women—The perplexing cares & troubles of their household life are far greater to them than the broader activities of ours." Rowland Howard's assessment of women's burdens in the Civil War, and men's responsibility for them, might have surprised his brother. Otis Howard tried, at least in writing, to be a tender, sensitive husband, frequently acknowledging Lizzie's burdens on the Maine homefront. And Lizzie, though admittedly lonely, did her work with little obvious complaint.[1]

Elizabeth Howard was to some degree the Civil War's ideal wartime wife. She was an inspiration to her husband, she maintained the household and family in his absence, she worked in soldier's aid, and she did all of this without bitterness. Her husband said he appreciated her efforts, and declared that if women like her stopped supporting the war, the soldiers would "go down."[2]

In Gettysburg, there were many stoical women like Lizzie Howard. They not only served the cause unnoticed when the war was elsewhere, but served the cause calmly when the war came home, and a battle descended upon them. At the same time, however, there were a number of Gettysburg women who, while modest, nevertheless sought some acknowledgment of their efforts during the battle. They wrote their stories down, they spoke to reporters, they edited their memories for publication. Women like Fannie Buehler, Harriet Bayly, and Sadie Bushman told their tales publicly, letting readers know of their tireless but exhausting work under fire, of their resilience and engagement, and of their physical and emotional struggles. A few other women went further than this, questioning, as years went by, why the women of Gettysburg in 1863 remained mostly invisible.

To some degree, women needn't have wondered why they were left out of the proliferating narratives of Gettysburg. They were served repeated reminders that were they to become too public, their sacrifice or heroism too well known, their reputations or even their virtue might be called into question. The public accounts of Georgia McClellan's sister, Jennie Wade, and, to a lesser extent, Elizabeth Thorn evolved into these sorts of reminders. They emphasized the degree to which the most honored women of Gettysburg were either briefly noted or barely recognizable. They also underscored the power of the chivalric ideal of warfare, in which men defended the homeland and women stayed out of sight.

ANGELS OF MERCY

In the years immediately following the battle, it was not uncommon for writers and speakers to pay some respect to white women's work at Gettysburg. One typical observer, commenting in the press in July 1863, characterized local women as angels, called to their loving duty. "Amid the very horrors of the conflict, with the missiles of death flying around them," he said, "the ladies of Gettysburg brought forth food and drink for our faint, and for a little time retreating soldiers. Thoughtful and anxious, yet calm and self possessed, they gave themselves to the ministrations of mercy." "No tongue can tell," he added, "what treasure of love is in a Christian woman's heart."[3]

Gettysburg women, this commentator suggested, were wonders of healing who performed their battle work out of their intrinsic goodness. Echoing common sentiments about women's service and sacrifice, other writers, too, stressed how local women's benevolence was so naturally and sweetly given, so disinterested, so much the outgrowth of their hearts, that it overcame physical exhaustion and political principle. The romances that allegedly grew between soldiers and their local caretakers at Gettysburg seemed emblematic of the way that women let their generous sensibilities govern their actions. Special friendships not only blossomed between Union soldiers and their nurses, but between Confederate soldiers and Gettysburg women.[4]

Gettysburg women's empathy was not only beautifully natural, it was distinctly quiet. Among the most honored contributors to the battle's aftermath were visiting Sisters of Charity, who nursed the wounded. A local paper lauded these nuns for the way that they "glide noiselessly about the hospitals, with nourishment for the feeble convalescent, with soothing palliatives for those writhing in the grasp of fell disease, and mutely kneeling by the bedsides of the dying. On battle-fields, amidst hurling shot and hissing shells, they have calmly walked to seek and save the wounded."[5]

Women ideally did soft and soothing work, and then they soundlessly disappeared. Truly feminine dispositions did not harbor any desire for compensation, or any hankering for formal acknowledgment. One Gettysburg businessman, writing in 1888—the twenty-fifth anniversary of the battle, when some women's battle accounts were making an appearance—remarked in a published essay that a woman's "innate refinement and modesty makes publicity repellent to her, the idea of being conspicuous is distasteful." When public officials noted what borough women had accomplished, they frequently commented that women's work offered its own reward. Congressman Edward Everett, who had praised women's contributions to the Union cause in his Gettysburg address, suggested that women deserved "our highest admiration and gratitude." "Happily," he said, "the labor and the service are their own reward." He also reminded women that they would reap further recognition in Heaven, where they would be credited with having done Christ's work. Private soldiers conveyed the same sentiments about women's efforts. Otis Howard wrote to Lizzie in Maine that he felt "badly that you have worked so hard," but reminded her that "God will reward you."[6]

Women's work at the Battle of Gettysburg was not only supposed to be about noiseless empathy rewarded in the hereafter; it was also about a distinct kind of courage. Women's courage was not considered equivalent to or synonymous with battle courage. It ideally had little to do with heroic assertion. Linked as it was to domesticity, maternity, and self-sacrifice, it was regarded as relatively passive. It was, in short, more like fortitude. Women were indeed acknowledged to have worked under fire, and the word "courage" was sometimes used, but their work was social service, not martial bravery, and while they might on occasion be singled out for their intrepidity, celebrated courage was reserved for soldiers.[7]

These male writers were not simply writing abstractly, or putting forth what they wanted the public to believe. Many wartime women in Gettysburg seem to have chosen to become models of unassuming bravery. They surfaced in public only when ex-soldiers referred to them, or when "women" were re-called generically. Or perhaps best of all, they came into view when veterans or journalists searched for them, and plucked them—reluctantly of course—from their private lives.

A number of Gettysburg women received this unsought-for commendation when they were "discovered" by soldiers long after the battle. Anna Hoke, for example, emerged when veteran cavalryman Merritt Lewis sought her out. Lewis, who was fifteen years old in 1863, had been injured in the battle, and had suffered a double amputation. He was sent to the Hoke house to recover. Anna had been a seven-year-old at the time, and had visited Lewis and other wounded soldiers every morning with a pail of milk, and then had played at the piano for hours with "pure, childish tones." The soldiers regarded her visits as "a gleam of sunshine," and while she worked her magic they would "forget their pains." Lewis had lost sight of Anna after the war, but finally succeeded in tracking her to Illinois decades later. The meeting of the grown-up Miss Hoke with the grown-up soldier was "joyous."[8]

Soldiers sought out the angels who had ministered to them, and also the girls and women who had inspired them to fight. Oliver Otis Howard claimed he could not forget the sight of a young woman on the first day of the battle, as his troops were pushing through to the north of town. A young girl seemed to be the only soul around, he said, and she stood on her porch waving her handkerchief. "A vision like that," Howard remarked, "had in it a tender, tear-ful inspiration; but it gave heart and firmness of tread to the marching men." After the war, he claimed he went house to house "to get the name of the brave girl who did us such a service." Decades after the battle he found her father living—he was in his eighties—but she had died years before.[9]

Veterans planning reunions also singled out women who had served them during the battle. Soldiers in one regiment would never forget twenty-seven-year-old Josephine Rodgers, for instance, who had insisted on baking bread for troops even after she was advised to evacuate her home. On July 2nd her house along the Emmitsburg Road was enveloped by gunfire, and the next day Pickett's Charge surged past her, but she persisted. Twenty-three years after the war, soldiers found Rodgers living in Ohio and brought her back to Gettysburg for a reunion. They "decorated her with a score of army badges, and sent her back a happy woman." The scene was repeated with other sol-diers, other women. At the fiftieth battle reunion in 1913, one reporter de-scribed veterans gathered in clusters along Cemetery Ridge. At the center of many groups sat a woman wearing a badge, reminiscing.[10]

Of all the Gettysburg women who were called on for an "appearance," none elicited more tender recollections than those who, as girls, had waved handkerchiefs and sung to Union cavalry the day before the battle began. In 1891, ex-troopers recalled the girls as "veritable angels" who, dressed in white, "awoke every feeling of chivalry in our souls." At the fortieth anniversary of the battle, these "Singing Girls"—now solidly old women—moistened eyes with their renditions of "Just Before the Battle Mother" and "When This Cruel War Is Over" and "The Battle Cry of Freedom." At the fiftieth reunion the "girls" were called on again. Gray-haired, with "tears in their eyes" and in "quavering tones," they sang the wartime melodies. "I'm afraid we can't sing like we sang fifty years ago," apologized one of them. It doesn't matter, the veterans said, and everybody cried.[11]

Former soldiers not only honored local women in their rituals but often brought in outsiders to add a symbolic female presence to their monument dedications and reunions. Visiting girls and women, sometimes the daughters or sisters of soldiers, unveiled statues, sang airs, or recited verse. Decorative and devoted, they reflected the way wartime women were depicted in postwar histories and ritual events across America. Throughout the country, one historian has commented, "Memorial Day ceremonies usually placed orphaned children and widows in important roles—though often in a silent and supportive capacity—in a way that would highlight their dependence on the manly heroism of the former soldiers."[12]

Of the many "angels of mercy" to surface in the story of Gettysburg, Sadie Bushman stands out. Emerging as she did at the turn of the twentieth century, when, thanks to the suffrage debate, discussions about women's place and women's character were prominent in the media, Sadie offered readers a "true" American girl. Only nine years old in 1863, she had had the courage to help others in one of the country's critical moments. After being rescued from crossfire by a soldier, she became a brave and steadfast nurse. To top it off, Sadie's fame, which was as brief as it was bright, rose without her efforts. Far from seeking public credit for her battle work, Sadie was discovered through a remarkable "accident." And in recalling the details to a reporter, she did not boast of her accomplishments. In fact, she "simply shivered at the memory."[13]

Sadie's story went like this. In 1880, a veteran of the battle wrote a letter to a newspaper editor in Missouri, describing how he had had his "leg shattered" by a shell during the first day's battle at Gettysburg, and had been carried to a nearby farm for treatment. There a brave young girl—a mere child—helped him endure the amputation of his leg. The young nurse "did all she could" for the wounded, and soldiers "loved that innocent little girl." He ended his account with a plea: "Now, boys, see justice done her, the heroine of Gettysburg." But the old soldier never finished the letter, and it remained unread until another man discovered it tucked into a book in a store. Moved by the poignant story, he sought to carry out the wishes of the old soldier—no doubt now dead—and sent the letter to a Chicago newspaper, which published it. Other papers picked up the account of the brave girl and the grateful soldier.[14]

Living in San Francisco at the turn of the century was a wealthy, eccentric doctor. Although his eyesight was failing, he still read the papers, and one day while sitting in a restaurant, he noted an article of interest, reprinted from the Midwest. It was the letter from the soldier. The elderly doctor realized that he had come to the end of a long search. None other than the surgeon who had put the plucky young girl to work as an assistant, he claimed that he, too, had been looking for "the little nurse." And what surprised him most was not the discovery of her married name, but her present location. She lived in San Francisco just as he did, and they were "almost within range of each others' voices."[15]

And so the surgeon thanked Sadie for her wartime work. He invited her to come to his offices in the city, and they were reunited. Sadie Bushman, now Sadie Jungerman, was relatively poor, and her husband, Edward Jungerman, was sick. The wealthy doctor expressed his gratitude to Sadie for her Gettysburg help by giving her a "cozy" little home on his large estate. "I am happy again," he wrote, "to be of service to the little nurse of Gettysburg." She demonstrated during those trying times, he said, "all the qualities of American womanhood."[16]

Sadie Bushman, a paragon of wartime girlhood, had grown into a model American woman. Her public persona—embodying virtue, modesty, and selfless dedication—suggested an image that many Civil War women might emulate. Her quiet pursuit of a life outside the public domain, her disinterest in seeing her name in print (until a reporter insisted), seemed nothing short of exemplary.

CAUTIONARY TALES

Sadie Bushman—to her credit, obviously—was not the most well-known woman of Gettysburg. Other women were better recognized, and, not coincidentally, attracted less positive attention. Elizabeth Thorn and Jennie Wade became celebrities of sorts, and the stories that circulated about them reveal how hard it was—how unadvisable it was—for a woman to share renown with soldiers.

According to her son, all Elizabeth Thorn wanted was a simple memento of the battle—some sign that she had been there, too, and that she had served. What she got was public attention, along with mixed consequences. Thorn knew she had done an extraordinary thing on the night of July 1, 1863—she had braved shells to reveal the lay of the land for Union troops. She had also scraped together a dinner for generals who gathered in her home. But as a female civilian, she had no reports to make, no correspondence to file. Neither historians nor investigators nor committees sought her out after the battle to flesh out their stories or to add dimension to their monuments or memorials. If Elizabeth Thorn wanted some record of her service in battle, she would have to go looking for it.

And she eventually did. In 1883, twenty years after the battle, Elizabeth Thorn asked her old employer at the cemetery, David McConaughy, to write to General Howard to see if he, at least, remembered what she had done. She was still poor, too, so testimony to her work on behalf of the army might yield some monetary damages. It was no longer shameful to ask for some compensation from the government—the uproar around her family's note was over. McConaughy tried to jog Howard's memory. Lizzie Thorn, he reminded the general, "behaved most bravely in accompanying an officer from the Lodge to the crest of the Hill & pointing out and naming the different public roads serving as approaches under the fire of the enemy's artillery . . . and she believes that she prepared supper for you on the evening of the 1st, at the Lodge."[17]

But General Howard could not help. Of all the circumstances of those eventful days that he himself had pored over, that he had searched in detail to bolster his own name, none included a clear memory of Elizabeth Thorn, wife of the keeper of the cemetery on Cemetery Hill. "I remember distinctly being at the Cemetery gate & that a woman was there," Howard wrote back. "I believe the woman gave me a cup of coffee, but the recollection is too indistinct to base any material statement upon. We gathered information from every source & doubtless I asked the woman some questions. For her sake & her husband's I would be very glad to furnish something of more value but I cannot. Very truly yours O. O. Howard Bvt. Major General U.S.A."[18]

Elizabeth Thorn did not give up. As the Battle of Gettysburg gained ground as one of the century's critical moments, so did her determination grow. And she continued to hope for recognition the way so many soldiers enjoyed it: in writing. In the spring of 1894, she enlisted her son, George Thorn, to write to the aging Howard. He did so, explaining that of all things, "the proudest heritage of [my mother's] memory is the experience she had in the battle of Gettysburg when she had . . . so unexpectedly entertained one of our commanding Generals." Couldn't General Howard offer her anything else? "As she is getting on in years," the son wrote, "she would like above all things something from you in black and white which she could treasure, and hand down to her children as a memento of that awful and sorrowful time." It was hard to keep asking, too. George Thorn worried, as he closed his letter, that his request might be "annoying" to General Howard.[19]

Otis Howard guarded his own reputation like a terrier, but he was generous and kind, and he must have realized by this time that Mrs. Thorn was persistent. The least he could do was to acknowledge her memory, if not his own. He wrote back that, indeed, on a past visit to Gettysburg, "You reminded me then as you had done before that your husband was a soldier and away from home and that you had entertained several officers besides myself, giving coffee and refreshments, on the night after the first days battle July 1st 1863." And he offered her thanks. "It was a great refreshment to me and those with me, when so weary and worn, to meet a little family like yours and to receive a cup of hot coffee at your hands. I have a very distinct recollection of it all, and am happy to reiterate my hearty thanks."[20]

While Elizabeth Thorn's service on the battlefield continued, significantly, to escape Howard's regard, her cooking had finally gained her some credit. Ultimately, in fact, it became a recollection with a life of its own. Howard's memory of the meal at the gatehouse grew even more "clear" as years went by, and each time Thorn benefited from the improvement. In 1896, Howard acknowledged not only coffee but a "splendid supper on the night of the first day's fight." Six years later, in 1902, the general called on Elizabeth Thorn in Gettysburg and thanked her for the "best supper he ever ate in his life." One of the papers reporting the event jumped into the act, too, by describing the meal as a "feast spread by Mrs. Thorn."[21]

Elizabeth Thorn did not rely entirely on Otis Howard's recollections to certify her battle work. While in her seventies, she told her story herself, to reporters, and she was careful to include the account Howard had forgotten—of her reconnaissance work under fire. Obviously, Thorn wanted her efforts at the Battle of Gettysburg to be remembered as she saw fit. Along the way, however, she became a public figure. And once she was generally known, she was molded into whatever any writer or artist desired. On one occasion she was turned into a "fearful" Mrs. Thorn, a "snug-built little woman running in and out of the cottage carrying her tray bearing cake and coffee" but "trembling" when she asks General Howard, "Is it all safe here, General?" "What must we do? Where can we go?" In other accounts, she became the only brave soul in the borough. In one case, Mrs. Thorn leads Howard himself into the fray, with the general explaining that "I could not get a man to come, they were all afraid." In a later cartoon, Howard, with his arm miraculously reattached, is asked by his soldiers, "Why have a woman for a guide, General?" "Because every man I asked was too cowardly to come!" replies General Howard.[22]

Why did Elizabeth Thorn's story take the shape of these two extremes? These stories may have served, even if unintentionally, as cautionary tales—suggesting what happened to reputations when women asserted themselves in wartime and in the public sphere of the press. Once Thorn's work at Gettysburg became known, it may also have been appropriated by those debating women's rights at the turn of the twentieth century. People could project onto this woman their hopes and fears for other females who had the audacity to go not only into the world of battle but into the voting booth. In Gettysburg, the issues of "men's" historical space and women's rights came to the forefront in 1913, when suffragists accompanied some veterans to the fiftieth reunion celebration, pitched tents, and attempted to call attention to voting rights. One veteran commented that if the suffragists prevailed and remained on the battlefield "there's going to be a war between the sexes, and the next reunion at Gettysburg will be between the black and blue instead of the blue and gray."[23]

The misrepresentations of Thorn may, then, reflect bigger social and political battles. They were also, of course, a comment on the ever-powerful, ever-prominent character of "courage." Physical courage in the context of battle was necessarily male. If a woman was physically brave, in a battle especially, it threw an established social system out of alignment, and in this tight world of opposites, men became womanly. In a world where battle served as a measure of manhood, there was little room for this sort of complication.[24]

Elizabeth Thorn's stories certainly spoke to widespread conversations about war and gender. It is less clear whether they had much to do with the status of immigrants in America. During the heyday of published civilian reminiscences around the turn of the century, many native-born Gettysburg citizens still sought to stake a claim to courage by contrasting themselves with "timid" German-born residents. They still discussed the story of General Schimmelfennig in his pigpen. Yet the Thorns, by 1900, lived in a town far more welcoming to people of German descent than it had been fifty years earlier. The Gettysburg that had once hosted street protesters shouting against indigent immigrant hordes, now offered these older citizens favorable comment. Two months after Elizabeth Thorn's husband, Peter, died in 1907, a local historian publicly lauded his courage and his "manhood." And he contrasted both of the German-born Thorns with the immigrants "vomited upon our shores to-day," and spoke of their great honor, good hearts, hard work, thrift, and energy. They were, in sum, "good American citizens."[25]

By the time Elizabeth Thorn died, in October 1907, ten months after her husband, she was a well-known local figure in Gettysburg's history. Unlike German-American soldiers, whose monuments and markers arose as unwavering counters to the vicissitudes of opinion, she was repeatedly buffeted in print. As the twentieth century progressed, however, her reputation became less volatile. And like most women of Gettysburg, she faded from the scene. Then again, as historians began toward the turn of the next century to recognize the role of some women in the Civil War, there was renewed interest in Thorn. And this time, there was a monument, too. In 2002, the superintendent of Evergreen Cemetery, who held the historic job that Peter Thorn had performed, raised money and put up a statue to Elizabeth. It stands in honor of all Civil War women, on the cemetery's private grounds.[26]

Even better known than Elizabeth Thorn, and even more decidedly manipulated in public opinion, was Georgia McClellan's sister, Jennie Wade. Jennie, it seemed, had everything going for her in Civil War posterity. She was a young woman who gave not only her time and energy to the soldier's cause, but her life as well. To Georgia's never-ending frustration, however, Jennie was guaranteed no safe home in Gettysburg's public memory. Like Elizabeth Thorn, but in a magnified way, the figure of Jennie Wade carried more than the burden of one girl's untimely death. It reflected feelings not only about the borough and the battle, but about the fundamental relationship between men and women, and war.

For a brief and sanctified time, Jennie Wade was as honored as any other selfless woman. Shot in the back during the battle, she had made the ultimate sacrifice, and newspaper reports of her death spoke of a woman valiant and true. One Gettysburg paper summed up initial public sentiment: "The saddest incident connected with the battle at this place was the killing of Mary Virginia Wade, by the rebel sharpshooters posted in the outskirts of town. She was attending a sick sister at the time, and the house standing in an exposed position, she was in constant danger. A minnie ball from one [of] their rifles struck her . . . and killed her instantly. Miss Wade was aged 20 years 1 month and 7 days, and was a young lady of good character and much respected." Other local and regional papers concurred. In Harrisburg the dead woman was a "lady of most excellent qualities of head and heart."[27]

For a century and more afterward, Jennie continued to have supporters like these. They included veterans who testified on her behalf to her biographer, and honored her memory and awarded her sister with a badge; they were poets and songwriters who tried to immortalize her bright spirit (not to mention her sweet voice, white hands, and red blood); and they were historians who painstakingly detailed her life and death, and emphasized not only her virtue but her patriotism—even her descent from Revolutionary War heroes. And they were men and women who erected tablets to her memory at her birthplace and residence. And, finally, her champions were a group of women who erected a statue over her grave in Evergreen Cemetery, and dedicated it in 1901. Jennie's defenders sometimes simply recounted the story of her death, but many—particularly those who honored her in commercial culture—also suggested her martyrdom. One publication pictured her bloodstains on the floorboard of her house, a relic of her death; the house in which she died became a museum, featuring "her" bullet holes in its front door; a Gettysburg restaurant offered "Jennie Wade bread," in honor of the food she served, certainly, but also suggestive of a kind of eucharist.[28]

But the martyred Jennie Wade was matched in the public imagination by her antithesis. It was not long after she was killed, in fact, that people, local and national, began to cast doubts on Jennie's character. As early as 1864, it was widely reported that Gettysburg people did not believe that Jennie Wade was a heroine "at all." Two years later another Gettysburg civilian wrote to an influential historian of women in the war and asserted "the less said about her the better." The fact of her "being killed while serving Union soldiers," he said, "was a fiction"; she was instead a "she-rebel." He could not comment further because he wished to be kind to "her reputation," but he could refer the historian to two of the most influential men of the town for corroboration.[29]

Other Gettysburg residents also shared their doubts about Jennie Wade. According to one local paper in the late 1870s, she was the "so-called" heroine of Gettysburg. Ten years later, a local woman published a thinly disguised story about Jennie's irascibility during the battle, concluding that "her sympathies were not as much for the Union as they should have been." Residents also speculated about why, when the "singing" girls crowded onto borough streets to inspire General Buford's cavalry on June 30, 1863, Jennie was not present. Didn't her absence hint of disloyalty?[30]

And then there were concerns about her virtue. A letter written by her soldier "sweetheart," Jack Skelly, to his mother before the battle referred to concerns about Jennie's late-night visitors while he was away. The gossip could not be settled because Skelly died shortly after Jennie did. So Jennie's story became even more titillating.[31]

In the twentieth century, Jennie continued to attract unwholesome attention. Reporters discussing the battle at the seventy-fifth reunion in 1938 spoke of "rumors" regarding her. A half-century later, one historian described Jennie Wade as "locally controversial," while another lamented that she was "almost a local joke." And at her museum in Gettysburg in the 1990s, personnel protested, with hushed remarks, that Jennie was associated with prostitution. Web site discussants also wondered whether or not Jennie was baking bread or entertaining soldiers. One Park Service official even pondered whether or not her death might have been an inside job.[32]

Emblematic of the recent mix of respect and irreverence directed at Jennie Wade is the way she has been remembered in material culture, and the way she has become a commodity. Jennie has been accorded dignified treatment in the privately run Evergreen Cemetery for over a century, where she stands as a statue, robed and saintly appearing. But she has gained wider publicity in the house (Georgia's house) where she was killed. In the popular, privately run museum, visitors can hear the story of Jennie's final day, and they can see her dead "body," too, lying disheveled beneath a quilt. In stark contrast to the granite military men who stand upright and inviolate up at the National Military Park, and whose dignified figures are protected by federal authority, this Jennie Wade has been sensationalized to appeal to history consumers. It would be hard to imagine even General Schimmelfennig "sold" in a similar way.[33]

Jennie Wade, revered by some, scorned by others, made the subject of scandal and admiration, has, by virtue of her notoriety, stood in for all women at Gettysburg. All the diverse ways that women engaged in the battle, all the vastness of their work and sacrifice have been boiled down to this one girl. Just as Alexander Schimmelfennig became, in a sense, all German Americans at Gettysburg, and just as his legend obscured the contributions of thousands of others, so Jennie has become *the* Gettysburg female. Perhaps, then, it is the burden of carrying the multiple records of so many women that has made Jennie Wade seem like such a contradictory person. But why else has she suffered?

Certainly Jennie's mixed reputation is anchored in nineteenth-century social opinion. Like Elizabeth Thorn, she became a news item at a time when a much-discussed "lady" was an oxymoron. It may also have been rooted in economic clashes. Jennie's family had spent time in the poorhouse, and her father, James, was known as a troublemaker and ne'er-do-well. Jennie's celebrity may have irritated the borough's elite, and they had the power, through the local press and gossip both, to bring her name down.[34]

The figure of Jennie Wade was also pulled into the damning attacks, launched by the New York press in 1863, and joined by other Pennsylvania newspapers, which suggested that cowardly (and often German and Democratic) men from Gettysburg had abandoned their social duty at the time of the battle. *New York Times* reporter Lorenzo Crounse had claimed that the borough's "male citizens mostly ran away, and left the women and children to the mercy of their enemies."[35]

It did not help that John Burns, Gettysburg's most notorious male civilian, added his weight to accusations against local men. Burns was a seventy-year-old former constable who took a musket, fought alongside Union troops on the first day of the battle, and was wounded. He quickly became a Gettysburg legend, even attracting the attention of Abraham Lincoln. According to some accounts, Burns readily denounced fellow citizens who had not taken up arms as he had, and, in one case, accused a neighbor who refused to fight of being a "damned coward, a chicken hearted squaw, a tallow faced sissy." What Burns himself did not say, his supporters expressed. Humorist Bret Harte disparaged Gettysburg men in a poem about Burns that he published in 1864. In the nationally run "John Burns of Gettysburg," Harte summed up Burns as "The only man who didn't back down, when the rebels rode through his native town." Burns, he continued, "held his own in the fight next day, when all his townsfolk ran away."[36]

One way to defend the borough's men against accusations of skedaddling or absenteeism was to deny the charges, repeatedly. This was the strategy of choice for borough editors for decades after the Civil War. Another, less obvious and perhaps less overt approach was to suggest that Gettysburg women who were left alone were not defenseless, but resilient and capable. Borough women who printed battle accounts and talked to reporters suggested this, even though they did not pointedly engage in the public debate. A further means of defusing accusations against Gettysburg men might have been to point to Jennie Wade. The shooting of Jennie in her kitchen suggested a breakdown of traditional chivalry. Jennie's house should not have been caught between battle lines and Jennie should have been shielded, not shot, by soldiers. But what if Jennie did not deserve chivalric protection? If she was a she-rebel, or if her morality was suspect, then she was less of a "protectable" person. Civil War gender codes worked both ways. Men—civilians and soldiers both—had obligations as guardians but only to vulnerable, innocent, and patriotic women.

For her part, Georgia Wade McClellan never ceased to regret the way that her sister's life and death became subject to public innuendo. Not long after the war's close, she, her veteran husband, and her battle-born son, Kenneth, left Gettysburg for good and settled in Iowa. She remained connected with individuals who remembered Jennie, including ex-cavalry men who had been stationed in Gettysburg during the war, and she occasionally traveled east to be present at ceremonies that honored her sister. But until the end of her life, the Gettysburg Jennie, the rumored-about Jennie, continued to haunt her.

In 1920, a man who had for years operated her Gettysburg house as a commercial museum reminded Georgia "about all the stories that were in circulation here," and about how he had "fought valiantly every defamer." Another man became Jennie's champion, producing a detailed history of her death. Yet Georgia remained concerned that "the name of Jennie Wade [would] be disgraced with misrepresentations." It is not clear how much hope she held out for ever clearing her sister's name, or how kindly she felt toward the borough where her family was subjected to ongoing scrutiny. She hoped to make a visit to Gettysburg in 1920, when she was close to eighty, but felt embittered. "I care very little for Gettysburg people," she wrote to the historian who had written about Jennie. "They are envious and back numbers according to my thought." In other words, she held no special fondness for her former town.[37]

Georgia's own work at Gettysburg in 1863 resembled that of so many women of the borough—necessary and valiant, and forgettable. While her mother had watched over her newborn son, she had cared for wounded soldiers in the borough and in the general hospital camp, and had later continued nursing in Washington, D.C. It was not until she was in her mid-eighties, living in Iowa, that suddenly people wanted to know more about her. She was one of the "few volunteer nurses of the Civil War yet living," and with her eyesight mostly gone, her health failing, the press suddenly rallied around her. "With phantom bugles of Gettysburg ringing in her ears," one reporter eulogized in 1927, "an old, old woman waits . . . for the roll of muffled drums." The reporter commented on her faulty memory as well as the paralysis that made it hard for her to talk. Georgia McClellan was so close to the end, he said, that she did not recognize her own children and could not recall events of the last decade. But mention the Civil War and she sprang to attention. She remembered the day she heard Lincoln give the Gettysburg Address. And Civil War business seemed to her to be urgent and current and real. "There's a boy across the hall who wants a letter written to his mother," she said to her attending nurse. "He's wounded so bad he'll never live. I do wish you'd write it for him."[38]

Georgia McClellan died in September 1927, when she was eighty-six years old. There was plenty of regret at her death, because nobody had captured her reminiscences. "Her sister's story," commented a local paper, "had romance in it, and her own was never set down." "We haven't anything at all," added her granddaughter, "We never wrote down any of the stories she used to tell. But now I'd give anything if we had."[39]

A MODEST REMEMBRANCE

Georgia Wade McClellan, who had nursed Union soldiers, borne a child in an occupied town, and suffered the death of a sister, was the mostly unremembered Wade. So was her mother, the parent of Union soldiers, a dead civilian, and a volunteer nurse. These Wade women had plenty of company, of course. After an initial flurry of speeches and a few publications honoring female sacrifice, most Gettysburg women, like most Northern women, slipped into oblivion. Regimental histories and soldiers' memoirs were produced to public applause toward the end of the nineteenth century, and monuments to soldiers' valor were dedicated with regularity, but women's work in both the battle and the war seemed increasingly unimportant. Gettysburg veterans occasionally took women to their hearts, pinned badges on their chests, and told them they were unforgettable and heroic, but it was clear to anyone who looked around at the memorial park that, unlike soldiers, women of the Battle of Gettysburg would be remembered only as long as the Civil War generation itself survived.[40]

To some people, the eclipsing of women's work in the public record was appropriate and seemly. To others it was regrettable. Just after the turn of the century, a local historian described the dismissal of women as a "neglect of oblivion that has enshrouded the deeds heroic of hundreds of maids and matrons of Gettysburg and vicinity," and another, a speaker at a Gettysburg Memorial Day address in 1898, called on his audience not to forget "the patriotic women of our land" who had, in the war, encouraged, cheered, nursed, raised money, and been tender in grief. He suggested a monument to women, "leaning toward" a monument to fallen sons, "as if to support it." Another woman regretted that there "was never any record made by either State or Federal Government of the services" of women "unknown and unrecognized."[41]

Rarely, a battle survivor put herself forward in print, to ask publicly why women like her had been so decidedly bypassed. Mary Montfort Melchior had been a young girl during the battle, and in 1886 she had a question for those who would ignore the work she and others performed. Why was it, she wondered, that people knew Gettysburg only by the names of Wade and Burns? Jennie Wade, she said, "was not the only woman who baked bread for the hospitals during the hours of the battle. But she lost her life in the act, and was immortalized; the others saved their lives for future work for the cause and are nameless." And as for John Burns—why, there were "women as old as John Burns" who went from house to house caring for injured men. Did a citizen have to shoulder a musket in order to be acknowledged? In questioning a society that made soldiers and shooting the highest measure of significance, Melchior stood up for all the forgotten civilians of Gettysburg. But she had especially harsh words for the people who dismissed women. Local women had done everything asked of them, and more. "Did their work," she wondered, "count as nothing?"[42]

Concerned that the answer to such a question was effectively "yes," some people put their heads and pocketbooks together to recognize women at Gettysburg. A "small company" of Iowa Relief Corps members, inspired by a visit to the borough and by their (now) fellow Iowan Georgia McClellan, dedicated a statue to Jennie Wade in 1901 in Evergreen Cemetery. They recognized that their efforts were a drop in the memorial bucket. It was, said one of the party, "the only monument for a woman among all these." Georgia McClellan herself, in attendance at the dedication, commented that she was proud of Iowa for "placing the first monument to the memory of women who served their country in the Civil War."[43] The location of Jennie Wade's statue was as unobtrusive as it was modest. It stood in the citizen's cemetery, not the federal park. The memorialization of men and women remained segregated: private and public, local and "national," less important and more important.

There were more routes to posterity than through stone and marble, however. There was print. Female survivors of the battle granted interviews to newspaper reporters, circulated memoirs, and produced short accounts of their battle days. But they spoke and wrote carefully. They repeatedly avowed their gratitude to Union soldiers at Gettysburg, and they cautiously addressed the male subject of battle and warfare. They did their best, in short, to frame their narratives in "womanly" fashion.

Many female narrators, for instance, honored the era's injunctions (and probably their own priorities) by claiming that they transcribed their stories for private or family purposes. Sadie Bushman's mother said she was "a bit sensitive" about her story, especially "telling it to outsiders," but she made it clear that "some day when I am gone you may tell it to one of your children or grandchildren." (Her granddaughter went further than that; she allowed it to be printed.) Fannie Buehler printed her memories of the battle, but insisted that her words appeared only for the sake of her children. "I do not do this for self-gratification," Fannie explained, "but to please my children, my grandchildren, possibly my great-grandchildren, and many friends whom I dearly love." Another woman printed her account—she insisted it was not "published"—to help benefit the local Sanitary Commission.[44]

These white women infused their battle stories with domestic character. They spoke of the way they baked bread and cooked food, of the way they bandaged and soothed soldiers, of the way they washed away the residue of battle and calmed the fears of their children. They showed how they shaped the battle by being good women. But their stories had many dimensions. Some women described how, once they had had a taste of life beyond their front doors in the horrific days of 1863, they did not look back. Georgia McClellan, for example, explained how she gave her baby to her mother and went to help soldiers in the nation's capital. Sadie Bushman was so committed to wartime nursing that in the next American war, in 1898, she applied to work in the Philippines. She was told she was too old.[45]

These women also revealed how the battle gave them an enlarged sense of capacity and skill and an ability to move in public and work with men. It allowed them to identify with male citizens and soldiers and with a narrative of national renown. Publicly acknowledged or not, they *belonged* to "Gettysburg," with all that that name implied. Sometimes, in fact, they talked like veterans. One woman related her battle stories to her children and friends "for many an evening," and on the occasion of World War One, her experience helped her identify with that conflict. "Her recollections of the battle," said her daughter, "were always most vivid, and helped to make the World War seem very realistic to her." Fannie Buehler emphasized her maternity in her account, but, perhaps inadvertently, also identified herself as a veteran. "I am only telling what I saw, what I did, what I know about it," she said in the introduction to her narrative of the battle, "for those who in future years may read or listen to the story, sitting around the fireside, as I, when a child, loved to sit and listen to the story of the Revolutionary War, as it fell from my grandfather's lips, who served in that war."[46] These women suggested that they had served, too.

By discussing their personal travails and transformations, these women called into question prevailing ideas about women in war. Much of what they accomplished at Gettysburg was not, as politicians and reporters would have it, instinctual, seamless, and romantic. It was instead deliberate, and extraordinary, involving risk-taking and physical and social struggle. Like other Northern women who called attention to their remarkable wartime service, these writers emphasized the many obstacles they faced at Gettysburg, and what they accomplished by surmounting them.[47]

Among the girls and women who described the rough and romantic sides of battle work were Sadie Bushman and Harriet Bayly. This young girl and this middle-aged farmer's wife both chafed at the limits placed around them by the men in their families. Harriet Bayly ran headlong into her husband's objections when she ventured out onto the battlefield on July 1 to assist injured soldiers. Her husband told her to stay home from then on, and she did. But she "never ceased to regret it" and put those regrets into print. And "angelic" Sadie Bushman disobeyed her father, in particular, when she expanded her girlhood horizons to work with wounded men. She was expected to stay home following the battle, but she slipped out to do hospital work, repeatedly. She endured regular whippings as a result. Thwarting male authority and then paying for it may have been something of a Bushman tradition; Sadie's mother was also punished for her curiosity during the shelling. She went to an upper-story window, looked out, dodged a bullet, and was picked up and carried downstairs by her husband. He said she "should be spanked" and demanded that from then on she "will obey orders, so help me God."[48]

White Gettysburg women and girls not only divulged how they bumped up against social boundaries during the battle; they also described how they faced conflicts between political and moral principle and the demands of caretaking. For every romance that blossomed between a nurse and soldier, in fact, there seems to have been a story that was less than sweet. In one hospital, for example, a young woman nursed a Confederate soldier who had lost both of his arms. As she fed him soup, he looked up at her "with a sneer." "We wouldn't let our ladies do this at home," he said. "This is what one of our niggers would do." She put down the bowl. "Get one of your niggers to do it for you then," she said, and walked out of the room. An eighteen-year-old girl also found herself unable to accept the compromise that caring for Confederates represented. An injured Confederate soldier allegedly developed affection for Sarah Miller during the time he recuperated at her house. A proposal of marriage left him rejected, though, because Sarah, who had two brothers fighting for the Union, could not "find it in her heart to give herself to a confederate." She did give him a lock of her hair, however. Twenty-five years later, a lawyer sent back the lock of hair, along with a check for thousands of dollars. The ex-soldier had died, and "his last wishes" had included returning to her the hair, along with the money. She lived in Brooklyn, New York, and he in New Orleans, but he had tracked her—the girl who had stood firm against romance—all his life.[49]

Women's stories not only cast doubts on nursing's romantic relationships but on nursing's "romantic" work. Women's accomplishments at Gettysburg were ideally fueled by natural empathy, but these women show us that they were actually driven by unimaginable toil, and they filled their accounts with details of exhaustion, illness, and debilitation. Their accounts of risk-taking and exposure further challenge the customary partitioning of "courage" into exemplary courage in combat and less celebrated displays of domestic fortitude. These women did not carry guns, and did not use weapons to defend themselves against attack, nor did they shoot the enemy, but some of them bore the markers of public peril and exposure nonetheless. Gettysburg casualties are often revealed in photographs as disemboweled and bloated men on fields, or as soldiers shot dead behind boulders. But these women suggest that there might have been a set of less dramatic pictures, never taken: dresses ripped by bullets and dirtied by mud; hands blistered by water pumps, by bread tins, by ovens; women soaked with the blood of the wounded; women dazed and shattered and shell-shocked. Only one of these residents queried why it was that women needed to prove they had a soldier's bravery in order to be acknowledged and remembered as brave at all. Most women sought simply to demonstrate that they, too, had experienced something painful and overwhelmingly hard.[50]

Women seeking some recognition for their courage faced remarkably steep obstacles, however, especially as the Battle of Gettysburg became more of a definer of manhood than a marker of moral victory. Gettysburg had always signified a powerful rite of passage, where white soldiers had distinguished themselves, through courage, as "men." But by the turn of the twentieth century, talk about manhood saturated veterans' reminiscences and public discussions of the battle's meaning. People spoke of how Gettysburg not only facilitated manhood; it exemplified manhood; it established the *standard* for manhood. If anybody had any doubts about the matter, they could consult the battlefield, where growing numbers of shafts and columns and statues reinforced the link between Gettysburg and men and bravery. Women's claims to courage necessarily fell on the public's deaf ears. To a great extent, "women" and "Gettysburg" were mutually exclusive.[51]

The extent to which Gettysburg served as a measure of masculinity, and the extent to which women's "weakness" figured into that calculation, can be seen in some of the accounts of male civilians at Gettysburg. Some of these boys and men were able and eager to set the record "straight." Gettysburg's John Charles Wills, for example, filled his account with "ladies" who were emotionally overcome by the battle's horrors, and who needed his assistance to reach safety on July 1. Borough men had been advised, he wrote in 1915, "to take our women and children and go into our cellars . . . and upon no occasion let them go out on the streets." But, he added, men disobeyed, and while "no women were seen on the streets . . . many men as well as myself went about in many different places of town to see what could be seen, as for myself I had no fear or thought of danger."[52]

Daniel Skelly, the brother of Jennie Wade's friend Jack, also printed an account of a "boy's experiences" during the battle. His account describes wide-ranging activity. He spent the battle days, he says, roaming about the town, openly meeting soldiers, climbing trees and rooftops. Skelly did not, according to a friend who introduced his account, "spend his time in the cellar," but was "in and through the thrilling experiences of those days, hearing and seeing." He was not only out and about when others (namely women) were presumably basement-bound, but he was tough when women were skittish. In one makeshift hospital, soldiers were so badly wounded that "a lady could not go near them" and deliver water. Skelly, not so intimidated, went around with his bucket while the timorous woman attended men who were not so "frightfully" hurt.[53]

Harriet Bayly's son William also contrasted his courage and daring with that of the women in his household. At thirteen years old, he had been too young, he said, to fight in the army, and that left him home alone with the womenfolk at the time of the battle. This had been a distinct burden: "I, being the oldest responsible male member of our family at home, must see that the horses are concealed, the cows driven to shelter, and the feminine portion of the family protected. All of which, of course, I saw to at once. But the question was, how could I look after a number of hysterical women." William Bayly did admit that his own mother was not at home during critical moments on July 1, and thus exempted her from the hysteria. Harriet Bayly, of course, told her own tale.[54]

While these male civilians tended to highlight women's fearfulness, the borough's newspaper editors were more equivocal. They were responsible, of course, for periodically bringing women's accounts into print, and they did so because they believed women's experiences commanded and demanded attention. Some of them could not help framing the female reminiscences, however. In introducing one young woman's narrative, editors remarked that they were pleased to offer "the experience of citizens during those three awful days" because there had been "no end" of "thrilling battle incidents and deeds of valor." There were citizens on the one hand, then, and "battle" and "valor" and "thrilling" on the other. Editors also on occasion printed news items that contradicted women's narratives of bravery. One paper printed an account of a "typical" border experience in 1885, which described how a Pennsylvania woman in one of the Confederate raids had died of fright, and described other females as "terror stricken" and "screaming, fainting and fleeing."[55]

A few editors also minimized the active involvement of Gettysburg women by linking women with the cause of pacifism. Most female storytellers described themselves as partisan battle players, fully supportive of Union fighting, as grim and horrific as it was. But in the early twentieth century, when peace movements and sectional reconciliation efforts called into question the idea of a "just war," women's accounts of blood and gore at Gettysburg were sometimes reinterpreted as a commentary on war's wastefulness. One account, published in Gettysburg in 1913 (coincident with the fiftieth reunion of the battle), was described by the editors who published it as a plea for peace. If Jane Smith's diary, said editors, "written with no idea that [it] would ever be printed, will help to make war hideous, or cause those in authority to pause before drawing the sword, this short diary will serve a purpose she dreamed not of."[56]

Dreamed not of indeed. Women who sought some recognition of the active role they played in the battle, including helping soldiers fight hard, might have been mortified that their words were twisted into pacifist critique. But they might have been gratified by the recognition. As the twentieth century progressed, the part that women played in the Battle of Gettysburg—pacifist or not—remained obscure. Local editors occasionally published reminiscences, mostly at battle anniversaries, and writers of fiction once in a while chose a girl or a woman as a protagonist. Then there was Jennie Wade, pilloried, worshipped, and sensationalized, who came to represent all women at Gettysburg, and none of them. The battle grew as a story about men who fought men to become better men. Best-selling historians rarely accorded women more than a few sentences in their tomes on Gettysburg. And best-selling novelists didn't do much more. In Michael Shaara's celebrated work about the Battle of Gettysburg, published in 1974, women appear fleetingly, as blurs behind windows or as visions of domestic loveliness. One woman briefly wields a gun, but she shoots a black man by mistake—a case of one unimportant character doing away with another. The soldiers bent on battle do not have time for any female distractions. They are fully absorbed in their separate, seemingly distant, world. Pennsylvania women are invisible and even soldiers' own wives are chimerical—inspiring them from a distance, opposing their going to war. Women are strangers to the way men conduct this war, and, the book suggests, to the way men love it.[57]

Gettysburg as a federally funded park paralleled Gettysburg's written history. It was a site throughout the twentieth century that honored veterans' maneuvers and operations, and where women appeared on monuments, if they appeared at all, dressed in togas. They were muses and symbols, almost all of them ahistorical. The story of the first day of the battle, in which women figured most prominently, was eclipsed in National Park Service tours by the story and the monuments of the Round Tops, Culp's Hill, and Seminary and Cemetery Ridges. The borough houses that were caught in crossfire, the farms where women served and protested enemy occupation, the churches and hospitals where they labored, remained in private hands, or, if they were Park property, they were shuttered to the public. In the wake of the revolution in American history in the 1960s, when narratives began to be researched and written "from the bottom up," including from women's perspectives, a few pioneers began documenting and discussing women's experiences at Gettysburg. But many of them worked in isolation.[58]

The long-standing dismissal of women in the public history of the Battle of Gettysburg would not have surprised the Civil War generation. Some of them would have wanted it this way. Theirs was a world where the good work that women did, even in trying times, was best left untrumpeted, and the way that women had changed in wartime was not a matter suitable for public discussion. Theirs was a world where the people who underwent celebrated trials in battle were men.

But other women looked beyond the dictates of modesty and chivalry to hope for some—even a modicum of—remembrance. Harriet Bayly was one of these women. She related her story of the battle to a reporter, telling him about her travails on July 1st, about the loss of her daughter's special horse, about her work with the wounded. She claimed she was telling "a woman's story," and her name was not printed. But her account appeared with her blessing, and so entered the public sphere where it could one day stand side by side with the tales of soldiers, less to challenge theirs for supremacy than to ask for a broad-minded and full telling. War, she asserted in her opening sentence, was a wide affair. Do not be fooled at Gettysburg, she said, by the "well known and well marked." The armies of 1863 took in many miles and many sites and many actors, all of them doing "brave deeds." She did not state that she was an actor at Gettysburg. Instead, she showed us.[59]

10

* * *

MAKING A LIVING ON HALLOWED LAND

PERHAPS NO ONE STOOD more squarely at the crossroads of black and white history in Gettysburg than Basil Biggs. Biggs, a leader of the borough's black community, had barely escaped before Confederate soldiers blasted into town in 1863. He had seen his rented farm ruined by the invading army. Hard-pressed, he had then taken on the grim task of disinterring Union soldiers and hauling them to the Soldier's National Cemetery for reburial. His work had helped make the words of Abraham Lincoln and Edward Everett concrete and specific: the orator and the president spoke over the neat, new graves of actual men.[1]

The part Biggs played in the evolution of Gettysburg's sacred ground did not stop with the cemetery. Not long after the war, Biggs bought and inherited land on Cemetery Ridge, close to other black landowners like Abraham Brian. Included in Biggs's property was a stand of trees—the kind that would sustain him with firewood, for buildings and fences, and for sale. One day, he was sawing away at some of his trees—he had already got a number of them down—when a man approached him. We do not know what words were exchanged, but the stranger—a white man—probably spoke with some urgency, and must have asked Biggs what he was doing. It is likely that the man informed the woodcutter that he was endangering a national treasure, that the trees were not just any small grove, but *the* copse of trees, the point toward which Pickett's Charge had moved, the place where—or nearly where—the Confederates had briefly penetrated the Federal line. The trees were a sacred grove, he must have said, which were worth a fortune in sentiment to veterans and citizens alike. The man, who was named John Bachelder, and who was already Gettysburg's preeminent battle historian, remembered that he "expostulated" with the landowner "without effect." Then he tried a different approach. He suggested to Biggs "that if he cut them then he was only getting for them their value as rails, whereas, if he allowed them to stand to mark the spot he would eventually get ten times as much for them." Biggs apparently stopped sawing.[2]

Basil Biggs left the trees standing, but he could not escape ongoing controversy over the future of the land—land that some people believed was close to holy, but that others believed—because they were poor enough that they had to believe—was serviceable. In 1881, the Gettysburg Battlefield Memorial Association, dedicated to the preservation and purchase of the battleground, lobbied to build a road from Cemetery Hill to the Round Tops to facilitate tourist traffic. The road would usurp and cut through land, including the now legendary copse. Biggs and other owners along Cemetery Ridge were asked how much they wanted for compensation. Biggs set a price of $125 an acre, which was deemed too high, and he was paid only $68 an acre. In 1882, Basil Biggs took the Association to court. A jury, convinced that the man deserved more money for his land and the trees, gave him a thousand dollars, plus eight months interest.[3]

Biggs's personal history of the battle, from the time that he fled Confederate kidnappers in 1863, to the days he exhumed dead soldiers, to his claims to "hallowed" land, suggests some of the competing meanings of Gettysburg. Biggs and other African Americans had been inescapably connected to the Gettysburg campaign—they had been threatened by invaders, they had sought to participate in the fight, they had suffered from the armies' destructive violence, and the battle's victory had significance for them and their brothers and sisters in slavery. Gettysburg's popular chroniclers, however—white veterans, editors, reporters, politicians, historians—showed little interest in black trials or black fortitude. Fewer still cared to acknowledge black contributions to the borough's reconstruction and to the battle's memorial events. Furthermore, with the dawning of the era of reconciliation at the end of the nineteenth century, Gettysburg's role in the history of emancipation faded in public importance. Black Americans became multiply estranged from Gettysburg's battle.

The record of Basil Biggs, as well as the stories of other people of color from the battle generation, like Lloyd Watts, Randolph Johnston, Owen Robinson, and Mag Palm, reveal this estrangement. They also show how hard it was for black residents to fully escape the dominant historical narrative. The battle was big business, and for people who struggled to make ends meet, it was business they could not afford to ignore. Even those African Americans who were drawn into the vortex of white battle commemoration, however, sustained their own histories of the battle, and claimed the Civil War past for themselves. Their children and grandchildren continued their efforts. This meant that by the turn of the twenty-first century, segregated histories persisted at Gettysburg, kept distinct and intact by people who were still trying to determine whether the work of the war was over or whether it had barely begun.

CLASPING HANDS ABOVE THE CHASM

For local African Americans, the Battle of Gettysburg had a two-sided history. It was an event that carried with it painful memories of loss and dislocation. And it was also a national symbol of a successful struggle for freedom. For many years after the battle, black people—not simply local folk—wanted to honor this second side of Gettysburg, and for many years they could. The popular history of the battle was infused with the story of the Union army's victory in the fight for emancipation, and the battlefield itself, and the borough that it surrounded, was welcoming to black and white visitors alike. From the 1880s until the First World War, trainloads of "colored excursionists" made their way to the battlefield and spent the day. They came as church groups and fraternal societies and as families, and some of them spent the night at local boardinghouses. Often they came to picnic, party, and dance at the commercial pavilions established near the Round Tops. But some of them also wanted to tour the sites where the Union army had triumphed. African Americans from nearby Baltimore came in biggest numbers on the September anniversary of the Emancipation Proclamation, thus celebrating, at least in spirit, the link between the battle and black freedom.[4]

The contest won by Union soldiers attracted black audiences in the late nineteenth century, and so did the white "heroes" of emancipation. In 1868, Gettysburg's black residents honored Abraham Lincoln in public rituals. Dressed in sashes and gloves, and marching to martial music, they cheered mightily for the "great emancipator." A year later they cheered Frederick Douglass when he spoke of Lincoln as "honest of purpose, large hearted." Fifteen years later, they still retained affection for Lincoln, albeit a different man. Robert Lincoln, the dead president's son, came to town with General Philip Sheridan, and the "colored people" were very "anxious" to see him, and to shake his hand. "They have not forgotten the Great Emancipator," commented a local reporter.[5] There were other shared heroes. Local black leaders celebrated the life and legacy of the committed abolitionist Thaddeus Stevens when he died in 1868. They honored their "great friend" with toasts, and Lloyd Watts spoke at Stevens' memorial service. That same year they also issued a special camp meeting invitation to General Oliver Otis Howard's brother, Charles, a veteran of the battle at Gettysburg, a commander of a black regiment in 1865, and an officer with the Freedmen's Bureau.[6]

For several decades after the Civil War, Gettysburg continued to be a place that honored the battle's role in the struggle against slavery. Visiting orators and dignitaries stressed the centrality of black freedom in Civil War history. Echoing Edward Everett, lecturers at Memorial Days or Battle anniversaries used words like "monstrous" to describe slavery, and "unholy" to describe slaveowners, and emphasized the moral success of the Civil War.[7] Toward the turn of the century, however, rhetoric softened significantly, and many speakers began to talk more about forgiving their former enemies than about Northern moral achievements. The movement toward reconciliation made many people happy. Commercial investors had been promoting sectional reunion since the 1870s and national politicians were eager to find new white constituencies. Popular nervousness about new immigrants and suspicions about immigrant-fueled labor strikes encouraged other white Americans to close ranks. Wars abroad also helped silence sectional disagreements, as all American men were "needed" to pull together and protect American interests (and white prerogatives) in Cuba and the Philippines. While some Union veterans remained distinctly reluctant to embrace their former enemies, other ex-soldiers willingly allowed the passage of time to diminish old divisions.[8]

Public discourse at Gettysburg reflected this sectional "healing." The subject of slavery and emancipation, which united white and black remembrance, began to be phased out, and veterans' reunions, commemoration rituals, and monument dedications began to feature new gestures of respect between the white North and South. While the battlefield itself remained an ever-expanding display of Union achievement—it had been studded with almost 200 Union monuments by 1888—it began to record Confederate actions as well. By 1890, a Maryland regimental monument had appeared, the Confederate High Water Mark—Basil Biggs's trees—had been enclosed with a fence, and the nearby spot where Confederate general Lewis Armistead penetrated Union lines had been honored with a memorial.[9]

Speeches delivered at the battlefield underscored new generosity toward former enemies. At the twenty-fifth anniversary of the battle in 1888, the governor of Pennsylvania, James Beaver, courted the reunion crowd by asserting that "there was not anything of personal animosity or bitterness or hate involved in the contest," and that the war had been fueled by "abstract ideas largely." At the same occasion, Confederate general James Longstreet employed the popular analogy of a bride and a bridegroom to describe the romantic détente between the white North and South. Over the next two decades, this "romance," and Gettysburg's key role in facilitating it, took on more explicit racial overtones. In 1913, an Alabama congressman gave a Memorial Day address that emphasized how Union and Confederate soldiers had mingled their blood in order to "do and to die for what they believed was right." A month later, at the fiftieth reunion of the battle, speakers spent four days expressing sectional forgiveness and white consanguinity. Thanks to those who had been "baptized in their life blood" at Gettysburg, one observer wrote, soldiers were now so closely linked "that difference of birth, employment, age, circumstance, politics, faith or section can never rend them apart." Gettysburg's importance, these speakers made clear, was not that it had helped deliver a death blow to slavery; rather, it helped tighten white blood ties.[10]

The story of the Civil War as a divisive fight over freedom did not fade without objection, at least before the turn of the century. Not only did some battle veterans resent the call for forgiveness, but local editors continued to allude to the specter of slavery, and to the fact that in Pennsylvania in 1863, "right" and "wrong" were at stake. And in 1888, the year that General James Longstreet talked about nuptial love between the North and South, protest flickered briefly as a counter-event to the veterans' reunion: A group of people in Adams County announced to the local press that they hoped the sons and daughters of the anti-slavery society of Adams County would also be having an anniversary—a "gathering" of their own.[11]

Visiting lecturers sometimes bitterly denounced the prevailing shift in public memory. Kansas senator John Ingalls, who spoke at Gettysburg in 1890, condemned the assertion that each side "died for what they believed to be their duty and God only knows which was right." I have, he said, "my opinion which was right. If we were not right, if liberty be not better than slavery, if nationality be not better than secession, then these solemn ceremonies that we now observe to-day are without significance and without consecration. If we were not right, then the war for the Union was the greatest crime of all centuries."[12]

There were some black Americans who, while hardly eager to make peace with former slaveholders, and hardly happy to witness new white alliances, also wanted to keep a distance from the painful subject of slavery. They wanted to put that horror behind them and move forward. There were other African Americans, though, Frederick Douglass among them, who were adamant that people not forget the hard past of American history as well as the key triumphs of emancipation. In the late 1880s, Douglass cautioned Americans—all Americans—against forgetting slavery and its uneasy legacies in the postwar period. He confessed he was worried when he saw white men begin to reconcile and "to shake hands over the bloody chasm." Social amnesia, he feared, was being paired with growing intolerance, especially new hardship for black people.[13]

Douglass's fears, of course, were well grounded. White reconciliation was accompanied and to some extent fueled by increased oppression of African

Americans. The decades around the turn of the twentieth century saw the repeal of civil rights legislation, the hardening of segregation, and the rise of racial violence, particularly lynching. By 1913, the year of Gettysburg's fiftieth anniversary, many of the civil rights triumphs of the Reconstruction period had become distant memories. An African American newspaper in Baltimore grimly put it this way: "with the single exception of slavery, everything [the South] fought for during the days of the Civil War, it has gained by repression of the Negro within its borders." For African Americans elsewhere in the country, including the border country of Pennsylvania, the sense of things was no different, leading one black leader to pronounce 1913 as a year when black communities were feeling more "discouraged and bitter" than ever.[14]

BLACK GETTYSBURG IN WHITE MEMORY

At the same time that all black Americans were beginning to "lose" the Battle of Gettysburg as a site and story of freedom, local African Americans witnessed the public repudiation of their personal battle experiences. The white Republican press in Gettysburg had sometimes spoken sympathetically of black civilians during the Civil War, and after the war it had, to a limited degree, continued to chronicle black concerns. A few white writers also occasionally acknowledged black experience in their work. They published accounts of old-time life in the Gettysburg area, took down oral histories, and made local black residents prominent characters in their fiction.[15]

Despite the recognition accorded to a few people of color, however, African-American experience during the Gettysburg Campaign was largely cast aside. Local newspapers set the precedent for the dismissal in 1863 by simply ignoring the distinct ordeals of black communities. One reporter, for instance, commented that Confederate soldiers had "behaved themselves very well" in Chambersburg, and noted that citizens and private property had generally been "respected and left inviolate." He admitted that "contrabands were taken, and free blacks; no distinction whatever was made in favor of any who were born free, either in the North or South; all were hurried away with all the horses and cattle that could be mustered in the neighborhood." But all in all he wanted to say that "we have had some exciting scenes, but nothing critical; no burning this time, and no real trouble." Another reporter was similarly indifferent. He noted how enemy soldiers plundered, "taking horses, negroes, and a large amount of store goods." And he expressed particular concern about the horses. "We are sorry to say," the paper commented, "that Capt. States of Bloody Run, had fourteen fine horses taken. A number of our citizens succeeded in getting their horses back again through the pleading of the ladies."[16]

This breezy dismissal of black suffering was rooted in racial indifference, of course, but also in the genuine relief that white Pennsylvania residents had felt when the invaders did not do as much damage as they anticipated—to them. By and large, white women had not been assaulted, and most white homes and businesses, even if looted, stood intact and unburned. Then, too, Confederate officers had engaged white residents in curbside chats and had permitted free speech and heartfelt but civil differences of opinion. Confederate soldiers had, on occasion, flirted with local girls. Many white residents confirmed that, all things considered, the Confederates had been gentlemanly in Pennsylvania.[17]

As the nineteenth century progressed, black residents faced new and equally belittling renditions of their experiences. White borough residents, anxious to answer critics about alleged civilian shortcomings in the battle, or eager to bequeath honorable accounts to their children, compared themselves favorably to timid and frightened blacks. "We were particularly uneasy before the Battle of Gettysburg," wrote one woman. "But none of the whites were scared quite as badly as the darkies." Descriptions of black families stumbling and running in panic, or mothers chiding their children to hurry, highlighted their own composure. The newspapers that printed many of these accounts added corroborative anecdotes. One noted how a black woman caught in the crossfire of a Civil War battle had been found seven months later in a neighboring state "an she handn't got done wid de hysterics yit."[18] All of these writers omitted from their stories the reasons for black flight, as well as details of kidnapping, social dislocation, or the damage done to black property, jobs, and psyches. Some white civilians expressed concern about black tribulations, but at the same time explained that they could only treat African American experience cursorily. Albertus McCreary, who diligently recorded the ordeal of the woman named "Old Liz" and her escape from would-be captors, wished that he could detail her story, but it was "more than I can undertake." Another white woman who reported the plight of the "colored people" explained that "if time permitted we might insert some curious scenes which occurred among them."[19]

Time did not "permit" discussions of black experience during the battle. Nor did it permit sympathetic accounts of black residents afterward. Once again, white stories centered on black fright, and in one prominent case the subject was Owen Robinson. This former slave, who had lived "in constant dread of being captured and taken South," had survived the invasion with his family. He was now a safely free man, and back in the food business. Employed by a white church, and a leader in the AME Zion church, he was the "well to do" father of ten children. But Robinson was still a black man who had spent his childhood in slavery. And that meant that, among other things, he might be fun to fool. As sexton of the Presbyterian church, he had the job of locking up at night. The church had served as a hospital during the battle, and Robin-son felt that it might be haunted. Young Gettysburg men made sure it seemed so. "Certain prankish youths in the congregation," remembered a white boy, "arranged that he should have convincing proof of his belief [in ghosts]," and they gave him an "unhappy" time closing down the church. They also passed along the story of his "gullibility."[20] White people also told tales of two other "scared" black men. Anthony and Billy Jackson, brothers, had been hired after the war as laborers on white-owned farms. The young men rarely visited each other at night because they were afraid of passing through an orchard where Confederate soldiers were buried. The brothers believed that they could "hear chains rattling up there." This story, too, needed to be shared.[21]

African Americans appeared prominently in wartime accounts as confused and frightened; they also appeared in battle accounts in more symbolic—and grotesque—ways. White writers not infrequently, and perhaps not consciously, associated men of color with passivity and vileness. They noted how corpses lying on the ground after the battle resembled black men, and how they pro-duced fear and loathing. One white woman explained to her cousin in a letter that after the battle she had visited the fields where men had died. "When we first went out the fields were lying full of dead rebs," she wrote. "They looked dreadful, all swollen up, they looked like colored men." Another woman, who had been a twelve-year-old girl in 1863, described a frightening experience in the battle's aftermath. When she was sent out to pick up some fruit for her mother on the edge of town just days after the battle, she passed through a lane and saw three dead men. She was forced to travel home the same way. Sixty years later, she could still remember how horrible it was to "pass those dead 'colored' men again."[22]

THE GREENING OF MEMORY

Black veterans and their families found it difficult to disentangle themselves from the web of white battle history. After all, the "mecca of American recon-ciliation" enveloped them, and white opinion, not to mention white story-telling, surrounded them. But some people of color insulated themselves from prevailing battle history and folktales both. Others created counternarratives. From the time of the battle into the late twentieth century, in fact, African Americans shaped and sustained autonomous memories of both the battle and the war.[23]

Black residents who had endured the battle, for example, passed along their own tales about bravery and manhood and contested, even if tongue-in-cheek, popular stories of exclusively white courage. One black woman (who barely escaped kidnapping) recalled how Confederate soldiers had scouted out the town just before the battle, dressed in female apparel. "Some time before the battle," she reported, "they come ridin' all around here dressed in women's clothes spyin' out." And then they had skedaddled. After a few days of fighting, "they'd just heard of some great army comin', and they run." Another woman, born years later, remembered hearing stories of how her family had remained in their house on Breckenridge Street, and when the cannonballs had come rolling down the middle of the floor nearby, "they'd throw em out." Others insisted that the stories of black residents taking flight from kidnappers—both local and Confederate—were exaggerated. Mag Palm's great-great-granddaughter repeated the family story of how Mag had not only fought off Gettysburg kidnappers before the war, but had bit one of their thumbs off and "spit it out!"[24]

The black community in Gettysburg told its irreverent tales and passed on its stories of resistance. It did not, apparently, spend much of its energy commemorating the battle itself. Black speakers, like white speakers, relegated civilian experience to history's backwater. Furthermore, this civilian experience was synonymous with trauma. Although Frederick Douglass might have disapproved, speakers and community leaders sought to stress the proud rather than the painful past. They also were well aware of the way that the public's Battle of Gettysburg had shifted away from their history, and their interests. Then, too, they may have regarded the summer of 1863 as something less than a watershed. Emancipation was an event that everyone cherished, of course, but the Confederate invasion and subsequent kidnappings in Pennsylvania were an extreme expression of threats they had faced for decades before the war. They had encountered the same threat one year later, in 1864, when Confederates had again moved into Pennsylvania. Finally, the racialized violence that had arisen in America since the war ended, and that seemed to be expanding year by year, also minimized the war's accomplishments. It seemed that every triumph, from Emancipation to the passage of the Fourteenth and Fifteenth Amendments, had its counterweight in hardship and hate. Life for black Americans, on some levels, had been a continuum.[25]

The black Gettysburg community did honor some aspects of the Civil War, however. It focused on the Civil War heroes everybody focused on: soldiers. It celebrated men like Randolph Johnston and Lloyd Watts. Gettysburg's Johnston had challenged white skeptics back in 1863 when he organized a black militia unit, drilled men, and offered to help defend the state. The United States government turned his services down in 1863, but he and Lloyd Watts and a number of other Gettysburg men eventually enlisted in the Union army. Along with nearly 180,000 other African American soldiers, including 8000 from Pennsylvania, these troops collectively rebuked the public that had questioned their readiness. Some Gettysburg men were sent to Florida, where they fought at the Battle of Olustee in early 1864. Some took part in assaults against Petersburg, Virginia, including the infamous battle of the "Crater." Some were assigned to duty in South Carolina and, in February 1865, when Charleston finally fell into Union hands, they served under a man who knew their hometown all too well: General Alexander Schimmelfennig.[26]

Lloyd Watts and Randolph Johnston joined Company B of the 24th United States Colored Infantry in early 1865. Within a week of enlisting, Johnston had been appointed first sergeant and Watts sergeant, and they were on their way to soldiering in a wasteland. Point Lookout, Maryland, wrote Watts sarcastically, was a "great looking place." "There is nothing," he said, "but warter [sic] as far as your eyes can carry you it is a narrow strip of land ninety miles from Baltimore and there is only one way to get out." Assigned to help guard 25,000 Confederate prisoners, Watts worried that he could not honor Sunday with rest. Johnston, whose years of training men to be soldiers now amounted to gang labor and guard duty, lost his health. In the summer of 1865, when his regiment marched to Roanoke, Virginia, for peacekeeping and supply work, he could barely keep up. He suffered increasingly from piles, and by the time they had marched into Virginia, he could no longer drill the company.[27]

Watts and Johnston and Gettysburg's other black soldiers returned home to a Pennsylvania borough that was beginning to remake itself as a war memorial. Already historians were engrossed in measuring and studying the battlefield, and the press was extolling Gettysburg's white Union soldiers. The local men of color who had been eager to stem the invasion, and who with other black American soldiers had also worked to win the war, attracted little attention. That did not mean that local black soldiers had been totally ignored. During the war, the borough's Democratic paper had devoted considerable column space to these men. Editors reported that black troops were among the first "to turn tail and run" outside of Petersburg in the summer of 1864 and that engagements in Florida earlier that year were disastrous thanks to African American soldiers. Certainly aware that Gettysburg's own black men were fighting at the Battle of Olustee, the paper had insulted them viciously. "It is now reported," the paper said, "that the Florida disaster is mainly due to the cowardice of the colored troops. We do not know how true this report is, but we are very certain that before the war is over the negro will not be found as brave, enduring, or efficient as the white." At least two black Gettysburg soldiers died fighting at Olustee, and more were wounded. John Watts, Lloyd's brother, had been shot in the shoulder and hospitalized.[28]

Long used to carving out a proud place for themselves, though, black veterans took up the task of honoring each other and of celebrating the war's social revolution. In 1866, Johnston and Watts, along with Owen Robinson, Basil Biggs, and nearly twenty other black men, formed a branch of a fraternal society called the "Sons of Good Will." Johnston was the association's first president, Watts the association's first secretary. The Sons of Good Will had several charges, including taking care of the sick, honoring the dead with a proper burial place, and celebrating with speeches and festivities Emancipation Day on January 1. Contributions at the first Emancipation Day celebration amounted to three dollars and thirty-five cents.[29]

Laboring under the shadow of the Soldier's National Cemetery, the Sons of Good Will struggled to find and maintain a place to bury black veterans. Ultimately purchasing a lot of land along Long Lane, members bought plots for their families and put in a fence and a gate. But it was time-consuming and expensive to keep the cemetery "in repair." And in 1879, when a group of white veterans went out looking for the "colored graveyard," they were "unable to find any one who could point out their graves, they being unmarked." They returned to Cemetery Hill, where distinguished guests spoke poignantly over the white dead, carriages brought the wealthy by, and children strewed flowers.[30]

The growing distance between black and white Civil War commemoration did not go unremarked. In 1873, during exercises at one of the black graveyards, a speaker reminded his audience of the meaning of the war. It had been, he said, a fight against "traitors" whose Confederacy had as its "corner stone Involuntary Servitude." Black soldiers had enlisted and fought with "heroic, self-sacrificing spirit" for a country that they hoped would recognize their "Manhood." But what had happened? Here in Gettysburg, while black men and women were now invited to decorate the graves of the white men who died in the Civil War, who honored men of color? The answer was obvious. "The colored people [were] requested to decorate the graves of the colored soldiers." The speaker was horrified. Did not these African American men "fraternize with their white comrades on many well contested fields of carnage and blood?" With this sort of segregation, he wondered, "where is the boasted civilization of America?" He called for flowers on the black soldiers' graves, so that the heroism of these men would not be lost, but rather be "green in our memories."[31]

Through the 1880s and 1890s, the black community continued to witness the public segregation of memory—civilian and military, black and white. While it seems that white veterans and community leaders occasionally honored black veterans, especially on Memorial Day, there was a growing disparity in public ritual. The "American" ceremonies held at the National Cemetery or on the battlefield were steadily funded and publicly recognized. These white men's graves were, after all, "our dead," according to local papers. The veteran graves in the "colored" cemeteries were "their" dead.[32] By the mid-1880s, "our dead" began to include, on a symbolic level, at least, some Confederates. Even as the Sons of Good Will struggled to make its graveyard "look respectable," Confederate veterans began arriving to considerable fanfare to identify their battle positions. In 1882, for example, former Confederate soldiers appeared in the borough to help "mark" the battlefield, and enjoyed a reception and a luncheon replete with toasts to and from Union veterans. The occasion, reported a newspaper, had "Union and Confederate ex-Soldiers vying with each other in sentiments of reconciliation." Black veterans did not have a lot of means to respond to these white army reunions, but they did have some. While Confederate and Union veterans were saluting each other in 1882, a local paper reported that "the colored ex-soldiers of this place are thinking of organizing a [separate] G.A.R. post."[33]

The Pennsylvania branch of the Grand Army of the Republic, the country's largest veteran organization, had admitted black veterans from its earliest days (albeit in largely segregated posts) and many white veterans in the postwar period had routinely collaborated with African Americans in honoring war dead.[34] Black veterans had at the same time struggled to persuade their white G.A.R. comrades to acknowledge their contributions in the war, as well as the importance of emancipation. Ultimately, they took matters into their own hands. They made speeches, they wrote recollections, they rallied, and they raised funds. A few of them also organized to try to install monuments to their army service, to place at least one dark face in an American landscape dotted with white stone men. Black veterans and other citizens in Philadelphia petitioned the Commonwealth of Pennsylvania in 1888, as "a matter of equal rights," to grant them money to install a monument to the "valor of our comrades." They were turned down. By 1900, there were just three monuments to black soldiers in the northern United States, none in Pennsylvania. In the South, monuments to African Americans went up with little white objection. They depicted loyal slaves.[35]

THE MYTH OF MAGGIE BLUECOAT

Public disinterest in African American veterans jarred the black community at Gettysburg and occasioned a sense of betrayal. There seems to have been no parallel disappointment over the disregard of black women. Women of color continued to have a voice in black civic affairs and sought to take part in Emancipation Day celebrations, but there was no visible effort to honor their achievements or sacrifice. The war, of course, had served as a monumental competition in masculinity, and service in the Union army had helped black veterans stake a claim to "manhood." The little recognition that was accorded to black residents went to the men who had served as soldiers, and who, like white men, established the standard for renown.[36]

Black womanhood in wartime was, by public definition, as invisible as it was tireless. During the Civil War, black women had helped hold the home-front together, serving their families and their employers alike. During the Gettysburg campaign, they had been subject to special fears and threats, and with their children had been targeted for kidnapping. They had been key to mobilizing evacuations and to finding safe haven. Some of them had provided vital support to white families during the Confederate occupation of Gettysburg. After the battle, they had rallied to rebuild the community, and worked to support their soldier heroes. But unlike white women, who were occasionally honored for their wartime contributions, these women slipped deep into the recesses of history.[37]

Public apathy toward black women's role in the Battle of Gettysburg meant that, around the turn of the century, stories began to disappear with their bearers. Some accounts would be carried into the future as fragments of oral history, but much was lost. Keziah Kuff's life largely disappeared. Keziah, a pipe-smoking woman who lived in a one-room wooden "shack," was known in Gettysburg to "almost every man, woman and child." She was, some claimed, over 120 years old when she died in 1926. While her birth date later came into dispute, there was no doubt that she could remember parts of the earlier century that most people only read about. A writer who published a short story drawn from Kuff's eccentricities noted her intense dislike of Jefferson Davis and her "delusions"—she believed she had been "sold from master to master, and that she had been beaten, and had run away and had come to Gettysburg," where she had been kidnapped yet again. Despite her "delusions," people who knew her described her "remarkable powers of recollection" and claimed Kuff could talk about antebellum events "vividly." She was also able to relate the story of the Battle of Gettysburg "clearly" and "always had a ready answer" for questions. The problem was, nobody wrote the ready answers down.[38]

Mag Palm also lacked note-takers. Stories continued to circulate about how she warned the black community on the eve of the invasion, about where she took refuge, and about how she survived, but few people knew her battle history for sure. Nobody could say, too, how much the Civil War changed life for Mag. She would never have to face enslavement again, that was for sure. But Mag may have otherwise picked up the cares she had known before. The war did not limit the way men could discipline or abuse women, for instance, and

Mag continued to have trouble with her husband Alf. He still drank, and occasionally came at her in a rage. Sometimes she took him to court, but she also stuck with him and served as his caretaker. When he was found about town drunk, she would load him into a wheelbarrow and roll him home. What also did not change for Mag was her life at the edge of want. She had succeeded more than some people of color, and she was eventually able to buy property for herself, along Long Lane, near other black residents. But the battle had thrown her world into disarray. And she could not stop working. She continued to scrub floors and beat rugs for white families, and she earned money meeting trains and hauling trunks through town. And it was still difficult to make ends meet. Mag had been raised partly at the almshouse, and it was to the almshouse that she turned toward the end of her life, for "relief" from the town.[39]

Mag Palm did not play a celebrated part in Gettysburg's rituals—black or white. Nor was she known for what she had accomplished or withstood. She was visible instead as a "character" about town. She "always had a pleasant word for everybody she met," and she was treasured for the way she made white folks laugh. Mag not only gave Gettysburg a chuckle; she amused other Americans as well. Elsie Singmaster, a prolific local writer, chose her as the basis for a lively character in *A Boy at Gettysburg* in 1924. Mag became the fearless former slave Maggie Bluecoat, who carried a musket with her, who weighed so much she "waddled," and who could not sit on a horse "without breaking his back." She also muttered in dialect and sang incessantly about "Marse Linkum." Bluecoat was so funny that other characters laughed, sometimes "hysterically," at her incantations. The book also translated Maggie Bluecoat's kidnapping ordeal into an adventure, featuring a daring rescue by white boys.[40]

The real Mag Palm may have enjoyed her reputation as an eccentric. She occasionally sent newspaper editors some of the natural oddities that she came across: a four-legged hen in 1876; a seven-inch egg three years later. There is no evidence, however, that Mag enjoyed serving as a laughingstock. In fact, she tried to take charge of some of the storytelling herself. She passed down her own accounts of her work and concerns in dialect that was not exaggerated "plantation," and told some of her tales to the people she worked for. They listened, and repeated them. In Mag's own story, she is no muttering fat lady; she is instead a woman who was attacked by local kidnappers and who defended herself fiercely and successfully. She is also a woman who armed herself with a shotgun and when one of her abductors appeared one day in the borough she went after him, saying "if she could have found him she would have shot him." Mag did more than talk about her ordeals. One day she went to a photographer and had her picture taken just the way she had looked when she had been bound up by would-be abductors. She is not laughing.[41]

Mag Palm would not be among the renowned actors or even the support-ing players in the story of Gettysburg. As a victim of attempted kidnapping, she had a lot at stake in 1863, and she lived smack in the middle of the battle's climactic space. She certainly had tales to tell. Because she was a black civilian woman, however, she had three strikes against her when it came to mattering to Civil War posterity. Mag died in 1896. One Sunday afternoon, late in Octo-ber, friends dropped by to call. They found that the "heart trouble" that had bothered her for some time had taken her at last, and they found her at home, sitting in her chair, gone.[42]

Toward the turn of the twentieth century, many of the other black residents from Gettysburg's Civil War era also passed away. Abraham Brian, who had rented a house to Mag Palm, and whose own farm on Cemetery Ridge was caught in the surge of Pickett's Charge, died in 1879. Basil Biggs, whose life had been affected not only by the battle but by the debate about the battle's meaning, passed away in 1906, at eighty-seven. In 1900, when Owen Robinson died, he was said to have been the oldest citizen of Gettysburg, and one of the oldest men in Pennsylvania. "Daddy" Robinson, born a slave in Maryland at the turn of the eighteenth century, had lived nearly a century in freedom. Like other African Americans, he never made much of a dent in the story of Civil War Gettysburg. Instead, his "gullibility" as a church caretaker attracted public comment, as did his cooking skills. His longevity also earned him honors. Six months before he died, he saw a photograph of himself in a Philadelphia paper. He was "much pleased."[43]

Randolph Johnston, who in 1863 had organized black soldiers to help re-pel Confederate invaders, left the Borough of Gettysburg in 1867. Shortly af-ter delivering some "spicy remarks" as the president of the Sons of Good Will (on an unknown subject), he moved with his wife to Maryland. There he taught school and became increasingly unwell. The piles he had suffered in the Civil War grew worse, and in his early fifties he complained that he could "hardly stand upon my feet." "I am oblige," he wrote in a pension affidavit, "to keep hot bricks to the soles of my feet to get to sleep." Johnston died suddenly in Baltimore in 1901 of a cerebral hemorrhage. He was sixty-one years old. His service to his country, his eagerness to fight invading Confederates, and his private strivings at home and at church barely grazed the public record.[44]

Randolph Johnston had missed Sunday school classes when he was a young man, but by the time he died he was a "Minister of the Gospel." Mag Palm barely surfaced in church minutes as a young woman, but after the Civil War she was active and involved; Owen Robinson and Abraham Brian were leaders of the church. All of these people point to the institution that centered their lives. While the battlefield became a shrine to white warriors everywhere, while Jim Crow insinuated itself into public life, Gettysburg's church community remained an oasis of safety and strength, continuing to promote strict Christian discipline, continuing to strive for racial justice, and continuing to offer support in troubled times.[45]

After soldiering in the Civil War, Lloyd Watts jumped into the task of church work. As secretary to the AME Zion church, Watts dutifully noted church doings and parishioner infractions. In the late 1860s and 1870s, he reported on the feisty women who skipped church classes or who quarreled or danced, the men who drank whiskey, and the members of both sexes who neglected church altogether. He also noted the people who recognized their failings, and who promised to live better lives. He acknowledged, too, the hard times that they all faced together, when the church had no money, and when they needed to "strive to work together" to salvage the institution that was their cherished taskmaster.[46]

Lloyd Watts was a church leader, a justice of the peace for the community, and one of the first black teachers in the borough. He was also active in the politics of Reconstruction—he worked on behalf of the Republican Party, and he spoke at ceremonies and town affairs. And he served in the battles over Civil War commemoration. As an active veteran, he not only helped the Sons of Good Will honor the work of fellow soldiers, but he campaigned independently to encourage the celebration of Emancipation Day. While many white veterans were trying to sideline the divisive issue of slavery, Watts did his best to keep the story of black freedom alive. At the same time, like so many other people of color in Gettysburg, he worked for the "other" war—the white man's war. And how could he not? The establishments that promoted the popular battle history—the history that increasingly skirted black experience—were some of the biggest employers around. Basil Biggs and other African Americans had begun their service in the history industry when they reburied soldiers in 1863. Thousands of others succeeded them, working in tourist hotels and restaurants, driving visitors around the battlefield, and cooking and cleaning for special memorial and dedication events.[47]

Lloyd Watts was employed, like many other men, directly on the field itself. He helped transform green fields and rocky inclines into one of the largest monument parks in the world. He helped erect statues to brave white men— men whom he believed were fighting in a war about slavery, but whom others argued fought for nothing of the sort. Watts did this work almost into his sixties, and the hard labor hurt him, literally. In the early 1890s, while laboring on the monuments, he suffered chest and joint pain. Soon afterward, he said, he became disabled.

In 1918, he died, a man steeped in the Civil War past, and bound up in the ironies of wartime memory.[48]

UNFINISHED BUSINESS

After people of the battle generation had passed away, their Gettysburg descendants continued to experience a relationship with the battle's public history that was fraught with contradiction. On the one hand they were estranged from a popular narrative that discounted black experience; on the other hand they could not ignore the business of that history that gave them work. Just as the Civil War generation had led double lives, these children and grandchildren also tried to make ends meet, and at the same time nurture a proud past. It wasn't easy.

The first decades of the twentieth century witnessed a solidification of the Battle of Gettysburg as a whites-only event. Occasional speakers at dedication ceremonies and memorial events continued to express gratitude to Union troops for their help in achieving the moral triumph of emancipation, but they were outnumbered by those who wanted to close their eyes to the subject of slavery and embrace Confederate veterans—and their descendants. Then, in the 1920s, the ceremonial mood, reflecting the prevailing national mood, moved from forgiveness of the Confederate South to its redemption. The Ku Klux Klan came to town. The white-sheeted hordes gathered on Gettysburg's fields by the tens of thousands. They marched through the streets of the Third Ward, the "negro section" of town, and posed for photographs on the battlefield. Some local Klan supporters seemed embarrassed at commandeering the town so brazenly, and a number of Gettysburg businessmen kept themselves hooded and gowned during the marches. One black resident remembered, however, that they had not fooled very many people.[49]

Not surprisingly, African American visitors to the battlefield at Gettysburg dwindled. It was not simply the tone of the place that discouraged black tourists, however. Local white residents had expressed concern about the rowdyism of black tourists for years, and during World War I, they closed the borough's bars during Emancipation Day. "Negro train specials" were also discontinued. Problems for people of color also centered on food and accommodations. By the middle of the twentieth century, as segregation fastened on the borough, touring African Americans found it nearly impossible to spend the night in Gettysburg. Of the thirty-six hotels and boardinghouses in the area in the early 1950s, none accepted guests of color and only three (out of fourteen) restaurants served them food, "depending on the 'situation.'" If they wanted to experience the Battle of Gettysburg on its home ground, then, black visitors had to drive in, pack food, tour quickly, and get out.[50]

Changes in transportation, as well as social segregation, affected local black people as well. As Gettysburg became a place to visit by the day by car, rather than by train for an overnight visit, many of Gettysburg's hotels, boarding-houses, and livery stables began to close down, and their black employees, particularly men, found themselves out of work as porters, bellboys, waiters, and especially as hack drivers. Some found work they could commute to outside of the borough, but others left Gettysburg for good.[51]

Black residents, squeezed out of battle-related service jobs by changes in transportation, had a hard time finding work in stores and shops that catered to Gettysburg tourists. The trends in American society that helped make the battlefield of Gettysburg an awkward neighbor to the borough's African Americans at the turn of the century grew more pronounced as the century progressed, and as segregation hardened. People of color continued to work for white employers as laborers and domestic help in the borough, but between 1925 and 1950, they were turned away from jobs in retail stores. "White folks don't want them waiting on them," commented one man. Another explained that his white "employees won't work with them." And it was next to impossible to get a job working at the National Military Park, even as a laborer.[52]

Gettysburg became a place that challenged local and visiting African Americans alike. According to one study, black residents found it difficult at mid-century to find a restaurant where they could eat, a bar where they could drink, or even a place where they might have their hair cut. Black families also had trouble finding places to live. There was only one area in town, the Third Ward, on the borough's southwest side, where people of color could easily buy and sell property.[53]

It is debatable whether segregation in Gettysburg was any worse than it was elsewhere in mid-twentieth-century America, but some observers argued that the borough, thanks to prevailing battle history, was indeed a special case. Gettysburg shop owners tapped into a battle story that gave increasing respect to Confederates and short shrift to the topic of emancipation. Their white employees catered to white Southern and Northern patrons, who outnumbered and outspent African Americans. A local judge explained what he saw as the commercial bottom line: "I believe the business people of Gettysburg discriminate toward the Negroes not because of personal feelings but because of the fear of losing tourist business, which is the life blood of the town." A hotel owner, he said, "had to protect his guests. . . . If he were to rent a room to a Negro who was a law breaker and if any crime occurred involving other guests, he would be responsible. . . . This community is unique because we have tourists from all over the United States in our hotels and restaurants every day in the year."[54]

As the Borough of Gettysburg divided into black and white worlds, the Battle of Gettysburg at the National Military Park was told in parallel narratives. Through the middle to late twentieth century, the Park, which came under federal jurisdiction in 1895, continued to focus on the battle's clash of muscle and strategic might, and to celebrate the valor of both armies. Yet at the same time it sustained a link, however tenuous, to Gettysburg's role in the "moral" Civil War. In 1912, for example, it established for visitors an emancipationist enclave, with a small but strategically placed Lincoln speech memorial, and much later in the century it introduced a basement exhibit on black troops (mostly Massachusetts regiments). Visitors sometimes came looking for this "other," this earlier Gettysburg. The "casual tourist," wrote one student of the scene in the 1950s, carries around with him the words of the "Great Emancipator," and even residents sometimes assert that "here is where the South lost the war," and "here the Negro was freed from his chains."[55]

The rise of the Civil Rights Movement in the 1950s and 1960s inspired not only local biracial groups to challenge discrimination and segregation in the borough, but encouraged resistance to Gettysburg's double histories: the predominant white "American" history seen in businesses and in "monument valley," and the nominal black history. Ironically, it was Lincoln, not Confederates, who began to lose ground as a compelling attraction at this time, as black Americans sought a positive and usable past, one in which their ancestors had played more than passive or subservient parts. Lincoln was a leading agent of Civil War freedom, but also a paternalistic one.[56]

The Civil Rights Movement had other effects on Gettysburg's public discourse. The celebration of the centennial of the battle, which took place shortly before the March on Washington in the summer of 1963, featured a number of speakers who called for an end to America's "unfinished business." Governor Richard Hughes of New Jersey threw down the gauntlet to those who had downplayed slavery and emancipation as driving issues of the Civil War. The Civil War, he said, "was fought to save America's soul." It was not fought "to preserve the Union 'lily white' or 'Jim Crow.' It was fought for liberty and justice for all." Hughes put it bluntly: "It is our shame at this moment that the full benefits of freedom are not the possession of all Americans."[57]

These interjections of moral meaning into Civil War memory, as well as the calls to correct ongoing injustice, were ultimately overpowered at the celebration, however. The former president of the United States, Dwight D. Eisenhower, deftly skirted the subject of slavery and its legacies by arguing that the

Civil War taught Americans the value of self-government, which was especially relevant in the contemporary struggle against "Communist dictator-
ships." President John F. Kennedy sent along a message extolling the manhood
and courage of the two armies—each, he said, having fought for the "right" it
believed in. Governor George Wallace of Alabama, famous for his stands
against integration, laid a wreath on the Alabama monument and spoke of
constitutional privileges.[58]

Despite the resistance of politicians like George Wallace, the Civil Rights
Movement made significant headway in widening political and social free-
doms in America. Among other things, it inspired a new generation of historians to reintroduce the subject of freedom into American narratives and to put
African Americans at the center of Civil War studies. What it did not inspire,
to a large degree, was a makeover of battle histories. Most of these narratives,
whether written or exhibited or displayed in stone, and whether nonprofit or
commercial, were distinctly resistant to the "new" social history in general and
to African American history in particular. The Battle of Gettysburg was no exception. For most of the late twentieth century, "Gettysburg," in all its manifestations, sidestepped scholarly developments and kept things the way they
had been for decades—socially and geographically circumscribed.

One of the most influential examples of this circumscribed history appear
as a best-selling novel. *The Killer Angels*, Michael Shaara's 1974 blockbuster,
extolls the deep brotherhood running beneath enemy lines in Pennsylvania
in 1863. Drawing from his rich imagination, rather from the historical
record that gives him most of his white characters, Shaara introduces into his
story a cringing, savage-looking black man whom Union soldiers discover en
route to Pennsylvania. Brutish and uncomprehending, with red eyes and
cannonball muscles, he appears to be freshly imported from Africa. Colonel
Joshua Chamberlain, a key character in the novel, finds himself both sympathetic and repulsed, and speculates on the man's awareness of his surround-
ings. "What could this man know of borders and states' rights and the
Constitution and Dred Scott?" the Colonel wonders. "What did he know of
the war?"[59]

This character throws Shaara's soldier protagonists into courageous and in-
telligent relief, and casts African Americans into ignoble shadows. For Shaara's
millions of readers, this man stands in for the real people of color who actually suffered the brunt of General Lee's invasion in 1863 and who knew as
much about borders and states' rights as anybody around. But there does not
seem to be a role for real black people in a book where soldiers fight in a social
vacuum and where slavery is the "lost" cause.

The Killer Angels, along with movies that it inspired, spoke to people who were primed to listen. They were also primed to act. White visitors flocked to the National Military Park in the last decades of the twentieth century to create makeshift shrines to Union and Confederate heroes both. Many of them wanted to do more than honor their heroes, too; they also sought to recapture and relive the Union and Confederate past. They wanted to "be there." Some of them attempted authenticity with old-time dress and battle reenactment. They spoke in period vocabulary, used period gestures, ate, slept, and fought like nineteenth-century men. And sometimes, even this wasn't enough. One visitor to Gettysburg lamented the fact that the past could not be truly restored: "I firmly believe," he commented, "that what should have been done was turn the entire town and environs into a frozen moment in time: July 1863."[60]

Contemporary African Americans—tourist and resident both—were not interested in recovering the past of 1863. Many were also not interested in surrounding themselves with monuments that celebration the Confederacy, or in fraternizing with people dressed as Lee's soldiers. Some black residents were offended by the thousands of Confederate soldiers who annually marched past their houses at the end of the century, in celebration of Remembrance Day. Remembrance Day honored the 1863 delivery of Lincoln's Gettysburg Address, but by 1997 its publicity featured Confederate flags and rituals paid "tribute to soldiers on both sides." Eventually, black residents avoided the battlefield and its businesses, and black tourists stayed away almost entirely. Guides sometimes offered their clients commentary on the historic black community, took them past Abraham Brian's house and the Lincoln speech memorial, and spoke about the battle's role in the history of abolition, but they talked to mostly white audiences. Close to two million people visited the park annually at the end of the 1990s, and the number of African American visitors who did not come with school groups or tours was, according to park personnel, less than one percent.[61]

One black visitor noted, in a prominent essay in the *New York Times* at the turn of the twenty-first century, why he in particular felt like such a foreigner at the battlefield. He was put off by the commercialism of the borough, he said, and by a "feeling of detachment from the battle, since no African American soldiers had taken part in it." He found himself an isolated visitor to the exhibits, a lonely man of color on Little Round Top, awkwardly encountering Confederate re-enactors and "Dixie"-whistling tourists. He had seen the Park Service exhibit on black soldiers in the Visitor's Center, and had read about Abraham Brian's house. Yet the place seemed to him alien land. He felt, he said, "like an uninvited guest."[62]

LIVING HISTORY

If in the late twentieth century black tourists could turn their backs on a historical site and a popular narrative that seemed irrelevant or unfriendly, local African Americans did not have that privilege. They could dismiss the dominant history as unimportant, or treat it with bemusement. They could avoid or picket stores and restaurants flaunting Confederate flags. They could privately bemoan living under the shadow of a war that didn't seem over. Many of them still needed, however, to keep body and soul together, and this meant that, on occasion, they worked for the company that ran the company town.

Catherine Carter and Margaret Nutter knew how this was. At the end of the 1990s, they were the living legacies of a woman and a man who had seen the Civil War firsthand. Catherine Carter, who was born in 1921, had heard a lot about her great-great-grandmother Mag Palm. Catherine herself passed down some of the stories, especially the ones about how Mag stood up to her enemies and fought back. As diminutive as Mag Palm was tall, Carter was tough-talking and had an expansive laugh, and she had grown up in Gettysburg. Descended from Alf and Mag Palm on her mother's side, and a Union veteran and a former slave on her father's, Catherine did what Mag did to get by—work for white families. And even though slavery was four generations away, it still festered as bad dreams and horror stories. Catherine's grandmother had told her tales about women "having to submit to the slaver." Her uncles were fathered by the slaveowner's nephew. What happened back then, she believed, "was not sanctioned by God."[63]

Margaret Nutter was two years older than Catherine Carter, and her best friend. The two women had lived out old age together, talking with each other every day. Margaret had begun working for families in Gettysburg when she was nine years old, and now, at the end of the century, she was beginning to slow down. Like her friend, she too had long links back to nineteenth-century Gettysburg. Her grandfather was the tireless Lloyd Watts, the man who wanted to make black men upstanding and black history memorable. Watts had passed on to his granddaughter many things, and one of them was his capacity to daydream. As a young girl, Margaret recalled, she was so distracted by the wonders of the everyday world that one year she was marked "tardy" nearly every day at school. She liked to lie down and stretch out in the cornfields between the north ends of Cemetery and Seminary Ridges, watch the clouds, and "wonder what made them move." Margaret Nutter was proud of her grandfather and everything he did for Gettysburg. She did not talk so much about the other connection she may have had to the Civil War. Family records, family artifacts, and "word of mouth" told her she had another grandfather, a man named Moses Thomas, who had once been enslaved by Robert E. Lee.[64]

Like Catherine Carter, Margaret Nutter had grown up sensitive to the long tentacles of slavery. In her house on South Washington Street, in Gettysburg's "black" section, Margaret used to read late into the evening. "At a certain time of night," she remembered, "I'd hear the clip clop of the horse and the wagon" at the corner. It would stop there and turn around, and then go back out. "It kept up until dawn." It was, she said, the sound of runaway slaves, getting out of a wagon and getting help at the Gettysburg stop in the Underground Railroad. Some people thought she was crazy to have heard things like that, but she knew what she had heard, and she believed in ghosts.

For Nutter, slavery lived in the shadows of dark nights, but not in the battlefield that surrounded her. For her family and friends, the historic site had no hallowed meaning—it was instead a playground, with cannons to play on and trees to climb, and it was a place of opportunity. "After Sunday School," she remembered, "was the battlefield." She and her friends would go to the "rec field and dig a little bit" and "get five cents." There were "bullets galore." When she got older, it was the reunions that really paid. The most important one was the seventy-fifth anniversary of the battle—in 1938. It was the last "living" reunion, the last time aged veterans of the battle came en masse to town. Tottering men tented with their attendants, reminisced with their former enemies, and listened to dignitaries dedicate a peace memorial. While some Union veterans still objected to sharing ceremonial space with ex-Confederates, the dominant mood was cordial. President Franklin Roosevelt issued a statement before the reunion and claimed that "the issues that divided America in that great struggle no longer exist."[65]

Behind the scenes, black women and men—Margaret Nutter and Catherine Carter included—worked to keep veterans healthy and fed. For people who needed cash, it was the chance of a lifetime—a week's worth of getting good pay and "good tips." The work, taking care of "old men ready to conk out," was hard, though. Some of the women and girls washed the men's clothes. And at least one worker, Margaret remembered, went through reunion latrines looking for coins to hook out. The reunion may have exacted more from black workers than toil. It brought in hundreds of ex-Confederate soldiers, and, as needy as some residents were, they were not needy enough to work for them. Margaret Nutter drew the line. Other people might be willing to make their beds or sweep their floors, but for her that was going too far. Catherine, on the other hand, had to cross the line. She had no choice. Her father had been killed the year before, and "so we had to scramble to get the tax money ready." She was sixteen at the time. She arrived at the veteran encampments early in the morning, in time to have a free breakfast with coffee that tasted like "mule piss," before making beds. She made over sixty beds a day, until she felt like she was putting on mattress covers in her sleep. Her sister gave her a hard time for working for the Southern soldiers. "They're gonna lynch you," she said. Nobody did. The men were "grabby," especially for their age, she remembered, but she had no other trouble.

But if she didn't have much trouble, she didn't take much pleasure, either. The battle reunion was the province of a foreign community. The battle's history had long ago veered away from people like her great-great-grandmother. Catherine Carter may have summed up the sentiment of many African Americans about the seventy-fifth anniversary of the Battle of Gettysburg. "It was," she said "the most uneventful thing in the world."

If the dominant history of the Battle of Gettysburg offered them more money than meaning, Catherine Carter and Margaret Nutter still had feelings for what the Civil War generation had accomplished. They remembered with fondness the black community's Memorial Day celebrations when they had been young—the parade, and the speeches in the historic black cemetery. One year, Margaret was asked to say the Gettysburg Address, as the community did annually, and she put on a blue linen dress with white piping and earned a dollar for doing it. These Memorial Day events were distinct from the bigger celebration the white folks put on, Catherine said, but not out of choice. "We weren't Jim Crowin' ourselves," she explained. Like nineteenth-century African American leaders who had looked for mutual acknowledgment and not found much, the contemporary black community turned inward to honor veterans of color and the struggle for emancipation.

In the early 1990s, these Memorial Day celebrations, which had been curtailed after the Second World War, were expanded. Their revival echoed new energy that was focused on African American history at Gettysburg. Women and men, some descended from the borough's oldest families, began probing written records, noting old-time stories, and writing a history that began to capture, finally, the complexity of Gettysburg's past. Some of these researchers maintained a distance from the prevailing story of the battle, but others began to insist on representing African American history at the National Military Park. They collaborated with the Park Service, which was itself reconsidering its slant on the battle, to put up a sign at the Abraham Brian house. Now tourists could know that besides Confederate and Union soldiers, there were "other people" who inhabited Cemetery Ridge. They worked with archaeologists to help survey and excavate African American sites, including the old Good Will cemetery that Lloyd Watts and Basil Biggs had helped establish.[66]

Changing interest in African American experience would not come soon enough or fast enough for Margaret Nutter or Catherine Carter, though. They both talked about the past and present in Gettysburg in what turned out to be the last years of their lives. They spoke about how the church sustained them, comforted them, honored them, just as it had their ancestors. And they spoke, still, of Gettysburg's separate spheres. "As far as the downtown is concerned," Nutter said, "it's still the same. You don't see a black face in a store. You don't see a black business down there. It's still the same." Carter felt comfortable eating in only one restaurant; there was only one lunchroom, she said, where she felt truly "welcome."[67]

Catherine Carter told most of her stories inside her small blue trailer on South Washington Street, in the neighborhood where her family had lived for at least six generations. Just one block over, almost within earshot, stood a parallel world, where "The Battle of Gettysburg" hummed. There, on Baltimore Street in the evening, men and women in Confederate and Union costume beckoned to tourists, bookshops and souvenir stores glowed neon, and ghost tour guides thrilled visitors as they crowded in and around restored houses. Once in a while a truck blasted down the thoroughfare, flapping the Stars and Bars on its bumper. A stone's throw away, on Carter's street, however, "history" was gone and the area was dark.

Shortly before she died in 1998, Catherine Carter sat in her trailer and spoke about the hope she had for different days ahead. "We're here," she said, "for such a short time." She brought out the book she had written about her family. With Sugar, her small, barrel-shaped poodle, on her lap, she described how proud she was of the research she had done on everyone from Mag Palm to people in the present, even as she revealed that she was having trouble placing the book in stores. As she talked, her police scanner blinked with the latest incident in the neighborhood. She got it, she explained, after she woke up one night to find a strange man in her house and bullets winging by outside. She also kept a gun nearby to stay safe—she had learned to shoot when she was little. "I was," she insisted, "never meant to be prey." Her resolve echoed earlier Gettysburg women who, in 1863, had been besieged by gunfire. But that, of course, was in a battle that lasted three days. By the late twentieth century, Catherine Carter had fought for a lifetime.

AFTERWORD

IN 1863, GETTYSBURG WAS the site of many battles. People who have read histories of the military campaign know a lot about one of them. Tourists who have traveled to south central Pennsylvania and who have visited the National Military Park and its surrounding fields know about one of them, too. They have walked the clean, green-sided slopes, scrambled up the bare and wooded hillsides, and taken the time to read stories etched on monuments and stamped on markers. They have learned about men with vigor and strength and impetuous courage. They have studied mistakes in judgment and errors in command. They have come to appreciate and to honor the generals who led the armies and the tens of thousands of soldiers who served in them.

Fewer people have paid attention to Gettysburg's other battles, including those that have been the subject of this book. In the contests here, men fought each other, even on the same side. Native-born and German-American Union soldiers inflicted injury, in fact, even before they shouldered weapons and even after they put them down. Their battles were about belonging and respect—about who got to be called a man, who got to be called an "American," and who got to be credited with courage—labels and identities, of course, that were usually synonymous. These hostilities were played out in the armies, particularly in the big battles of 1863 in the east, but they were not always limited to combatants. After the Battle of Gettysburg, Pennsylvania Germans were also swept up in public derogation. Like German-American soldiers, they were accused of fearfulness, but unlike soldiers, they were also accused of one of wartime's worst crimes: disloyalty. Across the United States, the public weighed in on these contests, throwing its approval in one direction—usually to the native-born majority—and its rebukes in another—usually to immigrants.

Ultimately, however, attacks and counterattacks on these noncombatants became backdrop at Gettysburg, as civilian history faded from battle memory,

233

and as immigrants from Western Europe gained acceptance in America. Criticism of German-American soldiers persisted in print, but by the early twentieth century, diverse soldiers began to stand side by side in monuments at the military park, everybody stalwart and firm and brave. And by the turn of the twenty-first century, as more people began to appreciate America's complex cultural character, scholars began giving German-American soldiers their due. But remnants of the old thinking remained. "Cowardly" Germans persisted in popular and commercial culture and in whispered stories at the battle site. Old animosities had lost some of their virulence, but not all of their appeal.

While men of the Eleventh Corps became better understood and appreciated during the twentieth century, their commander garnered less, rather than more, respect. If "ethnic" appreciation fostered better understanding of German-American soldiers, entrenched ideas about manhood did not give Oliver Otis Howard the benefit of the doubt. The vogue of rugged, tough, and secular masculinity left little room for the Howards of the military world. And Howard's moral courage, like Carl Schurz's moral courage, played to mixed reviews. As advocates for black civil rights and racial justice grew in number in the twentieth century—or, perhaps, because they grew—the history of abolitionism in the American Civil War was frequently edited out of popular memory. In the century-long celebration of "both sides," the commitment of these men to "right" over "wrong" was an unwanted reminder of white division. Schurz's "mighty cause" of emancipation and Howard's mighty work for freedmen and women were lost in the North–South commemoration of manhood.

This book has been about battles fought by civilian women as well as soldiers. White women in occupied Gettysburg were taken aback, literally, by the brutality that enveloped them in 1863, but they braced their families against the explosive violence and vigorously negotiated with the Confederate enemy. Sometimes they prevailed in these engagements, but occasionally they did not, and they suffered unhappy, even tragic, consequences. Women at Gettysburg fought, too, against strictures imposed by their own families, and after the battle some of them resisted social dictates that said that what they did in the summer of 1863 should be kept quiet.

Not all of these women experienced the battle or the battle's aftermath in the same manner. White native-born women of means, for example, had resources to cope with Confederate invaders, while poorer immigrant women, like Elizabeth Thorn, had a harder time meeting the demands of the emergency. Even though women engaged in the battle in distinct ways, however, historians have generally treated them all alike—and ignored them. With very few exceptions, writers between the time of the battle to the present have devoted themselves to soldiers focused on other soldiers in combat. They have chosen a time frame for the battle, too, a three-day span, that has obscured the many months of women's work. Battle, these historians have continued to suggest, is a male-defining event, epitomizing and idealizing a cultural divide between the sexes. Some nineteenth-century women of Gettysburg readily supported these divisions, and despite their own experience in battle's passable boundaries, willingly yielded the spotlight to soldiers. But some women—including the many women who publicly chronicled their experiences—challenged the neat partitioning of war.

Like most written histories, the federal battlefield park has shored itself against the presence of women and civilians. Its well-ordered fields suggest no messiness, no chaotic carryover of battle into homefront, no bold intrusion of homefront into battle. To a large extent it has not acknowledged the presence of local women either on the fighting fields, or in houses and churches, or in hospitals. Private organizations, commercial businesses, and persistent individuals in the borough have labored to recognize women's place and women's space in the battle of Gettysburg, but the massive, publicly funded park has focused on the men who fought and left quickly, not the women who were swept up in the violence, or who cared for soldiers left behind. Visitors to the park can still come and go and fully believe that women were barely around in 1863. The chivalrous model of war, where soldiers fought "far afield," is alive and well.[1]

Of Gettysburg's many battles, perhaps the struggle most overtly lost, in every sense of the word, has been the struggle of African Americans. Black women and men fought for their freedom in 1863, not, like Otis Howard or Carl Schurz, by taking up weapons and contending with Confederates. Most black men were not permitted military action in the summer of the invasion. These people fought instead in an unarmed struggle against overwhelming odds. And it was a battle with everything at stake: their personal liberty, the safety of their children, the security of their property, the integrity of their community.

The story of African Americans in the Gettysburg campaign was related, often casually, by observers at the time, but it became a tale few people sought to pass on. Some people believed it to be, or pretended it was, unimportant. Others, black and white, found it too painful to be repeated. Few of them knew enough about the experiences of women and men of color to realize that there was courage on display in this story, too, as well as resolute action.

And not many people realize that it still can be seen and imagined. It is there, at Gettysburg, in Abraham Brian's house, close to where Pickett's Charge failed. Unlike the stone and brass monuments on Cemetery Hill that honor brave sacrifice and martial boldness, and that celebrate the Confederate's high achievement, this wooden house narrates a different tale of determination. Visitors can see Brian's story in the fields he and his family planted in 1863, but could not harvest, and they can see the mile the Brian children walked to school, to get the education their parents never had. They can see the site where Mag Palm once lived, down by the Emmitsburg Road. They can also see the road that all of them probably took, late in June, to save themselves from the coming threat of slavery. And even though it is hard to say that Abraham Brian's house was a high water mark in a strictly military sense, visitors can see that it commemorates a battle—a momentous battle—of another kind.

Gettysburg was the site of these many battles, and its contours are large. It is long in topography, and wide in time. And it belongs to many people. For nearly a century and a half, Gettysburg has had a representative history—its familiar protagonists have stood in for everyone. It has also had a segregated history. In the borough itself the compartmentalization of the past is evident—here is the story of white fighting; over there is the story of Lincoln and "freedom"; and downtown, if you look hard enough, you can find some women. But the battle's boundaries were never that firm; its issues never that particularized. Its history was in many ways comprehensive. So, too, now, are its stories to be shared. Its dark account of terror and its tales of social cruelty are for all audiences; its multiple accounts of courage, on and off the battlefield, are to be celebrated broadly. Its soldiers are part of everyone's past and so are its civilians. The men who risked their lives for freedom at Gettysburg fought for all people, everywhere.

Gettysburg has been granted high purpose and meaning. It is possible, though, that the battle has not been momentous and telling enough. Perhaps it is time to go back to two of the earliest interpreters of the event, back to Edward Everett and Abraham Lincoln in November of 1863. Edward Everett told a long, inclusive story of Gettysburg, one that acknowledged, even if briefly, the "wide-spread" nature of war in Pennsylvania as well as the war's many players—its soldiers, its female civilians, its nurses, its people of color, and its overlapping battlefield and homefront. Perhaps Everett—the orator of the lost address—can inspire us to a grander Gettysburg. And maybe we can go back, too, to Abraham Lincoln's compact but lofty words, to his "unfinished work" and to his "great task remaining." Perhaps a way to move forward with that work and that task is to actually move back—to acknowledge the broad dimensions of war and the many people who shaped the dynamic past.

NOTES

INTRODUCTION

1. Amy J. Kinsel, "'From These Honored Dead': Gettysburg in American Culture, 1863–1938," Ph.D. diss., Cornell University, 1992, pp. 1–4. Gettysburg was referred to as the American Waterloo within weeks of the battle. See, for example, the *Star and Banner,* 9 July 1863.

2. Stephen W. Sears, *Gettysburg* (Boston: Houghton Mifflin, 2003), p. 38, refers to the Eleventh Corps as the "outcast" corps.

3. A classic use of these groups for less-than-favorable comparison can be found in Michael Shaara's *The Killer Angels* (New York: Ballantine Books, 1974). For a discussion of other uses of these groups as negative referents, see Chapters 8, 9, and 10.

4. On the rigid definitions of courage in the Civil War period see Gerald F. Linderman, *Embattled Courage: The Experience of Combat in the American Civil War* (New York: The Free Press, 1987), p. 17.

5. Edward Tabor Linenthal, *Sacred Ground: Americans and Their Battlefields* (Urbana: University of Illinois Press, 1993), p. 89.

6. Among the recent books that raise these questions with regard to twentieth-century Americans are David W. Blight, *Race and Reunion: The Civil War in American Memory* (Cambridge: Harvard University Press, 2001), and Tony Horwitz, *Confederates in the Attic* (New York: Random House, 1999).

7. Ronald F. Reid, *Edward Everett: Unionist Orator* (New York: Greenwood Press, 1990), pp. xi, 1; Paul A. Varg, *Edward Everett: The Intellectual in the Turmoil of Politics* (Cranbury, N.J.: Associated University Presses, 1992), pp. 15–68, 204.

8. On Everett's oratory at Gettysburg, see Paul Revere Frothingham, *Edward Everett: Orator and Statesman* (Boston: Houghton Mifflin, 1925), pp. 451–457. Everett's text can be found in Garry Wills, *Lincoln at Gettysburg: The Words That Remade America* (New York: Simon & Schuster, 1992), pp. 213–247 (Appendix III).

9. Everett, in Wills, *Lincoln at Gettysburg*, p. 229.

10. Everett, in Wills, *Lincoln at Gettysburg*, pp. 225–233, 241.

11. Wills, *Lincoln at Gettysburg*, pp. 34, 261; see also Blight, *Race and Re-union*, p. 13.

12. Garry Wills' entire book provides a provocative analysis of both the substantive gaps in and context for Lincoln's address.

13. See, for example, Shelby Foote's Remembrance Day address in Gettysburg, 1993. "Shelby Foote Cites Lincoln Intent of Unity, Forgiveness," *The Gettysburg Times*, 20 November 1993.

14. Reid, *Edward Everett*, pp. 100–101.

15. Frothingham, *Edward Everett*, p. 458.

16. Wills, *Lincoln at Gettysburg*, p. 211.

17. Studies of northern soldiers that have been particularly helpful include Bell Wiley, *The Life of Billy Yank: The Common Soldier of the Union* (Baton Rouge: Louisiana State University Press, 1979); Reid Mitchell, *Civil War Soldiers* (New York: Viking, 1988) and *The Vacant Chair: The Northern Soldier Leaves Home* (New York: Oxford, 1993); and Linderman, *Embattled Courage*. Important studies that acknowledge the vital importance of the northern homefront to the war's trajectory and that explore the intersections between soldier and civilian experience include Catherine Clinton and Nina Silber, eds., *Divided Houses: Gender and the Civil War* (New York: Oxford University Press, 1992); J. Matthew Gallman, *The North Fights the Civil War: The Home Front* (Chicago: Ivan R. Dee, 1994); Joan E. Cashin, ed., *The War Was You and Me: Civilians in the American Civil War* (Princeton: Princeton University Press, 2002); and Paul A. Cimbala and Randall M. Miller, eds., *Union Soldiers and the Northern Home Front: Wartime Experiences, Postwar Adjustments* (New York: Fordham University Press, 2002); on Pennsylvania in particular, see J. Matthew Gallman, *Mastering Wartime: A Social History of Philadelphia During the Civil War* (Cambridge: Cambridge University Press, 1990), and William Blair and William Pencak, eds., *Making and Remaking Pennsylvania's Civil War* (University Park: Pennsylvania State University Press, 2001). Influential scholars who have introduced northern women into Civil War history (and wartime history into the analysis of women's experience) include Elizabeth D. Leonard, *Yankee Women: Gender Battles in the Civil War* (New York: W.W. Norton, 1994) and *All the Daring of the Soldier: Women of the Civil War Armies* (New York: W.W. Norton, 1999); Jeanie Attie, *Patriotic Toil: Northern Women and the American Civil War* (Ithaca: Cornell University Press, 1998); and, for Pennsylvania women in particular, see Rachel Filene Seidman, "Beyond Sacrifice: Women and Politics on the Pennsylvania Homefront During the Civil War" (Ph.D. diss., Yale University, 1995).

18. On German Americans see David L. Valuska and Christian B. Keller, *Damn Dutch: Pennsylvania Germans at Gettysburg* (Mechanicsburg, Penn.: Stackpole Books, 2004); on borough civilians, see Robert L. Bloom, "'We Never Expected a Battle': The Civilians at Gettysburg, 1863," in *Pennsylvania History* 55 (October 1988): 161–200; Gerald R. Bennett, *Days of "Uncertainty and Dread"*:

The Ordeal Endured by the Citizens at Gettysburg (Littlestown, Penn.: Gerald R. Bennett, 1994); William A. Frassanito, *Early Photography at Gettysburg* (Gettysburg: Thomas Publications, 1995); Timothy H. Smith, "'These Were Days of Horror': The Gettysburg Civilians," in Barbara J. Finfrock, ed., *Unsung Heroes of Gettysburg: Programs of the Fifth Annual Gettysburg Seminar* (Gettysburg: The National Park Service, 1996); and J. Matthew Gallman and Susan Baker, "Gettysburg's Gettysburg: What the Battle Did to the Borough," in Gabor S. Boritt, ed., *The Gettysburg Nobody Knows* (New York: Oxford University Press, 1997); on African American civilians see Harry Bradshaw Matthews, "Whence They Came: The Families of United States Colored Troops in Gettysburg, Pennsylvania, 1815–1871," privately printed, Adams County Historical Society; Peter C. Vermilyea, "The Effect of the Confederate Invasion of Pennsylvania on Gettysburg's African American Community," in *The Gettysburg Magazine* 24 (2001): 112–128; Betty Dorsey Myers, *Segregation in Death: Gettysburg's Lincoln Cemetery* (Gettysburg: Lincoln Cemetery Project Association, 2001); and oral history work by Jean Odom and Shelley Jones. On Gettysburg women in general see Eileen F. Conklin, *Women at Gettysburg 1863* (Gettysburg: Thomas Publications, 1993), and Christina Ericson, "'The World Will Little Note Nor Long Remember': Gender Analysis of Civilian Responses to the Battle of Gettysburg," in Blair and Pencak, eds., *Making and Remaking Pennsylvania's Civil War.*

19. See John S. Patterson, "A Patriotic Landscape: Gettysburg, 1863–1913," *Prospects* 7 (1982): 315–333; Edward Tabor Linenthal, *Sacred Ground: Americans and Their Battlefields* (Urbana: University of Illinois Press, 1993); Kinsel, "'From These Honored Dead'"; Jim Weeks, *Gettysburg: Memory, Market, and an American Shrine* (Princeton: Princeton University Press, 2003); and Thomas A. Desjardin, *These Honored Dead: How the Story of Gettysburg Shaped American Memory* (New York: Da Capo Press, 2003).

20. One historian who has tackled the cultural construction of war head on is Linda Grant De Pauw, in *Battle Cries and Lullabies, Women in War from Prehistory to the Present* (Norman: University of Oklahoma Press, 1998) (see Chapter 1 in particular); see also John S. Patterson, "Zapped at the Map: The Battlefield at Gettysburg," *Journal of Popular Culture* 7 (1974): 825–837; Stephen Cushman, *Bloody Promenade: Reflections on a Civil War Battle* (Charlottesville: University Press of Virginia, 1999); and James M. McPherson, "Foreword," in Clinton and Silber, eds., *Divided Houses.*

21. Thomas Desjardin provides a good overview of source criticism at Gettysburg in *These Honored Dead,* especially Chapter 2.

PROLOGUE

1. Charles H. Glatfelter, "Gettysburg, Pennsylvania: A Very Brief History," typescript, Adams County Historical Society (hereafter ACHS), 1977, pp. 1–2.

2. Andrew Brown, *Geology and the Gettysburg Campaign* (Harrisburg: Bureau of Topographic and Geologic Survey, 1972), pp. 6–13; for the panorama

see Carl Schurz, *The Reminiscences of Carl Schurz*, Vol. III (New York: The Mc-Clure Company, 1908), pp. 5–6.

3. Robert L. Bloom, *A History of Adams County, Pennsylvania, 1700–1990* (Gettysburg: Adams County Historical Society, 1992), pp. 70–83 (quotation on p. 71), pp. 107, 127, 158–159.

4. Bloom, *History of Adams County*, pp. 102–103; Alice Powers, "A Timely Backward Glance," *The Compiler*, 27 June 1903. Gettysburg newspapers went through a succession of name modifications and owners in the nineteenth and early twentieth centuries. This book will cite names in common use at the time of the battle: *The Compiler*, *The Adams Sentinel*, *The Star and Banner*, and, later, *The Star and Sentinel* and *The Gettysburg Times*.

5. Joan R. Hankey, "Gettysburg Residents, 1860–1863" (Gettysburg: Privately printed, 1996).

6. *The Star and Banner*, 11 September 1846; 20 October 1848; 6 September 1850; *The Compiler*, 23 September 1861.

7. Bloom, *History of Adams County*, pp. 129, 172; Adams County Poor House Records, 1854–1864, private collection. African American population figures are derived from *The Star and Sentinel*, 22 September 1871; "Negroes in 1860 Cumberland Township" and "Gettysburg 1860 Census," compilations at Gettysburg National Military Park, Historian's Office (File 796); Sarah Sites Rodgers, ed., *The Ties of the Past: The Gettysburg Diaries of Salome Myers Stewart, 1854–1922* (Gettysburg: Thomas Publications, 1996), p. 160; C. M. W. Foster, "The Story of the Battle by a Citizen Whose Home Was Pierced by Flying Shells," *The Compiler*, 29 June 1904.

8. *The Star and Banner*, 12 June 1846; 15 June, 19 June 1849.

9. *The Compiler*, 26 January 1863.

10. *The Compiler*, 14 July 1862; 29 September 1862; 26 May 1862; 28 July 1862; 16 March 1863; 10 October 1862; 3 November 1862; on Adams County and Gettysburg political divisions see Gerald R. Bennett, *Days of "Uncertainty and Dread": The Ordeal Endured by the Citizens at Gettysburg* (Littlestown, Penn.: Privately published, 1994), pp. 2–3.

11. *The Compiler*, 5 January 1863.

12. *The Compiler*, 20 October 1862; 3 November 1862; 4 May 1863.

13. *The Star and Banner*, 7 May 1863; *The Compiler*, 11 May, 18 May 1863.

CHAPTER ONE

1. Carl Schurz, *The Reminiscences of Carl Schurz*, Vol. II (New York: The McClure Company, 1907), pp. 407–408; John J. Hennessy, "We Shall Make Richmond Howl: The Army of the Potomac on the Eve of Chancellorsville," in Gary Gallagher, ed., *Chancellorsville: The Battle and Its Aftermath* (Chapel Hill: University of North Carolina Press, 1996), pp. 10–11; Gary Gallagher, "Introduction," in *Chancellorsville*, p. ix.

2. Schurz, *Reminiscences,* Vol. II, p. 410; Stephen W. Sears, *Chancellorsville* (Boston: Houghton Mifflin, 1996), p. 97, 138.

3. Gary W. Gallagher, *The Battle of Chancellorsville: Civil War Series* (Fort Washington, Penn.: Eastern National Park and Monument Association, 1995), p. 12; Sears, *Chancellorsville,* p. 192; Schurz, *Reminiscences,* Vol. II, p. 410.

4. Schurz, *Reminiscences,* Vol. II, pp. 411–412; Louise Winkler Hitz, ed., *Letters of Frederick C. Winkler 1862–1865* (n.p.: William K. Winkler, 1963), pp. 46, 49–50.

5. Schurz, *Reminiscences,* Vol. II, p. 412; Sears, *Chancellorsville,* p. 193.

6. Sears, *Chancellorsville,* pp. 231, 239.

7. Gallagher, *The Battle of Chancellorsville,* p. 24.

8. The number of men in the Eleventh Corps is taken from Sears, *Chancellorsville,* p. 138; James S. Pula, *For Liberty and Justice: The Life and Times of Wladimir Krzyzanowski* (Chicago: Polish American Congress Charitable Foundation, 1978), p. 73.

9. Agricultural problems were many: Farms had dwindled in size as the population grew, and blights and crop failures had compounded the suffering. See Bruce Levine, *The Spirit of 1848: German Immigrants, Labor Conflict, and the Coming of the Civil War* (Urbana: University of Illinois Press, 1992), Chapters 1 and 2. Thanks, too, to Steve Hochstadt.

10. Robert L. Peterson and John A. Hudson, "Foreign Recruitment for Union Forces," *Civil War History* 7 (1961): 176–186.

11. Pension File WC 30.320 (Adam Muenzenberger), National Archives and Records Administration, Washington, D.C.; James S. Pula, *The Sigel Regiment,* available at www.russscott.com/~rscott/26thwis/franzsig.htm.

12. Adam Muenzenberger to Barbara Muenzenberger, 14 October 1862; 29 November 1862; typescript, State Historical Society of Wisconsin, Madison (hereafter SHSW); also available at www.russscott.com/~rscott/26thwis/adammuen.htm.

13. Pula, *The Sigel Regiment;* Adam Muenzenberger to Barbara Muenzenberger, 14, 30 October 1862; 19, 25, 29 November 1862; 16 February 1863, SHSW; John S. Applegate, ed., *Reminiscences and Letters of George Arrowsmith of New Jersey* (Red Bank, N.J.: John R. Cook, 1893), p. 184 (28 November 1862).

14. Adam Muenzenberger to Barbara Muenzenberger, 19 November 1862; 7, 9, 21 December 1862; 7, 16, 27 February 1863; 23 March 1863, SHSW; Barbara Muenzenberger to Adam Muenzenberger, 8 December 1862, SHSW.

15. See Christian B. Keller, "Diverse German Immigrants and Ethnic Identity on the Eve of the Civil War," in David L. Valuska and Christian B. Keller, *Damn Dutch: Pennsylvania Germans at Gettysburg* (Mechanicsburg, Penn.: Stackpole Books, 2004), p. 12; see also Frederick C. Luebke, "Images of German Immigrants in the United States and Brazil, 1890–1918: Some Comparisons," in Frank Trommler and Joseph McVeigh, eds., *America and the Germans: An Assessment of a Three-Hundred-Year History,* Vol. 1 (Philadelphia: University of Pennsylvania Press, 1985), p. 208; Valentin Bechler, a German in the Union

army, and a Republican, said he spoke for others when he shifted his allegiance after a hard dose of army life. He wrote home in late 1862: "Dear wife democrats will win. If I were home they would have one vote more. I don't want to fire another shot for 'die Neker' and I wish that all the abolitionists were in hell, before the country is ruined. That's what everybody I know is saying." Valentin Bechler to Leokadia Bechler, 11 November 1862, in Robert C. Goodell and P. A. M. Taylor, eds., "A German Immigrant in the Union Army: Selected Letters of Valentin Bechler," *Journal of American Studies* 4 (February 1971): 146, 161; Bruce Levine, *The Spirit of 1848*, pp. 9, 150–151, 196, 234–238.

16. James M. McPherson, *For Cause & Comrades: Why Men Fought in the Civil War* (New York: Oxford University Press, 1997), pp. 117–130.

17. Hans L. Trefousse, *Carl Schurz: A Biography* (Knoxville: University of Tennessee Press, 1982), p. 59; Joseph Schafer, ed., *Intimate Letters of Carl Schurz, 1841–1869* (Madison: State Historical Society of Wisconsin, 1928); Carl Schurz to William Seward, 17 November 1861, Schurz Papers, Library of Congress.

18. Schurz, *Reminiscences*, Vol. II, pp. 28, 37, 67–70; Schafer, ed., *Intimate Letters*, pp. 190–231.

19. Ezra Warner, *Generals in Blue: Lives of the Union Commanders* (Baton Rouge: Louisiana State University Press, 1996), pp. 426–428; Trefousse, *Carl Schurz*, pp. 123, 129–130.

20. Pula, ed., *For Liberty and Justice*, p. 65. The Polish-born Wladimir Krzyzanowski had, like Schurz, been exiled. See James S. Pula, ed., *The Memoirs of Wladimir Krzyzanowski* (San Francisco: R & E Research Associates, 1978), pp. 1, 2, 8, 9, 10, 40–43; Schurz, *Reminiscences*, Vol. II, pp. 41–43; Diary of Friedrich August Braeutigam, 3 January 1863, Civil War Miscellaneous Collection, United States Army Military History Institute (hereafter USAMHI), Carlisle Barracks, Penn.

21. Schafer, *Intimate Letters*, p. 109 (19 April 1852); Gerald F. Linderman, *Embattled Courage: The Experience of Combat in the American Civil War* (New York: The Free Press, 1987), p. 45.

22. Pula, *For Liberty and Justice*, p. 32; Applegate, ed., *Reminiscences of Arrowsmith*, p. 178 (24 November 1862); Martin Oefele, "German-Americans and the War up to Gettysburg," in Valuska and Keller, *Damn Dutch*, p. 36.

23. Adam Muenzenberger to Barbara Muenzenberger, 7 December 1862, SHSW.

24. Keller, "Diverse German Immigrants," pp. 9, 14; Ronald Takaki, *A Different Mirror: A History of Multicultural America* (Boston: Little, Brown, 1993), p. 139.

25. Schurz, *Reminiscences*, Vol. II, p. 404; Ella Lonn, *Foreigners in the Union Army and Navy* (Baton Rouge: Louisiana State University Press, 1951), pp. 179–180; Sears, *Chancellorsville*, p. 64–65.

26. Sears, *Chancellorsville*, p. 65.

27. John A. Carpenter, *Sword and the Olive Branch: Oliver Otis Howard* (Pittsburgh: University of Pittsburgh Press, 1964), pp. 32–33; O. O. Howard to Elizabeth Howard, June 1862, Bowdoin College Special Collections (hereafter BCSC).

28. O. O. Howard to Elizabeth Howard, 15 March to 22 March 1863, BCSC.

29. O. O. Howard to Elizabeth Howard, 29 October 1861, BCSC.

30. O. O. Howard to John Gilmore, 27 July 1851, BCSC; E. Anthony Rotundo, *American Manhood: Transformations in Masculinity from the Revolution to the Modern Era* (New York: Basic Books, 1993), pp. 172–173, 271–272; Carpenter, *Sword and Olive Branch*, pp. 7–9.

31. Carpenter, *Sword and Olive Branch*, pp. 20–21.

32. Rotundo, *American Manhood*, pp. 172–173; Reid Mitchell, "Soldiering, Manhood, and Coming of Age: A Northern Volunteer," in Catherine Clinton and Nina Silber, eds., *Divided Houses: Gender and the Civil War* (New York: Oxford University Press, 1992), p. 44; Frank Haskell, quoted in "Major General Oliver Otis Howard," www.rocemabra.com/~roger/tagg/generals/general26 .html; Schurz, *Reminiscences*, Vol. II, p. 405.

33. On Jackson see James McPherson, *Battle Cry of Freedom: The Civil War Era* (New York: Oxford University Press, 1988), pp. 454–457.

34. O. O. Howard to Elizabeth Howard, 20 December 1861, BCSC. Hooker was reputed to have turned headquarters into a brothel of sorts; Sickles had been at the center of a notorious love triangle, and had shot his wife's lover. See Warner, *Generals in Blue*, pp. 235, 446.

35. Sears, *Chancellorsville*, pp. 232–234.

36. Adam Muenzenberger to Barbara Muenzenberger, 6 April 1863, SHSW; Schurz, *Reminiscences*, Vol. II, p. 405.

37. Hennessy, "We Shall Make Richmond Howl," p. 24; *Letters of Frederick C. Winkler*, p. 42; Pula, *Memoirs of Krzyzanowski*, p. 74.

38. Mitchell, "Soldiering, Manhood, and Coming of Age," p. 46; McPherson, *For Cause & Comrades*, pp. 62–64.

39. Adam Muenzenberger to Barbara Muezenberger, 6 April 1863; 20 April 1863, SHSW.

40. O. O. Howard to Elizabeth Howard, 10 and 12 April, 1863, BCSC; O. O. Howard to Eliza Gilmore, 12 April 1863, BCSC.

41. *Letters of Frederick C. Winkler*, p. 43.

42. Schurz, *Reminiscences*, Vol. II, pp. 405, 407–408.

43. Adam Muenzenberger to Barbara Muenzenberger, 7 May 1863, SHSW; Elizabeth Howard to O. O. Howard, 10 August 1861; O. O. Howard to Elizabeth Howard, 28 March 1863; 12 April 1863; 1 May 1863, BCSC.

44. Donald C. Pfanz, "Negligence on the Right: The Eleventh Corps at Chancellorsville," Morningside Notes (Dayton, Ohio: 1984), accessed at www.morningsidebooks.com/notes/eleventh.htm; Stephen Sears explains that Hooker "posted Howard on the far right to keep him out of the most likely fire"(Sears, *Chancellorsville*, pp. 236–238, 270).

45. Sears, *Chancellorsville*, pp. 244–247; Oefele, "German-Americans," pp. 39–40.

46. Pfanz, "Negligence on the Right"; Sears, *Chancellorsville*, p. 266.

47. Sears, *Chancellorsville*, pp. 256, 262–263.

48. Sears, *Chancellorsville,* p. 266, 269; D. G. Brinton Thompson, "From Chancellorsville to Gettysburg, a Doctor's Diary" [Dr. Daniel Brinton's Diary], *Pennsylvania Magazine of History and Biography* 89 (July 1965): 300.

49. Alfred C. Raphelson, "Alexander Schimmelfennig: A German-American Campaigner in the Civil War," *Pennsylvania Magazine of History and Biography* 87 (April 1963): 168; Pfanz, "Negligence on the Right"; Sears, *Chancellorsville,* p. 279; Robert Hoffsommer, ed., "The Rise and Survival of Private Mesnard, Part One," *Civil War Times Illustrated* (January 1986): 24; Brinton Thompson, "From Chancellorsville to Gettysburg," p. 299; James L. Morrison, Jr., ed., "The Memoirs of Henry Heth, Part II," in *Civil War History* 8 (1962): 301.

50. See Sears, *Chancellorsville,* pp. 269–275; Hoffsommer, ed., "The Rise of Mesnard, Part One," p. 24; Brinton Thompson, "From Chancellorsville to Gettysburg," pp. 299–300; Raphelson, "Schimmelfennig," p. 169.

51. Hoffsommer, ed., "The Rise of Mesnard, Part One," p. 24; Devens himself joined the fight, but, wounded in the foot, was helped away by a man who described him as "drunk." Sears, *Chancellorsville,* p. 284.

52. Schurz, *Reminiscences,* Vol. II, p. 426; Sears, *Chancellorsville,* p. 277; Oliver Otis Howard, *Autobiography of Oliver Otis Howard,* Vol. I (New York: The Baker & Taylor Company, 1908), pp. 370–372; Rice C. Bull, *Soldiering: The Civil War Diary of Rice C. Bull, 123rd New York Volunteer Infantry* (San Rafael, Calif.: Presidio Press, 1977), p. 51; Pfanz, "Negligence on the Right." Special thanks to John Hennessy for information on Jackson's attack and on the perceptions of General Howard and his men at the time.

53. Darwin D. Cody to Parents, 9 May 1863, Fredericksburg & Spotsylvania National Military Park (hereafter FSNMP); Lucius B. Swift, [28th New York], Memoirs, Bigelow Papers, Library of Congress.

54. Ernest B. Furgurson, *Chancellorsville 1863: The Souls of the Brave* (New York: Knopf, 1992), p. 181; James H. Peabody, "The Battle of Chancellorsville," G.A.R. War Papers, Vol. I (Cincinnati: Fred C. Jones, c. 1891), p. 53; Historian Donald Pfanz cautions readers against accepting at face value Peabody's observations of Howard. See Pfanz, "Negligence on the Right," footnote 36.

55. Calvin S. Heller, Diary, 2 May 1863, Civil War Miscellaneous Collection, USAMHI; William H. Clark to his sister, 8 May 1863, Leigh Collection, USAMHI; Schurz *Reminiscences,* Vol. II, p. 426; Oefele, "German-Americans," pp. 40–41; Sears, *Chancellorsville,* pp. 277, 285.

56. On Eleventh Corps resistance, see William H. Clark to his sister, 8 May 1863, USAMHI; Charles Wickesberg to his family, 21 May 1863, in Donald Woods, ed., *Civil War Letters of Sergeant Charles Wickesberg* (Milwaukee: Alfred Wickesberg, 1961), pp. 15–18 (thanks to Wolfgang Hochbruck); Schurz, *Reminiscences,* Vol. II, p. 426; *The War of the Rebellion: The Official Records of the Union and Confederate Armies,* Ser. I, Vol. 25, Pt. I (Washington, D.C.: Government Printing Office, 1889), p. 655, Report of Gen. Carl Schurz, Chancellorsville Campaign, 12 May 1863; Adam Muenzenberger to Barbara Muenzenberger, 7 May 1863, SHSW; Pula, *The Sigel Regiment*; Sears, *Chancellorsville,* p. 546 (note 6).

57. Gallagher, *Chancellorsville*, p. 50; Schurz, *Reminiscences*, Vol. II, pp. 427, 431.

58. Mark H. Dunkelman and Michael J. Winey, *The Hardtack Regiment: An Illustrated History of the 154th Regiment, New York State Infantry Volunteers* (Rutherford, N.J.: Fairleigh Dickinson University Press, 1981), p. 65; Friedrich Kappelman to his parents, 10 May 1863, Civil War Times Illustrated Collection, USAMHI.

59. Schurz, *Reminiscences*, Vol. II, pp. 432–434; *The New York Times*, 5 May 1863; 6 May 1863; 3 June 1863; *The New York Herald*, 26 May 1863.

60. Carl Schurz carried on an angry, blame-sharing exchange with Brigadier General Adolph von Steinwehr. See Schurz to von Steinwehr and von Steinwehr to Schurz, 16 June 1863, Carl Schurz Papers, Reel 2, Library of Congress; Francis C. Barlow to his family, 8 May 1863, Massachusetts Historical Society, Boston (hereafter MHS); Barlow to his mother, 29 May 1863, MHS; Barlow to Charles Dalton, 2 June 1863, MHS.

61. Raphelson, "Alexander Schimmelfennig," pp. 162–163; Applegate, ed., *Reminiscences of George Arrowsmith*, p. 184 (28 November 1862).

62. Raphelson, "Alexander Schimmelfennig," p. 168–169, 171–172; Schurz, *Reminiscences*, Vol. II, p. 434.

63. L. L. Crounse, *The New York Times*, 5 May 1863; *The Compiler*, 18 May 1863.

64. Schurz, *Reminiscences*, Vol. II, pp. 434–435; Carl Schurz to O. O. Howard, 12 May 1863, Schurz Papers, Library of Congress.

65. *The New York Times*, 4 June 1863.

66. Barlow to family, 8 May 1863; Barlow to Charles Dalton, 2 June 1863; Barlow to "Richard," 26 June 1863, MHS.

67. Charles Wickesberg, quoted in A. Wilson Greene, "From Chancellorsville to Cemetery Hill: O. O. Howard and Eleventh Corps Leadership," in Gary W. Gallagher, ed., *The First Day at Gettysburg: Essays on Confederate and Union Leadership* (Kent, Ohio: Kent State University Press, 1992), p. 59; Adam Muenzenberger to Barbara Muenzenberger, 7 May 1863, SHSW.

68. Adam Muenzenberger to Barbara Muezenberger, 7 May 1863, SHSW.

69. Henry Blakeman to his mother, 2 June 1863, USAMHI; Dunkelman and Winey, *The Hardtack Regiment*, pp. 67–68.

70. O. O. Howard to Elizabeth Howard, 9 May 1863, BCSC.

71. O. O. Howard to Carl Schurz, 8 May 1863, Schurz Papers, Library of Congress; O. O. Howard to Elizabeth Howard, 12 May 1863, BCSC.

72. Carl Schurz to O. O. Howard, 26 May 1863, Schurz Papers, Library of Congress.

73. Ibid.

74. O. O. Howard to Elizabeth Howard, 26, 31 May 1863, BCSC; Larry Tagg, *The Generals of Gettysburg: The Leaders of America's Greatest Battle* (Campbell, Calif.: Savas Publishing, 1998), p. 122.

75. O. O. Howard to Rowland Howard, 16 May 1863; O. O. Howard to Eliza Gilmore, 17 May 1863, BCSC.

76. O. O. Howard to Eliza Gilmore, 17 May 1863; Thomazine M. Potter to O. O. Howard, 6 March 1863; O. O. Howard to Elizabeth Howard, 28 March 1863, 26, 31 May 1863, BCSC.

77. Carpenter, *Sword and Olive Branch,* p. 8; Charles Howard to his mother, 29 December 1861; O. O. Howard to Elizabeth Howard, 17 May 1862, BCSC.

78. Charles Howard to his mother, 13 January 1862; 12 August 1861, BCSC.

79. Rowland Howard to O. O. Howard, 12 May 1863; O. O. Howard to Rowland Howard, 16 May 1863, BCSC.

80. Carl Schurz also said he did not want to leave the corps because he did not want to "confirm the slanders circulating about me," and because it "will seem as if I were shaken off." See Carl Schurz to O. O. Howard, 21 and 26 May 1863, Schurz Papers, Library of Congress; Carl Schurz to Theodore Petrasch, 3 October 1863, in Schafer, ed., *Intimate Letters,* p. 287.

CHAPTER TWO

1. Andrew Brown, *Geology and the Gettysburg Campaign* (Harrisburg: Bureau of Topographic and Geologic Survey, 1972), pp. 6–13; Carl Schurz, *The Reminiscences of Carl Schurz,* Vol. III (New York: The McClure Company, 1908), pp. 5–6.

2. Another South Mountain gap would serve as an important feature in the Gettysburg campaign, too, although not as the same kind of advance gateway. Southwest of Gettysburg, the Fairfield Gap raised considerable concern in late June. Confederate troopers made their way through this gap on June 21, thwarting the efforts of Gettysburg men who tried to block their passage by felling trees. The Confederate infantry retreated through this gap as well. See Stephen W. Sears, *Gettysburg* (Boston: Houghton Mifflin, 2003), p. 480.

3. Women served in unprecedented numbers as nurses, working alongside surgeons in public settings, making life-determining decisions, and sometimes taking charge of acute medical care. They also developed increased political awareness and took part in more and more public engagements. But, ultimately, as some historians have pointed out, their work was infused with domestic overtones or content. Army nursing was nurturing work, not utterly different from caretaking at home. Even women who served armies as wartime spies, who demonstrated physical courage and independence, often depended on the feminine cover of gentility and delicacy to carry out their deceptions. For a discussion of the "time-honored" divisions of men, women, and war, see Jean Bethke Elshtain, *Women and War* (New York: Basic Books, 1987), and Linda Grant de Pauw, *Battle Cries and Lullabies, Women in War from Prehistory to the Present* (Norman: University of Oklahoma Press, 1998). On Civil War women who bent, but who often did not fully undermine the nineteenth-century gender system, see Mary P. Ryan, *Women in Public: Between Banners and Ballots, 1825–1880* (Baltimore: Johns Hopkins University Press, 1990), pp. 141–143; Elizabeth D.

Leonard, *Yankee Women: Gender Battles in the Civil War* (New York: W.W. Norton, 1994), pp. xxi–xxii, 198; and Leonard, *All the Daring of the Soldier: Women of the Civil War Armies* (New York: W.W. Norton, 1999).

4. See Leonard, *Yankee Women,* pp. xvii–xviii; Jeanie Attie, "Warwork and the Crisis of Domesticity in the North," in Catherine Clinton and Nina Silber, eds., *Divided Houses: Gender and the Civil War* (New York: Oxford University Press, 1992), pp. 247–259; Rachel F. Seidman, "Beyond Sacrifice: Women and Politics on the Pennsylvania Homefront During the Civil War," Ph.D. diss., Yale University, 1995.

5. On the 1862 raids, see Timothy H. Smith, ed., "The Story of Albertus McCreary: A Boy's Experience of the Battle," in *The Gettysburg Magazine* 17 (1997): 118–119 (esp. footnote 8).

6. Fannie J. Buehler, *Recollections of the Rebel Invasion and One Woman's Experience During the Battle of Gettysburg* (Gettysburg: Star and Sentinel Print, 1900; reprint, Gary T. Hawbaker, n.d.), pp. 6–7; "A Woman's Story," *The Star and Sentinel,* 25 September 1888; "Gettysburg's Fight," *The Compiler,* 12 January 1892.

7. "Mrs. Thorn's War Story," in "Woman, Keeper of Cemetery in 1863, Describes Battle," *The Gettysburg Times,* 2 July 1938.

8. The account here uses the spelling Möser, found in the Thorn Bible, for the family surname. During the battle, a note sent by Elizabeth Thorn's father uses Moeser (see Chapter 7). Later, the family adopted the spelling Masser, and this spelling appears on family headstones. Thanks to Brian Kennell, superintendent of Evergreen Cemetery, for this information (conversation on 29 January 2004). See also the Thorn Family file, Adams County Historical Society (hereafter ACHS), especially research note, 9 November 1986.

9. Marilyn Brownfield Rudawsky, "After July: The Effects of the Battle of Gettysburg on the People of Adams County," M.A. thesis, Youngstown State University, 1979, pp. 7, 9, ACHS; *The Star and Banner,* 20 July 1849; 2 January 1852; 11 June 1852; 24 March 1854; 1 June 1849; 5 October 1855; 18 November 1853; 15 December 1854; 26 January 1855; 16 February 1855; *The Star and Banner,* 8 February 1856; 3 April 1857; J. Matthew Gallman with Susan Baker, "Gettysburg's Gettysburg: What the Battle Did to the Borough," in Gabor Boritt, ed., *The Gettysburg Nobody Knows* (New York: Oxford University Press, 1997), p. 148.

10. Linda S. Pickle, "Stereotypes and Reality: Nineteenth Century German Women in Missouri," in *Missouri Historical Review* 79 (1985): 291–292; Harriet Beecher Stowe, *Household Papers and Stories* (Cambridge: The Riverside Press, 1896; originally published in 1839), pp. 487–493; on Frederick Stowe, who was seriously wounded at Gettysburg, see Calvin Stowe to O. O. Howard, 3 November 1864, Bowdoin College Special Collections (hereafter BCSC); Christian B. Keller, "The Pennsylvania Dutch and 'the Hard Hand of War,'" in David L. Valuska and Christian B. Keller, *Damn Dutch: Pennsylvania Germans at Gettysburg* (Mechanicsburg, Penn.: Stackpole Books, 2004), pp. 58–71; *The Star and Banner,* 5, 26 October 1855; 5 January 1849.

11. *The Star and Banner,* 6 January 1854; 13 June 1856; Eileen Conklin, *Women at Gettysburg, 1863* (Gettysburg: Thomas Publications, 1993) p. 166. Additional conclusions about the Thorns' way of life are drawn from genealogical and biographical notes, Chief Historian's Office, Gettysburg National Military Park (hereafter GNMP), and conversations with Brian Kennell, superintendent of Evergreen Cemetery.

12. *The Star and Banner,* 23 November 1855.

13. The *Adams Sentinel,* 22 June 1857; 29 June 1857; 6 July 1857.

14. "List of Paupers Commencing January 1st, 1846," Poor House Records, private collection. See also William A. Frassanito, *Early Photography at Gettysburg* (Gettysburg: Thomas Publications, 1995), pp. 121–123; Cindy L. Small, *The Jennie Wade Story* (Gettysburg: Thomas Publications, 1991), pp. 9–12; "Erect Tablets in Woman's Memory," *The Gettysburg Times,* 22 May 1922.

15. This account uses the historically familiar name "Jennie" to refer to Mary Virginia Wade, although it recognizes the fact that "Ginnie" may have been more commonly used by friends and family. See also "Erect Tablets in Woman's Memory."

16. Small, *Jennie Wade Story,* p. 13.

17. Frassanito, *Early Photography at Gettysburg,* pp. 121, 123.

18. *The Compiler,* 22 July 1861; see also *The Compiler,* 22 June 1863, for a description of women opposing the draft.

19. On this sort of advice (delivered to women in Philadelphia and Pittsburgh), see Rachel Filene Seidman, "Beyond Sacrifice: Women and Politics on the Pennsylvania Homefront," pp. 19–24.

20. *The Star and Banner,* 6 July 1855; 6 October 1854.

21. *The Star and Banner,* 10 April 1846; 6 October 1854 (quotations); *The Compiler,* 25 June 1860; 22 July 1861; Ryan, *Women in Public,* pp. 141–143; Rachel Filene Seidman, "'We Were Enlisted for the War': Ladies Aid Societies and the Politics of Women's Work During the Civil War," in William Blair and William Pencak, eds., *Making and Remaking Pennsylvania's Civil War* (University Park: Pennsylvania State University Press, 2001), pp. 59–79; Attie, "Warwork and the Crisis of Domesticity," pp. 248–252.

22. On the Wade sisters' friendliness toward Union cavalry see Samuel Leigh to J. W. Johnston, 18 May 1920, Rochester Museum and Science Center (hereafter RMSC); Anon. to Jennie Wade, 2 November 1862, RMSC; diaries that describe the routine of women's work in antebellum Gettysburg include Sarah Sites Rodgers, ed., *The Ties of the Past: The Gettysburg Diaries of Salome Myers Stewart 1854–1922* (Gettysburg: Thomas Publications, 1996), and diaries of Anna Cecilia Haupt and Mary Elizabeth Haupt, Herman Haupt Papers, Sterling Memorial Library, Yale University.

23. Judith Walzer Leavitt, *Brought to Bed: Childbearing in America 1750–1950* (New York: Oxford University Press, 1986), pp. 20–21.

24. Small, *Jennie Wade,* p. 9.

25. Evergreen Cemetery Burial Permit #309 (Jane Bayly), 11 March 1862, ACHS; Harriet Hamilton Bayly, "A Woman's Story," *The Star and Sentinel*, 25 September 1888; *The Star and Banner*, 22 December 1848; 12 January 1849; 8 June 1849.

26. Sir William Osler, *The Principles and Practice of Medicine* (New York: D. Appleton and Company, 1912), pp. 57–71.

27. Journal of Anna C. K. Haupt, 31 May 1843, Herman Haupt Papers, Sterling Library, Yale University.

28. Bayly, "A Woman's Story."

29. Buehler, *Recollections of the Rebel Invasion*, pp. 6–7; Seidman, "'We Were Enlisted for the War,'" pp. 60–61.

30. Buehler, *Recollections of the Rebel Invasion*; on David Buehler's editorial opinions and Fannie's good works, see *The Star and Banner*, 5 October 1855; 19 October 1855; 26 October 1855; 16 November 1855; 23 November 1855; 19 December 1856.

31. Buehler, *Recollections of the Rebel Invasion*, p. 17.

32. *The Star and Banner*, 8 December 1854; 6 November 1846; 7 September 1849; 24 August 1849; *The Compiler*, 12 July 1858; Anne M. Boylan, "Growing Up Female in Young America, 1800–1860," in Joseph M. Hawes and N. Ray Hiner, *American Childhood: A Research Guide and Historical Handbook* (Westport, Conn.: Greenwood Press, 1985), pp. 160–161.

33. James Marten, *The Children's Civil War* (Chapel Hill: University of North Carolina Press, 1998), pp. 117–118, 180–181; *The Compiler*, 1 June 1863; 22 May 1861; 23 October 1861; 9 December 1861; 29 September 1862; 2 March 1863; 14 July 1863.

34. For advice to young girls see *The Adams Sentinel*, 20 February 1861; see also the obituary of thirteen-year-old Louisa Myers, 4 August 1848, in *The Star and Banner*.

35. Indeed, one newspaper reported in 1862 that a girl had died from the fright of simply seeing a rat in her cellar. See *The Compiler*, 4 August 1862.

36. *The Compiler*, 6 May 1861.

37. *The Star and Banner*, 18 December 1846; *The Adams Sentinel*, 18 September 1861; *The Compiler*, 13 April 1863.

38. Leander Warren, "Recollections of the Battle of Gettysburg," typescript, no date, ACHS; Gerald R. Bennett, *Days of "Uncertainty and Dread": The Ordeal Endured by the Citizens at Gettysburg* (Littlestown, Penn.: Privately printed, 1994), p. 4.

39. *The Adams Sentinel*, 7 May 1860.

40. "Report of General Robert E. Lee," 31 July 1863, in *The War of the Rebellion: A Compilation of the Official Records of the Union and Confederate Armies*, Ser. I, Vol. 27, Pt. II (Washington, D.C.: Government Printing Office, 1889), p. 305; Edwin B. Coddington, *The Gettysburg Campaign: A Study in Command* (New York: Simon & Schuster, 1997; reprint of 1968 edition), pp. 3–7, 51. Both

the invasion and the Confederate advance north are discussed in Glenn Tucker, *High Tide at Gettysburg: The Campaign in Pennsylvania* (Gettysburg: Stan Clark Military Books, 1995), p. 20; Coddington, *Gettysburg Campaign,* p. 51; Sears, *Gettysburg,* pp. 14–15, 59–60.

41. Coddington, *Gettysburg Campaign,* p. 6; Sears, *Gettysburg,* p. 59; James M. McPherson, *Battle Cry of Freedom: The Civil War Era* (New York: Oxford University Press, 1988), p. 648.

42. Tucker, *High Tide at Gettysburg,* p. 22.

43. McPherson, *Battle Cry of Freedom,* p. 649; Coddington, *Gettysburg Campaign,* p. 16; Philip Schaff, "The Gettysburg Week," *Scribner's Magazine* 16 (1894): 25.

CHAPTER THREE

1. *The Compiler,* 22 June 1863; *The (Harrisburg) Patriot and Union,* 16, 25, 26 June 1863; 26 June 1863; 1 July 1863.

2. Many of the refugees from the Cumberland Valley were of German descent, and their property and livestock were critical to their agricultural way of life. See Christian B. Keller, "The Pennsylvania Dutch and 'the Hard Hand of War,'" in David L. Valuska and Christian B. Keller, *Damn Dutch: Pennsylvania Germans at Gettysburg* (Mechanicsburg, Penn.: Stackpole Books, 2004), pp. 59, 63. The actions of Jenkins' men are described in more detail in Chapter 6.

3. For discussions of what black women might fear in wartime, see Ervin L. Jordan, Jr., "Sleeping with the Enemy: Sex, Black Women, and the Civil War," *The Western Journal of Black Studies* 18 (1994): 57–58; Darlene Clark Hine and Kathleen Thompson, *A Shining Thread of Hope: The History of Black Women in America* (New York: Broadway Books, 1998), pp. 170–171; Linda Grant de Pauw, *Battle Cries and Lullabies: Women in War from Prehistory to the Present* (Norman: University of Oklahoma Press, 1998), p. 165; Joan E. Cashin, "Into the Trackless Wilderness: The Refugee Experience in the Civil War," in Edward D. C. Campbell, Jr., and Kym S. Rice, eds., *A Woman's War: Southern Women, Civil War, and the Confederate Legacy* (Richmond: Museum of the Confederacy, 1996), pp. 47–48. An enumeration of sexual assaults carried out by Union and Confederate soldiers, based largely on official military reports, can be found on the Web site www.hometown.aol.com/cwrapes.

4. *The Pennsylvania Freeman,* 9 May 1844; Carol Wilson, *Freedom at Risk: The Kidnapping of Free Blacks in America, 1780–1865* (Lexington: University Press of Kentucky, 1994), pp. 16–17, 42.

5. See Julie Winch, "Philadelphia and the Other Underground Railroad," in *The Pennsylvania Magazine of History and Biography* 3 (1987): 3–4. Most of the men witnessed in the act of kidnapping were identified as white. Samuel McAllister, son of one of Gettysburg's prominent abolitionist families, alleged in 1904, however, that a "yellow kidnapper" in town was active as well. His relatives, McAllister claimed, "would say it was a Lie" if they were confronted with

word of his involvement. See "Letter of S. R. McAllister," in G. Craig Caba, ed., *Episodes of Gettysburg and the Underground Railroad as Witnessed and Recorded by Professor J. Howard Wert* (Gettysburg: G. Craig Caba Antiques, 1998), p. 59.

6. The account of the kidnapping of Mag Palm, who was Margaret Devid (or Devit) at the time, is found in *The Compiler,* 15 February 1858; 26 April 1858. Mag Palm was under thirty years old when this happened. Her rough age is indicated in obituaries, *The Compiler,* 27 October 1896, and *The Star and Sentinel,* 27 October 1896. Further details of the incident, as Mag allegedly related them, can be found in a letter from David Schick to Elsie Singmaster Lewars, 24 April 1952, Palm Family File, Adams County Historical Society (hereafter ACHS).

7. "Negroes in 1860 Cumberland Township" and "Gettysburg 1860 Census," compilations at Gettysburg National Military Park (hereafter GNMP), Historian's Office (File 796); *The Star and Sentinel,* 22 September 1871; Sarah Sites Rodgers, ed., *The Ties of the Past: The Gettysburg Diaries of Salome Myers Stewart 1854–1922* (Gettysburg: Thomas Publications, 1996), p. 160; C. M. W. Foster, "The Story of the Battle by a Citizen Whose Home Was Pierced by Flying Shells," *The Compiler,* 29 June 1904; William A. Frassanito, *Early Photography at Gettysburg* (Gettysburg: Thomas Publications, 1995), p. 109.

8. Frederick Douglass, Address to the American Anti-Slavery Society, 4 December 1863, in John W. Blassingame, ed., *The Frederick Douglass Papers,* Ser. 1, Vol. 3 (New Haven: Yale University Press, 1985), pp. 605–606.

9. *The Star and Banner,* 28 August 1846; *The Pennsylvania Freeman,* 14 August 1845; *The Compiler,* 18 August 1845.

10. *The Pennsylvania Freeman,* 5 December 1844; Winch, "The Other Underground Railroad," p. 4.

11. For the case of kidnapping from a barbershop, see *The Star and Banner,* 24 April 1846; while chopping wood, *The Star and Banner,* 29 November 1850; while milking, *The Pennsylvania Freeman,* 25 September 1845; in a quiet place, *The Star and Banner,* 5 October 1855; under the pretense of a broken carriage, *The Star and Banner,* 10 January 1851; shake of the hand, *The Star and Banner,* 28 May 1852; in a shed, *The Star and Banner,* 28 January 1853.

12. Wilson, *Freedom at Risk,* p. 14, tells of the special vulnerability of children, and of two brothers in Philadelphia kidnapped near their home.

13. *The Star and Banner,* 14 June 1850.

14. *The Star and Banner,* 11 June 1847.

15. Thomas P. Slaughter, *Bloody Dawn: The Christiana Riot and Racial Violence in the Antebellum North* (New York: Oxford University Press, 1991), p. ix.

16. Charles L. Blockson, *The Underground Railroad in Pennsylvania* (Jacksonville, N.C.: Flame International, 1981), p. i, 145–146.

17. Untitled Record Book, Gettysburg, Pennsylvania, 24 November 1840, private collection; *The Pennsylvania Freeman,* 10 February 1841; Gail A. Stanislow, "Antislavery Sentiment and Opposition in Adams County, Pennsylvania," n.d., p. 7, typescript in the ACHS.

18. Blockson, *The Underground Railroad in Pennsylvania*, p. 144; this legend was likely promoted through the fiction of Gettysburg author Elsie Singmaster. Mag's descendants were told tales of her efforts on behalf of refugees, but acknowledge that this may have been simply "family talk." (Author discussions with Palm descendants, July 1997.)

19. "The McAllister Mill, an 'Underground' Station Where the Battle of Gettysburg Was Fought," in *The Millers' Review*, 15 March 1912, ACHS; George M. Neely, Jr., "The Anti-Slavery Movement and the Underground Railroad in Adams County," B.A. thesis, Gettysburg College, May 1930, pp. 17–21, ACHS.

20. Edward R. Turner, *The Negro in Pennsylvania: Slavery–Servitude–Freedom, 1639–1861* (Washington, D.C.: American Historical Association, 1911), pp. 227–239, 247; *The Pennsylvania Freeman*, 11 February 1847.

21. *The Star and Banner*, 3 November 1848; 16 February 1849; 12 May 1848; 1 November 1850.

22. *The Star and Banner*, 28 August 1846; 20 November 1846; *The Pennsylvania Freeman*, 14 August 1845; 1 October 1846.

23. Stanislow, "Antislavery Sentiment," p. 13; Thaddeus Stevens apparently had a dubious beginning in Gettysburg, when he took on a case that sent a fugitive woman back to slavery. Soon afterward, however, he became committed to defending slave refugees. See Hans L. Trefousse, *Thaddeus Stevens: Nineteenth-Century Egalitarian* (Chapel Hill: University of North Carolina Press, 1997), pp. 12–51; Betty D. Myers, "The Progression of Black Education in Gettysburg," lecture to the Adams County Historical Society, tape recording, n.d.

24. *The National Enquirer*, 27 July 1837; *The Pennsylvania Freeman*, 21 May 1840; 7 January 1847.

25. *The Pennsylvania Freeman*, 8 May 1845; 31 July 1845.

26. *The Star and Banner*, 21 January 1848; 23 May 1851; 31 January 1851; 7 November 1851; Robert L. Bloom, *A History of Adams County, Pennsylvania, 1700–1990* (Gettysburg: Adams County Historical Society, 1992), p. 173.

27. *The National Enquirer*, 1 July 1837; *The Star and Banner*, 19 June 1846; 11, 18 June 1847; 12 October 1849; 14, 21 February 1851; 9 September 1853.

28. *The Star and Banner*, 13 July 1855.

29. *The Compiler*, 16 June 1862; 29 December 1862; 16 March 1863; 18 August 1862; 22 April 1861; 23 March 1863.

30. Turner, *The Negro in Pennsylvania*, pp. 204–205.

31. See Donald H. Becker, "Trends in Negro Segregation in Gettysburg from 1900 to 1953," M.A. thesis, University of Maryland, 1953, copy in Abdel Ross Wentz Library, Lutheran Theological Seminary, Gettysburg, p. 80; and Chapter 10.

32. R. C. Smedley, *History of the Underground Railroad in Chester and the Neighboring Counties of Pennsylvania* (Lancaster, Penn.: Office of the Journal, 1883), p. 36, says that "there was a very friendly feeling in Gettysburg toward the abolitionists. The professors at the College and at the Theological Seminary were anti-slavery in sentiment and contributed to the cause; but they had to do it cautiously, as many of their students were from the Southern States"; see also

The Pennsylvania Freeman, 5 July 1838, and Bloom, *A History of Adams County,* pp. 173–176.

33. Joan R. Hankey, "Gettysburg Residents, 1860–1863"(Gettysburg: Privately printed, 1996); 1860 Cumberland Township Census, GNMP.

34. Marcella Sherfy, "The Brien [*sic*] Farm and Family," GNMP Report, June 1972; Memorandum, Senior Historian to Chief, I&VP, Brian Files, GNMP; Adams County Court records, Quarter Session G, 1836–1866, August Sessions, 1855; Mag Palm lived in the Brian's tenant house in 1860, according to census reports (ACHS).

35. Harry Matthews estimated that in 1840 half of the free blacks in Gettysburg were living within white households. See Harry Bradshaw Matthews, "Whence They Came: The Families of United States Colored Troops in Gettysburg, Pennsylvania, 1815–1871," privately printed, ACHS, p. 113.

36. It was, says one historian, as if the school directors had to keep reminding themselves that there were black children to teach, too. The school was shunted from pillar to post, from the teachers' personal rooms, to the basement of a lecture hall, to the black church. See Betty Myers, "The Progression of Black Education in Gettysburg"; Peter Vermilyea, "'We Did Not Know Where Our Colored Friends Had Gone': The Effect of the Confederate Invasion of Pennsylvania on Gettysburg's African-American Community," Undergraduate history paper, Gettysburg College, 25 April 1994, p. 7, Appendix A.

37. Payne would go on to the elevated position of bishop in the AME church. Bishop Daniel Alexander Payne, *Recollections of Seventy Years* (New York: Arno Press, 1968), pp. 44, 56–64.

38. This work will refer to this Gettysburg church as the AME (African Methodist Episcopal) church in the antebellum period and the AME Zion church for the period from 1859 on, following the apparent practice of church leaders. Among the black denominations formed in the United States in the early nineteenth century from the biracial (but segregated) Methodist church was the AME Zion, which added "Zion" in 1848, in order to distinguish itself from other secessionist denominations. Two decades after the Civil War the AME Zion church in Gettysburg added the name St. Paul. Thanks to Betty Myers for some of this information. See also AME Zion Leaders' Minutes Books, 1852–1881, private collection; "St Paul AME Zion Church, 1838–1994: A Version of Its History," typescript, private collection; Clarence E. Walker, *A Rock in a Weary Land: The African Methodist Episcopal Church During the Civil War and Reconstruction* (Baton Rouge: Louisiana State University Press, 1982), pp. 4–14; Becker, "Trends in Negro Segregation," pp. 73–75.

39. From a comparison of the 1860 U.S. census for the Borough of Gettysburg and AME church leaders' minutes, well over half of the black population of the borough receives mention in church activities. See census books, ACHS; also AME Zion Leaders' Minutes, 1838–1863, private collection.

40. *The Compiler,* 16 January 1900; AME Leaders' Minutes, 20 January 1840, private collection.

41. Betty Dorsey Myers, *Segregation in Death: Gettysburg's Lincoln Cemetery* (Gettysburg: Lincoln Cemetery Project Association, 2001), pp. 74–75; Matthews, "Whence They Came," pp. 134–135; Notebook of Lloyd Francis Asbury Watts, 1854–1858, private collection, Gettysburg.

42. AME Leaders' Minutes, 13 April 1861; 2 June 1856; 28 April 1856. Church officials were hardly exempt from scrutiny; in fact, in this democratic institution, they were often a target of complaint. AME Leaders' Minutes, 7 April 1852; 2 June 1856; 9 February 1858; 2 September 1859; 8 September 1860.

43. AME Leaders' Minutes, September 1852; 6 April 1861, 13 April 1861.

44. AME Leaders' Minutes, September 1852; 2 June 1853; 4 June 1858; 15 June 1859; 21, 23 November 1859.

45. AME Leaders' Minutes, 24 September 1859; 7, 8, 11 August 1860.

46. AME Leaders' Minutes, 29 October 1859.

47. Mag might have been a member of one of the other, smaller, black congregations, but she later joined this church. *The Adams Sentinel,* 30 January 1861; 24 January 1859; Cumberland Township Census (Adams County), 1860, ACHS.

48. AME Leaders' Minutes, 23 November 1860; Hankey, "Gettysburg Residents," p. 14.

49. See, for example, *The Star and Banner,* 2 April 1863, which reported that "An Act to Prevent the Immigration of Negroes and Mulattoes into this State had Passed the Pa. House of Representatives"; David Herbert Donald, *Lincoln* (New York: Simon & Schuster, 1995), pp. 343–344.

50. Gary W. Gallagher, ed., *The Antietam Campaign* (Chapel Hill: University of North Carolina Press, 1999), p. 14; Alan T. Nolan, *Lee Considered: General Robert E. Lee and Civil War History* (Chapel Hill: University of North Carolina Press, 1991), p. 17.

51. Charles M. McCurdy, "Gettysburg: A Memoir" (Pittsburgh: 1929), p. 19; *The Star and Sentinel,* 15 August 1900; Records of the AME Zion Church, 1840–1870, private collection; *The Pennsylvania Freeman,* 10 February 1841.

52. *The Star and Banner,* 11 June 1863; Randolph Johnston Enlistment Papers, National Archives, Washington, D.C.; on Johnston's company, see David Wills to Andrew Curtin, 15 June 1863, Military Dispatch Books, Book 18, RG 19.181, Pennsylvania State Archives. Thanks to Timothy H. Smith for this information. See also Frassanito, *Early Photography at Gettysburg,* p. 110.

53. This account assumes that Mag still rented the Emmitsburg Road house at the time of the battle, but acknowledges that we cannot be absolutely sure of that fact. (The 1860 census put her in that house, but since the building was largely destroyed on July 3, 1863, it is not referenced in the 1870 census.)

CHAPTER FOUR

1. Gen. Joseph Hooker to John C. Babcock, 20 June 1863, in *The War of the Rebellion: The Official Records of the Union and Confederate Armies,* Ser. 1, Vol.

27, Pt. 3 (Washington, D.C.: Government Printing Office, 1889), p. 225 (hereafter cited as *Official Records*).

2. Edwin B. Coddington, *The Gettysburg Campaign: A Study in Command* (New York: Touchstone, 1997), pp. 49–50, 70.

3. Charles Howard to Rowland Howard, 3 June 1863, Bowdoin College Special Collections (hereafter BCSC).

4. Charles Howard to Rowland Howard, 3 June 1863, BCSC; Charles Howard to Eliza Gilmore, 6 June 1863, BCSC; O. O. Howard to Elizabeth Howard, 6, 17 June 1863; Howard Papers, BCSC.

5. Charles Howard to Eliza Gilmore, 15, 19 June 1863.

6. D. G. Brinton Thompson, ed., "From Chancellorsville to Gettysburg, a Doctor's Diary [Daniel G. Brinton]," in *The Pennsylvania Magazine of History and Biography* 89 (July 1965): 305-306, 308 (14–19 June 1863); Adam Muenzenberger to Barbara Muenzenberger, June 1863, typescript, State Historical Society of Wisconsin, Madison (hereafter SHSW); Mark H. Dunkelman and Michael J. Winey, *The Hardtack Regiment: An Illustrated History of the 154th Regiment, New York State Infantry Volunteers* (Rutherford, N.J.: Fairleigh Dickinson University Press, 1981), pp. 68–69; John Michael Priest, ed., *John T. McMahon's Diary of the 136th New York, 1861–1864* (Shippensburg, Penn: White Mane Publishing, 1993), 12 June 1863 to 15 June 1863; Diary of Calvin S. Heller, 12 June 1863, Civil War Miscellaneous Collection, United States Army Military History Institute (hereafter USAMHI), Carlisle, Penn.

7. Albert Wallber, "From Gettysburg to Libby Prison," MOLLUS, Wisconsin Commandery, War Papers, Vol. 4 (Milwaukee: 1914), p. 191; Heller diary, 12 June 1863; Coddington, *Gettysburg Campaign*, p. 621 (note).

8. Heller diary, 22 June to 27 June 1863; Louise Winkler Hitz, ed., *Letters of Frederick C. Winkler, 1862–1865* (n.p.: William K. Winkler, 1963), p. 63; Brinton diary, 19 June 1863, p. 308; O. O. Howard to Elizabeth Howard, 19 June 1863; Rowland Howard to Elizabeth Howard, 26 June 1863; Coddington, *Gettysburg Campaign*, pp. 123, 631 (note).

9. Adam Muenzenberger to Barbara Muenzenberger, 31 May 1863; 7, 22 June 1863, SHSW.

10. Adam Muenzenberger to Barbara Muenzenberger, 22, 24 June 1863, SHSW.

11. Adam Muenzenberger to Barbara Muenzenberger, 24 June 1863, SHSW.

12. Brinton diary, 25 June 1863, p. 309; Heller diary, 22 June to 27 June 1863.

13. Dunkelman and Winey, *The Hardtack Regiment*, p. 70.

14. C. M. W. Foster, "The Story of the Battle by a Citizen Whose Home Was Pierced by Flying Shells," *The Compiler*, 29 June 1904; Gerald R. Bennett, *Days of "Uncertainty and Dread": The Ordeal Endured by the Citizens at Gettysburg* (Littlestown, Penn.: Privately printed, 1994), p. 6; John Charles Wills, "Reminiscences of the Three Days Battle of Gettysburg at the 'Globe Hotel,'" typescript, c. 1910, ACHS; [Sue Myers], "Some Battle Experiences as Remembered by a Young

School Girl," *The Compiler*, 24 April 1907; Fannie J. Buehler, *Recollections of the Rebel Invasion and One Woman's Experience During the Battle of Gettysburg* (Gettysburg: Star and Sentinel Print, 1900; reprint, Gary T. Hawbaker, n.d.), p. 6; [Alice Powers], "A Timely Backward Glance," *The Compiler*, 27 June 1903; Sarah Sites Rodgers, ed., *The Ties of the Past: The Gettysburg Diaries of Salome Myers Stewart, 1854–1922* (Gettysburg: Thomas Publications, 1996), p. 160.

15. Sarah Broadhead, *The Diary of a Lady of Gettysburg, Pennsylvania from June 15 to July 15 1863* (Hershey, Penn.: Gary T. Hawbaker, 1990; reprint), pp. 3, 7; Buehler, *Recollections*, pp. 8–9.

16. Bennett, *Days of "Uncertainty,"* p. 7; "The Bank Clerk," in Clifton Johnson, *Battleground Adventures* (Boston: 1915), p. 193; Tillie Pierce Alleman, *At Gettysburg, or What a Girl Saw and Heard of the Battle* (New York: W. Lake Borland, 1889; reprint, Baltimore: Butternut and Blue, 1994), pp. 19–20; Powers, "A Timely Backward Glance."

17. Rodgers, ed., *Ties of the Past*, p. 160; Alleman, *At Gettysburg*, pp. 19–20.

18. Bennett, *Days of "Uncertainty,"* pp. 6–8. Republican newspapers committed to Lincoln stressed the atrocities of the invading Confederates and tended to demonize the invaders. See the *(Harrisburg) Daily Telegraph*, 15 June 1863. (Quotes from this paper.)

19. Broadhead, *Diary of a Lady*, pp. 8–9. The cultural, as well as economic, imperatives of removing horses to safety for Pennsylvania Dutch farmers are discussed by Christian B. Keller, in David L. Valuska and Christian B. Keller, *Damn Dutch: Pennsylvania Germans at Gettysburg* (Mechanicsburg, Penn.: Stackpole Books, 2004), pp. 5, 61, 63; John Charles Wills, "Reminiscences"; "A Woman's Story" [Harriet H. Bayly], *The Star and Sentinel*, 25 September 1888.

20. Foster, "Story of the Battle"; James Cole et al., "Civil War Hostages Remembered," *Hanover Sun*, 3 December 1994.

21. Adams County enlistment numbers courtesy of Tim Smith.

22. Rodgers, ed., *Ties of the Past*, p. 162; Foster, "Story of the Battle." On the subject of where battles were supposed to be, see Jennie Croll [?], "Days of Dread: A Woman's Story of Her Life on a Battle-Field," *(Philadelphia) Weekly Press*, 16 November 1887. [Elwood Christ and Tim Smith suggest that "Croll's" account is more likely that of Catherine Horner.]; Henry Eyster Jacobs, quoted in Robert L. Bloom, "'We Never Expected a Battle': The Civilians at Gettysburg, 1863," *Pennsylvania History* 55 (October 1988): 165.

23. Rodgers, ed., *Ties of the Past*, p. 160; Broadhead, *The Diary of a Lady*, pp. 9–10; Bennett, *Days of "Uncertainty,"* pp. 8–9; Robert L. Bloom, *A History of Adams County, Pennsylvania, 1700–1990* (Gettysburg: Adams County Historical Society, 1992), p. 194; Coddington, *The Gettysburg Campaign*, p. 167.

24. Sarah Barrett King, "Battle Days in 1863," *The Compiler*, 4 July 1906; Buehler, *Recollections*, p. 10.

25. David L. Valuska, "The Pennsylvania Dutch as First Defenders," in Valuska and Keller, *Damn Dutch*, p. 51.

26. Bennett, *Days of "Uncertainty,"* p. 9; Broadhead, *Diary of a Lady,* p. 8.

27. Harry W. Pfanz, *The Battle of Gettysburg* (Fort Washington, Penn.: Eastern National, 1994), p. 3.

28. [Myers], "Some Battle Experiences."

29. Buehler, *Recollections,* pp. 9–10.

30. Bayly, "A Woman's Story"; William Hamilton Bayly, "William Hamilton Bayly's Story of the Battle," *Gettysburg Compiler Scrapbook,* reprint, n.d., ACHS.

31. Cindy L. Small, *The Jennie Wade Story* (Gettysburg: Thomas Publications, 1991), p. 18; "Dear Comrade," letter from Georgia Wade McClellan to unknown, *The Madison (Wisconsin) Democrat,* n.d., Rochester Museum and Science Center (hereafter RMSC).

32. Elizabeth Thorn, "Mrs. Thorn's War Story," *Gettysburg Times,* 2 July 1938.

33. Bloom, "'We Never Expected a Battle,'" p. 167; Broadhead, *Diary of a Lady,* p. 11 (26 June 1863); Wills, "Reminiscences," pp. 7-10; Bennett, *Days of "Uncertainty,"* pp. 13–14.

34. Some of these recollections, written toward the turn of the century in an era of sectional reunion, are, not surprisingly, generous to the Confederates. Contemporary accounts also expressed pity for the invading men at this time, however. *Days of "Uncertainty,"* p. 15; Broadhead, *Diary of a Lady,* p. 11; Alleman, *At Gettysburg,* p. 27; King, "Battle Days in 1863," *The Compiler,* 4 July 1906; Buehler, *Recollections,* p. 10.

35. Buehler, *Recollections,* p. 12; Anna Garlach Kitzmiller, "Mrs. Kitzmiller's Story: Battle Days Between Union and Confederate Lines," *The Compiler,* 23 August 1905; Sarah Barrett King, "A Mother's Story of the Battle of Gettysburg," *Compiler Scrapbook,* n.d., ACHS.

36. Hoke, *The Great Invasion of 1863,* p. 184; King, "Battle Days in 1863," *The Compiler,* 4 July 1906; "Mrs. Thorn's War Story." The reference to Winchester may allude to the "regime" of Union general Robert Milroy, whose forces reigned over the Shenandoah town with "tyrannical" fierceness in 1863—until Confederates pushed him out on their way north. General Milroy was known to have confiscated civilian belongings to furnish his headquarters, and he created a scandal by throwing a disabled woman out of her home so his wife could inhabit it. See Stephen Sears, *Gettysburg* (Boston: Houghton Mifflin, 2003), p. 77; James P. Gannon, *Irish Rebels, Confederate Tigers: A History of the 6th Louisiana Volunteers, 1861–1865* (Mason City, Iowa: Savas Publishing Company, 1998), p. 172.

37. Broadhead, *Diary of a Lady,* p. 9; Buehler, *Recollections,* pp. 11–12.

38. Mark Grimsley, in *The Hard Hand of War: Union Military Policy Toward Southern Civilians 1861–1865* (New York: Cambridge University Press, 1995), pp. 143–144, describes how the practice of war changed for the Federal army in the South after the second year of the war; on representations of Southern men see Ronald G. Walters, "The Erotic South: Civilization and Sexuality in American Abolitionism," *American Quarterly* 25 (1973): 177–201; Gerald Linderman,

Embattled Courage: The Experience of Combat in the American Civil War (New York: The Free Press, 1987), p. 195; Everard H. Smith, "Chambersburg: Anatomy of a Confederate Reprisal," *American Historical Review* 96 (April 1991): 448; on the fears of Confederate soldiers see Leander Warren, "Recollections of the Battle of Gettysburg," typescript, n.d., ACHS; Rodgers, *Ties of the Past,* p. 162; Alleman, *At Gettysburg,* p. 22; Edwin B. Coddington, "Prelude to Gettysburg: The Confederates Plunder Pennsylvania," *Pennsylvania History* 30 (1963): 129.

39. Buehler, *Recollections,* pp. 11–12; see also Gannon, *Irish Rebels,* p. 181.

40. Terry L. Jones, *Lee's Tigers: The Louisiana Infantry in the Army of Northern Virginia* (Baton Rouge: Louisiana State University Press, 1987), pp. xii, 7–8, 14–18, 52–53, 91–93, 124; Richard Taylor, *Destruction and Reconstruction: Personal Experiences of the Late War* (New York: D. Appleton and Company, 1879), pp. 24–25; Clyde Lottridge Cummer, ed., *Yankee in Gray: The Civil War Memoirs of Henry E. Handerson* (Cleveland: Press of Western Reserve University, 1962), pp. 33–34.

41. Gannon, *Irish Rebels,* pp. 165–166; Jones, *Lee's Tigers,* pp. 146–147.

42. Jones, *Lee's Tigers,* p. 127; Terry L. Jones, *Cemetery Hill: The Struggle for the High Ground, July 1–3, 1863* (New York: Da Capo Press, 2003), p. 20.

43. Coddington, *Gettysburg Campaign,* pp. 88–89; Merl E. Reed, ed., "The Gettysburg Campaign—A Louisiana Lieutenant's Eye-Witness Account," *Pennsylvania History* 30 (April 1963): 185–186; Sears, *Gettysburg,* pp. 78–80; Small, *The Jennie Wade Story,* p. 16.

44. Reed, ed., "The Gettysburg Campaign," pp. 186–187; Thomas Benton Reed, *A Private in Gray* (Camden, Ark.: T.B. Reed, 1905), pp. 39, 67–68.

45. Ibid.

46. Broadhead, *Diary of a Lady,* p. 10; Buehler, *Recollections,* pp. 12, 15. Fannie Buehler "thought the bulk of Union soldiers was far away and their way was clear, and no one dreamed of a battle being fought in our town, or any place near us."

47. "Mrs. Thorn's War Story"; Bloom, "'We Never Expected a Battle,'" p. 169; Bennett, *Days of "Uncertainty,"* pp. 16–17.

48. Alice Powers, "Dark Days of the Battle Week"; *The Compiler,* 1 July 1903; Buehler, *Recollections,* p. 15; Broadhead, *Diary of a Lady,* p. 11; Bennett, *Days of Uncertainty,* p. 16.

49. Brinton diary, p. 312; Winkler letters, pp. 66–67; Heller diary, 9 June to 30 June; Dunkelman and Winey, *The Hardtack Regiment,* p. 70; Priest, ed., *McMahon's Diary,* p. 53; Adam Muenzenberger to Barbara Muenzenberger, 30 June 1863, SHSW.

50. Charles W. McKay, "'Three Years or During the War,' with the Crescent and Star," *The National Tribune Scrap Book* (Washington, D.C.: The National Tribune, 1909), p. 130.

51. Adam Muenzenberger to Barbara Muenzenberger, 30 June 1863, SHSW.

52. O. O. Howard to Elizabeth Howard, 10 June 1863; 27 June 1863.

53. O. O. Howard to Elizabeth Howard, 27 June 1863; Winkler letters, p. 64 [11–27 June 1863]; A. Wilson Greene, "From Chancellorsville to Cemetery Hill: O. O. Howard and Eleventh Corps Leadership," in Gary W. Gallagher, ed., *The First Day at Gettysburg: Essays on Confederate and Union Leadership* (Kent, Ohio: Kent State University Press, 1992), p. 66.

54. Winkler letters, p. 65; Dunkelman and Winey, *Hardtack Regiment,* p. 69; Christian Keller has found that Union soldiers received a warmer welcome in Maryland than in "Dutch" (and often Democratic) Pennsylvania. Certainly, the loyalties and politics of the borderland population were mixed, and different troops may have encountered different kinds of welcome. See Christian B. Keller, "The Pennsylvania Dutch and 'the Hard Hand of War,'" in Valuska and Keller, *Damn Dutch*, pp. 69–70.

55. Coddington, *The Gettysburg Campaign,* pp. 218–220, 234–235, 240, 260–261; Winkler letters, p. 67; O. O. Howard, *Autobiography of Oliver Otis Howard, Major General United States Army,* Vol. 1 (New York: The Baker and Taylor Company, 1908), pp. 402–403.

56. Greene, "From Chancellorsville to Cemetery Hill," pp. 72, 68; Coddington, *The Gettysburg Campaign,* pp. 261, 237.

57. D. Scott Hartwig, "'The Unlucky 11th': The 11th Army Corps on July 1, 1863," *The Gettysburg Magazine* 2 (January 1990): 33; Winkler letters, p. 69.

58. Carl Schurz, "The Battle of Gettysburg," *McClure's Magazine* 29 (July 1907): 272–273; Carl Schurz, *Reminiscences,* Vol. III (New York: The McClure Company, 1908), pp. 4–5.

59. Schurz, *Reminiscences,* Vol. III, pp. 4–5; McKay, "Three Years," p. 130.

60. L. A. Smith, "Recollections of Gettysburg," *War Papers Read Before the Michigan Commandery of the Military Order of the Loyal Legion of the United States,* Vol. 2, 7 December 1893–5 May 1898 (Detroit: James H. Stone, Co., Printers, 1898), p. 298.

61. O. O. Howard, "Campaign and Battle of Gettysburg, June and July, 1863," *Atlantic Monthly Magazine* 38 (July 1876): 53; O. O. Howard, *Autobiography,* Vol. I, p. 410.

62. Ibid.

63. Greene, "From Chancellorsville to Cemetery Hill," p. 71; Hartwig, "'The Unlucky 11th'", p. 35; Alfred Wickesberg, ed., Ingeborg Wolferstetter, trans., *Civil War Letters of Sergeant Charles Wickesberg* (Milwaukee: Alfred Wickesberg, 1961), p. 19 (thanks to Wolfgang Hochbruck for this reference); John S. Applegate, ed., *Reminiscences and Letters of George Arrowsmith of New Jersey* (Red Bank, N.J.: John H. Cook, 1893), p. 211; Alice Powers, "Dark Days of the Battle Week," *The Compiler,* 1 July 1903; C. M. W. Foster, "The Story of the Battle"; Winkler letters, p. 71; Annie Young to "Mina," in Catherine Merrill, *The Soldier of Indiana in the War for the Union* (Indianapolis: 1866), pp. 119–120.

64. Schurz, "The Battle of Gettysburg," pp. 275–276.

65. Howard had assumed command of all Union forces following Gen. Reynolds' death; Schurz, "The Battle of Gettysburg," pp. 275–276.

66. Greene, "Howard and Eleventh Corps Leadership," pp. 76–78; Schurz, "The Battle of Gettysburg," pp. 276–277.

67. Hartwig, "'The Unlucky 11th,'" pp. 40–41; Greene, "Howard and Eleventh Corps Leadership," pp. 78–79.

68. Francis Channing Barlow to Robert Treat Paine, 12 August 1863, Barlow Papers, Massachusetts Historical Society, Boston (hereafter MHS); Francis Channing Barlow to his mother, 2 June 1863, Barlow Papers, MHS. Like many men of his time, Barlow segregated his prejudice. He expressed disgust over the "Dutch" and at the same time was a keen anti-slavery man. For instance, while he was disciplining the German Americans in his command, he was also considering an appointment as "Superintendent" of freed African Americans. See Francis Channing Barlow to his mother, c. 4 July 1863, MHS.

69. Joseph Tyler Butts, ed., *A Gallant Captain of the Civil War* (New York: 1902), pp. 72–75; see also O. O. Howard to L. von Gilsa, 28 June 1863, BCSC.

70. Wickesberg, ed., *Letters of Charles Wickesberg*, pp. 15–16.

71. Barlow to Paine, 12 August 1863, MHS; Barlow to his mother, 7 July 1863, MHS; Greene, "Howard and Eleventh Corps Leadership," p. 79; Scott Hartwig, "The Campaign and Battle of Gettysburg," in Valuska and Keller, *Damn Dutch*, p. 91.

72. Reed, *A Private in Gray*, p. 42; Greene, ed., *Howard and Eleventh Corps Leadership*, pp. 79–80.

73. Hartwig, "The Campaign and Battle of Gettysburg," in Valuska and Keller, *Damn Dutch*, pp. 91–92; Martin Oefele, "German-Americans and the War up to Gettysburg," in Valuska and Keller, *Damn Dutch*, p. 25; Christian B. Keller, "Pennsylvania's German-Americans, a Popular Myth," in Valuska and Keller, *Damn Dutch*, pp. 143–145.

74. Hartwig, "'The Unlucky 11th,'" pp. 47–49; Pfanz, *Gettysburg—The First Day*, pp. 261, 294, 339.

75. Pfanz, *Gettysburg—The First Day*, pp. 260–266; Winkler letters, p. 70; McKay, "Three Years," p. 131; Keller, "Pennsylvania's German-Americans," p. 146; Sears, *Gettysburg*, p. 217.

76. Reed, ed., "The Gettysburg Campaign," pp. 185–188; Hartwig, "'The Unlucky 11th,'" p. 49; Keller, "Pennsylvania's German-Americans," p. 146; Sears, *Gettysburg*, pp. 79, 109, 217.

77. Greene, ed., *Howard and Eleventh Corps Leadership*, p. 82; McKay, "Three Years," pp. 131–132; Sears, *Gettysburg*, p. 221.

78. Alfred C. Raphelson, "Alexander Schimmelfennig: A German-American Campaigner in the Civil War," *The Pennsylvania Magazine of History and Biography* 87 (April 1963): 175–176.

79. Schurz refers to Schimmelfennig's shelter as a "pig-sty." The Garlach family that owned the shelter described it as more of a space between a woodpile and swill barrels. See Raphelson, "Alexander Schimmelfennig," pp. 175–176; Schurz, *Reminiscences,* Vol. III, pp. 35–37; Anna Garlach Kitzmiller, "Story of a Brig. General," *The Compiler,* 9 August 1905.

80. Winkler letters, p. 71 (6 July 1863).

81. *Official Records,* Ser. I, Vol. 27, Pt. 1, p. 703; Charles Howard to [Major Whittlesey], 9 July 1863, BCSC; Thomas L. Elmore, "A Meteorological and Astronomical Chronology of the Gettysburg Campaign," *The Gettysburg Magazine* 13 (July 1995): 11.

82. *Official Records,* Ser. I, Vol. 27, Pt. 1, p. 697; Sears, *Gettysburg,* p. 224.

83. Schurz, *Reminiscences,* Vol. III, p. 20.

84. McKay, "Three Years," pp. 131–132; Greene, "Howard and Eleventh Corps Leadership," pp. 83–84; Narrative of Simon Hubler, Civil War Misc. Coll., USAMHI, p. 6; Adam Muenzenberger to Barbara Muenzenberger, 30 August 1863, SHSW.

85. Alice Powers, "Dark Days of the Battle Week"; Reed, *Private in Gray,* p. 42; Cummer, ed., *Yankee in Gray,* pp. 63–64.

86. "Story of a Brig. General in Hiding," *The Compiler,* 9 August 1905; Anna Garlach Kitzmiller, "Mrs. Kitzmiller's Story."

87. Elizabeth Thorn, "Experience During Battle: A Woman's Thrilling Experiences of the Battle," *The Compiler,* 26 July 1905.

88. Schurz, *Reminiscences,* Vol. III, p. 19; Alleman, *At Gettysburg,* p. 93; *Official Records,* Ser. I, Vol. 27, Pt. 1, p. 705; O. O. Howard, "Campaign and Battle of Gettysburg," p. 60.

89. Sears, *Gettysburg,* pp. 234–239.

CHAPTER FIVE

1. Lydia Catherine Ziegler Clare, "A Gettysburg Girl's Story of the Great Battle," c. 1900, typescript, Adams County Historical Society (hereafter ACHS); John Charles Wills, "Reminiscences of the Three Days Battle of Gettysburg at the 'Globe Hotel,'" typescript, c. 1910, ACHS.

2. Harriet Hamilton Bayly, "A Woman's Story," *The Star and Sentinel,* 25 September 1888; Harriet Hamilton Bayly, "Mrs. Joseph Bayly's Story of the Battle," typescript, from *The Compiler Scrapbook,* n.d., ACHS. All references to Harriet Bayly in the following two pages derive from these sources.

3. William Hamilton Bayly, "William Hamilton Bayly's Story of the Battle," *The Compiler Scrapbook,* n.d., Gettysburg National Military Park (hereafter GNMP).

4. Jennie Croll, attrib., "Days of Dread," *Philadelphia Weekly Press,* 16 November 1887.

5. Sarah C. Shriver to Elizabeth J. Myer, 29 June 1863, ACHS; Tillie (Pierce) Alleman, *At Gettysburg or What a Girl Saw and Heard of the Battle* (New York: W. Lake Borland, 1889; reprint, Baltimore: Butternut and Blue, 1994), p. 54.

6. O. O. Howard to Major Henry Burrage, 9 February 1894, Bowdoin College Special Collections (hereafter BCSC); Edwin B. Coddington, *The Gettysburg Campaign: A Study in Command* (New York: Touchstone, 1997), p. 302; [Croll], "Days of Dread"; Sarah M. Broadhead, *The Diary of a Lady of Gettysburg, Pennsylvania, from June 15 to July 16, 1863* (N.p.: Privately printed, 1864; reprint, Hershey, Penn.: Gary T. Hawbaker, 2002), p. 18, mentions how soldiers at Gettysburg were engaged in "saving us."

7. [Croll], "Days of Dread"; C. M. W. Foster, "The Story of the Battle by a Citizen Whose Home Was Pierced by Flying Shells," *The Compiler,* 29 June 1904; Annie Young to Annie _____, 5 July 1863, ACHS (orig. Edward McPherson Papers, Library of Congress); Gerald R. Bennett, *Days of "Uncertainty and Dread"* (Littlestown, Penn.: Privately printed, 1994), p. 54; Lt. Col. W. W. Blackford, *War Years with Jeb Stuart* (New York: Charles Scribner's Sons, 1945), p. 231.

8. Broadhead, *The Diary of a Lady,* pp. 13–14; [Croll], "Days of Dread."

9. Lavinia Bollinger to Susan White, 9 September 1863, ACHS; Annie Young to Annie _____, 5 July 1863, ACHS.

10. Annie Young to "My Dear Mina," 17 July 1863, in Catherine Merrill, *The Soldier of Indiana in the War for the Union* (Indianapolis: 1866), pp. 119–120, clipping, ACHS; May Garlach Hoffman/Mary McAllister, "Woman Lifts Curtain on Gettysburg History," *Philadelphia Inquirer,* 26 June 1938.

11. Hoffman/McAllister, "Woman Lifts Curtain"; May Garlach Hoffman/Mary McAllister, "Gettysburg Terrors Made to Live Again in Woman's Account of Great Battle," *Philadelphia Inquirer,* 27 June 1938.

12. McAllister/Hoffman, "Gettysburg Terrors"; Broadhead, *The Diary of a Lady,* p. 18; Alice Powers, "Dark Days of the Battle Week," *The Compiler,* 1 July 1903; Jennie McCreary to her sister, 22 July 1863, in "Girl Saw Streets Filled with Dead and Wounded at Gettysburg," in *The (Philadelphia) Evening Bulletin,* 2 July 1938, clipping, ACHS; Salome Myers to Mr. Russell, 19 August 1863, ACHS.

13. Broadhead, *The Diary of a Lady,* p. 14; Bayly, "A Woman's Story"; Annie Young to "My Dear Mina," pp. 119–120; Powers, "Dark Days of the Battle Week."

14. Bayly, "A Woman's Story"; Bennett, *Days of "Uncertainty and Dread,"* p. 40–41; Elwood W. Christ (preparer), Pennsylvania Historical Resource Survey Form, Emanuel Bushman House, n.d., ACHS; Sue Myers, "Some Battle Experiences as Remembered by a Young School Girl," *The Compiler,* 24 April 1907; Sue Elizabeth Stoever, "A Woman's Story of the Battle," *The Compiler,* 24 June 1903; Fannie J. Buehler, *Recollections of the Rebel Invasion* (Gettysburg: Star and Sentinel Print, 1900; reprint, Hershey, Penn.: Gary T. Hawbaker, n.d.).

15. Buehler, *Recollections of the Rebel Invasion,* pp. 19, 22.

16. "Mrs. Joseph Bayly's Story"; "William Bayly's Story"; Leander H. Warren, "Recollections of the Battle of Gettysburg," n.d., typescript, p. 7, ACHS; William McClean, "The Days of Terror in 1863," *The Compiler,* 1 June 1908.

17. Broadhead, *The Diary of a Lady*, p. 16; Foster, "The Story of the Battle by a Citizen"; Annie Young to Annie _____, 5 July 1863, ACHS.

18. Bayly, "A Woman's Story"; Bayly, "Mrs. Joseph Bayly's Story."

19. General Robert E. Lee, General Orders No. 73, in the *Official Records of the War of the Rebellion*, Ser. I, Vol. 27, Pt. III, pp. 942–943.

20. Mary Bushman Power Deardorff, "Grandmother Bushman's Friendship Quilt," *The Gettysburg Times*, July 1938; Louie Dale Leeds, ed., and Nellie E. Aughinbaugh, "Personal Experiences of a Young Girl During the Battle of Gettysburg," privately printed, c. 1926–1938, p. 9.

21. Powers, "Dark Days of the Battle Week"; Sarah Barrett King, "A Mother's Story of [the] Battle of Gettysburg," *The Compiler Scrapbook*, n.d., GNMP; William Bayly, "William Bayly's Story," p. 14.

22. Mrs. Jacob A. Clutz (Liberty Augusta Hollinger), "The Battle of Gettysburg," *Pennsylvania History* 5 (1938): 173; Leeds/Aughinbaugh, "Personal Experiences of a Young Girl," p. 13.

23. Sarah Barrett King, "A Mother's Story"; Annie Young to Annie _____, 5 July 1863, ACHS.

24. Clutz, "Battle of Gettysburg," p. 172; Leeds/Aughinbaugh, "Personal Experiences of a Young Girl," p. 7.

25. Leeds/Aughinbaugh, "Personal Experiences of a Young Girl," p. 7; King, "A Mother's Story."

26. Clutz, "Battle of Gettysburg," p. 170; comments on the Eleventh Corps can be found in Shriver to Myer, 2 July 1863; Salome Myers also makes an equivocal remark about the "gallant" Eleventh Corps crowding into her basement (Myers to Russell, 19 August 1863).

27. See Nina Silber, *The Romance of Reunion: Northerners and the South, 1865–1900* (Chapel Hill: University of North Carolina Press, 1993).

28. O. O. Howard, "Campaign and Battle of Gettysburg, June and July, 1863," in *Atlantic Monthly Magazine*, 38 (July 1876): 61; Carl Schurz, *Reminiscences*, Vol. III (New York: The McClure Company, 1907), p. 20.

29. Howard, "Campaign and Battle of Gettysburg," p. 61; Schurz, *Reminiscences*, Vol. III, pp. 20–21.

30. Harry W. Pfanz, *Gettysburg: The Second Day* (Chapel Hill: University of North Carolina Press, 1987), pp. 26–28; Sears, *Gettysburg*, pp. 234, 254.

31. Schurz, *Reminiscences*, Vol. III, pp. 21–22.

32. Whitelaw Reid, "The Battles of Gettysburgh," [*sic*] *Cincinnati Gazette*, 4 July 1863.

33. O. O. Howard, "Campaign and Battle of Gettysburg," p. 63; Harry W. Pfanz, *Gettysburg: Culp's Hill and Cemetery Hill* (Chapel Hill: University of North Carolina Press, 1993), pp. 128, 180.

34. Howard, "Campaign and Battle of Gettysburg," p. 63; Schurz, *Reminiscences*, Vol. III, p. 22; Pfanz, *Gettysburg: The Second Day*, p. 113.

35. Pfanz, *Gettysburg: Culp's Hill*, p. 194; Schurz, *Reminiscences*, Vol. III, p. 23; Pfanz, *Gettysburg: The Second Day*, Chap. 8; Adin B. Underwood, *The Three*

Years' Service of the Thirty-third Mass. Infantry Regiment 1862–1865 (Boston: A. Williams & Co., 1881), p. 124.

36. Schurz, *Reminiscences,* Vol. III, p. 23; Underwood, *Thirty-third Mass.,* p. 127.

37. Stephen Sears, *Gettysburg* (Boston: Houghton Mifflin, 2003), Chapter 10.

38. Harry W. Pfanz, *The Battle of Gettysburg: Civil War Series* (Fort Washington, Penn.: Eastern National Publishers, 1994), pp. 36–41; Underwood, *Thirty-third Mass.,* p. 128.

39. Terry L. Jones, *Lee's Tigers: The Louisiana Infantry in the Army of Northern Virginia* (Baton Rouge: Louisiana State University Press, 1987), pp. 233–254, carries a useful appendix with information on soldiers' birthplaces; on Irish immigrants and gendered prejudice see Michael Kimmel, *Manhood in America: A Cultural History* (New York: The Free Press, 1996), p. 32.

40. On Virginia see James P. Gannon, *Irish Rebels, Confederate Tigers: The 6th Louisiana Volunteers, 1861–1865* (Mason City, Iowa: Savas Publishing, 1998), pp. 40–46.

41. Edwin B. Coddington, *The Gettysburg Campaign: A Study in Command* (New York: Simon & Schuster, 1997), p. 435; Pfanz, *Gettysburg: Culp's Hill,* p. 250; Sears, *Gettysburg,* p. 326; Gannon, *Irish Rebels,* pp. 190–191.

42. Coddington, *The Gettysburg Campaign,* p. 435; Schurz, *Reminiscences,* Vol. III, p. 24; Underwood, *Thirty-third Mass.,* p. 129; Pfanz, *Gettysburg: Culp's Hill,* p. 252; Oliver Otis Howard, *Autobiography of Oliver Otis Howard* (New York: The Baker & Taylor Company, 1908), pp. 428–429.

43. Coddington, *The Gettysburg Campaign,* p. 436; Pfanz, *Gettysburg: Civil War Series,* pp. 39–40; Gannon, *Irish Rebels,* p. 195.

44. Coddington, *The Gettysburg Campaign,* pp. 436–437; Schurz, *Reminiscences,* Vol. III, pp. 24–25; Charles W. McKay, "'Three Years or During the War,' with the Crescent and Star," *The National Tribune Scrap Book* (Washington, D.C.: 1909), p. 132; Gannon, *Irish Rebels,* pp. 198–199; Christian B. Keller, "Pennsylvania's German-Americans, a Popular Myth, and the Importance of Perception," in David L. Valuska and Christian B. Keller, *Damn Dutch: Pennsylvania Germans at Gettysburg* (Mechanicsburg, Penn.: Stackpole Books, 2004), pp. 146–147; Scott Hartwig, "The Campaign and Battle of Gettysburg," in Valuska and Keller, *Damn Dutch,* pp. 102–104; Sears, *Gettysburg,* pp. 335–339; Terry L. Jones, *Cemetery Hill: The Struggle for the High Ground, July 1–3, 1863* (New York: Da Capo Press, 2003), pp. 80–95.

45. Schurz, *Reminiscences,* Vol. III, p. 25; Underwood, *Thirty-third Mass.,* p. 130; Gannon, *Irish Rebels,* p. 198.

46. Robert Dale Mitchell and Robert Hoffsommer, eds., "The Rise and Survival of Private Mesnard," Pt. II, *Civil War Times Illustrated* (February 1986): 13; Schurz, *Reminiscences,* Vol. III, pp. 24–25.

47. Pfanz, *Gettysburg: Civil War Series,* pp. 31 –38; Pfanz, *Gettysburg: The Second Day,* pp. 231–236; Sears, *Gettysburg,* pp. 326–331.

48. McKay, "Three Years," p. 132; Diary of Charles Moore, July 1863, Robert Brake Collection, United States Army Military History Institute, Carlisle, Penn.

49. Agnes Barr, Untitled account of the Battle of Gettysburg, typescript, n.d., ACHS; "An Echo of the Battle" [Diary of Jane Smith], *The Star and Sentinel,* 2 July 1913; Buehler, "Recollections of the Rebel Invasion," p. 22; "Mrs. Thorn's War Story," *The Gettysburg Times,* 2 July 1938.

50. King, "A Mother's Story."

51. Jane Smith, "An Echo of the Battle"; Merl E. Reed, ed., "The Gettysburg Campaign—A Louisiana Lieutenant's Eye-Witness Account," *Pennsylvania History* 30 (April 1963): 186–187; Thomas Benton Reed, *A Private in Gray* (Camden, Ark.: T. B. Reed, 1905), p. 39.

52. [Croll], "Days of Dread," p. 2; Elizabeth McClean, "The Rebels are Coming," in *The Compiler,* 8 July 1908; Leander H. Warren, "Recollections of the Battle of Gettysburg," p. 8, typescript, n.d., ACHS; William Bayly, "William Bayly's Story of the Battle"; Lavinia Bollinger to Susan White, 9 September 1863, ACHS; Elma Epley Gerbeling, ed., "Account of Sophia Culp Epley," n.d., GNMP.

53. Sue King Black to Belle Miller Willard, n.d., ACHS; G. F. Minter to "Dear Cousin," 27 July 1863, ACHS; Albertus McCreary, "Gettysburg: A Boy's Experience of the Battle," *McClure's Magazine* 33 (July 1909): 250.

54. Broadhead, "Diary of a Lady," pp. 15, 16; William Bayly, "William Bayly's Story of the Battle."

55. *Lancaster Daily Evening Express,* 2 July 1863. This is a rare public report of an incident of rape during the Gettysburg campaign. Thanks to Tim Smith for bringing it to my attention.

56. May Garlach Hoffman/Mary McAllister, "Rebels at Gettysburg Ate Molasses in Hunger," *Philadelphia Inquirer,* 28 June 1938; Jennie McCreary to her sister, 22 July 1863; Leeds/Aughinbaugh, "Personal Experiences of a Young Girl"; Bayly, "A Woman's Story"; Bayly, "Mrs. Joseph Bayly's Story"; King, "A Mother's Story."

57. Gerald Linderman describes how Federal soldiers in the South also sought to punish "unwomanly" behavior. See *Embattled Courage: The Experience of Combat in the American Civil War* (New York: The Free Press, 1987), p. 195.

58. Lydia Meals Panebaker, "Reminiscences of the Battle of Gettysburg," c. 1926, ACHS.

59. Powers, "Dark Days of the Battle Week"; Hoffman/McAllister, "Rebels Ate Molasses"; "Burning of M'Lean Home on the First Day's Battle of Gettysburg Told by a Young Girl Driven from the House When Set on Fire," *The Compiler,* 15 July 1915; Caroline S. Sheads, "Scenes of the Battle of Gettysburg," *(Washington) National Republican,* 28 November 1863.

60. Smith, "An Echo of the Battle."

61. Bayly, "A Woman's Story"; William Bayly, "William Bayly's Story of the Battle."

62. E. D. McSwain, ed., *Crumbling Defenses: Memoirs and Reminiscences of John Logan Black, Colonel CSA* (Macon, Ga.: 1960), p. 45, clipping, ACHS; *The*

Star and Sentinel, 16 July 1913; Hoffman/McAllister, "Rebels Ate Molasses". See also William McClean, "The Days of Terror in 1863," *The Compiler,* 1 June 1908.

63. Clutz, "Some Personal Recollections," pp. 4, 7, ACHS; Hoffman/McAllister, "Gettysburg Terrors"; Anna Garlach Kitzmiller, "Mrs. Kitzmiller's Story: Battle Days Between Union and Confederate Lines," *The Compiler,* 23 August 1905, ACHS. The use of "feminine" disadvantage, weakness, or wiles was a strategy employed widely by women and girls in the Civil War, albeit in varying circumstances. Elizabeth Leonard describes how women engaged in spy operations sometimes drew on their charms, their purported sweetness and innocence to accomplish their covert goals. See Elizabeth D. Leonard, *All the Daring of the Soldier: Women of the Civil War Armies* (New York: W.W. Norton, 1999), pp. 96–97.

64. Sheads, "Scenes of the Battle of Gettysburg."

65. Clutz, "The Battle of Gettysburg"; "Nonagenarian Buys Bond Thursday," *The Gettysburg Times,* 10 September 1943; King, "A Mother's Story." Widow Mary Thompson also refused to make meals for the Confederate officer in her house. When asked about it later, in fact, she grew "indignant." "No," she recollected, "I guess I didn't cook for any Rebel. They had to do their own cooking." In this case the "Rebel" was Robert E. Lee, who used her house as his headquarters. See Timothy H. Smith, *The Story of Lee's Headquarters: Gettysburg, Pennsylvania* (Gettysburg: Thomas Publications, 1995), pp. 48–49.

66. Gerbeling, ed., Sophia Culp Epley Account; Bayly, "A Woman's Story"; Buehler, "Recollections of the Rebel Invasion," p. 20.

67. Foster, "The Story of the Battle."

68. Buehler, "Recollections of the Rebel Invasion," p. 18.

69. "Mrs. Junge[r]man's Story of her Girlhood Experience: After Thirty Years She Meets the Army Surgeon," in *The (San Francisco) Bulletin,* 9 March 1902; "Gettysburg's Fight: The Part That a Brave Little Girl Played During the Battle," *The Compiler,* 12 January 1892. Sadie's account here is an amalgam of the two reports. There are some inconsistencies. In the 1892 account, for example, Sadie has a younger brother with her; in the 1902 account she travels through the battle zone alone. Questions also exist about the identity of the surgeon she assisted, and the dates of his service in a field hospital. There is some evidence that at least one of the men she helped did not arrive at Gettysburg until after the battle. Thanks to Tim Smith.

70. "Mrs. Junge[r]man's Story"; "Gettysburg's Fight."

71. Barr, Untitled account of the Battle; Henry N. Blake, *Three Years in the Army of the Potomac* (Boston: 1865), pp. 206–208; Mary M. Melchior, "John Burns at Gettysburg," *Doyleston (Penn.) Democrat,* 14 August 1886, clipping, ACHS; [Carrie Sheads] in Frank Moore, *Women of the War; Their Heroism and Self-sacrifice* (Hartford: S. S. Scranton & Co., 1867), pp. 241–242; John Chisolm Horn, trans., "A Vivid Story of the Mighty Conflict from the Lips of Rev. Dr. Jacobs, Who Was a Gettysburg Boy," *The Baltimore American,* 29 June 1913, copy, ACHS.

72. This account represents common elements in three different versions of Thorn's story: "A Gettysburg Heroine," *The Compiler,* 29 July 1884; "Experience

During Battle: A Woman's Thrilling Experiences of the Battle," *The Compiler,* 26 July 1905; and "Mrs. Thorn's War Story," *The Gettysburg Times,* 2 July 1938.

73. The Bayly account of Nellie derives from three separate sources: Bayly, "A Woman's Story"; William Bayly, "William Bayly's Story of the Battle"; and Bayly, "Mrs. Joseph Bayly's Story of the Battle."

74. "Grand Army Corner: Jennie Wade, Heroine," in *The Madison (Wisconsin) Democrat,* n.d., clipping, Rochester Museum and Science Center (hereafter RMSC); J. W. Johnston, *The True Story of "Jennie" Wade: A Gettysburg Maid* (Rochester: Privately printed, 1917), p. 15.

75. Cindy L. Small, *The Jennie Wade Story* (Gettysburg: Thomas Publications, 1991), p. 22; Georgia Wade McClellan to Dear Comrade, in untitled, n.d., *The Madison (Wisconsin) Democrat,* RMSC.

76. Johnston, *True Story,* p. 19.

77. Johnston, *True Story,* pp. 21–22.

78. Johnston, *True Story,* pp. 22–23.

CHAPTER SIX

1. Richard Rollins, ed., *Pickett's Charge: Eyewitness Accounts* (Redondo Beach, Calif.: Rank and File Publications, 1994), p. 72; Edwin B. Coddington, *The Gettysburg Campaign: A Study in Command* (New York: Touchstone, 1997), p. 484; Thomas L. Elmore, "Torrid Heat and Blinding Rain: A Meteorological and Astronomical Chronology of the Gettysburg Campaign," in *The Gettysburg Magazine* 13 (July 1995): 7–19; T. S. Potter, "The Battle of Gettysburg," *The National Tribune,* 5 August 1882.

2. Coddington, *The Gettysburg Campaign,* pp. 442, 479; Rollins, ed., *Pickett's Charge,* p. 75; Elmore, "A Meteorological Chronology," p. 13.

3. Coddington, *The Gettysburg Campaign,* p. 484; Rollins, ed., *Pickett's Charge,* p. 72; Carl Schurz, *Reminiscences,* Vol. III (New York: The McClure Company, 1907), p. 27.

4. Rollins, ed., *Pickett's Charge,* pp. 62, 68, 58–59; Harry W. Pfanz, *The Battle of Gettysburg* (Fort Washington, Penn.: Eastern National, 1994), pp. 41–43.

5. William Faulkner, *Intruder in the Dust* (New York: Vintage Books, 1991), p. 190.

6. James C. Mohr, ed., *The Cormany Diaries: A Northern Family in the Civil War* (Pittsburgh: University of Pittsburgh Press, 1982), pp. 328–329.

7. Mohr, *Cormany Diaries,* p. 329; W. P. Conrad and Ted Alexander, *When War Passed This Way* (Shippensburg, Penn.: Beidel Printing House/Greencastle Bicentennial, 1982), pp. 131–132; Jacob Hoke, *The Great Invasion of 1863 or General Lee in Pennsylvania* (Gettysburg: Stan Clark Military Books, 1992; reprint), pp. 99–102. The appearance of Jenkins' cavalry apparently contrasted sharply with the look of more neatly trimmed Confederate cavalry units, such as those associated with Jeb Stuart.

8. Mohr, ed., *Cormany Diaries,* pp. 329–330.

9. Hoke, *The Great Invasion*, p. 108.

10. Conrad and Alexander, *When War Passed This Way*, p. 135; "The Chambersburg Telegrams," in *The New York Herald*, 19 June 1863; *The Philadelphia Inquirer*, 19 June 1863; *Franklin Repository*, 8 July 1863, quoted in Alan T. Nolan, *Lee Considered: General Robert E. Lee and Civil War History* (Chapel Hill: University of North Carolina Press, 1991), p. 17.

11. *The Compiler*, 29 June 1863; Philip Schaff, "The Gettysburg Week," *Scribner's Magazine* 16 (July 1894): 22–26.

12. Isaac V. Reynolds to his wife, 9 August 1863, accessed at www.rhobard .com/russell/letters/reynolds2.html; Conrad and Alexander, *When War Passed This Way*, p. 137; Schaff, "Gettysburg Week," pp. 26–29; J. D. Edmiston Turner, ed., "Diary of Rev. Thomas Creigh, 19 June–1 July 1863," paper read before the Kittochtinny (Pa.) Historical Society, 29 February 1940, available at www.jefferson.village.virginia.edu/vshadow2/KHS/creigh.html.

13. Schaff, "Gettysburg Week," p. 24. See also Coddington, *The Gettysburg Campaign*, p. 162.

14. Mohr, ed., *Cormany Diaries*, p. 330; Schaff, "Gettysburg Week," p. 24; Hoke, *The Great Invasion*, p. 107.

15. Schaff, "Gettysburg Week," p. 25; Hoke, *The Great Invasion*, p. 111.

16. Schaff, "Gettysburg Week," p. 26; Hoke, *The Great Invasion*, pp. 111, 108.

17. Hoke, *The Great Invasion*, p. 108; Conrad and Alexander, *When War Passed This Way*, pp. 135–136.

18. Mohr, ed., *Cormany Diaries*, p. 330; Luis F. Emilio, *A Brave Black Regiment: History of the Fifty-Fourth Regiment of the Massachusetts Volunteer Infantry, 1863–1865* (Boston: The Boston Book Company, 1891), pp. 339–392.

19. Sarah Sites Rodgers, *The Ties of the Past: The Gettysburg Diaries of Salome Myers Stewart, 1854–1922* (Gettysburg: Thomas Publications, 1996), p. 162; Tillie Pierce Alleman, *At Gettysburg, or What a Girl Saw and Heard of the Battle* (New York: W. Lake Borland, 1889; reprint), p. 22; Edwin B. Coddington, "Prelude to Gettysburg: The Confederates Plunder Pennsylvania," *Pennsylvania History* 30 (1963): 129.

20. See Ervin L. Jordan, Jr., "Sleeping with the Enemy: Sex, Black Women, and the Civil War," *The Western Journal of Black Studies* 18 (1994): 57–58; Darlene Clark Hine and Kathleen Thompson, *A Shining Thread of Hope: The History of Black Women in America* (New York: Broadway Books, 1998), pp. 141–142; Linda Grant De Pauw, *Battle Cries and Lullabies: Women in War from Prehistory to the Present* (Norman: University of Oklahoma Press, 1998), p. 165; Joan E. Cashin, "Into the Trackless Wilderness: The Refugee Experience in the Civil War," in Edward D. C. Campbell, Jr., and Kym S. Rice, *A Woman's War: Southern Women, Civil War and the Confederate Legacy* (Richmond: Museum of the Confederacy, 1996), pp. 47–48. An enumeration of sexual assaults carried out by Union and Confederate soldiers, based largely on official military reports, can be found on the Web site www.hometown.aol.com/cwrapes.

21. William A. Frassanito, *Early Photography at Gettysburg* (Gettysburg: Thomas Publications, 1995), p. 110; *Pittsburgh Evening Chronicle,* 28 July 1863. Thanks to Tim Smith for information on Colonel Christian.

22. Mohr, ed., *Cormany Diaries,* p. 330; Schaff, "Gettysburg Week," pp. 24–26.

23. David G. Smith, "Race and Retaliation: The Capture of African Americans during the Gettysburg Campaign" (unpublished paper, 2004), pp. 10–13. (Thanks to David Smith for sharing his important work.)

24. Smith, "Race and Retaliation," pp. 13, 16–19; Conrad and Alexander, *When War Passed This Way,* p. 133; Coddington, *The Gettysburg Campaign,* p. 161; Gary W. Gallagher, ed., *The Antietam Campaign* (Chapel Hill: University of North Carolina Press, 1999), p. 14; Nolan, *Lee Considered,* p. 17.

25. "War Story by Prof. Harry," in *The Compiler,* 28 June 1911.

26. Jane Dice Stone, ed., "Diary of William Heyser," *The Kittochtinny (Pa.) Historical Society Papers* 16 (1978): 54–88 (18 June 1863), accessed at http://valley .vcdh.virginia.edu/personal/wmheyser.html; *The (New York) Anglo-African,* 4 July 1863; *The Harrisburg Patriot and Union,* 16 June 1863; 1 July 1863.

27. "War Story by Prof. Harry," *The Compiler,* 28 June 1911; on the Underground Railroad in Adams County see G. Craig Caba, ed., *Episodes of Gettysburg and the Underground Railroad as Witnessed and Recorded by Professor J. Howard Wert* (Gettysburg: G. Craig Caba Antiques, 1998).

28. *Philadelphia Inquirer,* 30 June 1863, quoted in James Elton Johnson, "A History of Camp William Penn and Its Black Troops in the Civil War, 1863–1865," Ph.D. diss., University of Pennsylvania, 1999, p. 39.

29. *The (New York) Anglo-African,* 4 July 1863; *The Harrisburg Patriot and Union,* 16, 19, 25 June 1863; 1 July 1863; "War Story by Prof. Harry," *The Compiler,* 28 June 1911.

30. *The (New York) Anglo-African,* 20 June 1863; *The Chambersburg Repository,* c. 20 June 1863; Chester K. Leach to Wife, 15 July 1863, in Ted Alexander, "'A Regular Slave Hunt': The Army of Northern Virginia and Black Civilians in the Gettysburg Campaign," *North & South* 4 (September 2001): 87.

31. David A. Murdoch, ed., "Catherine Mary White Foster's Eyewitness Account of the Battle of Gettysburg, with Background on the Foster Family Union Soldiers," *Adams County History* 1 (1995): 49.

32. Johnson, "The Bank Clerk," p. 193; "War Story by Prof. Harry," *The Compiler,* 28 June 1911; *The Patriot and Union,* 25 June 1863; Mohr, ed., *Cormany Diaries,* p. 330; Schaff, "Gettysburg Week," p. 25.

33. *The Star and Sentinel,* 15 August 1900; Charles M. McCurdy, *Gettysburg: A Memoir* (Pittsburgh: Reed & Witting, 1929), p. 19.

34. Marcella Sherfy, "The Brien [*sic*] Farm and Family," Gettysburg National Military Park (hereafter GNMP) Report, June 1972; Memorandum, Senior Historian to Chief, I&VP, 8 August 1995, Brian Files, GNMP; the Brian house was also the likely headquarters of Union General Alexander Hays. See Frassanito, *Early Photography,* pp. 232–233.

35. Memorandum, 1995, GNMP; Census of Adams County, 1860, Adams County Historical Society (hereafter ACHS); *The Compiler,* 15 February 1858; 26 April 1858; David Schick to Elsie Singmaster Lewars, 24 April 1952, ACHS; Elsie Singmaster, *A Boy at Gettysburg* (New York: Houghton-Mifflin Co., 1924), pp. 94, 169–170; author interview with Catherine Carter, 1997, and Jean Odom, 1997.

36. *The Star and Banner,* 11 June 1863; Frassanito, *Early Photography,* p. 110; Johnston Pension Records, National Archives, Washington, D.C.; *Harrisburg Patriot and Union,* 2 July 1863; Johnson, "History of Camp William Penn," p. 43; the correspondence between Wills and Curtin was discovered by Tim Smith in the Pennsylvania State Archives. See David Wills to Andrew Curtin, 15 June 1863; Andrew Curtin to David Wills, 15 June 1863, Military Dispatch Books, Box 18, RG 19.181.

37. *Harrisburg Patriot and Union,* 2 July 1863; *Harrisburg Daily Telegraph,* 10 July 1863; "Our Darkies Impressed," *The Compiler,* 29 June 1863.

38. See "Columbia," *Philadelphia Press,* 29 June 1863; "The Fight at Wrightsville," *Philadelphia Press,* 29 June 1863; *Lancaster Weekly Express,* 4 July 1863; Tim Smith, who has assembled a clippings file on this event, has identified this death as the third of the campaign, the first being a Union cavalryman killed in Greencastle on June 22; the second being George Sandoe outside of Gettysburg on June 26. See also Hoke, *The Great Invasion,* pp. 185–190; Johnson, "A History of Camp William Penn," pp. 36–38; Coddington, *The Gettysburg Campaign,* pp. 169–170.

39. Rodgers, ed., *Ties of the Past,* p. 160; Johnson, *Battleground Adventures,* pp. 192–193.

40. Mary Warren Fastnacht, "Memories of the Battle of Gettysburg, Year 1863" (York, Penn., 1927), photocopy in ACHS, p. 3; T. W. Herbert, "In Occupied Pennsylvania," *The Georgia Review* (Summer 1950): 104–105.

41. Fastnacht, "Memories of the Battle," p. 3; Rev. Creigh diary, 26 June 1863; Smith, "Race and Retaliation," p. 17.

42. Fannie J. Buehler, *Recollections of the Rebel Invasion and One Woman's Experience During the Battle of Gettysburg* (Gettysburg: Star and Sentinel Print, 1900; reprint, Gary T. Hawbaker, Hershey, Penn., n.d.), p. 11.

43. Johnson, *Battleground Adventures,* pp. 183–184, 187; John Charles Wills, "Reminiscences of the Three Days Battle of Gettysburg at the Globe Hotel," c. 1915, typescript, ACHS, p. 11; it is difficult to know how these employees fared during the battle.

44. Johnson, *Battleground Adventures,* pp. 183–184, 192–193; Albertus McCreary, "Gettysburg: A Boy's Experience of the Battle," *McClure's Magazine* 33 (July 1909): 250.

45. Rodgers, ed., *Ties of the Past,* p. 160.

46. Herbert, "In Occupied Pennsylvania," pp. 104–105.

47. Johnson, "The Colored Servantmaid," in *Battleground Adventures,* pp. 188–190.

48. Johnson, "The Colored Servantmaid," in *Battleground Adventures*, p. 189; Sarah B. King, "Battle Days in 1863," *The Compiler*, 4 July 1906; "Mrs. Thorn's War Story," *The Gettysburg Times*, 2 July 1938; General Robert E. Lee, "General Orders No. 73," in the *Official Records of the War of the Rebellion*, Ser. I, Vol. 27, Pt. III, pp. 942–943.

49. McCreary, "Gettysburg: A Boy's Experience," pp. 243–253 (quotation on p. 250).

50. Alexander, "A Regular Slave Hunt," p. 88; also see the request made to the Freedmen's Bureau in 1865 to help reunite a mother and three children taken from Pennsylvania in 1863 in William S. McFeely, *Yankee Stepfather: General O. O. Howard and the Freedmen* (New Haven: Yale University Press, 1968), pp. 203–204; Smith, "Race and Retaliation," pp. 3, 20 (note 5).

51. Coddington, *The Gettysburg Campaign*, p. 493.

52. Jennie McCreary to Julia Earnest, 22 July 1863, in "Girl Saw Streets Filled with Dead and Wounded at Gettysburg," *The (Philadelphia) Evening Bulletin*, 2 July 1938; Sarah M. Broadhead, "The Diary of a Lady of Gettysburg, Pennsylvania, from June 15 to July 15, 1863" (reprint, Gary T. Hawbaker, Hershey, Penn., n.d.).

53. McCreary, "Gettysburg: A Boy's Experience," p. 246; Henry Eyster Jacobs, "A Vivid Story of the Mighty Conflict," transcript from *The Baltimore American*, 29 June 1913, ACHS.

54. L.A. Smith, "Recollections of Gettysburg," in *War Papers Read Before the Michigan Commandery of the Military Order of the Loyal Legion of the United States*, Vol. 2 (1893–1898) (Detroit: James H. Stone & Co., Printers, 1898), pp. 303–304.

55. Smith, "Recollections of Gettysburg," pp. 304–305.

56. Coddington, *The Gettysburg Campaign*, p. 514; Sears, *Gettysburg*, pp. 428–454.

57. Sears, *Gettysburg*, pp. 454, 468.

CHAPTER SEVEN

1. A. Wilson Greene, "From Gettysburg to Falling Waters: Meade's Pursuit of Lee," in Gary W. Gallagher, ed., *The Third Day at Gettysburg & Beyond* (Chapel Hill: University of North Carolina Press, 1994), p. 164; Edwin B. Coddington, *The Gettysburg Campaign: A Study in Command* (New York: Touchstone, 1997), pp. 536–539; Stephen Sears, *Gettysburg* (Boston: Houghton Mifflin, 2003), pp. 464–473; "Civil War Hostages Remembered," *Hanover Sun*, 3 December 1994.

2. Bernhard Domschcke, *Twenty Months in Captivity: Memoirs of a Union Officer in Confederate Prisons*, ed. and trans. by Frederic Trautmann (Rutherford, N.J.: Fairleigh Dickinson University Press, 1987), pp. 29–31.

3. Charles Howard to Major Whittlesey, 9 July 1863, Bowdoin College Special Collections (hereafter BCSC); O. O. Howard to Elizabeth Howard, 6, 9, 14, 16 July 1863, BCSC; Greene, "From Gettysburg to Falling Waters," pp. 171–172; Sears, *Gettysburg*, p. 490.

4. Gerald R. Bennett, *Days of "Uncertainty and Dread": The Ordeal Endured by the Citizens at Gettysburg* (Littlestown, Penn.: Gerald R. Bennett, 2002, rev. ed.), pp. 68–69; John Charles Wills, "Reminiscences of the Three Days Battle of Gettysburg at the 'Globe Hotel,'" c. 1915, typescript, ACHS, p. 22; Clifton Johnson, *Battleground Adventures* (Boston: 1915), p. 180; Fannie J. Buehler, *Recollections of the Rebel Invasion and One Woman's Experience During the Battle of Gettysburg* (Gettysburg: Star and Sentinel Print, 1900; reprint, Gary T. Hawbaker, n.d.), p. 24.

5. Bennett, *Days of "Uncertainty,"* pp. 69–71; C. M. W. Foster, "The Story of the Battle by a Citizen Whose Home Was Pierced by Flying Shells," *The Compiler*, 29 June 1904; Henry E. Horn, ed., *Memoirs of Henry Eyster Jacobs: Notes on a Life of a Churchman* (Huntingdon, Penn.: Church Management Service, 1974), p. 59.

6. Harriet Bayly, "A Woman's Story," *The Star and Sentinel*, 25 September 1888.

7. Report, Committee on Pensions, U.S. Senate, 8 July 1882, typescript, Johnston Collection, Rochester Museum and Science Center, Rochester, N.Y.; J. W. Johnston, *The True Story of "Jennie" Wade* (Rochester, N.Y.: Privately printed, 1917), pp. 25–27; Cindy L. Small, *The Jennie Wade Story* (Gettysburg: Thomas Publications, 1991), p. 48.

8. *The Compiler*, 20 July 1863; Brian A. Kennell, *Beyond the Gatehouse: Gettysburg's Evergreen Cemetery* (Gettysburg: Evergreen Cemetery Association, 2000), pp. 44–45; Bennett, *Days of "Uncertainty,"* p. 74.

9. *The Compiler*, 13, 20 July 1863; Bayly, "A Woman's Story"; Mrs. Jacob A. Clutz [Liberty Hollinger], "Some Personal Recollections of the Battle of Gettysburg," privately printed, n.d. (c. 1925), Adams County Historical Society (hereafter ACHS).

10. Leander H. Warren, "Recollections of the Battle of Gettysburg," n.d., typescript in the ACHS; *The Compiler*, 20 July 1863; 24 August 1863.

11. Albertus McCreary, "Gettysburg: A Boy's Experience of the Battle," *McClure's Magazine* 33 (July 1909): 250–251; *The Compiler*, 20 July 1863; 24 August 1863.

12. Lydia Catherine Ziegler Clare, "A Gettysburg Girl's Story of the Great Battle," typescript in the ACHS, c. 1900; Louie Dale Leeds, ed., Nellie E. Aughinbaugh, "Personal Experiences of a Young Girl During the Battle of Gettysburg," privately printed c. 1926–1938, ACHS, p. 11; Garry Wills, *Lincoln at Gettysburg* (New York: Simon & Schuster, 1992), p. 20; [William McClean], "The Days of Terror in 1863," *The Compiler*, 1 June 1908; Bennett, *Days of "Uncertainty and Dread,"* pp. 73–75.

13. William A. Frassanito, *Early Photography at Gettysburg* (Gettysburg: Thomas Publications, 1995), pp. 222, 230–231; Aughinbaugh, "Personal Experiences"; McCreary, "Gettysburg: A Boy's Experience," p. 251.

14. Clutz, "Some Personal Recollections"; "The Farmer's Son," in Johnson, *Battleground Adventures*, pp. 174–175; "The Colored Servantmaid," in Johnson, *Battleground Adventures*, pp. 190–191.

15. Charles M. McCurdy, *Gettysburg: A Memoir* (Pittsburgh: Reed & Witting Company, 1929), p. 28.

16. Buehler, *Recollections of the Rebel Invasion,* pp. 17, 25.

17. Robert L. Bloom, "'We Never Expected a Battle': The Civilians at Gettysburg, 1863," *Pennsylvania History* 55 (October 1988), reprint, n.d., ACHS, pp. 184–190; Bennett, *Days of "Uncertainty,"* pp. 79–83.

18. "Gleanings from Gettysburg," *Philadelphia Evening Bulletin,* 21 November 1863; [Carrie Sheads] in Frank Moore, *Women of the War; Their Heroism and Self-sacrifice* (Hartford: S. S. Scranton & Co., 1867), p. 244; Frances Cunningham Harper, "Native of Adams County Writes of Experiences of Parents During '63 Battle," *The Compiler,* 26 April 1941; Sarah Sites Rodgers, *The Ties of the Past: The Gettysburg Diaries of Salome Myers Stewart 1854–1922* (Gettysburg: Thomas Publications, 1996), p. 199.

19. Fannie Buehler, *Recollections of the Rebel Invasion,* p. 26.

20. See Peter C. Vermilyea, "The Effect of the Confederate Invasion of Pennsylvania on Gettysburg's African American Community, in *The Gettysburg Magazine* 24 (2001): 124, note 74.

21. Johnson, *Battleground Adventures,* pp. 190–191; Memorandum, Senior Historian to Chief, I&VP, 8 August 1995, Brian File, Gettysburg National Military Park (hereafter GNMP); "The Bryan Farm Buildings," typed report, n.d., Brian File, GNMP; Marcella Sherfy, "The Brien Farm and Family," typed report, June 1972, Brian File, GNMP; Frassanito, *Early Photography at Gettysburg,* p. 230; Sophia Devan Damage Claims File, National Archives, Washington, D.C.

22. Tim Smith deserves credit for uncovering quartermaster records at the National Archives (author conversation, 16 April 2004); *The Star and Banner,* 6 August 1863; J. Howard Wert, "In the Hospitals of Gettysburg," *Harrisburg Daily Telegraph,* 6 August 1907.

23. "What We Did at Gettysburg," in Moore, ed., *Women of the War,* pp. 142–143.

24. "What We Did at Gettysburg," p. 133.

25. *Harrisburg Patriot and Union,* 9, 10, 11, 13 July 1863; *Harrisburg Daily Telegraph,* 13 July 1863.

26. Elizabeth Thorn, "Experience During Battle: A Woman's Thrilling Experiences of the Battle," *The Compiler,* 26 July 1905; "Mrs. Thorn's War Story," *The Gettysburg Times,* 2 July 1938; author interview, Brian Kennell, Superintendent, Evergreen Cemetery, 27 February 1999.

27. The child was a girl, Rosie Meade Thorn, who died at age fourteen; "Mrs. Thorn's War Story"; Frassanito, *Early Photography,* p. 152.

28. "Introduction" and "Report of David Wills," in *Revised Report Made to the Legislature of Pennsylvania Relative to the Soldiers' National Cemetery, at Gettysburg* (Harrisburg: Singerly & Myers, 1867), pp. 3–6.

29. "Report of David Wills," in *Revised Report,* p. 7; Basil Biggs' damage claim, 22 October 1868, in "Gettysburg Area Residents Claims File," GNMP; "Leading Colored Citizen" (Biggs' obituary), *The Compiler,* 13 June 1906.

30. Massachusetts sent its own burial squad to handle reinterments. That squad buried 158 men, making the total number removed to the National

Cemetery to be 3512, according to the official report of 1864. See "Report of Samuel Weaver," in *Revised Report*, p. 161.

31. "Specifications," in *Revised Report*, p. 14; Leander H. Warren, "Recollections of the Battle of Gettysburg," typescript, n.d., ACHS; "Report of Samuel Weaver," 19 March 1864, in *Revised Report*, p. 163.

32. "Report of Samuel Weaver," in *Revised Report*, p. 162; "List of Articles," in *Revised Report*, pp. 144–153; "Report of David Wills," in *Revised Report*, p. 7.

33. Frassanito, *Early Photography at Gettysburg*, pp. 167–169; "Report of Samuel Weaver," in *Revised Report*, p. 161; Warren, "Recollections of the Battle of Gettysburg"; McCreary, "Gettysburg: A Boy's Experience of the Battle," p. 252.

34. Mary Hunt Carson to her mother, 21 November 1863, private collection; Frassanito, *Early Photography*, p. 166, places the speaker's stand for the Gettysburg Address inside Evergreen Cemetery.

35. L. L. Crounse, "Further Details of the Battle of Gettysburgh," *The New York Times*, 9 July 1863; James Fulton, M.D., "Gettysburg Reminiscences," in *The National Tribune*, 20 October 1898; Bloom, "We Never Expected a Battle," p. 188; *Harrisburg Patriot and Union*, quoting *The New York Herald*, 4 July 1863. Tim Smith has done a thorough study of newspaper coverage of civilian behavior at Gettysburg. See Timothy H. Smith, "'These Were Days of Horror': The Story of the Gettysburg Civilians," in Barbara J. Finfrock, ed., *Unsung Heroes of Gettysburg: Programs of the Fifth Annual Gettysburg Seminar* (Gettysburg: Gettysburg National Military Park/The National Park Service, 1996), pp. 82–84.

36. Crounse, "Further Details of the Battle of Gettysburgh"; *The New York Herald*, 30 May 1863.

37. "What We Did at Gettysburg," in Moore, *Women of the War*, p. 138; Christian B. Keller, "The Pennsylvania Dutch and 'the Hard Hand of War,'" in David L. Valuska and Christian B. Keller, *Damn Dutch: Pennsylvania Germans at Gettysburg* (Mechanicsburg, Penn.: Stackpole Books, 2004), pp. 58–59, 69–71.

38. See Valuska and Keller's important account of "Pennsylvania Dutch" in the context of the Confederate invasion, *Damn Dutch*, pp. 50–54, 56–73. Keller and Valuska explain that most "Pennsylvania Dutch" were neither Dutch nor Amish. Most were members of the Lutheran and German Reformed churches (Chap. 1, p. 9). On the reluctance of some Pennsylvanians to rise to the defense of their state, see also Marilyn Brownfield Rudawsky, "After July: The Effects of the Battle of Gettysburg on the People of Adams County," M.A. thesis, Youngstown State University, Youngstown, Ohio, 1979, pp. 22–23, ACHS.

39. "Memories Unlocked at Gettysburg Anniversary for Geo. D. Thorn," *The Compiler*, 9 July 1932; Thorn, "Experience During Battle," *The Compiler*, 26 July 1905; "Mrs. Thorn's War Story," *The Gettysburg Times*, 2 July 1938.

40. "Memories Unlocked at Gettysburg Anniversary"; "Experience During Battle"; "Mrs. Thorn's War Story."

41. John Möser to O. O. Howard, 2 July 1863, BCSC. The note appears to have been written for Möser, a non-English speaker, by someone else, possibly a

soldier, who was unfamiliar with Gettysburg. He writes the town as "Get-tysville." In the press, another note (or a misrepresentation of this note) de-scribes a claim of $1700 for damage done to the cemetery. See Smith, "These Were Days of Horror," p. 83.

42. There is some possibility that John Möser wrote on behalf of Elizabeth Thorn, or that she had a separate list drawn up; the historical evidence is un-clear. See David McConaughy to O. O. Howard, 17 January 1883, BCSC.

43. Buehler, *Recollections of the Rebel Invasion.*

44. J. T. Trowbridge, "The Field of Gettysburg," *The Atlantic Monthly* 16 (November 1865): 616, 623.

45. "L. L. Crounse and Gettysburg; Gettysburg, July 11 1863," in *The Adams Sentinel,* 21 July 1863; *The Star and Banner,* 30 July 1863; lecture on Gettysburg civilians by Timothy H. Smith, 23 May 2001, Gettysburg College.

46. David McConaughy to O. O. Howard, 29 July 1863, BCSC.

47. David McConaughy to O. O. Howard, 17 January 1883, BCSC.

48. By the beginning of the twenty-first century, this was beginning to change. Markers, thanks to "Main Street Gettysburg," identified civilian battle sites, and commercial enterprises—like house and ghost tours—also focused on civilian experience. The National Military Park continued to concern itself pri-marily with combat engagements.

CHAPTER EIGHT

1. Harriet Bayly, "Mrs. Joseph Bayly's Story of the Battle," *The Compiler Scrapbook,* n.d., typescript, Gettysburg National Military Park Library (hereafter GNMP); Bernhard Domschcke, *Twenty Months in Captivity: Memoirs of a Union Officer in Confederate Prisons,* ed. and trans. by Frederic Trautmann (Rutherford, N.J.: Fairleigh Dickinson University Press, 1987), pp. 30–31.

2. Domschcke, *Twenty Months,* p. 30.

3. Domschcke, *Twenty Months,* pp. 31, 33–34.

4. Domschcke, *Twenty Months,* pp. 34–35, 53.

5. Domschcke, *Twenty Months,* pp. 43–47, 52, 57; Neal Dow, *The Reminis-cences of Neal Dow: Recollections of Eighty Years* (Portland, Maine: The Evening Express Publishing Co., 1898), p. 719.

6. Dow, *Reminiscences,* pp. 723–724; Richmond articles reprinted in the *New York Times,* 8–13 November 1863; Domschcke, *Twenty Months in Captivity,* pp. 53–54.

7. Adam Muenzenberger to Barbara Muenzenberger, 30 August 1863, State Historical Society of Wisconsin, Madison (hereafter SHSW).

8. Adam Muenzenberger to Barbara Muenzenberger, 30 August 1863; 9 Jan-uary 1863; 2 April 1863; 3, 31 May 1863, SHSW.

9. Adam Muenzenberger to Barbara Muenzenberger, 27 September 1863, SHSW.

10. Adam Muenzenberger to Barbara Muenzenberger, 22 October 1863; Barbara Muenzenberger to Adam Muenzenberger, 4 November 1863; Robert Mueller to Barbara Muenzenberger, 14 November 1863, SHSW.

11. *The New York Times*, 6, 14, 28 November, 1863.

12. Death certificate, Adam Muenzenberger, National Archives, Washington, D.C.; Frank L. Byrne, "A General Behind Bars: Neal Dow in Libby Prison," in William B. Hesseltine, ed., *Civil War Prisons* (Kent, Ohio: Kent State University Press, 1962), p. 70.

13. See Christian B. Keller, "Pennsylvania's German-Americans, a Popular Myth, and the Importance of Perception," in David L. Valuska and Christian B. Keller, *Damn Dutch: Pennsylvania Germans at Gettysburg* (Mechanicsburg, Penn.: Stackpole Books, 2004), p. 140; Carl Schurz, *The Reminiscences of Carl Schurz*, Vol. III (New York: The McClure Company, 1908), p. 50.

14. *The New York Times*, 3, 4, 6 July 1863; *Harrisburg Patriot and Union*, 4 July 1863; Keller, "Pennsylvania's German-Americans," in Valuska and Keller, *Damn Dutch*, pp. 140–142, 157–160.

15. Keller, "Pennsylvania's German-Americans," in Valuska and Keller, *Damn Dutch*, pp. 149–153; Francis C. Barlow to Robert T. Paine, 12 August 1863, in D. Scott Hartwig, "The 11th Army Corps on July 1, 1863—'The Unlucky 11th,'" *The Gettysburg Magazine* 2 (January 1990): 35; Oliver Otis Howard to General Henry Halleck, 29 July 1863, Bowdoin College Special Collections (hereafter BCSC); Schurz, *Reminiscences*, Vol. III, pp. 50–52; Trefousse, *Schurz*, p. 138; see also on the tenacity of the Flying Dutchman moniker, Augustus Choate Hamlin, *The Battle of Chancellorsville* (Bangor, Maine: Privately printed, 1896), pp. 31–32, 154–155.

16. *Harrisburg Patriot and Union*, 17 July 1863; *The Star and Banner*, 16 July 1863.

17. "Gen. Schimmelfennig," *National Tribune*, 13 August 1885; Anna Garlach Kitzmiller, "Story of a Brig. General, in Hiding Surrounded by Rebels During Battle," *The Compiler*, 9 August 1905.

18. *The Star and Banner*, 3 September 1863; Frank Moore, *Women of the War; Their Heroism and Self-sacrifice* (Hartford: S. S. Scranton & Co., 1867), p. 138.

19. John Charles Wills, "Reminiscences of the Three Days Battle of Gettysburg at the 'Globe Hotel,'" typescript, c. 1910, pp. 24, 42, ACHS; Mrs. Jacob A. Clutz (Liberty Augusta Hollinger), "Some Personal Recollections of the Battle of Gettysburg," privately printed, c. 1925, Adams County Historical Society (hereafter ACHS); Annie Skelly, "Recollections of the Battle of Gettysburg, Lincoln, and Other Incidents," 1941, typescript, ACHS; Mary Bushman Power Deardorff, "Grandmother Bushman's Friendship Quilt," *Gettysburg Times 75th Anniversary Edition*, July 1938, ACHS clipping.

20. Bayly, "Mrs. Joseph Bayly's Story"; Fannie J. Buehler, *Recollections of the Rebel Invasion and One Woman's Experience During the Battle of Gettysburg*

(Gettysburg: Star and Sentinel Print, 1900, reprint, Gary T. Hawbaker, Hershey, Penn., n.d.), pp. 19, 22–23.

21. Fannie Buehler's husband was likely descended from early German settlers; he had decidedly nativist inclinations, however. Differences in politics, religion, and/or wealth may have alienated him from recent immigrants.

22. Alfred C. Raphelson, "Alexander Schimmelfennig: A German-American Campaigner in the Civil War," *The Pennsylvania Magazine of History and Biography* 87 (1963): 177–178.

23. Sophia Schimmelfennig Pension File, National Archives, Washington, D.C.; Raphelson, "Alexander Schimmelfennig," pp. 179–180; Steven D. Smith, "Whom We Would Never More See: History and Archaeology Recover the Lives and Deaths of African American Civil War Soldiers on Folly Island, South Carolina," S.C. Department of Archives and History, n.d. (1990s).

24. *The Berks and Schuylkill (Penn.) Journal,* 16 September 1865; Alfred C. Raphelson, "General Schimmelfennig in Berks," *Historical Review of Berks County* (Autumn, 1962): 109–110.

25. *The Berks and Schuylkill (Penn.) Journal,* 16 September 1865; *The Reading Gazette and Democrat,* 16 September 1865; "Resolutions," forwarded to Sec. Edwin Stanton, New York, 3 October 1865, in Sophia Schimmelfennig Pension Application file, National Archives, Washington, D.C.

26. Informant response, Author Battlefield Guide Survey, 2000–2001; Keller, "Pennsylvania's German-Americans," in Valuska and Keller, *Damn Dutch,* pp. 154, 204.

27. Trefousse, *Schurz,* pp. 140–143; Schurz, *Reminiscences,* Vol. III, pp. 52–55, 80–84.

28. Trefousse, *Schurz,* pp. 138–144; Schurz, *Reminiscences,* Vol. III, pp. 85–95; Ella Lonn, *Foreigners in the Union Army and Navy* (Baton Rouge: Louisiana Staate University Press, 1951), p. 181.

29. Hamlin, *The Battle of Chancellorsville,* p. 154; Schurz, *Reminiscences,* Vol. III, pp. 51, 89.

30. Frederick C. Luebke, "Images of German Immigrants in the United States and Brazil, 1890–1918: Some Comparisons," in Frank Trommler and Joseph McVeigh, eds., *America and the Germans: An Assessment of a Three-Hundred-Year History,* Vol. 1 (Philadelphia: University of Pennsylvania Press, 1985), p. 211; Matthew Frye Jacobson, *Whiteness of a Different Color: European Immigrants and the Alchemy of Race* (Cambridge: Harvard University Press, 1998), pp. 76–77.

31. Jacobson, *Whiteness,* p. 47; Hon. Joseph H. Choate, "Address in Memory of Carl Schurz," in *Addresses in Memory of Carl Schurz* (New York: Committee of the Carl Schurz Memorial, 1906), pp. 7–8.

32. See Gerald F. Linderman, *Embattled Courage: The Experience of Combat in the American Civil War* (New York: The Free Press, 1987), p. 277.

33. *The Star and Sentinel,* 6 April 1886; 14 December 1886; 2, 9 October 1888.

34. Hamlin, *The Battle of Chancellorsville*, p. 29.

35. Hamlin, *Chancellorsville*, pp. 128, 154–155.

36. Schurz, *Reminiscences*, Vol. III, p. 38; Carl Schurz, "The Battle of Gettysburg," *McClure's Magazine* 29 (July 1907): 285; Carl Schurz to Agathe Schurz, 9 November 1863, in Joseph Schafer, ed., *Intimate Letters of Carl Schurz* (Madison: State Historical Society of Wisconsin, 1928), p. 291.

37. Schurz, *Reminiscences*, Vol. III, pp. 158–185 (quotation, 185); Trefousse, *Schurz*, pp. 147, 156–158.

38. According to scholars, Schurz wavered on social reform in the South. He shifted away from the Republican Party, then back again, and then away, and in the 1870s he urged rapprochement between the white South and the white North. He then devoted himself to civil service reform and other humanitarian causes: denouncing anti-Semitism and America's expansionism at the turn of the century. At the end of his life, he turned back to the South and its race relations, drawing unpopular connections between racial oppression in the South and United States, imperial ambitions in Cuba and the Philippines. See Trefousse, *Schurz*, pp. 174, 235–255, 188–209; Schurz, *Reminiscences*, Vol. III, pp. 331, 451–452.

39. Schurz, *Reminiscences*, Vol. III, pp. 38, 124–126.

40. Hamlin, *Chancellorsville*, p. 32.

41. Luebke, "Images of German Immigrants," p. 216; Steven Rowan, trans., and Don Heinrich Tolzmann, Werner D. Mueller, and Robert E. Ward, eds., Wilhelm Kaufmann, *The Germans in the American Civil War* (Carlisle, Penn.: John Kallmann, Publishers, 1999), p. iv.

42. *The Gettysburg Times*, 30 May 1918.

43. On Gettysburg's rising status as a standard of manhood, see Amy J. Kinsel, "'A Monument to American Manhood': How the War Department Shaped the Gettysburg National Military Park," paper delivered at the Organization of American Historians Meeting, Toronto, April 1999.

44. Rowan et al., Kaufmann, *The Germans in the American Civil War*, p. iv. A definitive account of "foreigners" in the Civil War that helped to pave the way for Kaufmann's translation is Ella Lonn, *Foreigners in the Union Army and Navy* (Baton Rouge: Louisiana State University Press, 1951). Thanks to Christian B. Keller for thoughts on Kaufmann's history.

45. Keller, "Pennsylvania's German-Americans," in Valuska and Keller, *Damn Dutch*, p. 155, describes the historical treatment of German soldiers in the twentieth century; Keller and Valuska's entire book is a powerful examination of the "Flying Dutchman" stereotype as it applied to Pennsylvania Germans during the Civil War. See also Scott Hartwig, "The 11th Army Corps," pp. 33–49. For other prominent depictions of the Eleventh Corps at Gettysburg, see Edwin B. Coddington, *The Gettysburg Campaign: A Study in Command* (New York: Touchstone, 1968; reprint, 1997), pp. 305–306; Michael Shaara, *The Killer Angels* (New York: Ballantine Books, 1974), p. 123; Sears, *Gettysburg*, pp. 216, 495.

46. Ezra J. Warner, *Generals in Blue: Lives of the Union Commanders* (Baton Rouge: Louisiana State University Press, 1996), pp. 238–239.

47. Senator James Grimes of Iowa, who moved that Howard's name be added, commented that "the man who selected the position where the battle of Gettysburg was fought, and who, indeed fought it the first day, was General Howard, and to him the country is indebted as much for the credit of securing that victory as to any other person." John A. Carpenter, "General O. O. Howard at Gettysburg," *Civil War History* 9 (1963): 261.

48. Carpenter, "O. O. Howard at Gettysburg," p. 273.

49. General Joseph Hooker to O. O. Howard, 3 July 1863; O. O. Howard to Elizabeth Howard, 16 July 1863, BCSC; O. O. Howard to Major Henry Burrage, 9 February 1894; O. O. Howard, "Campaign and Battle of Gettysburg, June and July, 1863," *Atlantic Monthly Magazine* 38 (July 1876): 70.

50. Carpenter, "Howard at Gettysburg," pp. 265–271; Abner Doubleday's criticism is summed up in *The Star and Sentinel,* 29 March 1882; see also Glenn Tucker, *High Tide at Gettysburg: The Campaign in Pennsylvania* (Gettysburg: Stan Clark Military Books, 1958; reprint, 1995), pp. 123–124.

51. Hooker quotation, *San Francisco Chronicle,* 23 May 1872, in Carpenter, *Sword and Oliver Branch,* pp. 24–25 (see also www.fredericksburg.com/Civil War/Battle/chanc_story?dy=0824002&fn=705813); Oliver Otis Howard, *Autobiography of Oliver Otis Howard,* Vol. 2 (New York: The Baker and Taylor Company, 1908), p. 16.

52. O. O. Howard to Elizabeth W. Howard, 25 September 1863; 1 October 1863; O. O. Howard to General-in-Chief Halleck, 29 July 1863 (even though he favored breaking up the corps, Howard had kind words for his officers, and seemed relatively close to one of his division commanders, Adolph von Steinwehr); O. O. Howard to Elizabeth W. Howard, 22, 31 July 1863, BCSC.

53. Howard was not the only senior officer that Schurz criticized; not surprisingly, he also vehemently attacked Hooker. Schurz, *Reminiscences,* Vol. II, pp. 442–443; Vol. III, pp. 85–86, 93; O. O. Howard to Secretary Carl Schurz, 17 March 1881, BCSC.

54. O. O. Howard to General Orland Smith, 18 December 1896, BCSC.

55. Hamlin, *The Battle of Chancellorsville,* pp. 158, 175, 34.

56. Oliver Otis Howard to [General] John T. Lockman, 24 December 1896. And the counterattacks went on, too. As late as 1900, Howard was associated with insult to Schurz and other immigrant soldiers. At a banquet honoring Howard in New York City, a commemorative booklet featured a sketch of Howard at Chancellorsville. Pictured on a white horse, his empty sleeve clutching the American flag, Howard is described as "the only man in his own command that was not running at that moment." He pleads with his men, "literally weeping as he entreated the unheeding horde." See "Banquet to Major-General Oliver Otis Howard," Commemorative Booklet, 8 November 1900, BCSC.

57. O. O. Howard to Orland Smith, 18 December 1896.

58. See, for example, Schurz, *Reminiscences*, Vol. III, pp. 79–80. Schurz attributes the "Christian soldier" comment to General William T. Sherman.

59. E. Anthony Rotundo, *American Manhood: Transformations in Masculinity from the Revolution to the Modern Era* (New York: Basic Books, 1993), pp. 222–239. Howard's piety got in the way of his reputation, and so, ironically, did his desire to clear his name. He recognized that his efforts to "keep my record bright and honorable" were seen by some as "unworthy." See Carpenter, "Howard at Gettysburg," p. 274.

60. Howard speech, *The Star and Sentinel*, 5 February 1889; O. O. Howard to J. McKim, 11 January 1866, BCSC.

61. When Howard was a young boy, his father hired a young African American as a farmhand, and Howard later claimed that the boy's living with him, as his friend, was "a providential circumstance, for it relieved me from that feeling of prejudice which would have hindered me from doing the work for the freedmen." After the war, Howard sought to integrate his white church in Washington, D.C., and his home community of Leeds, Maine. O. O. Howard to Elizabeth W. Howard, 24 September 1864; Geoffrey R. Stanwood, "On Oliver Otis Howard, Bowdoin College, and Howard University," prepared for Special Collections, Bowdoin College, 1992; Howard, *Autobiography*, Vol. 1, p. 13; Eliza Gilmore to O. O. Howard, 24 November 1865, BCSC; William S. McFeely, *Yankee Stepfather: General O. O. Howard and the Freedmen* (New Haven: Yale University Press, 1968), pp. 103–104, 211–213. (Thanks to Laura Juraska for information on Leeds.) William T. Sherman to Oliver Otis Howard, 17 May 1865, BCSC.

62. McFeely, *Yankee Stepfather*, Chaps. 7–9; O. O. Howard to William Hayward, 23 December 1865, BCSC.

63. McFeely, *Yankee Stepfather*, p. 237, Chap. 6. William McFeely makes a good case for General Rufus Saxton as the kind of Civil War veteran, leader, and serious advocate of the freedmen who might have led the Bureau to more positive results. See *Yankee Stepfather*, Chap. 3; Carpenter, *Sword and Olive Branch*, p. 169; W. E. B. Du Bois, *The Souls of Black Folk* (New York: Vintage, 1990), pp. 26, 31. Howard felt the enmity of abolitionists who believed he compromised away substantive freedom for African Americans, but he did have wide-ranging support, from conservative white abolitionists like Harriet Beecher Stowe to more radical abolitionists like Thaddeus Stevens. And he had consistent support from much of the black community—people who, in the words of one historian, were "doggedly loyal" even in the roughest times. One of those rough moments included the failure of the Freedmen's Bank during the depression of 1873, when many depositors lost their savings. "My dear General," wrote a disappointed but gracious Frederick Douglass, "take nothing of this to yourself." "Friend Howard," echoed Sojourner Truth, "I pray to God that you may live to overcome the persecutors." See McFeely, *Yankee Stepfather*, p. 3; Harriet Beecher Stowe to O. O. Howard, 12 November 1878, BCSC; Sojourner Truth to O. O.

Howard, 23 December 1873, BCSC; Frederick Douglass to O. O. Howard, 18 February 1875, BCSC; O. O. Howard to Charles Douglass, 14 February 1895.

64. Blight, *Race and Reunion,* p. 390 and epilogue. Howard, not surprisingly, had difficulty with the movement toward reconciliation. While he was cordial to ex-Confederates, he was not eager to socialize with them. In 1889, responding to an invitation to join a get-together, Howard explained that these sorts of meetings "were not altogether wholesome in their tendency. It seems too much like brothers making up after a quarrel, where the two are equally at fault." Howard believed that less-than-friendly work remained: "The hard thing now is to secure the faithful carrying out [of] measures secured by the war, namely, the positive equality of rights of every citizen before the law." He did not see how veterans' reunions would help matters. Carpenter, *Sword and Olive Branch,* p. 282.

65. Paul A. Cimbala, "Introduction," p. ix, in Carpenter, *Sword and Olive Branch,* 1999 edition.

66. See Frederick W. Hawthorne, *Gettysburg: Stories of Men and Monuments* (Gettysburg: Association of Licensed Battlefield Guides, 1988), p. 9; Battlefield Guide Survey, 2001; author's battlefield tours, 2001–2002; see also Cimbala, "Introduction," *Sword and the Olive Branch,* p. xii.

CHAPTER NINE

1. Rowland Howard to O. O. Howard, 31 March 1865, Bowdoin College Special Collections (hereafter BCSC).

2. Elizabeth Howard to O. O. Howard, 5 August 1861; O. O. Howard to Elizabeth Howard, 22 August 1861, BCSC.

3. *The Star and Banner,* 16 July 1863.

4. Elizabeth D. Leonard, *Yankee Women: Gender Battles in the Civil War* (New York: W.W. Norton & Company, 1994), pp. 169–179; Jeanie Attie, "Warwork and the Crisis of Domesticity in the North," in Catherine Clinton and Nina Silber, eds., *Divided Houses: Gender and the Civil War* (New York: Oxford University Press, 1992), pp. 251–252; Mrs. Jacob A. Clutz (Liberty Augusta Hollinger), "Some Personal Recollections of the Battle of Gettysburg" (privately printed, c. 1925), p. 14, Adams County Historical Society (hereafter ACHS); Jennie Croll[?] "Days of Dread," *Philadelphia Weekly Press,* 16 November 1887.

5. *The Star and Sentinel,* 15, 22 April 1874; *The Compiler,* 26 October 1863.

6. [Charles M. McCurdy] *The Star and Sentinel,* 6 March 1888; Edward Everett, oration at Gettysburg, in Garry Wills, *Lincoln at Gettysburg: The Words That Remade America* (New York: Simon & Schuster, 1992), pp. 231, 233; O. O. Howard to Elizabeth Howard, 22 September 1862, BCSC.

7. See "Courage," in Helen A. Hawley, *Friendly Letters to Girls* (New York: Anson D. F. Randolph & Company, 1888), pp. 25–28; see also E. Anthony Rotundo, *American Manhood: Transformations in Masculinity from the Revolution*

to the Modern Era (New York: Basic Books, 1993), pp. 42–43, who describes how boys taught each other stoicism and physical daring. Teddy Roosevelt, writing at the turn of the century, when many women's reminiscences were published, commented that women's courage was the courage to be faithful to their sex, to be mothers and wives. "The woman must be the housewife . . . the wise and fearless mother of many healthy children," he said just before the turn of the century. "When men fear . . . righteous war, when women fear motherhood, they tremble on the brink of doom" (*The Strenuous Life,* 1899, available at www.bartleby.com/58/1.html).

8. *The Star and Sentinel,* 9 September 1890.

9. *The Star and Sentinel,* 18 July 1903; "Memories of Gettysburg: Recalled by Maj.-Gen. O. O. Howard Before His Death," *The Compiler,* 23 March 1910.

10. *The Star and Sentinel,* 29 September 1891; see also Timothy H. Smith, "Josephine Miller: A Heroine of the Battle," *Blue & Gray Magazine* 20 (Holiday 2002): 21–24; "Pickett's Men Listen to Heroine of the Battle," *Philadelphia Press,* 4 July 1913.

11. *The Star and Sentinel,* 1 September 1891; 8 July 1903; *New York Herald,* 1 July 1913.

12. *The Star and Sentinel,* 27 May 1868; 3 June 1868; 27 May 1870; 6 October 1885; 8 July 1903; Nina Silber, *The Romance of Reunion: Northerners and the South, 1865–1900* (Chapel Hill: University of North Carolina Press, 1993), p. 59.

13. "Gettysburg's Fight: The Part That a Brave Little Girl Played During the Battle," *The Compiler,* 12 January 1892. On the popular currency of the "angel of mercy" image of Civil War women, see Leonard, *Yankee Women,* p. 171.

14. "The Part That a Brave Girl Played," *The Compiler,* 12 January 1892.

15. "Mrs. Jungerman's Story of Her Girlhood Experience," *The (San Francisco) Bulletin,* 9 March 1902; Ilza Veith, "Hygeia by the Bay—A City of Health," *The Western Journal of Medicine* 127 (November 1977): 442–449. Thanks to Dr. David Steinhardt for information on Benjamin Lyford.

16. "Mrs. Jungerman's Story." There is some confusion as to the date that Lyford picked up Sadie Bushman's story. The story seems to have first circulated in San Francisco in late 1891 (according to the 12 January 1892 *Gettysburg Compiler*), but the reunion was featured in a San Francisco paper ten years later.

17. David McConaughy to O. O. Howard, 17 January 1883, BCSC.

18. O. O. Howard to David McConaughy, 7 February 1883, BCSC.

19. George D. Thorn to O. O. Howard, 2 March 1894, BCSC.

20. O. O. Howard to George D. Thorn, 4 April 1894, BCSC.

21. *Harrisburg Telegraph,* 25 October 1896, described in "Memories Unlocked at Gettysburg Anniversary Fete for Geo. D. Thorn," *The Compiler,* 9 July 1932; *The Compiler,* 23 September 1902; *The Star and Sentinel,* 8 October 1902.

22. Elizabeth Thorn, "Experience During Battle: A Woman's Thrilling Experiences of the Battle," *The Compiler,* 26 July 1905; "Memories of Gettysburg,"

The Compiler, 23 March 1910; *The Compiler,* 29 July 1884 (quoting the *South Haven Michigan Sentinel,* 19 July 1884; "Gettysburg Heroine," editorial cartoon in the *Harrisburg Evening News,* 29 May 1937, clipping, ACHS.

23. *The Washington Post,* 30 June 1913.

24. The Thorn cartoon may also have been aimed at the town itself. The drawing of Elizabeth Thorn with "cowardly" men was printed not in Gettysburg but in Harrisburg, one year before the borough was to receive national attention for the battle's seventy-fifth anniversary. The borough had fallen under attack from neighboring communities before other anniversaries. See, for instance, *The Star and Sentinel,* 16 July 1913.

25. Census note, Thorn family, Historian's Office, Gettysburg National Military Park (hereafter GNMP); J. Howard Wert, "Old Time Notes of Adams County," *The Star and Sentinel,* 13 March 1907. On native-born depictions of immigrant civilians during the battle, see Chapter Eight.

26. Evergreen Cemetery's superintendent Brian Kennell raised money for the statue that honors Thorn. The statue depicts her pregnant, as she was at the time of the battle. See also Brian A. Kennell, *Beyond the Gatehouse: Gettysburg's Evergreen Cemetery* (Gettysburg: Evergreen Cemetery Association, 2000), and www.evergreencemetery.org.

27. *The Star and Banner,* 9 July 1863; *The Compiler,* 13 July 1863; *Harrisburg Patriot and Union,* 23 July 1863.

28. See J. W. Johnston, *The True Story of "Jennie" Wade: A Gettysburg Maid* (Rochester, N.Y.: Privately printed, 1917); Cindy L. Small, *The Jennie Wade Story: A True and Complete Account of the Only Civilian Killed During the Battle of Gettysburg* (Gettysburg: Thomas Publications, 1991); Mary H. Eastman, "Jenny Wade of Gettysburg" (Philadelphia: J. B. Lippincott & Co., 1864); R. Stewart Gibbs, "The Maid of Gettysburg," *The Compiler,* 22 July 1903; Anon., "The Heroine of Gettysburg," in *Iowa Woman's Relief Corps Messenger,* 1922, Rochester Museum and Science Center (hereafter RMSC); "Georgia Wade-McClellan Died at Hospital Monday Morning," *The Carroll Times,* 7 September 1927; Warren Irish to John Johnston, 5 June 1923, RMSC; author visits to Jennie Wade Museum; and Farnsworth House Restaurant, Gettysburg, 1997–2003.

29. *Pittsburgh Evening Chronicle,* April 21 1864, in John S. Patterson, "John Burns and Jennie Wade: The Hero and Heroine of Gettysburg," paper presented at the American Folklore Society Meeting, 19 October 1989, p. 11 (copy in GNMP). This analysis takes its bearings from the pioneering work of Patterson. One of the two "influential" people in town who could "confirm" Jennie's unpatriotic status was Postmaster David Buehler, Fannie's husband. See Timothy H. Smith, *John Burns: "The Hero of Gettysburg"* (Gettysburg: Thomas Publications, 2000), p. 117.

30. *The Star and Sentinel,* 25 July 1878; Tillie (Pierce) Alleman, *At Gettysburg or What a Girl Saw and Heard of the Battle: A True Narrative* (New York: W. Lake Borland, 1889; reprint, 1994), pp. 26–27; Johnston, *The True Story,* pp. 10–11.

31. Johnston H. Skelly to his mother, 7 April 1863, in E. F. Conklin, *Women at Gettysburg 1863* (Gettysburg: Thomas Publications, 1993), pp. 387–388.

32. *The Gettysburg Times,* 2 July 1938; William A. Frassanito, "Introduction," in Alleman, *At Gettysburg,* p. v; Conklin, *Women at Gettysburg,* p. 131; Web site, for example, www.arthes.com/dtindi.html#; author conversation with battle-field guides and National Park Service rangers, 1999.

33. Author visit to cellar exhibit, Jennie Wade House Museum, 2000.

34. Adams County Poor House Records, 1854–1874, private collection. Per-sonnel of the National Military Park in the mid-twentieth century continued to find that the "social status of the Wade family is definitely a sensitive subject." "Her family is not considered," one staff member asserted, "as 'society' in Get-tysburg." See GNMP memo, c. 1950s–1960s, cited in Patterson, "John Burns and Jennie Wade," p. 15 (note 11).

35. Timothy H. Smith, "'These Were Days of Horror': The Gettysburg Civil-ians," in *Unsung Heroes of Gettysburg: Programs of the Fifth Annual Gettysburg Seminar* (Gettysburg: Gettysburg National Military Park, 1996), p. 82. Gettys-burg and Harrisburg were two of the towns slinging accusations at each other. Not long after the battle, a newspaper in Harrisburg called Gettysburg's patriot-ism into question when it declared that Jennie Wade "was the only sacrifice which the people of that locality had to offer on the shrine of their country." Gettysburg responded by asking if Harrisburg would have preferred "the slaughter of more of our innocent women and children." See *The Harrisburg Daily Telegraph* and *The Adams Sentinel,* c. 1 December 1863, in Small, *The Jen-nie Wade Story,* pp. 43–44.

36. Smith, *John Burns,* pp. 44–45, 151.

37. Johnston, *The True Story of Jennie Wade,* p. 3; Robert Miller to Georgia Wade McClellan, 12 June 1920, RMSC; Georgia Wade McClellan to John W. Johnston, 22 January 1920, RMSC.

38. "Carroll Woman is Honored at State G.A.R. Meeting," in *The Carroll (Iowa) Times,* 29 June 1927; "Georgia Wade-McClellan Died at Hospital Mon-day Morning."

39. "Georgia Wade-McClellan Died at Hospital Monday Morning."

40. Historian Alice Fahs describes how recognition of Union women in liter-ature evaporated not long after the war. The two most important volumes on women's wartime work, Frank Moore's *Women of the War: Their Heroism and Self-Sacrifice* (1866) and Linus P. Brockett and Mary C. Vaughan's *Women's Work in the Civil War: A Record of Heroism, Patriotism, and Patience* (1867), had few followers. Thomas Brown explains that monumentation acknowledging Union women's contributions was similarly nonexistent and the first major construc-tion honoring women on a national level, the Red Cross Headquarters, dedi-cated in 1917, commemorated women of both sections. See Alice Fahs, "The Feminized Civil War: Gender, Northern Popular Literature, and the Memory of

War, 1861–1900," *The Journal of American History* 85 (March 1999):1464; and Thomas J. Brown, *The Public Art of Civil War Commemoration: A Brief History with Documents* (Boston: Bedford/St. Martin's, 2004), pp. 58–61.

41. J. Howard Wert, "Old Time Notes of Adams County," 3 March 1907, *The Star and Sentinel; The Star and Sentinel,* 7 June 1898; Mary M. Melchior, "John Burns at Gettsyburg," *Doyleston (Penn.) Democrat,* 14 August 1886, ACHS; Louie Dale Leeds, inscriber, "Nellie E. Aughinbaugh, Personal Experiences of a Young Girl During the Battle of Gettysburg," privately printed, c. 1926–1938, ACHS.

42. Melchior, "John Burns at Gettysburg."

43. "Dedication Ceremonies of the Jennie Wade Monument at Gettysburg, Penn., September 16th, 1901," pamphlet, RMSC.

44. Mary Bushman Powers Deardorff, "Grandmother Bushman's Friendship Quilt," in *The Gettysburg Times,* 75th Anniversary Edition, July 1938; Lydia Catherine Ziegler Clare, "A Gettysburg Girl's Story of the Great Battle," c. 1900, typescript, ACHS; Clutz, "Some Personal Recollections"; Fannie J. Buehler, *Recollections of the Rebel Invasion and One Woman's Experience During the Battle of Gettysburg* (Gettysburg: Star and Sentinel Print, 1896; reprint, Gary T. Hawbaker, Hershey, Penn., n.d.); Sarah M. Broadhead, *The Diary of a Lady of Gettysburg, Pennsylvania, from June 15 to July 15 1863* (Gettysburg: Privately printed, 1864; reprint, Gary T. Hawbaker, Hershey, Penn., 2002).

45. "Mrs. Jungerman's Story"; "Carroll Woman is Honored at State G.A.R. Meeting."

46. Leeds/Aughinbaugh, "Personal Experiences of a Young Girl During the Battle of Gettysburg," p. 3, 15; Buehler, *Recollections of the Rebel Invasion,* p. 5.

47. On the many ways American women contested the prevailing image of their war work as instinctual, see Jeanie Attie, "Warwork and the Crisis of Domesticity in the North," in Clinton and Silber, eds., *Divided Houses,* pp. 258–259.

48. Harriet Hamilton Bayly, "A Woman's Story," *The Star and Sentinel,* 25 September 1888; "Mrs. Jungerman's Story"; Deardorff, "Grandmother Bushman's Friendship Quilt."

49. Leeds/Aughinbaugh, "Personal Experiences," p. 12; *The Star and Sentinel,* 11 September 1888.

50. For details of women's injuries, see Chapter 7; Melchior, "John Burns at Gettysburg."

51. Amy J. Kinsel, "'A Monument to American Manhood': How the War Department Shaped the Gettysburg National Military Park," paper delivered at the Organization of American Historians Meeting, April 1999; David W. Blight, "'What Will Peace Among the Whites Bring?': Reunion and Race in the Struggle over the Memory of the Civil War in American Culture," *The Massachusetts Review* 34 (Autumn 1993): 402; John Patterson, "Zapped at the Map: The Battlefield at Gettysburg," *Journal of Popular Culture* 7 (1974): 835.

52. John Charles Wills, "Reminiscences of the Three Days Battle of Gettysburg at the Globe Hotel," c. 1915, typescript, ACHS.

53. Daniel Alexander Skelly, *A Boy's Experiences During the Battles of Gettysburg* (Gettysburg: Privately printed, 1932; reprint, Gary T. Hawbaker, n.d.). (Daniel Skelly had actually been eighteen at the time of the battle.)

54. William Hamilton Bayly, "William Hamilton Bayly's Story of the Battle," *Gettysburg Compiler Scrapbook*, n.d., typescript, GNMP.

55. *The Star and Sentinel,* 30 July 1889; 20 January 1885.

56. *The Star and Sentinel,* 2 July 1913.

57. For fiction see the works of Elsie Singmaster, and on girls see Alice Turner Curtis, *Kathleen: A Yankee Girl at Gettysburg* (New York: Gramercy Books, reprint, 1995); Michael Shaara, *The Killer Angels* (New York: Ballantine Books, 1974), pp. 36, 42, 167–172, 236.

58. Writers who produced important work on Gettysburg women around the turn of the twenty-first century include Eileen Conklin, Christina Ericson, Sarah Sites Rodgers, and Cindy Small. Janet Bucklew and Rebecca Lyons launched a women's history symposium as well, sponsored in part by the National Military Park.

59. Bayly, "A Woman's Story."

CHAPTER TEN

1. Basil Biggs Damage Claim, 22 October 1868, in "Gettysburg Area Residents Claims File," Gettysburg National Military Park (hereafter GNMP); William A. Frassanito, *Early Photography at Gettysburg* (Gettysburg: Thomas Publications, 1995), p. 169.

2. John B. Bachelder, "Report to Colonel C. H. Buehler, Gettysburg Battlefield Memorial Association," 1 February 1894, in Bachelder Papers, Microfilm #5, M6–008, GNMP.

3. Gettysburg Battlefield Memorial Association Minutes, 9 November, 16 November, 22 December 1881, GNMP; *The Star and Sentinel,* 22, 29 November 1882.

4. African Americans came to Gettysburg on other "Emancipation Days" as well. See *The Star and Sentinel,* 22 July 1884; 26 July 1887; 2 August 1887; 2 June 1891; Donald H. Becker, "Trends in Negro Segregation in Gettysburg, 1900–1953," M.A. thesis, University of Maryland, 1953, p. 44 (Abdel Ross Wentz Library, Lutheran Theological Seminary, Gettysburg); Garry E. Adelman and Timothy H. Smith, *Devil's Den: A History and Guide* (Gettysburg: Thomas Publications, 1997), pp. 78–91; Jim Weeks, *Gettysburg: Memory, Market, and an American Shrine* (Princeton: Princeton University Press, 2003), pp. 91–98. Weeks discusses the conflicted feelings about these excursions among the black community in Baltimore.

5. *The Star and Sentinel,* 19 February 1868; 29 January 1869; 12 August 1884.

6. *The Star and Sentinel,* 19 February 1868; 28 August 1868.

7. *The Star and Sentinel,* 9 July 1869; 3 June 1890.

8. Nina Silber, *The Romance of Reunion,* pp. 95, 101–106; David W. Blight, *Race and Reunion: The Civil War in American Memory* (Cambridge: Harvard University Press, 2001), pp. 175, 198, 209, 216; *The Star and Sentinel,* 7 June 1898.

9. W. Fitzhugh Brundage, "Race, Memory, and Masculinity: Black Veterans Recall the Civil War," in Joan E. Cashin, ed., *The War Was You and Me: Civilians in the American Civil War* (Princeton: Princeton University Press, 2002), p. 142; Frederick W. Hawthorne, *Gettysburg: Stories of Men and Monuments as Told by Battlefield Guides* (Gettysburg: Association of Licensed Battlefield Guides, 1988). Thanks especially to Wayne Motts.

10. *The Star and Sentinel,* 10 July 1888; John S. Patterson, "A Patriotic Landscape: Gettysburg, 1863–1913," *Prospects* 7 (1982): 328–329; *The Compiler,* 4 June 1913; *The Gettysburg Times,* 31 May 1913; David W. Blight, "'What Will Peace Among the Whites Bring?': Reunion and Race in the Struggle Over the Memory of the Civil War in American Culture," *The Massachusetts Review* (Autumn 1993): 400–407; *The Compiler,* 23 July 1913; *The Gettysburg Times,* 31 May 1913; *The New York Times,* 29 June 1913; Blight, *Race and Reunion,* p. 326.

11. *The Star and Sentinel,* 31 March 1885; 2 June 1885; 17 September 1889; 7 June 1892; 13 March 1888.

12. *The Star and Sentinel,* 3 June 1890. Evidence that slavery was becoming a nontopic among speech-givers and evidence of the racial language of reconciliation in Gettysburg is abundant. In Gettysburg see, for example, *The Compiler,* 11 July 1893; 16 July 1913; *The Star and Sentinel,* 9 July 1913.

13. Blight, *Race and Reunion,* pp. 311–318; "What Will Peace . . . Bring?" pp. 404–405; Blight, *Frederick Douglass' Civil War,* pp. 220–222; Barbara A. Gannon, "Sites of Memory, Sites of Glory: African American Grand Army of the Republic Posts in Pennsylvania," in William Blair and William Pencak, eds., *Making and Remaking Pennsylvania's Civil War* (University Park: Pennsylvania State University Press, 2001), p. 181.

14. Blight, *Race and Reunion,* pp. 390–391 (quotations).

15. *The Star and Sentinel,* 4 September 1868; 30 June 1871; 28 June 1882; for other local history, see J. Howard Wert, "Old Time Notes of Adams County," published regularly in the *Star and Sentinel* at the turn of the century; for oral histories see Clifton Johnson, *Battleground Adventures* (Boston: 1915); and for fiction, for example, see Elsie Singmaster, *A Boy at Gettysburg* (New York: Houghton-Mifflin Company, 1924).

16. *The Star and Banner,* 25 June 1863; 6 August 1863; see also "The Chambersburg Telegrams," *New York Herald,* 19 June 1863, and *The Compiler,* 29 June 1863 (from the *McConnellsburg [Penn.] Democrat*).

17. Philip Schaff, "The Gettysburg Week," *Scribner's Magazine* 16 (July 1894): 22–23; Jacob Taughenbaugh, "In Occupied Pennsylvania," edited by T. W. Herbert, *The Georgia Review* (1950): 108; Fannie J. Buehler, *Recollections of the Rebel*

Invasion and One Woman's Experience During the Battle of Gettysburg (Gettysburg: Star and Sentinel Print, 1900; reprint, Gary T. Hawbaker, Hershey, Penn., n.d.), p. 12; Harriet H. Bayly, "A Woman's Story," *The Star and Sentinel,* 25 September 1888; Annie Young to "My dear Mina," 17 July 1863, in Catherine Merrill, *The Soldier of Indiana in the War for the Union* (Indianapolis: 1866), pp. 119–120.

18. Johnson, *Battleground Adventures,* pp. 192–193 (footnote); *The Star and Sentinel,* 21 August 1888.

19. Albertus McCreary, "Gettysburg: A Boy's Experience of the Battle," *McClure's Magazine* 33 (July 1909): 250; Catherine Mary White Foster, "The Story of the Battle by a Citizen Whose Home Was Pierced by Flying Shells," *The Compiler,* 29 June, 6 July 1904.

20. Charles M. McCurdy, "Gettysburg: A Memoir" (Pittsburgh: Reed & Witting Company, 1929), pp. 19–20.

21. Frances Cunningham Harper, "Native of Adams County Writes of Experiences of Parents During '63 Battle," *The Compiler,* 26 April 1941.

22. Nellie E. Aughinbaugh, *Personal Experiences of a Young Girl During the Battle of Gettysburg,* edited by Louie Dale Leeds (N.p.: Privately printed, c. 1926–1938), p. 12; Lavinia Bollinger to Susan White, 9 September 1863, Adams County Historical Society (hereafter ACHS); Mary Warren Fastnacht, "Memories of the Battle of Gettysburg," privately printed, 23 October 1928, ACHS.

23. Quotation, Blight, *Race and Reunion,* p. 199.

24. Johnson, *Battleground Adventures,* pp. 187–190; author interview with Margaret Nutter, Gettysburg, 17 April 1999; Catherine Carter, talk to Bates College class, Gettysburg, May 1997; Lauri Lebo, "History Overlooked," *The (Hanover) Evening Sun,* 8 February 1998, B1.

25. Everard H. Smith, "Chambersburg: Anatomy of a Confederate Reprisal," *American Historical Review* 96 (1991): 432–455; Blight, *Race and Reunion,* p. 327, discusses the spread of racially driven violence.

26. Frederick M. Binder, "Pennsylvania Negro Regiments in the Civil War," *Journal of Negro History* 37 (October 1952): 385; Betty Dorsey Myers, *Segregation in Death: Gettysburg's Lincoln Cemetery* (Gettysburg: Lincoln Cemetery Project Association, 2001), pp. 63–75, indicates Gettysburg troop assignments.

27. By the time Watts and Johnston enlisted, the army had formally dropped some of its most blatant discriminatory practices, such as unequal pay and work for black and white soldiers. See Ira Berlin, Joseph P. Reidy, and Leslie S. Rowland, *Freedom's Soldiers: The Black Military Experience in the Civil War* (New York: Cambridge University Press, 1998), pp. 26–37; Lloyd Watts to his wife, 28 May 1865, ACHS; Enlistment Papers, Randolph Johnston, National Archives, Washington, D.C.; Pension application [Disability Affidavits], John R. Johnston file, National Archives, Washington, D.C.

28. *The Compiler,* 22 August 1864; 7 March 1864; Betty Dorsey Myers, *Segregation in Death,* p. 74.

29. Sons of Good Will Record Book, n.d., 1866, 1 January 1868, private collection; AME Zion Leaders' Book, 12 November 1867, private collection; Myers, *Segregation in Death*, p. 14; Wade P. Catts et al., "An Archaeological and Geophysical Investigation of the Lincoln Cemetery, Borough of Gettysburg, Adams County Pennsylvania" (unpublished report prepared by John Milner Associates, Inc., West Chester, Penn., 2000), p. 7 (thanks to Dr. Walter Powell).

30. *The Star and Sentinel*, 5 June 1879; Myers, *Segregation in Death*, pp. 7, 14–16; AME Zion Leaders' Book, 23 June 1868; 11 March 1869.

31. *The Star and Sentinel*, 4 June 1873, quoted in Myers, *Segregation in Death*, pp. 89–90.

32. Patterson, "A Patriotic Landscape," pp. 315–333; *The Star and Sentinel*, 4 June 1873; 25 May 1886; 5 June 1888; 4 June 1889; 3 June 1890; 31 May 1892.

33. Myers, *Segregation in Death*, pp. 18–19; *The Star and Sentinel*, 14 June 1882.

34. See Gannon, "Sites of Memory," pp. 165–175, 180–181; Brundage, "Race, Memory, and Masculinity," pp. 140–141. Stuart McConnell describes how segregated, rather than integrated, G.A.R. posts were commonplace in the North in the late nineteenth century. The white members of the mammoth Union veterans' organization felt no particular obligation to be socially inclusive; most of them "viewed the conflict primarily as a battle to preserve an existing Union rather than a crusade to free slaves." See McConnell, *Glorious Contentment: The Grand Army of the Republic, 1865–1900* (Chapel Hill: University of North Carolina Press, 1992), pp. 213–215. Nina Silber, *The Romance of Reunion: Northerners and the South, 1865–1900* (Chapel Hill: University of North Carolina Press, 1993), p. 124.

35. Brundage, "Black Veterans Recall the War," p. 142; Gannon, "Sites of Memory," p. 180; Blight, *Race and Reunion*, pp. 196–197, 344.

36. On black women's voice in community affairs see Myers, *Segregation*, p. 14.

37. On black women's participation in Pennsylvania G.A.R. functions, see Gannon, "Sites of Memory," p. 175.

38. "Keziah Kuff, Said to be 122 Years Old, Dead," *The Gettysburg Times*, 2 July 1926; Charles H. Glatfelter, "You Shall Know the Truth, But it is a He—of a Lot Less Fun Than Fiction," in *Adams County Historical Society News Letter* 13 (October 1986); Elsie Singmaster, "Old Flo," *The Saturday Evening Post*, n.d., clipping, ACHS.

39. David Schick to Elsie Singmaster Lewars, 24 April 1852, ACHS; *The Star and Sentinel*, 17 March 1885; 3 May 1887; 6 March 1888.

40. For examples of Mag Palm as town "character," see *The Star and Sentinel*, 26 April 1872; 27 August 1873; 26 August 1875; Elsie Singmaster, *A Boy at Gettysburg* (New York: Houghton-Mifflin Company, 1924), pp. 4, 40, 52, 52–61.

41. *The Star and Sentinel*, 18 May 1876; 10 July 1879.

42. AME Zion Leaders' Minutes, 2 February 1878, private collection; *The Compiler*, 27 October 1896; *The Star and Sentinel*, October 1896.

43. *The Star and Sentinel,* 8 August 1900; 15 August 1900; *The Compiler,* 13 June 1906; 16 January 1900.

44. Sons of Good Will Record Book, n.d., private collection; Myers, *Segregation in Death,* p. 14; Affidavit, Randolph Johnston Pension Application, 1891, 1896, National Archives, Washington, D.C.; Vital Statistics Record, City of Baltimore, Johnston Pension File, National Archives.

45. Vital Statistics Record, City of Baltimore, in Johnston Pension File, National Archives; AME Zion Leaders' Record Book, 1851–1879, private collection.

46. AME Zion Leaders' Record Books, 1864–1879; quotation from 2 April 1866, private collection.

47. Watts was also a strong spokesperson for the black community, having little patience with Gettysburg editors who took comic pleasure in arguments and physical flare-ups among African Americans. When, for example, a local Republican newspaper characterized a disagreement in the AME Zion church with the double-barreled headline "Trouble in the Wigwam," Watts shot a note back arguing that the issues had been intellectual ones, over church doctrine, and that the article had been "entirely false." See *The Star and Sentinel,* 1 March 1872; 4 March 1872. On black work in the battle industry, see *The Star and Sentinel,* 7 August 1867; 19 February 1868; 31 May 1872; 5 June 1879; 21 December 1881; 8 August 1883; *The Compiler,* 21 June 1898; William A. Frassanito, *Early Photography at Gettysburg* (Gettysburg: Thomas Publications, 1995), pp. 216–217; Blight, *Race and Reunion,* p. 386; author interviews with Betty Myers (1997–1998), Catherine Carter (1996–1997), and Margaret Nutter (1999).

48. Lloyd Watts, National Archives pension application, 6 April 1897; *The Star and Sentinel,* 1 June 1918.

49. A local Republican paper had expressed alarm over the beginnings of the KKK in the late 1860s, sympathizing with African Americans over attacks on innocent citizens, but then it, too, had eased into fear mongering. By the 1880s, it regularly reported incidents of black males who preyed on white females, and it pictured lynchings not as lawless atrocities but as coolly managed private affairs. By the time the Klan staged rallies in Gettysburg in the 1920s, the local white media was, if not receptive to the white supremacists, at least hospitable to them. See *The Star and Sentinel,* 9 June 1885; 2 March 1886; 10 August 1886; 3 May 1887; Joan Vannorsdall and Roxy Bream, "The Ku Klux Klan," student paper, May 1968, typescript, ACHS; see also *The Gettysburg Times,* 18 September 1925; 30 September 1926; 28 and 30 May 1928. The popular links between Civil War memory and white redemption were, of course, reinforced by D. W. Griffiths' highly acclaimed film *Birth of a Nation,* which opened in 1915. In Griffiths' film (based on Thomas Dixon's 1905 novel *The Clansman*), the Ku Klux Klan rescues white women and elite Southerners from threatening black men and their carpetbagger accomplices (Blight, *Race and Reunion,* pp. 394–395).

50. Becker, "Trends in Segregation," pp. 44–45, 61–62, 65; Lebo, "History Overlooked"; Lee Emmons, film director, Ray Gouker, producer, "African Amer-

ican Heritage in Gettysburg: An Oral History," 2000 (Adams County Teachers Association).

51. The population of African Americans in Adams County grew at a much slower pace than the white population, being only 267 in 1950. See Becker, "Trends in Segregation," p. 19 (Becker's thesis, based on interviews with nearly 800 residents, as well as statistical information, provides a wealth of information on the borough in the mid-1900s).

52. Becker, "Trends in Segregation," pp. 23–27.

53. Becker, "Trends in Segregation," pp. 44–45, 61–62, 65; Lebo, "History Overlooked"; Emmons/Gouker, "African American Heritage in Gettysburg."

54. Becker, "Trends in Segregation," pp. 46–47.

55. Becker, "Trends in Segregation," p. 6. Among those who worked for racial justice in Gettysburg were people connected with Gettysburg College and the Lutheran Theological Seminary. Those on the front lines personally challenging and testing discrimination in stores, shops, and swimming pools included Adam Myers and Jean Odom. Thanks to Betty Myers, 16 April 2004.

56. Local people of color rejected Lincolnian paternalism in 1952 at a 100th anniversary of the Western Maryland Railway Company. The company sponsored a re-enactment of Lincoln's arrival by rail in Gettysburg. Professional actors were brought in to play major characters, and black residents were asked to take minor parts: servants, liverymen, and porters. They declined. Becker, "Trends in Segregation," pp. 59–61.

57. "Field Mass Attracts 5000; Rev. Fr Hesburgh Calls for Americans to be Emancipators," *The Gettysburg Times*, 1 July 1963; Edith Evans Asbury, "Hughes Charges Moral Failure to Aid Negroes Since Civil War," *The New York Times*, 2 July 1963.

58. "Eisenhower Tells Audience of 6000 That Lincoln Gave True Meaning of Battle Here," *The Gettysburg Times*, 1 July 1963.

59. Michael Shaara, *The Killer Angels* (New York: Ballantine Books, 1974), pp. 169–171.

60. One popular film derived from Shaara's acclaimed book was TNT's *Gettysburg*, produced in 1993. On re-enactors' desire for time travel, see Jim Weeks, *Memory, Market, and an American Shrine* (Princeton: Princeton University Press, 2003), pp. 195–225, quotation on p. 201; it must be noted, too, that African Americans do play a part in the re-enactment community. USCT black regiments, like the 54th and 55th Massachusetts, have strong national membership.

61. Remembrance Day parades are described in *The Gettysburg Times*, 16 November 1992; 19 November 1993; 18 November 1994; 17 November 1997; black visitors were reported to the author in a licensed Battlefield Guide Survey (fourteen respondents), December–January 2000/2001.

62. Allen B. Ballard, "The Demons of Gettysburg," *The New York Times*, 30 May 1999.

63. Catherine Stanton Carter, *Gettysburg's Oldest Family: Memoirs* (Gettysburg: Privately printed, 1998), pp. 1–4, 47–49; author interviews with Carter, July 1997 and May 1998, Gettysburg. (All subsequent quotations and references to Catherine Carter derive from these interviews.)

64. Shelley L. Jones, *Gettysburg Times* clipping, 28 August 1986, courtesy of Rogers Smith; Margaret Nutter, author interview, 17 April 1999. Subsequent references to Margaret Nutter derive from this interview.

65. Aubrey L. Thomas, "Blue and Gray in Final Meeting," *The Gettysburg Times*, 28 May 1938; Franklin D. Roosevelt to John S. Rice, 8 September 1936, in *Gettysburg Blue and Gray Reunion* (Gettysburg: Pennsylvania State Commission, n.d.), p. 5.

66. On Memorial Day celebrations, see Betty Dorsey Myers, *Segregation in Death*, pp. 8, 38–61; Wade P. Catts, "Executive Summary," Lincoln Cemetery Archaeological Investigations, 26 July 1999, courtesy of Walter Powell.

67. Emmons/Gouker, "African American Heritage in Gettysburg."

AFTERWORD

1. John S. Patterson, "Zapped at the Map: The Battlefield at Gettysburg," *Journal of Popular Culture* 7 (1974): 825–837. Patterson's eloquent essay is a provocative meditation on how the tidy (and technologically smooth) contemporary battlefield park obscures the battle's bloody and chaotic realities.

BIBLIOGRAPHY

This Bibliography lists materials used most commonly in this narrative, as well as those of general relevance to the social history of the Gettysburg campaign. Additional sources, primary and secondary, manuscript and printed, are indicated in the Notes section.

PRIMARY SOURCES: ARCHIVAL

Adams County Court House, Gettysburg, Penn.
 1. Adams County Quarter Session Books, 1836–1866
Adams County Historical Society, Gettysburg, Penn. (ACHS)
 1. Census Records, Adams County
 2. Adams County Family Files
 3. The Civilian Witness Collection (CWC)
     Unpublished Sources
         Agnes Barr Account
         Sue King Black Letter
         Lavinia Bollinger Letter
         Lydia Catherine Ziegler Clare Account
         Sophia Culp Epley Account
         Emma Gilbert Letter
         Sarah Barrett King Letters
         Salome Myers Letter
         Lydia Ann Meals Panebaker Letter
         Annie Skelly Account
         Leander Warren Account
         John Charles Wills Account
         Annie Young Letter
 4. Evergreen Cemetery Burial Permits
 5. Vital Statistics Index

Fredericksburg and Spotsylvania National Military Park, Fredericksburg, Va.
  1. The Darwin Cody Correspondence
George J. Mitchell Department of Special Collections, Bowdoin College, Brunswick, Maine
  1. The Howard Papers
Gettysburg National Military Park, Gettysburg, Penn. (GNMP)
  1. Bachelder Papers
  2. Civilian Files
  3. Clippings Files
  4. Historian Correspondence Files
  5. Park Reports
Library of Congress, Washington, D.C.
  1. The Carl Schurz Papers
Massachusetts Historical Society, Boston, Mass.
  1. The Francis C. Barlow Papers
National Archives, Washington, D.C.
  1. Service Records
  2. Pension Records
  3. Claims Files
Rochester Museum and Science Center, Rochester, N.Y. (RMSC)
  1. The John White Johnston Papers
State Historical Society of Wisconsin, Madison, Wisc. (SHSW)
  1. The Muenzenberger Papers
Sterling Memorial Library, Yale University, New Haven, Conn.
  1. The Herman Haupt Papers
United States Army Military History Institute, Carlisle, Penn. (USAMHI)
  1. The Civil War Miscellaneous Collection
  2. The Civil War Times Illustrated Collection
  3. The Leigh Collection
  4. The Robert L. Brake Collection
Private Collections
  1. AME Zion Leaders' Minutes Book, 1852–1881, Gettysburg, Penn.
  2. Mary Eliza Hunt Carson Correspondence, 1859–1863
  3. Lloyd F. A. Watts, Notebook, 1854–1858, Gettysburg, Penn.
  4. Adams County Poor House Records, Gettysburg, Penn.

PRIMARY SOURCES: PRINTED

Alleman, Tillie Pierce. *At Gettysburg, or What a Girl Saw and Heard of the Battle.* New York: W. Lake Borland, 1889. Reprint. Butternut and Blue, Baltimore, 1994.

Arrowsmith, George. *Reminiscences and Letters of George Arrowsmith of New Jersey,* edited by John S. Applegate. Red Bank, N.J.: John H. Cook, 1893.

Aughinbaugh, Nellie E. "Personal Experiences of a Young Girl During the Battle of Gettysburg," edited by Louie Dale Leeds. N.p.: Privately printed, 1926–1938. Copy, ACHS/CWC.

Bayly, Harriet H. "A Woman's Story." *The Star and Sentinel* (25 September 1888). Clipping, ACHS/CWC.

_____. "Mrs. Joseph Bayly's Story of the Battle." *The Compiler Scrapbook,* n.d. Copy, ACHS/CWC.

Bayly, William Hamilton. "William Hamilton Bayly's Story of the Battle." *The Compiler Scrapbook,* n.d. Copy, ACHS/CWC.

Blackford, W. W. *War Years with Jeb Stuart.* New York: Charles Scribner's Sons, 1945.

Blake, Henry N. *Three Years in the Army of the Potomac.* Boston: Lee and Shepard, 1865.

Blassingame, John W., ed. *The Frederick Douglass Papers,* Ser. 1, Vol. 3. New Haven: Yale University Press, 1985.

Brinton, Daniel G. "From Chancellorsville to Gettysburg, a Doctor's Diary," edited by D. G. Brinton Thompson. *The Pennsylvania Magazine of History and Biography* 89 (July 1965): 292–315.

Broadhead, Sarah M. *The Diary of a Lady of Gettysburg, Pennsylvania from June 15 to July 15, 1863.* Gettysburg: Privately printed, 1864. Reprint. Gary T. Hawbaker, Hershey, Penn., 2002.

Buehler, Fannie J. *Recollections of the Rebel Invasion and One Woman's Experience During the Battle of Gettysburg.* Gettysburg: Star and Sentinel Print, 1900. Reprint. Gary T. Hawbaker, Hershey, Penn., n.d.

Bull, Rice C. *Soldiering: The Civil War Diary of Rice C. Bull, 123rd New York Volunteer Infantry,* edited by K. Jack Bauer. San Rafael, Calif.: Presidio Press, 1977.

Bushman, Catherine. "Grandmother Bushman's Friendship Quilt," edited by Mary Bushman Power Deardorff. *Gettysburg Times 75th Anniversary Edition* (July 1938). Clipping, ACHS/CWC.

Bushman, Sarah. "Gettysburg's Fight: The Part That a Brave Little Girl Played During the Battle." *The Compiler* (12 January 1892).

_____. "Mrs. Jungerman's Story of Her Girlhood Experience." *The (San Francisco) Bulletin* (9 March 1902). Clipping, ACHS/CWC.

Caba, G. Craig, ed. *Episodes of Gettysburg and the Underground Railroad as Witnessed and Recorded by Professor J. Howard Wert.* Gettysburg: G. Craig Caba Antiques, 1998.

Clutz, Mrs. Jacob A. (Liberty A. Hollinger). "The Battle of Gettysburg." *Pennsylvania History* 5 (1938): 166–178.

[Croll, Jennie S.] "Days of Dread: A Woman's Story of Her Life on a Battlefield." *The (Philadelphia) Weekly Press* (16 November 1887). Clipping, ACHS/CWC.

Curtis, Alice Turner. *Kathleen: A Yankee Girl at Gettysburg.* Reprint. New York: Gramercy Books, 1995.

Domschcke, Bernhard. *Twenty Months in Captivity: Memoirs of a Union Officer in Confederate Prisons,* edited and translated by Frederic Trautmann. Rutherford, N.J.: Fairleigh Dickinson University Press, 1987.

Dow, Neal. *The Reminiscences of Neal Dow.* Portland, Maine: The Evening Express Publishing Company, 1898.

Du Bois, W. E. B. *The Souls of Black Folk.* Reprint. New York: Vintage, 1990.

Eastman, Mary H. *Jenny Wade of Gettysburg.* Philadelphia: J. B. Lippincott & Company, 1864.

Fastnacht, Mary Warren. "Memories of the Battle of Gettysburg, Year 1863." N.p.: Privately printed, 1928. Copy, ACHS/CWC.

Faulkner, William. *Intruder in the Dust.* Reprint. New York: Vintage Books, 1991.

Foster, Catherine Mary White. "The Story of the Battle by a Citizen Whose Home Was Pierced by Flying Shells." *The Compiler* (29 June, 6 July 1904). Copy, ACHS/CWC.

_____. "Catherine Mary White Foster's Eyewitness Account of the Battle of Gettysburg, with Background on the Foster Family Union Soldiers," edited by David A. Murdoch. *Adams County History* 1 (1995): 45–67.

Harper, Frances Cunningham. "Native of Adams County Writes of Experiences of Parents During '63 Battle." *The Compiler* (26 April 1941). Clipping, ACHS/CWC.

Henderson, Henry E. *Yankee in Gray: The Civil War Memoirs of Henry E. Henderson,* edited by Clyde Lottridge Cummer. Cleveland, Ohio: Press of Western Reserve University, 1962.

Heth, Henry. "The Memoirs of Henry Heth, Part II," edited by James L. Morrison, Jr. *Civil War History* 8 (1962): 300–326.

Heyser, William. "Diary of William Heyser," edited by Jane Dice Stone. *The Kittochtinny (Penn.) Historical Society Papers* 16 (1978): 54–88. Also http://valley.vcdh.virginia.edu/personal/wmheyser.html.

Hollinger, Liberty Augusta (Mrs. Jacob A. Clutz). "Some Personal Recollections of the Battle of Gettysburg." N.p.: Privately printed, 1925. Copy, ACHS/CWC.

Howard, Oliver Otis. "Campaign and Battle of Gettysburg, June and July, 1863." *Atlantic Monthly Magazine* 38 (July 1876): 48–70.

_____. *Autobiography of Oliver Otis Howard, Major General United States Army.* 2 vols. New York: The Baker & Taylor Company, 1908.

_____. "Memories of Gettysburg." *The Compiler* (23 March 1910). Clipping, ACHS/CWC.

Jackson, J. Warren. "The Gettysburg Campaign—A Louisiana Lieutenant's Eye-Witness Account," edited by Merl E. Reed. *Pennsylvania History* 30 (April 1963): 184–191.

Jacobs, Henry Eyster. *Memoirs of Henry Eyster Jacobs,* edited by Henry E. Horn. Huntingdon, Penn.: Church Management Service, Inc., 1974.

_____. "A Vivid Story of the Mighty Conflict from the Lips of Rev. Dr. Jacobs, Who Was a Gettysburg Boy," edited by John Chisolm Horn. *The Baltimore American* (29 June 1913). Transcription, 1982, ACHS/CWC.

Johnson, Clifton. *Battleground Adventures.* Boston: Houghton-Mifflin Company, 1915.

King, Sarah Barrett. "Battle Days in 1863." *The Compiler* (4 July 1906). Clipping, ACHS/CWC.

_____. "A Mother's Story of [the] Battle of Gettysburg." *The Compiler Scrapbook,* n.d. Copy, ACHS.

Kitzmiller, Anna Garlach. "Story of a Brig. General." *The Compiler* (9 August 1905). Clipping, ACHS/CWC.

_____. "Mrs. Kitzmiller's Story: Battle Days Between Union and Confederate Lines." *The Compiler* (23 August 1905). Clipping, ACHS/CWC.

Krzyzanowski, Wladimir. *The Memoirs of Wladimir Krzyzanowski,* edited by James S. Pula. San Francisco: R & E Research Associates, Inc., 1978.

McAllister, Mary. "Woman Lifts Curtain on Gettysburg History," edited by May Garlach Hoffman. *The Philadelphia Inquirer* (26 June 1938). Clipping, ACHS, CWC.

_____. "Gettysburg Terrors Made to Live Again in Woman's Account of Great Battle," edited by May Garlach Hoffman. *The Philadelphia Inquirer* (27 June 1938). Clipping, ACHS/CWC.

_____. "Rebels at Gettysburg Ate Molasses in Hunger," edited by May Garlach Hoffman. *The Philadelphia Inquirer* (28 June 1938). Clipping, ACHS/CWC.

_____. "Woman Describes Retreat of Rebels After Their Decisive Defeat at Gettysburg," edited by May Garlach Hoffman. *The Philadelphia Inquirer* (29 June 1938). Clipping, ACHS/CWC.

McClean, Elizabeth. "The Rebels are Coming!" *The Compiler* (8 July 1908). Clipping, ACHS/CWC.

McClean, William. "The Days of Terror in 1863." *The Compiler* (1 June 1908). Clipping, ACHS/CWC.

McCreary, Albertus. "Gettysburg: A Boy's Experience of the Battle." *McClure's Magazine* 33 (July 1909): 243–253.

_____. "The Story of Albertus McCreary: A Boy's Experience of the Battle," edited by Timothy H. Smith. *The Gettysburg Magazine* 17 (1997): 118–128.

McCreary, Jennie. "Girl Saw Streets Filled with Dead and Wounded at Gettysburg." *The (Philadelphia) Evening Bulletin* (2 July 1938). Clipping, ACHS/CWC.

McCurdy, Charles M. *Gettysburg: A Memoir.* Pittsburgh: Reed & Witting Company, 1929.

McKay, Charles W. "'Three Years or During the War,' with the Crescent and Star." In *The National Tribune Scrapbook.* Washington, D.C.: The National Tribune, 1909.

McMahon, John T. *John T. McMahon's Diary of the 136th New York 1861–1864,* edited by John Michael Priest. Shippensburg, Penn.: The White Mane Publishing Company, 1993.

Melchior, Mary Elizabeth Montfort. "John Burns at Gettysburg." *Doyleston (Penn.) Democrat* (1886). Clipping, ACHS/CWC.

_____. "How a 12-Year-Old Girl Saw Gettysburg," edited by Lester Trauch. *Daily Intelligencer (Doylestown, Penn.)* (30 May 1959). Transcript, ACHS/CWC.

Mesnard, Luther. "The Rise and Survival of Private Mesnard," edited by Robert Hoffsommer. *Civil War Times Illustrated* (January 1986): 18–25.

_____. "The Rise and Survival of Private Mesnard, Part II," edited by Robert Hoffsommer. *Civil War Times Illustrated* (February 1986): 10–17, 44–45.

Miller, Amelia E. Harman. "Burning of M'Lean Home." *The Compiler* (15 July 1915). Clipping, ACHS/CWC.

Mohr, James C., ed. *The Cormany Diaries: A Northern Family in the Civil War.* Pittsburgh: University of Pittsburgh Press, 1982.

Moore, Frank. *Women of the War: Their Heroism and Self-Sacrifice.* Hartford: S. S. Scranton & Company, 1867.

Myers, Sue. "Some Battle Experiences as Remembered by a Young School Girl." *The Compiler* (24 April 1907). Clipping, ACHS/CWC.

Payne, Daniel Alexander. *Recollections of Seventy Years.* New York: Arno Press, 1968.

Revised Report Made to the Legislature of Pennsylvania Relative to the Soldiers' National Cemetery at Gettysburg. Harrisburg: Singerly & Myers, 1867.

Rodgers, Sarah Sites, ed. *The Ties of the Past: The Gettysburg Diaries of Salome Myers Stewart 1854–1922.* Gettysburg: Thomas Publications, 1996.

Rollins, Richard, ed. *Pickett's Charge: Eyewitness Accounts.* Redondo Beach, Calif.: Rank and File Publications, 1994.

Schaff, Philip. "The Gettysburg Week." *Scribner's Magazine* 16 (July 1894): 21–30.

Schurz, Carl. "The Battle of Gettysburg." *McClure's Magazine* 29 (July 1907): 272–285.

_____. *Intimate Letters of Carl Schurz, 1841–1869,* edited by Joseph Schafer. Madison: State Historical Society of Wisconsin, 1928.

_____. *The Reminiscences of Carl Schurz.* 3 vols. New York: The McClure Company, 1907–1908.

Shaara, Michael. *The Killer Angels.* New York: Ballantine, 1974.

Sheads, Caroline S. "Scenes of the Battle of Gettysburg." *The National Republican* (28 November 1863). Clipping, ACHS/CWC.

Singmaster, Elsie. *A Boy at Gettysburg.* New York: Houghton Mifflin Company, 1924.

Skelly, Daniel Alexander. *A Boy's Experiences During the Battles of Gettysburg.* Gettysburg: Privately printed, 1932. Reprint. Gary T. Hawbaker, Hershey, Penn., n.d.

Smith, Jane. "An Echo of the Battle." *The Star and Sentinel* (2 July 1913). Clipping, ACHS/CWC.

Smith, L. A. "Recollections of Gettysburg." *War Papers Read Before the Michigan Commandery of the Military Order of the Loyal Legion of the United States,* Vol. 2. Detroit: James H. Stone & Company, 1898.

Taughenbaugh, Jacob. "In Occupied Pennsylvania," edited by T. W. Herbert. *The Georgia Review* (1950): 103–113.

Thorn, Elizabeth. "Experience During Battle." *The Compiler* (26 July 1905). Clipping, ACHS/CWC.

———. "Mrs. Thorn's War Story." *The Gettysburg Times* (2 July 1938). Transcription, ACHS/CWC.

Trowbridge, J. T. "The Field of Gettysburg." *The Atlantic Monthly* 16 (November 1865): 616–625.

U.S. War Department. *War of the Rebellion: A Compilation of the Official Records of the Union and Confederate Armies.* 128 parts in 70 vols. Washington, D.C.: Government Printing Office, 1880–1902.

Wickesberg, Charles. *Civil War Letters of Sergeant Charles Wickesberg.* Translated by Ingeborg Wolferstetter. Milwaukee: Alfred Wickesberg, 1961.

Winkler, Frederick C. *Letters of Frederick C. Winkler 1862–1865,* edited by Louise Winkler Hitz. N.p.: William K. Winkler, 1963.

NEWSPAPERS

The Adams Sentinel, Gettysburg
The Anglo-African, New York
The Christian Recorder, Philadelphia
The Compiler, Gettysburg
The Daily Telegraph, Harrisburg
The Gettysburg Times, Gettysburg
The National Enquirer, Philadelphia
The New York Herald, New York
The New York Times, New York
The Patriot & Union, Harrisburg
The Pennsylvania Freeman, Philadelphia
The Philadelphia Evening Bulletin, Philadelphia
The Philadelphia Inquirer, Philadelphia
The Star and Banner, Gettysburg
The Star and Sentinel, Gettysburg

SECONDARY SOURCES

Adelman, Garry E., and Timothy H. Smith. *Devil's Den: A History and Guide.* Gettysburg: Thomas Publications, 1997.

Alexander, Ted. "'A Regular Slave Hunt': The Army of Northern Virginia and Black Civilians in the Gettysburg Campaign." *North & South* 4 (September 2001): 82–89.

Attie, Jeanie. "Warwork and the Crisis of Domesticity in the North." In *Divided Houses: Gender and the Civil War,* edited by Catherine Clinton and Nina Silber. New York: Oxford University Press, 1992.

———. *Patriotic Toil: Northern Women and the American Civil War.* Ithaca: Cornell University Press, 1998.

Bennett, Gerald R. *Days of "Uncertainty and Dread": The Ordeal Endured by the Citizens at Gettysburg.* Littlestown, Penn.: Gerald R. Bennett, 1994.

Blair, William, and William Pencak, eds. *Making and Remaking Pennsylvania's Civil War.* University Park: Pennsylvania State University Press, 2001.

Blight, David W. *Frederick Douglass' Civil War: Keeping Faith in Jubilee.* Baton Rouge: Louisiana State University Press, 1989.

_____. "'What Will Peace Among the Whites Bring?': Reunion and Race in the Struggle over the Memory of the Civil War in American Culture." *The Massachusetts Review* 34 (1993): 393–410.

_____. *Race and Reunion: The Civil War in American Memory.* Cambridge, Mass.: Harvard University Press, 2001.

Blockson, Charles L. *The Underground Railroad in Pennsylvania.* Reprint. Jacksonville, N.C.: Flame International, 1981.

Bloom, Robert L. "'We Never Expected a Battle': The Civilians at Gettysburg, 1863." *Pennsylvania History* 55 (October 1988): 161–200.

_____. *A History of Adams County, Pennsylvania 1700–1990.* Gettysburg: Adams County Historical Society, 1992.

Boritt, Gabor S., ed. *The Gettysburg Nobody Knows.* New York: Oxford University Press, 1997.

Boylan, Anne M. "Growing Up Female in Young America, 1800–1860." In *American Childhood: A Research Guide and Historical Handbook,* edited by Joseph M. Hawes and N. Ray Hiner. Westport, Conn.: Greenwood Press, 1985.

Brockett, Linus P., and Mary C. Vaughan. *Woman's Work in the Civil War: A Record of Heroism, Patriotism, and Patience.* Philadelphia: Zeigler, McCurdy, 1867.

Brown, Andrew. *Geology and the Gettysburg Campaign.* Harrisburg, Penn.: Bureau of Topographic and Geologic Survey, 1972.

Brown, Thomas J. *The Public Art of Civil War Commemoration: A Brief History with Documents.* Boston: Bedford/St. Martin's, 2004.

Butts, Joseph Tyler, ed. *A Gallant Captain of the Civil War.* New York: F. Tennyson Neely, 1902.

Byrne, Frank L. "A General Behind Bars: Neal Dow in Libby Prison." In *Civil War Prisons,* edited by William B. Hesseltine. Kent, Ohio: Kent State University Press, 1962.

Carpenter, John A. "General O. O. Howard at Gettysburg." *Civil War History* 9 (1963): 261–276.

_____. *Sword and Olive Branch: Oliver Otis Howard.* Pittsburgh: University of Pittsburgh Press, 1964.

Cashin, Joan E. "Into the Trackless Wilderness: The Refugee Experience in the Civil War." In *A Woman's War: Southern Women, Civil War, and the Confederate Legacy,* edited by Edward D. C. Campbell, Jr., and Kym S. Rice. Richmond, Va.: Museum of the Confederacy, 1996.

_____, ed. *The War Was You and Me: Civilians in the American Civil War.* Princeton, N.J.: Princeton University Press, 2002.

Cimbala, Paul A. Introduction to *Sword and Olive Branch,* by John A. Carpenter. New York: Fordham University Press, 1999.

Cimbala, Paul A., and Randall M. Miller, eds. *Union Soldiers and the Northern Home Front: Wartime Experiences, Postwar Adjustments.* New York: Fordham University Press, 2002.

Clinton, Catherine, and Nina Silber, eds. *Divided Houses: Gender and the Civil War.* New York: Oxford University Press, 1992.

Coddington, Edwin B. "Prelude to Gettysburg: The Confederates Plunder Pennsylvania." *Pennsylvania History* 30 (1963): 123–157.

_____. *The Gettysburg Campaign: A Study in Command.* New York: Simon & Schuster, 1997.

Conklin, Eileen F. *Women at Gettysburg 1863.* Gettysburg: Thomas Publications, 1993.

Conrad, W. P., and Ted Alexander. *When War Passed This Way.* Shippensburg, Penn.: Beidel Printing House/Greencastle Bicentennial, 1982.

Cullen, Jim. *The Civil War in Popular Culture: A Reusable Past.* Washington, D.C.: Smithsonian Institution Press, 1995.

Cushman, Stephen. *Bloody Promenade: Reflections on a Civil War Battle.* Charlottesville: University Press of Virginia, 1999.

De Pauw, Linda Grant. *Battle Cries and Lullabies: Women in War from Prehistory to the Present.* Norman: University of Oklahoma Press, 1998.

Desjardin, Thomas A. *These Honored Dead: How the Story of Gettysburg Shaped American Memory.* New York: Da Capo Press, 2003.

Donald, David Herbert. *Lincoln.* New York: Simon & Schuster, 1995.

Dunkelman, Mark H., and Michael J. Winey, eds. *The Hardtack Regiment: An Illustrated History of the 154th Regiment, New York State Infantry Volunteers.* Rutherford, N.J.: Fairleigh Dickinson University Press, 1981.

Elmore, Thomas L. "Torrid Heat and Blinding Rain: A Meteorological and Astronomical Chronology of the Gettysburg Campaign." *The Gettysburg Magazine* 13 (July 1995): 7–19.

Elshtain, Jean Bethke. *Women and War.* New York: Basic Books, 1987.

Emilio, Luis F. *A Brave Black Regiment: History of the Fifty-Fourth Regiment of the Massachusetts Volunteer Infantry, 1863–1865.* Boston: The Boston Book Company, 1891.

Ericson, Christina. "'The World Will Little Note Nor Long Remember': Gender Analysis of Civilian Responses to the Battle of Gettysburg." In *Making and Remaking Pennsylvania's Civil War,* edited by William Blair and William Pencak. University Park: Pennsylvania State University Press, 2001.

Fahs, Alice. "The Feminized Civil War: Gender, Northern Popular Literature, and the Memory of the War, 1861–1900." *The Journal of American History* 85 (March 1999): 1461–1494.

Frassanito, William A. *Early Photography at Gettysburg.* Gettysburg: Thomas Publications, 1995.

_____. "Introduction." In *At Gettysburg, or What a Girl Saw and Heard of the Battle,* by Tillie Pierce Alleman. New York: W. Lake Borland, 1889. Reprint. Butternut and Blue, Baltimore, 1994.

Frothingham, Paul Revere. *Edward Everett: Orator and Statesman.* Boston: Houghton Mifflin Company, 1925.

Furgurson, Ernest B. *Chancellorsville 1863: The Souls of the Brave.* New York: Alfred A. Knopf, 1992.

Gallagher, Gary W., ed. *The First Day at Gettysburg: Essays on Confederate and Union Leadership.* Kent, Ohio: Kent State University Press, 1992.

_____. *The Third Day at Gettysburg & Beyond.* Chapel Hill, N.C.: University of North Carolina Press, 1994.

_____. *The Battle of Chancellorsville: Civil War Series.* Fort Washington, Penn.: Eastern National Park and Monument Association, 1995.

_____. *Chancellorsville: The Battle and Its Aftermath.* Chapel Hill, N.C.: University of North Carolina Press, 1996.

_____. *The Antietam Campaign.* Chapel Hill, N.C.: University of North Carolina Press, 1999.

Gallman, J. Matthew. *Mastering Wartime: A Social History of Philadelphia During the Civil War.* New York: Cambridge University Press, 1990.

_____. *The North Fights the Civil War: The Home Front.* Chicago: Ivan R. Dee, 1994.

Gallman, J. Matthew, with Susan Baker. "Gettysburg's Gettysburg: What the Battle Did to the Borough." In *The Gettysburg Nobody Knows,* edited by Gabor S. Boritt. New York: Oxford University Press, 1997.

Gannon, James P. *Irish Rebels, Confederate Tigers: A History of the 6th Louisiana Volunteers, 1861–1865.* Mason City, Iowa: Savas Publishing Company, 1998.

Greene, A. Wilson. "From Chancellorsville to Cemetery Hill: O. O. Howard and Eleventh Corps Leadership." In *The First Day at Gettysburg: Essays on Confederate and Union Leadership,* edited by Gary W. Gallagher. Kent, Ohio: Kent State University Press, 1992.

_____. "From Gettysburg to Falling Waters: Meade's Pursuit of Lee." In *The Third Day at Gettysburg & Beyond,* edited by Gary W. Gallagher. Chapel Hill, N.C.: University of North Carolina Press, 1994.

Grimsley, Mark. *The Hard Hand of War: Union Military Policy Toward Southern Civilians, 1861–1865.* New York: Cambridge University Press, 1995.

Hamlin, Augustus Choate. *The Battle of Chancellorsville.* Bangor, Maine: Privately printed, 1896.

Hankey, Joan R. "Gettysburg Residents, 1860–1863: A Comparison of 1860 Census and 1863 & 1864 Tax Lists." Gettysburg: Privately printed, 1996.

Hartwig, D. Scott. "The 11th Army Corps on July 1, 1863—'The Unlucky 11th.'" *The Gettysburg Magazine* 2 (January 1990): 33–49.

———. "The Campaign and Battle of Gettysburg." In *Damn Dutch: Pennsylvania Germans at Gettysburg,* edited by David L. Valuska and Christian B. Keller. Mechanicsburg, Penn.: Stackpole Books, 2004.

Haskell, Frank. "Major General Oliver Otis Howard." www.rocemabra.com/ ~roger/tagg/generals/general26.html.

Hawthorne, Frederick W. *Gettysburg: Stories of Men and Monuments.* Gettysburg: The Association of Licensed Battlefield Guides, 1988.

Hennessy, John J. "'We Shall Make Richmond Howl': The Army of the Potomac on the Eve of Chancellorsville." In *Chancellorsville: The Battle and Its Aftermath,* edited by Gary W. Gallagher. Chapel Hill, N.C.: University of North Carolina Press, 1996.

Hine, Darlene Clark, and Kathleen Thompson. *A Shining Thread of Hope: The History of Black Women in America.* New York: Broadway Books, 1998.

Hoke, Jacob. *The Great Invasion of 1863 or General Lee in Pennsylvania.* Reprint. Gettysburg: Stan Clark Military Books, 1992.

Horwitz, Tony. *Confederates in the Attic: Dispatches from the Unfinished Civil War.* New York: Random House, 1999.

Jacobson, Matthew Frye. *Whiteness of a Different Color: European Immigrants and the Alchemy of Race.* Cambridge, Mass.: Harvard University Press, 1998.

Johnston, J. W. *The True Story of "Jennie" Wade: A Gettysburg Maid.* Rochester, N.Y.: Privately printed, 1917.

Jones, Terry L. *Lee's Tigers: The Louisiana Infantry in the Army of Northern Virginia.* Baton Rouge, La.: Louisiana State University Press, 1987.

———. *Cemetery Hill: The Struggle for the High Ground, July 1–3, 1863.* New York: Da Capo Press, 2003.

Jordan, Ervin L., Jr. "Sleeping with the Enemy: Sex, Black Women, and the Civil War." *The Western Journal of Black Studies* 18 (1994): 55–63.

Kaufmann, Wilhelm. *The Germans in the American Civil War,* translated by Steven Rowan, edited by Don Heinrich Tolzmann, Werner D. Mueller, and Robert E. Ward. Carlisle, Penn.: John Kallmann Publishers, 1999.

Keller, Christian B. "The Pennsylvania Dutch and 'the Hard Hand of War.'" In *Damn Dutch: Pennsylvania Germans at Gettysburg,* edited by David L. Valuska and Christian B. Keller. Mechanicsburg, Penn.: Stackpole Books, 2004.

———. "Pennsylvania's German-Americans, a Popular Myth, and the Importance of Perception." In *Damn Dutch: Pennsylvania Germans at Gettysburg,* edited by David L. Valuska and Christian B. Keller. Mechanicsburg, Penn.: Stackpole Books, 2004.

Kennell, Brian A. *Beyond the Gatehouse: Gettysburg's Evergreen Cemetery.* Gettysburg: Evergreen Cemetery Association, 2000.

Kimmel, Michael. *Manhood in America: A Cultural History.* New York: The Free Press, 1996.

Leavitt, Judith Walzer. *Brought to Bed: Childbearing in America 1750–1950.* New York: Oxford University Press, 1986.

Leonard, Elizabeth D. *Yankee Women: Gender Battles in the Civil War.* New York: W. W. Norton & Company, 1994.

_____. *All the Daring of the Soldier: Women of the Civil War Armies.* New York: W. W. Norton & Company, 1999.

Levine, Bruce. *The Spirit of 1848: German Immigrants, Labor Conflict, and the Coming of the Civil War.* Urbana: University of Illinois Press, 1992.

Linderman, Gerald F. *Embattled Courage: The Experience of Combat in the American Civil War.* New York: The Free Press, 1987.

Linenthal, Edward Tabor. *Sacred Ground: Americans and Their Battlefields.* Urbana: University of Illinois Press, 1993.

Lonn, Ella. *Foreigners in the Union Army and Navy.* Baton Rouge, La.: Louisiana State University Press, 1951.

Luebke, Frederick C. "Images of German Immigrants in the United States and Brazil, 1890–1918: Some Comparisons." In *America and the Germans: An Assessment of a Three-Hundred-Year History,* edited by Frank Trommler and Joseph McVeigh. 2 vols. Philadelphia: University of Pennsylvania Press, 1985.

Marten, James. *The Children's Civil War.* Chapel Hill, N.C.: University of North Carolina Press, 1998.

McFeely, William S. *Yankee Stepfather: General O. O. Howard and the Freedmen.* New Haven: Yale University Press, 1968.

McPherson, James M. *Battle Cry of Freedom: The Civil War Era.* New York: Oxford University Press, 1988.

_____. Foreword to *Divided Houses: Gender and the Civil War,* edited by Catherine Clinton and Nina Silber. New York: Oxford University Press, 1992.

_____. *For Cause & Comrades: Why Men Fought in the Civil War.* New York: Oxford University Press, 1997.

Mitchell, Reid. *Civil War Soldiers.* New York: Viking, 1988.

_____. "Soldiering, Manhood, and Coming of Age: A Northern Volunteer." In *Divided Houses: Gender and the Civil War,* edited by Catherine Clinton and Nina Silber. New York: Oxford University Press, 1992.

_____. *The Vacant Chair: The Northern Soldier Leaves Home.* New York: Oxford University Press, 1993.

Myers, Betty Dorsey. *Segregation in Death: Gettysburg's Lincoln Cemetery.* Gettysburg: Lincoln Cemetery Project Association, 2001.

Nolan, Alan T. *Lee Considered: General Robert E. Lee and Civil War History.* Chapel Hill, N.C.: University of North Carolina Press, 1991.

Oefele, Martin. "German-Americans and the War up to Gettysburg." In *Damn Dutch: Pennsylvania Germans at Gettysburg,* edited by David L. Valuska and Christian B. Keller. Mechanicsburg, Penn.: Stackpole Books, 2004.

Patterson, John S. "Zapped at the Map: The Battlefield at Gettysburg." *Journal of Popular Culture* 7 (1974): 825–837.

_____. "A Patriotic Landscape: Gettysburg, 1863–1913." *Prospects* 7 (1982): 315–333.

Peterson, Robert L., and John A. Hudson. "Foreign Recruitment for Union Forces." *Civil War History* 7 (1961): 176–186.

Pfanz, Donald C. "Negligence on the Right: The Eleventh Corps at Chancellorsville." Accessed at www.morningsidebooks.com/notes/eleventh.htm. Dayton, Ohio, 1984.

Pfanz, Harry W. *Gettysburg: The Second Day.* Chapel Hill, N.C.: University of North Carolina Press, 1987.

_____. *Gettysburg: Culp's Hill and Cemetery Hill.* Chapel Hill, N.C.: University of North Carolina Press, 1993.

_____. *The Battle of Gettysburg: Civil War Series.* Fort Washington, Penn.: Eastern National Publishers, 1994.

_____. *Gettysburg—The First Day.* Chapel Hill, N.C.: University of North Carolina Press, 2001.

Pickle, Linda S. "Stereotypes and Reality: Nineteenth Century German Women in Missouri." *Missouri Historical Review* 79 (1985): 291–312.

Pula, James S., ed. *For Liberty and Justice: The Life and Times of Wladimir Krzyzanowski.* Chicago: Polish American Congress Charitable Foundation, 1978.

_____. *The Sigel Regiment.* www.russscott.com/~rscott/26thwis/franzsig.htm.

Raphelson, Alfred C. "General Schimmelfennig in Berks." *Historical Review of Berks County* (Autumn 1962): 107–110.

_____. "Alexander Schimmelfennig: A German-American Campaigner in the Civil War." *The Pennsylvania Magazine of History and Biography* 87 (April 1963): 156–181.

Reed, Thomas Benton. *A Private in Gray.* Camden, Ark.: T. B. Reed, 1905.

Reid, Ronald F. *Edward Everett: Unionist Orator.* New York: Greenwood Press, 1990.

Rotundo, E. Anthony. *American Manhood: Transformations in Masculinity from the Revolution to the Modern Era.* New York: Basic Books, 1993.

Ryan, Mary P. *Women in Public: Between Banners and Ballots, 1825–1880.* Baltimore: Johns Hopkins University Press, 1990.

Sears, Stephen W. *Chancellorsville.* Boston: Houghton-Mifflin Company, 1996.

_____. *Gettysburg.* Boston: Houghton-Mifflin Company, 2003.

Seidman, Rachel F. "'We Were Enlisted for the War': Ladies' Aid Societies and the Politics of Women's Work During the Civil War." In *Making and Remaking Pennsylvania's Civil War,* edited by William Blair and William Pencak. University Park: Pennsylvania State University Press, 2001.

Silber, Nina. *The Romance of Reunion: Northerners and the South, 1865–1900.* Chapel Hill, N.C.: University of North Carolina Press, 1993.

Slaughter, Thomas P. *Bloody Dawn: The Christiana Riot and Racial Violence in the Antebellum North.* New York: Oxford University Press, 1991.

Small, Cindy L. *The Jennie Wade Story: A True and Complete Account of the Only Civilian Killed During the Battle of Gettysburg.* Gettysburg: Thomas Publications, 1991.

Smedley, R. C. *History of the Underground Railroad in Chester and the Neighboring Counties of Pennsylvania.* Lancaster, Penn.: Office of the Journal, 1983.

Smith, Everard H. "Chambersburg: Anatomy of a Confederate Reprisal." *American Historical Review* 96 (1991): 432–455.

Smith, Timothy H. *The Story of Lee's Headquarters: Gettysburg, Pennsylvania.* Gettysburg: Thomas Publications, 1995.

———. "'These Were Days of Horror': The Story of the Gettysburg Civilians." In *Unsung Heroes of Gettysburg: Programs of the Fifth Annual Gettysburg Seminar,* edited by Barbara J. Finfrock. Gettysburg: Gettysburg National Military Park, 1996.

———. *John Burns: "The Hero of Gettysburg."* Gettysburg: Thomas Publications, 2000.

———. "Josephine Miller: A Heroine of the Battle." *Blue & Gray Magazine* 20 (2002): 21–24.

Tagg, Larry. *The Generals of Gettysburg: The Leaders of America's Greatest Battle.* Campbell, Calif.: Savas Publishing, 1998.

Trefousse, Hans L. *Carl Schurz: A Biography.* Knoxville, Tenn.: University of Tennessee Press, 1982.

———. *Thaddeus Stevens: Nineteenth-Century Egalitarian.* Chapel Hill, N.C.: University of North Carolina Press, 1997.

Trotter, Joe William, Jr., and Eric Ledell Smith, eds. *African Americans in Pennsylvania: Shifting Historical Perspectives.* University Park: Pennsylvania State University Press, 1997.

Tucker, Glenn. *High Tide at Gettysburg: The Campaign in Pennsylvania.* Reprint. Gettysburg: Stan Clark Military Books, 1995.

Turner, Edward R. *The Negro in Pennsylvania: Slavery–Servitude–Freedom, 1639–1861.* Washington, D.C.: American Historical Association, 1911.

Valuska, David L., and Christian B. Keller. *Damn Dutch: Pennsylvania Germans at Gettysburg.* Mechanicsburg, Penn.: Stackpole Books, 2004.

Varg, Paul A. *Edward Everett: The Intellectual in the Turmoil of Politics.* Cranbury, N.J.: Associated University Presses, 1992.

Vermilyea, Peter C. "The Effect of the Confederate Invasion of Pennsylvania on Gettysburg's African American Community." *The Gettysburg Magazine* 24 (2001): 112–128.

Walker, Clarence E. *A Rock in a Weary Land: The African Methodist Episcopal Church During the Civil War and Reconstruction.* Baton Rouge, La.: Louisiana State University Press, 1982.

Walters, Ronald G. "The Erotic South: Civilization and Sexuality in American Abolitionism." *American Quarterly* 25 (1973): 177–201.

Warner, Ezra J. *Generals in Blue: Lives of the Union Commanders.* Baton Rouge: Louisiana State University Press, 1996.

Weeks, Jim. *Gettysburg: Memory, Market, and an American Shrine.* Princeton, N.J.: Princeton University Press, 2003.

Wiley, Bell. *The Life of Billy Yank: The Common Soldier of the Union.* Baton Rouge, La.: Louisiana State University Press, 1994.

Wills, Garry. *Lincoln at Gettysburg: The Words That Remade America.* New York: Simon & Schuster, 1992.

Wilson, Carol. *Freedom at Risk: The Kidnapping of Free Blacks in America, 1780–1865.* Lexington, Ky.: University Press of Kentucky, 1994.

Winch, Julie. "Philadelphia and the Other Underground Railroad." *The Pennsylvania Magazine of History and Biography* 111 (1987): 3–25.

SECONDARY SOURCES: UNPUBLISHED

Becker, Donald H. "Trends in Negro Segregation in Gettysburg from 1900–1953." M.A. thesis, University of Maryland, 1953. Copy at Abdel Ross Wentz Library, Lutheran Theological Seminary, Gettysburg.

Glatfelter, Charles H. "Gettysburg, Pennsylvania: A Very Brief History." 1977. Copy, ACHS.

Johnson, James Elton. "A History of Camp William Penn and Its Black Troops in the Civil War, 1863–1865." Ph.D. dissertation, University of Pennsylvania, 1999.

Kinsel, Amy J. "'From These Honored Dead': Gettysburg in American Culture, 1863–1938." Ph.D. dissertation, Cornell University, 1992.

———. "'A Monument to American Manhood': How the War Department Shaped the Gettysburg National Military Park." Paper delivered at the Organization of American Historians Meeting, Toronto, April 1999.

Matthews, Harry B. "Whence They Came: The Families of the United States Colored Troops in Gettysburg, Pennsylvania 1815–1817." n.d. Copy, ACHS.

Myers, Betty D. "The Progression of Black Education in Gettysburg." Lecture, n.d. Tape recording, ACHS.

Neely, George M., Jr. "The Anti-Slavery Movement and the Underground Railroad in Adams County." B.A. thesis, Gettysburg College, 1930.

Patterson, John S. "John Burns and Jennie Wade: The Hero and Heroine of Gettysburg?" Paper presented at the American Folklore Society Meeting, 19 October 1989. Copy, GNMP.

Rudawsky, Marilyn Brownfield. "After July: The Effects of the Battle of Gettysburg on the People of Adams County." M.A. thesis, Youngstown State University, 1979. Copy, ACHS.

Seidman, Rachel F. "Beyond Sacrifice: Women and Politics on the Pennsylvania Homefront During the Civil War." Ph.D. dissertation, Yale University, 1995.

Sherfy, Marcella. "A Study of Local Newspaper Handling of the Battle of Gettysburg." Seminar Paper, January 1969. Copy, ACHS.

Smith, David G. "Race and Retaliation: The Capture of African Americans During the Gettysburg Campaign." 2004. Unpublished essay.

Stanislow, Gail A. "Antislavery Sentiment and Opposition in Adams County, Pennsylvania." n.d. Copy, ACHS.

ACKNOWLEDGMENTS

IT IS HARD TO know where to begin to thank the many people who have offered advice on this project, or who have exhorted, encouraged, or helpfully critiqued. Scores of people have assisted with the research of this book, and these comments will barely do them justice.

The place to begin is in the Borough of Gettysburg itself, and on Seminary Ridge. There, in the legendary Lutheran Theological Seminary building, sits the Adams County Historical Society. And there works a remarkable staff. I benefited from the experienced assistance of Charles Glatfelter, Russell Swody, Wayne Motts, Marge McConnell, and Randy Miller. I received outstanding help from Elwood Christ, the inimitable whistling historian who lives and breathes the Adams County past.

And I wouldn't have gotten anywhere without Tim Smith. Tim, who knows as much as anyone about Gettysburg civilians and the battle, spent hours setting me straight (and can't be blamed when he did not succeed). He also helped me dig into archives, he shared his own vast knowledge and his unique discoveries, and he took a detailed look at the manuscript. Tim's expertise, his generosity, and his contagious enthusiasm made him a wonderful ally in the effort to expand the history of the Battle of Gettysburg.

Other Gettysburg specialists deserve thanks as well, particularly Gerald Bennett and Walter Powell. Both were charitable with their time and knowledge. Brian Kennell was a great help with Evergreen Cemetery history, and carries on a historic tradition at the Gatehouse.

Personnel at the Gettysburg National Military Park were unbelievably supportive. Historians Kathy Harrison and Winona Peterson have labored long and hard to help people consider the cultural context of the battle, and they offered guidance and information with humor and panache. Becky Lyons and Louise Arnold also offered insight and assistance, not to mention rollicking good company. Scott Hartwig, John Heiser, and John Latschar were also obliging. Many Licensed Battlefield Guides answered questions, offered comments, and even filled in a questionnaire. Thanks to all of you.

The pursuit of African American history was made possible by many people. Catherine Carter, Margaret Nutter, and Jean Odom offered inspiration and assistance very early on, and kindly shared materials on nineteenth-century Gettysburg as well as oral histories. Alisha Hansen, Rogers Smith, and Shelley Jones were also forthcoming with material and insights. Betty Dorsey Myers has been on the vanguard of black history in Gettysburg for a long time, and has worked hard and carefully to get facts of the story down right. I have appreciated her thoughtful comments. Pete Vermilyea, also a pioneer in the black history of the battle, deserves special credit as well.

A number of historians read parts of this work as papers, offered comments in conferences, or shared information by e-mail, and I am very grateful for their advice. They include Jeanie Attie, Joan Cashin, Gary Gallagher, Linda Grant De Pauw, Michael Fellman, Amy Kinsel, Edward Linenthal, Michael Parrish, John Patterson, David Smith, and Jim Weeks.

And a few intrepid scholars took time out of their own hectic teaching, writing, or research schedules to take a long look at parts of the manuscript. John Hennessy, Christian Keller, and Marcus Bruce were thoughtful and helpful readers. Elizabeth Leonard deserves distinct thanks for her willingness to slog through multiple chapters and for providing an ever-sympathetic ear.

Gabor Boritt of Gettysburg College and the Civil War Institute offered early encouragement and steady support, and I very much appreciate all the remarkable ways he generates conversations among Civil War historians. Matt Gallman, with his canny take on American history, not to mention his clever wit, contributed immeasurably to my visits to Gettysburg. Chris Ericson also offered valuable insights into nineteenth-century women's history. And fellow Lincoln Prize sojourners John Quist and Lloyd Benson were wonderful cheerleaders.

I received additional tips and suggestions from John Mohr, Ron Young, William Conyngham, Steve Mohr, William Lamers, Litt Roden, Jim Cole, and Patrick Bowmaster, and I received kind attention in my home away from home at Gettysburg from Charles and Ruth Anne Wilcox.

In Maine, Bowdoin College Special Collections proved a delightful place to do research, and Bates College, my home base, supported me with research funds and terrific student assistants over the years: Jess Oas, Beth Kalinowski, Tracy Lyford, and Kate Marshall. I also received good help from Charlotte Hoffmann and Elizabeth Wallace. My computer guru, Greg Struve, deserves a big pat on the back, as does Laura Juraska of Ladd Library. Sylvia Hawks, the queen of bibliographies, was amazing. Members of the Department of History at Bates deserve credit for their patience and wisdom, and fellow faculty in the Program in African American and American Cultural Studies were equally generous. Steve Hochstadt was particularly helpful with German history, and Michael Jones, Hilmar Jensen, and Liz Tobin were great companions at Gettysburg itself. Glen Lawson, Lee Dionne, and David Heald of Company A of the 3rd Maine were terrific teachers of living history.

On the publishing end, Kathy Anderson of Anderson Grinberg and Don Fehr of Basic Books were encouraging and supportive, and copyeditor John Thomas did a skilled job of working his way through the wilderness of the manuscript. Sue Caulfield and Kay Mariea were also a pleasure to work with. I am happy to acknowledge, too, the generous assistance of Mary O'Meara, Deborah Oliver, and Ann Greenleaf.

And finally, thanks go to folks on the home front: to Deborah Strachan, Ann Kistler, and the rest of the South Street gang; to Steve Bachelder, king of cultural talk and fricassees both; to Rachel, Lew, and John, of Holman and Howard. My family stayed the course, remarkably. Some of them traveled with me to Gettysburg, walked the battlefield and waited in hotel rooms while I worked; others read parts of the manuscript and offered tough and timely criticism. All were forgiving and funny, and helped keep the project in perspective. Thanks to my husband Rob Smith, to my children Louisa, Malcolm, and Nick, and to my parents Jean Scott Creighton and James Alexander Creighton. My mother, a writer, offered her expertise in prose, and my father, a veteran of World War II, offered his insights into the experience of war.

INDEX